Unfinished Music

Unfinished Music

RICHARD KRAMER

OXFORD
UNIVERSITY PRESS
2008

OXFORD
UNIVERSITY PRESS

Oxford University Press, Inc., publishes works that further
Oxford University's objective of excellence
in research, scholarship, and education.

Oxford   New York
Auckland   Cape Town   Dar es Salaam   Hong Kong   Karachi
Kuala Lumpur   Madrid   Melbourne   Mexico City   Nairobi
New Delhi   Shanghai   Taipei   Toronto

With offices in
Argentina   Austria   Brazil   Chile   Czech Republic   France   Greece
Guatemala   Hungary   Italy   Japan   Poland   Portugal   Singapore
South Korea   Switzerland   Thailand   Turkey   Ukraine   Vietnam

Published by Oxford University Press, Inc.
198 Madison Avenue, New York, New York 10016

www.oup.com

Oxford is a registered trademark of Oxford University Press

Library of Congress Cataloging-in-Publication Data
Kramer, Richard, 1938–
Unfinished music / Richard Kramer.
p.   cm.
ISBN 978-0-19-532682-6
1. Music—Psychological aspects.   2. Music—Philosophy and aesthetics.
3. Composition (Music)—Psychological aspects.   I. Title.
ML3830.K7295 2007
781.1′7—cd22   2007009450

This volume is published with generous support from the Manfred Bukofzer
Publication Endowment Fund of the American Musicological Society.

9   8   7   6   5   4   3   2   1

Printed in the United States of America
on acid-free paper

For Alex, Adam, and ever Martha

Every perfect work is the death mask of its intuition.

The work is the death mask of conception.

WALTER BENJAMIN

PREFACE

When Walter Benjamin came to publish the aphorism that, in its two forms, serves as the motto of this book, he drew back from the notion of the *vollkommene* work.[1] All works, whether measurably perfect or not, partake of this axiomatic truth: that in their completion, they die. And he drew back as well from the sense of creation as, purely, intuition. *Konzeption* is the broader, the more common term. But the governing idea remains a breathtaking one. Stumbling upon it in a volume of Benjamin's letters, I was struck all at once how its central paradox resonates in each of the essays that follow.

The motto itself articulates no simple thesis. Each of its substantives is riddling. The death mask conjures a fleeting moment: the face frozen in death yet warm with life. At death, the features are fixed in a certain way. In this final instant of perfect resolution, of timeless calm, the vicissitudes of a life are effaced. Benjamin's stark image dares us to believe that a powerful undercurrent of meaning lies in what we can reconstruct of the complex, turbulent, rich processes antecedent to this moment in which a text is fixed. We have come to speak of this, in the old cliché, as a moment of birth. In the playing out of the creative process, a work is born. At the moment of its birth, something of essence in the work is muted. What happens subsequently is of little consequence, at least for an understanding of the work. If one must have a history of art, it will be a history of what lies beneath these masks. "The research of contemporary art history always amounts

---

1. "Jedes vollkommene Werk ist die Totenmaske seiner Intuition." *Walter Benjamin: Briefe,* ed. Gershom Scholem and Theodor W. Adorno (Frankfurt am Main: Suhrkamp Verlag, 1978), I: 327; *The Correspondence of Walter Benjamin, 1910–1940,* ed. and annotated by Gershom Scholem and Theodor W. Adorno, tr. by Manfred R. Jacobson and Evelyn M. Jacobson (Chicago and London: The University of Chicago Press, 1994), 227. "Jedes vollkommene Werk" suggests the sense of perfection more as a "making whole" than as an aesthetic absolute.

"Das Werk ist die Totenmaske der Konzeption." *Einbahnstraße,* in *Gesammelte Schriften,* ed. Rolf Tiedemann and Hermann Schweppenhäuser, in collaboration with Theodor W. Adorno and Gershom Scholem, IV/1, ed. Tillman Rexroth (Frankfurt am Main: Suhrkamp Verlag, 1972), 538; and Walter Benjamin, *Selected Writing, I: 1913–1926,* ed. Marcus Bullock and Michael W. Jennings (Cambridge, Mass., and London: Harvard University Press, 1996), 459, in which the aphorism is the thirteenth entry in the section "The Writer's Technique in Thirteen Theses." I have altered their rendering "of *its* conception" (my emphasis), which seems not quite what Benjamin intends.

merely to a history of the subject matter or a history of form," Benjamin wrote a month earlier, "for which the works of art provide only examples, and, as it were, models; there is no question of there being a history of the work of art as such."[2]

For years during the writing of this book, improvisation—the improvisatory as an act of music—figured in its imagined title. It continues to figure in the text, whether implicitly or as a topic of inquiry in itself. In music, improvisation is cherished as the emblem of intuition. Ephemeral by nature, the improvisatory act vanishes, as texts do not. Much of this creative process that we are at pains to document is a quest for the evidence of the improvisatory. Indeed, the act of composition may be said to emulate the spontaneity of improvisation, to capture intuition. In the fixing of text, intuition is embalmed, masked over.

This moment at which text is "fixed" is itself an epistemological problem of some magnitude. At precisely what moment can the work be said to be completed, finished, *vollendet?* The composers whose works are studied here trouble this question each in a different way. Emanuel Bach's obsession with the further *Veränderung*—alteration, variation of considerable substance—of works otherwise finished (and even published) now strongly implicates the act of performance as a text-defining moment, further complicating the very notion of *Vollendung.* For Haydn, the imagining of primal Chaos provokes the improvisatory urge to create. Beethoven's compulsive sketching, drafting, rehearing of even the least ambitious of his works, concretizing the process of mind in its struggle toward the notion of the completed work, seems a model for what Benjamin is after. This idealizing of the moment of finish and the anxieties that it induces in the Romantic artist was not lost on Schubert. A considerable repertory has survived of important work left unfinished. Fragments, they are: works in eternal limbo, not quite born, nor, in Benjamin's sense, yet dead. Fragments, like sketches, exist as texts. We have learned to construe them as early stages in a process. But they were not so construed at their conception. They, too, wear masks.

The final essay returns to Benjamin's aphorism, exploring the contexts and circumstances that nourished its conception. In Benjamin's interrogation of Goethe's *Wahlverwandtschaften,* in his pursuit of the idea of beauty, we are offered a dark and difficult prism through which to hear again the familiar music that is the subject of this book.

For Benjamin, the very condition of finish, of completion, signifies the end of a life. Whose life? Resisting an answer, the question yet forces us to think hard about the nature of artistic creation, to imagine the ephemeral moment during which the work is separated from its author. This moment is what Benjamin

---

2. In a letter of 9 December 1923 to Rang. *Briefe,* I: 322; *Correspondence,* 224.

seems intent upon actualizing. The separation is now labored, troubled, difficult, now imperceptible. That there exists such a moment of separation, both in the aesthetic sense, at which the autonomy of the work is established, and in the psychological sense, triggering the convoluted anxieties of the author, is an assumption that underlies each of the studies that follow. They each seek to apprehend the moment as an event, impalpable though it may seem, at which something called the work is now "finished," and all the disparate evidence of creation, of the author's engagement with composition and context, is swept away, the author along with it. But it is a condition of art that the work, alive in its afterlife, is in some sense never "finished," and that the evidence of its creation, and of its creator, is everywhere implicit in its text and constitutes a grain of its meaning.

Learning to live with the pleasurable discomforts of these paradoxes is the modest resolve of this book.

ACKNOWLEDGMENTS

A good many of the ideas in this book grew from talks given at conferences and seminars. I owe debts of gratitude to Stefan Litwin, whose seminar "Beethovens Spätstil. Probleme der Interpretation" at the Wissenschaftskolleg zu Berlin (Institute for Advanced Study) in June 2004 provoked the essay on Beethoven's Opus 109; to Richard Will and Marshall Brown for the invitation to deliver the keynote address at the annual meeting of the North American Society for the Study of Romanticism, in Seattle, August 2001, from which grew the chapter on Herder and Haydn; to Annette Richards, whose memorable conference on Emanuel Bach at Cornell in 1999 inspired the chapter on Diderot and Bach; and to Hans-Werner Küthen, whose symposium at the Beethoven-Haus Bonn in 2000 provided a lively environment for the essay on Opus 90 and the ghost of Emanuel Bach. Chapter 2, an essay on Emanuel Bach's music as conceived in escape from, if not in agon with, the music of his father, appeared in a collection of essays honoring Robert Marshall, and I profited greatly from his sage reflections on these discomforting allegations. Chapter 12 was earlier conceived for a conference at Harvard University in 1996—"Rethinking Beethoven's Late Period"—honoring Lewis Lockwood, whose inspiring seminars at Princeton long ago set in motion many of the themes and indeed the underlying thesis of this book. Chapter 15 was written for a celebration in 1998 at the Graduate Center of the City University of New York of the work of Leo Treitler, who then, predictably and to my great pleasure, subjected the essay to a penetrating inquiry of his own that only intensified the stimulation in writing it for him.

Several chapters appeared in earlier publications: chapter 2, in *Historical Musicology: Sources, Methods, Interpretations,* ed. Stephen A. Crist and Roberta Montemorra Marvin (Rochester: University of Rochester Press, 2002); chapter 6, in *C. P. E. Bach Studies,* ed. Annette Richards (Cambridge: University of Cambridge Press, 2006); chapters 9 and 14 in the journal *19th Century Music,* 15 (1991): 116–131, and 21 (1997): 134–148, © 1997 by the Regents of the University of California; and chapter 12, in *Beethoven Forum* 7 (Lincoln & London: University of Nebraska Press, 1999), 67–88, © 1999 by the University of Nebraska Press. Some paragraphs in chapter 1 appeared originally in "The Sketch Itself," in *Beethoven's Compositional Process*, ed. William Kinderman (Lincoln & London: University of Nebraska Press, 1991), 3–5, ©1991 by the University of Nebraska Press. I am grateful to these presses for granting permission to publish revised versions here. An earlier version of chapter 10 appeared as "Beethovens Opus 90 und die Fenster zur Vergangenheit," in *Beethoven und die Rezeption der Alten Musik: Die hohe Schule der Überlieferung*, ed. Hans-Werner Küthen (Bonn: Verlag Beethoven-Haus Bonn, 2002), 93–120; my thanks to Michael Ladenburger and Bernhard Appel for permission to publish this revision and a return to its original language. I am grateful to Roland Schmidt-Hensel and Clemens Brenneis of the Staatsbibliothek zu Berlin–Preußischer Kulturbesitz: Musikabteilung mit Mendelssohn Archiv; to Eike Zimmer of the Bildarchiv d. Österreichischen Nationalbibliothek; and to Dr. Otto Biba of the Gesellschaft der Musikfreunde in Wien, for granting permission to use, in illustration here, documents from their precious collections.

Many colleagues and friends responded to my desperate inquiries for advice and for help in securing documents. My deepest thanks to Paul Corneilson, Managing Editor of *Carl Philipp Emanuel Bach: The Complete Works*, at the Packard Humanities Institute; to Susan J. Clermont, of the Library of Congress, who graciously gave too much of her time to the solving of a publishing matter; to Darrell Berg, for sharing her rich store of Bach sources and an even richer wisdom about them; and to David Schulenberg, for graciously providing materials otherwise difficult of access. Blake Howe compiled the List of Works Cited deftly and swiftly, against an unfriendly deadline. Alexander Kramer expertly prepared several of the illustrations.

Scott Burnham read the entire manuscript with sympathy and searching insight, and I am profoundly indebted to him for that. Three chapters were exposed to the piercing critique of a brilliant cohort of theorists and scholars at the Mannes Theory Institute, held in New Haven in June of 2006; I shall be eternally grateful to those fifteen participants for their willingness to engage these ideas, and to Wayne Alpern, director of the Institute, for the invitation to conduct the seminar. I have profited from lively exchanges on the various ideas in this book with Siegmund Levarie, Kristina Muxfeldt, Maynard Solomon, James Hepokoski, James Webster, Alexander Rehding, Joseph Kerman, and many others in the course of the decade and more during which this book took shape. Among those others were several generations of students, at the Graduate Center of the City University of New York and at Stony Brook, who tackled these embryonic topics with bracing wit and, in the spirit of those seminars, a robust skepticism that I came to prize. I have learned from them more than they can ever know.

Trafficking in speculations regarding the obscure workings of the creative mind is not a project for the faint of heart. Undaunted, Suzanne Ryan, Senior Music Editor at Oxford University Press, offered unwavering enthusiasm from our earliest conversations. For this I shall be ever grateful, and as well for her keen, steady judgment and uncompromising support during the long haul of production.

As ever, Martha Calhoun endured with sanity and deflating humor the misanthropic moods of her reclusive husband. She listens with the musician's ear for prose and the lawyer's mind for argument. That this book was ever completed owes in no small measure to her cherished companionship.

CONTENTS

PART I

First Things

CHAPTER 1

Language and the Beginnings of Creation

> One cannot truly understand what men are saying by
> merely applying grammatical or logical or any other kind
> of rules, but only by an act of "entering into"—what
> Herder called "Einfühlung"—their symbolisms, and for
> that reason only by the preservation of actual usage, past
> and present. Consequently, while we cannot do without
> rules and principles, we must constantly distrust them
> and never be betrayed by them into rejecting or ignor-
> ing or riding roughshod over the irregularities and pe-
> culiarities offered by concrete experience.[1]

Isaiah Berlin here captures one aspect of the theory of language that is a central topic of his penetrating study of Johann Georg Hamann (1730–1788). The stubborn obscurity of Hamann's thought, and in particular its location of meaning at the cradle of language, before the exercise of reason and analysis, is strikingly pertinent to an understanding of the music of Carl Philipp Emanuel Bach (1714–1788), whose eccentricities set his contemporaries to similar feats of exegesis. If the two never met, the picture of a confrontation between two minds so uncompromisingly original challenges the imagination. Their place at the source of a new mode of thought affecting arts and letters—a place in the midst of *Aufklärung* (Enlightenment), askew in posture and even contrary to its common tenets, and yet a function of them—is uncommonly close.

---

1. Isaiah Berlin, *The Magus of the North: J. G. Hamann and the Origins of Modern Irrationalism* (London: J. Murray, 1993), 130.

"The Origins of Modern Irrationalism," the subtitle of Berlin's monograph, is suggestive as well for the place of Emanuel Bach's music in the course of a history that in some sense may be said to begin here, in these idiosyncratic works that touched his contemporaries as had no others. The privacy of Bach's language, indeed the tendency of his music to speak in linguistic neologisms, set it apart from the common currents of musical style in the 1790s and beyond, so that his music, in the genuineness of its expression, was valued by Haydn, Mozart, and Beethoven more for what it suggested of an aesthetics, of an attitude toward art, than for the artifices of its composition.

What, precisely, is this irrationalism that Berlin holds as a reactionary counterpoise to the power of reason that he understands as the foundational principle of the Enlightenment? For Berlin, the wing-span of the Enlightenment begins in the Renaissance and extends to the French Revolution "and indeed beyond it." Its tenets were clear, and Berlin's formulation of them clearer still: "The three strongest pillars upon which it rested were faith in reason . . . ; in the identity of human nature through time and the possibility of universal human goals; and finally in the possibility of attaining to the second by means of the first, of ensuring physical and spiritual harmony and progress by the power of the logically or empirically guided critical intellect."[2] To define the Enlightenment in these terms and with such enviable clarity is to marginalize as contrary and negligible a body of vigorous inquiry, no less enlightened, that ventured to understand the dissonance between what might be called the exercise of reason and the empirical play of sensibilities—to understand, that is, how reason and feeling (better, *Empfindung*, a word far richer in meaning) might be reconciled, and further, to locate the processes of thought itself. How, after all, can we know, in the course of our thinking, that we are in the presence of "rational" thought? It is a question of this kind that lurks behind a passage in Diderot's *Jacques le fataliste* that is as witty as it is unsettling: "It's that, not knowing what is written above, we know neither what we want nor what we do. So we follow our fantasy, which we call reason, or our reason, which is often only a dangerous fantasy that sometimes turns out well and sometimes badly."[3]

---

2. Berlin, *ibid.*, 28–29. Peter Gay, noting the tradition by which the Enlightenment is delimited to "within a hundred-year span beginning with the English Revolution and ending with the French Revolution," then compellingly identifies it as "the work of three overlapping, closely associated generations." See his *The Enlightenment: An Interpretation*; [I] *The Rise of Modern Paganism* (New York: Alfred A. Knopf, 1966), 17.

3. For a slightly different translation, see Denis Diderot, *Jacques the Fatalist and His Master*, tr. with an Introduction and Notes by J. Robert Loy (New York and London: W. W. Norton & Co, rev. ed., 1978), 11. As Thomas Kavanagh has it: "For Jacques, reason and fantasy, the tactical corollaries of a belief in determinism on the one hand and a resignation to chance on the other, become one and the same." See his *Enlightenment and the Shadows of Chance: The Novel and the Culture of Gambling in Eighteenth-Century France* (Baltimore and London: The Johns Hopkins University Press, 1993), 231.

Diderot plays more earnestly with the unpredictable causalities of thought in a memorable passage in the *Conversation Between D'Alembert and Diderot*. Seeking an explanation for how the mind can embrace not "vast chains of reasoning of the kind that range over thousands of ideas, but just one simple proposition," the mathematician d'Alembert cannot move past the observation that "we can think of only one thing at a time." Diderot, his interlocutor, now puts in play this grand conceit of the vibrating string that resonates "long after it has been plucked," and that sets other strings to vibrate sympathetically: "it is in this way that one idea calls up a second, and the two together a third, and all three a fourth, and so on. . . . This instrument can make astonishing leaps, and one idea called up will sometimes start an harmonic at an incomprehensible interval. If this phenomenon can be observed between resonant strings which are inert and separate, why should it not take place between living and connected points, continuous and sensitive fibres?" The philosopher is then a kind of clavichord:

> We are instruments possessed of sensitivity and memory. Our senses are so many keys which are struck by things in nature around us, and often strike themselves. . . . There is an impression which has its cause within the instrument or outside it, and from this impression is born a sensation, and this sensation has duration, for it is impossible to imagine that it is both made and destroyed in a single, indivisible instant. Another impression succeeds the first which also has its cause both inside and outside the animal, then a second sensation, and tones which describe them in natural or conventional sounds.[4]

The reasoning mind in action, so to say, is set in motion by the sensibilities of the entire nervous system. The mind and its thoughts do not exist outside this sensitive organ that is Man. Reasoned thought has its involuntary, irrational aspect.

The daring leap from Diderot's "thinking" clavichord to the machinery of the creative mind and the creation of art returns us to the theater of language. For Hamann, the beginnings of creative thought are one with the beginnings of language. Without language, thought itself is not possible. As Berlin puts it, Hamann is among the first "to be quite clear that thought *is* the use of symbols, that nonsymbolic thought, that is, thought without either symbols or images—whether visual or auditory, or perhaps a shadowy combination of the two . . .—is an unintelligible notion."[5] This notion of thought in lockstep with the creation of a

4. Denis Diderot, *Rameau's Nephew and D'Alembert's Dream,* tr. with Introduction by Leonard Tancock (Harmondsworth and New York: Penguin Books, 1966), 156–157.

5. Berlin, *Magus of the North,* 75.

language of symbols necessary for its expression is a provocative one for the imagining of how music is conceived. If it is a commonplace to acknowledge that musical thought and its actuality in some linguistic, voiced utterance constitute an inseparable identity, Hamann's account encourages us to think freshly about the complexity, the idiosyncrasy, the originality of the musical idea, to think of composition not as the clever play with inherited conventions, but as a bolder adventure in which language is always invented de novo.

In their very different ways, Diderot, Hamann, and Herder interrogate what, by the 1770s, had become the common currency of Enlightenment thought. The name itself—*Aufklärung*—had come to dominate the discourse in a self-conscious effort to understand what it signified. "Was ist Aufklärung?"—what is Enlightenment? The question, innocently put in a Berlin monthly of 1783, provoked a brace of replies by, among others, Moses Mendelssohn and Immanuel Kant. "*Enlightenment is mankind's exit from its self-incurred immaturity,*" begins Kant. "*Sapere aude!* Have the courage to use your *own* understanding! This," he claimed, "is the motto of enlightenment."[6] Hamann's reaction to Kant's essay, a cynical sneer wrapped in a characteristically impenetrable linguistic knot, is impatient with the question itself: "The enlightenment of our century," for Hamann, "is a mere northern light. . . . All prattle and reasoning [Raisonniren] of the emancipated immature ones, who set themselves up as guardians of those who are themselves immature."[7] A far clearer sense of his quarrel with Kant will be found in Hamann's "Metacritique on the Purism of Reason" (1784).[8] Here again it is the axiomatic priority of language that controls the discourse: "If it is still a chief question *how the faculty of thought is possible*—the faculty to think *right* and *left, before* and *without, with* and *beyond* experience—then no deduction is needed to demonstrate the genealogical superiority of *language.*"[9]

"The oldest language was music. . . . The oldest writing was painting and drawing," writes Hamann, casting the beginnings of thought in boldly aesthetic

---

6. Often translated, Kant's essay can be found in the company of others replies to the question in James Schmidt, ed., *What Is Enlightenment? Eighteenth-Century Answers and Twentieth-Century Questions* (Berkeley, Los Angeles, London: University of California Press, 1996), 58–64.

7. Hamann's response is contained in a letter to Christian Jacob Kraus of 18 December 1784. A translation, copiously annotated, may be found in Schmidt, *What Is Enlightenment,* 145–153.

8. The text, unpublished during Hamann's lifetime, first appeared in *Mancherley zur Geschichte der metakritischen Invasion,* ed. F. T. Rink (Königsberg, 1800), 120–134. For a translation of this version, see Schmidt, *What Is Enlightenment,* 154–167. A copy of the text that was sent to Johann Gottfried Herder in September 1784 is given in *Johann Georg Hamann: Briefwechsel,* ed. Walther Ziesemer and Arthur Henkel (Wiesbaden and Frankfurt: Insel Verlag, 1955–1979), V: 210–216.

9. Schmidt, *What Is Enlightenment,* 156.

terms.[10] This seems an echo of Vico's reflections on the primacy of metaphor in the evolution of the earliest languages, and of his penetrating notion that for the first poets every metaphor "is a fable in brief." In the extended and frequent exchanges with Herder on the nature of language and its origins at the beginning of thought, Hamann is vituperative, and he is obscure—intentionally so, it often seems. It is in this context—mindful of Hamann's notion that "language and the forms of art are indissolubly one with the art itself"[11]—that we turn to Emanuel Bach, whose music so pointedly exemplifies this refusal to separate out the "forms of art" from the thing itself, whose music seems (and assuredly seemed to his contemporaries) to wrestle with the creation of language.

A Rhetoric of Sonata

> Language is what we think with, not translate into: the meaning of the notion of "language" is of symbol-using. Images came before words, and images are created by passions.[12]

This sequence—"passion, image, word"—indeed, the very act of putting them in sequence, suggests perhaps the slightest dissonance with a phenomenon that Hamann (as Berlin understands him) is at pains to establish: the simultaneity of feeling and expression. The gestural aspect of Bach's music plays out this linguistic notion with a vividness unmatched in other arts.

That Bach's music was understood to negotiate its meaning in linguistic terms was manifest early on. In the entry "Sonata" written in the early 1770s for Sulzer's *Theorie der schönen Künste,* its author J. A. P. Schulz singled out Bach as the composer whose works demonstrate "the possibility to infuse character and expression in the sonata." Most of Bach's sonatas, he continues, "speak so clearly that one thinks he is hearing not notes so much as an understandable language that rouses and maintains our imagination and feelings."[13] Forkel went further, tak-

---

10. Schmidt, *ibid,* 156.

11. Berlin, *Magus of the North,* 77.

12. Berlin, *ibid.,* 76.

13. "Die mehresten derselben sind so sprechend, daß man nicht Töne, sondern eine verständliche Sprache zu vernehmen glaubt, die unsere Einbildung und Empfindungen in Bewegung setzt, und unterhält." Johann Georg Sulzer, *Allgemeine Theorie der Schönen Künste,* Neue vermehrte zweite

ing the Sonata in F minor, published in the third collection "für Kenner und Liebhaber" (1781), as a provocation to write seventeen pages—a "Sendschreiben" (a communication), he calls it—toward a definition of Sonata.[14] The prose has the experimental ring of the empiricist sorting through evidence of a new kind, for each of Emanuel Bach's new works was met with stunned acknowledgment of its originality. Forkel seeks to come to grips with a "difficult" work that was perceived to set loose conceptual challenges: the extreme case, forging its own rule, that must yet be reconciled with a formal concept resilient enough to accommodate the quiddities of this sonata within a repertory itself dense with idiosyncratic specimens.

"When I think of a sonata," Forkel begins, "I think to myself of the musical expression of a man transfixed by feeling or inspiration, who endeavors either to sustain his feeling at a certain point of spiritedness (when, for example, it is constituted in a desirably agreeable sensation); or, if it belongs to the class of unpleasant feelings, to reduce it in intensity, and to transform it from a disagreeable feeling to an agreeable one."[15] Who is this subject given to transform his feeling, his

---

Auflage, 4 vols. (Leipzig: Weidmann, 1792; reprint Hildesheim: Georg Olms, 1970), IV: 425. For a somewhat different translation, see Thomas Christensen, tr. and ed., "Johann Georg Sulzer, General Theory of the Fine Arts (1771–1774): Selected Articles," in *Aesthetics and the Art of Musical Composition in the German Enlightenment: Selected Writings of Johann Georg Sulzer and Heinrich Christoph Koch,* ed. Nancy Kovaleff Baker and Thomas Christensen (Cambridge and New York: Cambridge University Press, 1995), 104. Etienne Darbellay reminds us of this passage in his essay "C. P. E. Bach's Aesthetic as Reflected in his Notation," in *C. P. E. Bach Studies,* ed. Stephen L. Clark (Oxford: Oxford University Press, 1988), 62.

14. [Johann Nikolaus Forkel,] "Ueber eine Sonate aus Carl Phil. Emanuel Bachs dritter Sonatensammlung für Kenner und Liebhaber in F moll, S 30. Ein Sendschreiben an Hrn. von * *," in *Musikalischer Almanach für Deutschland auf das Jahr 1784* (Leipzig: im Schwickertschen Verlag, [n. d.]; reprint Hildesheim and New York: Georg Olms, 1974), 22–38. It was a famous piece, praised even before its publication in 1781. In a note on its publication, Johann Friedrich Reichardt, *Musikalisches Kunstmagazin,* I (Berlin: Im Verlage des Verfassers, 1782; repr. Hildesheim: Georg Olms, 1969), 87, singled it out as "by far the best" in the collection. "I can think of nothing that exceeds it in rhetoric, in lyricism, nothing more overpowering in every application of genius and art." And he could now reveal this as the sonata about which he'd written with unbridled enthusiasm in his *Briefe eine aufmerksamen Reisenden die Musik betreffend,* II (Frankfurt and Breslau, 1776), 10–11: "eine Clavier-Sonate, die ich von ihm in seiner Handschrift für mich allein erhielt. . . . Es ist dieses wirklich eines der alleroriginellesten Stücke, die ich jemals gehört habe: und jeder, jeder, dem ich sie vorspiele, bricht, wie verabredet, in die Worte aus: **So etwas hörte ich nie!**" (a keyboard sonata which I received from him in his handwriting for myself alone. . . . This is really one of the most original pieces that I have ever heard; and everyone, everyone for whom I play it breaks out, as though speechless, in these words: I've never heard anything like it!). The sonata was singled out as well in the brief review in the *Hamburgische unpartheische Correspondent,* No. 187 (1781), reprinted in *Carl Philipp Emanuel Bach im Spiegel seiner Zeit,* ed. with commentary by Ernst Suchalla (Hildesheim, Zurich, New York: Georg Olms, 1993), 157–158.

15. "Wenn ich mir eine Sonate denke, so denke ich mir den musikalischen Ausdruck eines in Empfindung oder Begeisterung versetzten Menschen, der sich bestrebt, entweder seine Emp-

inspiration, into expression? Is it the composer who is thus transfixed, or does the music construct some fictive inner voice, a figure of narrative? If there is a confusion of persona in Forkel's personification, the formulation yet suggests the spirit of Herder's *Einfühlung*, this "entering into their symbolisms" as a way of understanding what is being said in this language without cognates.[16] A few pages later, Forkel comes at the problem from another angle:

> A series of highly spirited concepts, as they follow upon one another according to the rules of an inspired imagination, is an Ode. Just such a series of spirited, expressive musical ideas [Ideen (Sätze)], when they follow upon one another according to the precept of a musically inspired imagination is, in music, the Sonata.[17]

The simile again has its root in something linguistic. Forkel is careful to avoid the suggestion that the form of the ode in any of its particulars—its verse structure, its rhyme patterns, its meter, its prosody—is at issue here. Rather, it is the elevated tone of the ode, the complexity of syntax trafficking in lofty concepts, that Forkel takes as exemplary for the sonata. In Forkel's equation, *Begriffe* (concepts) in the Ode become *Ideen* (*Sätze*) in the Sonata. In the sonata, ideas are indistinguishable from *Sätze:* the syntactical element—the phrase, the gesture, the theme as an elaboration of such morphemes—is itself the "idea."

Forkel returns to his opening conceit. The *Empfindungen* earlier ascribed to this fictive personification of the sonata now assume a substantive role in what might be called the meaning of the work. For Forkel, the aesthetic achievement of the sonata lies precisely here, in a natural tension between "*Begeisterung* [Inspiration], or the extremely spirited expression of certain feelings," and "*Anordnung* [Arrangement], or the appropriate and natural progression of these feelings into similar and related ones, or into those more distant."[18] In the end, it is this fine discernment "to join refined and abstract taste with passionate imagination,

---

findung auf einem gewissen Punkte von Lebhaftigkeit zu erhalten, (wenn es NB. eine wünschenswürdige angenehme Empfindung ist;) oder sie, wenn sie in die Classe der unangenehmen gehört, von ihrer Höhe herunter zu stimmen, und aus einer unangenehmen in eine angenehmere zu verwandeln." Forkel, "Sendschreiben," 25.

16. On Herder and *Einfühlung*, see chapter 2, footnote 19.

17. "Eine Reihe höchst lebhafter Begriffe, wie sie nach den Gesetzen einer begeisterten Einbildungskraft auf einander folgen, ist eine **Ode**. Eben eine solche Reihe lebhafter, Ausdrucksvoller musikalischer Ideen, (Sätze) wenn sie nach der Vorschrift einer musikalisch begeisterten Einbildungskraft auf einander folgen, ist in der Musik die **Sonate**." Forkel, "Sendschreiben," 27.

18. "Begeisterung, oder höchstlebhaften Ausdruck gewisser Gefühle" and "Anordnung, oder zweckmäßige und natürliche Fortschreitung dieser Gefühle, in ähnliche und verwandte, oder auch in entferntere." Forkel, "Sendschreiben," 29.

to induce order and design in the progress of *Empfindung*" that is "the summit of art both for the genuine composer of sonatas and the poet of odes."[19]

Forkel is much absorbed in the phenomenon of *Empfindung* as the principle matter in the work of art. This is not the implacable, fixed "affect" identified with *Figur* in the music of the Baroque. *Empfindungen* have a way of changing, often quixotically and unpredictably. Forkel advocates control. The work of art will be "governed" by "a principal *Empfindung;* similar secondary *Empfindungen; Empfindungen* dismembered, broken up, that is, into their separate components; and contradictory and opposed *Empfindungen,* which, when they are put into a fitting sequence, then constitute in the language of *Empfindungen* that which, in the language of ideas, or in true rhetoric, are the well-known figures, established in our natures: exordium, proposition, refutation, affirmation and the like."[20] Here, at the heart of Forkel's elaborate effort to get at such music, is a recognition of the aesthetic appeal of the irrational and the urgency to control it through the formal conventions of rhetoric: the ballast of tradition as counterpoise to the flight of inspiration.

Music, then, speaks in the "Sprache der Empfindungen" but emulates the linguistic syntax of the "Sprache der Ideen." The musical Idea, earlier equated with this linguistic notion of "*Satz,*" is now defined as "*Empfindung.*" This is the word without which Emanuel Bach's music cannot be construed. What, precisely, does it mean?[21] Forkel will no doubt have known the lengthy article under this entry in Sulzer's *Allgemeine Theorie,* whose opening lines are worth having: "This word possesses a psychological as well as a moral meaning. . . . Used in the first, more general sense, *Empfindung* is to be understood in contrast to clear knowledge, and signifies some image (*Vorstellung*) only in so far as it makes a pleasing or displeasing impression upon us, affects our desires, or awakens ideas of good or evil, the

---

19. "Diese feine Beurtheilung, diesen gebildeten und abgezogenen Geschmack mit der feurigen Einbildungskraft zu verbinden, Ordnung und Plan in den Fortgang der Empfindung zu bringen, ist der Gipfel der Kunst eines ächten Sonatencomponisten und Odendichters." Forkel, "Sendschreiben," 28.

20. "(1) eine Hauptempfindung, (2) ähnliche Nebenempfindungen, (3) zergliederte, das heißt, in einzelne Theile aufgelößte Empfindungen, (4) widersprechende und entgegengesetzte Empfindungen . . . die denn, wenn sie in eine gehörige Folge gestellt werden, in der Sprache der Empfindungen das sind, was in der Sprache der Ideen, oder in der eigentlichen Beredsamkeit die bekannten, und von guten, ächten Rednern noch immer beybehaltenen, auf unsere Natur gegründeten Exordien, Propositionen, Widerlegungen, Bekräftigungen, etc. sind." Forkel, "Sendschreiben," 32.

21. For reasons that will become clearer in chapter 6, given to "C.P.E. Bachs Empfindungen," I retain the German to avoid any distortion of the complexity of its meaning. The common English equivalents—sentiment, feeling, perception—each miss something.

pleasing or the repugnant."[22] For Sulzer, the foundational difference between *Empfindung* and *Erkenntniß* (cognitive knowledge, perception) allows that the one may even contradict the other: what the former calls good, the latter may reject.[23]

When Forkel speaks of "*Empfindungen* dismembered (zergliederte), broken up (aufgelöste), that is, into their separate components," he is describing what commonly happens to thematic material. The thematic substance of the work is understood to be linguistically conceived, and thus subject to the permutations of syntax. These syntactic constructions each express—better, embody—an *Empfindung*, by which Forkel must mean something akin to a sentiment conveyed in the thematic figure (broadly defined). It is not the sentiment that is broken up into smaller units, but the thematic figure that conveys it. For Forkel, the *Empfindung* is at once something observed and apprehended in the formal, syntactical sense, and something felt. Just how these two aspects are related, and even whether they are separable, is an imponderable that Forkel will not pursue.

"You've perhaps not found much beauty in that place in the second part of the first Allegro, where the modulation moves through A♭ minor, F♭ major, and from there returns in a rather rough manner to F minor," writes Forkel, coming finally, on the very last page of the essay, to the actual notes of the sonata. (The passage is shown in ex. 1.1). "I must confess that, considered quite apart from its connection to the whole, I too haven't found much beauty in it. But who finds beauty in the hard, rough, violent outbursts of an angry and resentful man? I am quite inclined to believe that Bach, whose sensibility is otherwise always so exceptionally correct, has not in this instance been betrayed by a false sentiment, and that under such circumstances, this difficult modulation is nothing other than the accurate expression of what should and must be expressed in this instance."[24]

Forkel was not the last to focus on this difficult passage in Bach's sonata—von

---

22. "Dieses Wort drükt sowol einen psychologischen als einen moralischen Begriff aus. . . . In dem erstern Sinn, der allgemeiner ist, wird die Empfindung der deutlichen Erkenntniß entgegen gesetzt, und bedeutet eine Vorstellung, in so fern sie einen angenehmen oder unangenehmen Eindruk auf uns macht, oder in so fern sie auf unsre Begehrungskräfte würkt, oder in so fern sie die Begriffe des Guten oder Bösen, des Angenehmen oder Widrigen erwekt." Sulzer, *Allgemeine Theorie,* II: 53. With only the slightest emendations, the translation is taken from Christensen, "Selected Articles," 27–28.

23. "Wer auf diesen bestimmten Unterschied zwischen Empfindung und Erkenntniß genau acht hat, wird daraus leicht begreifen, woher es komme, daß bisweilen die Empfindung der Erkenntniß widerspricht; das jene gut heißt, was diese verwirft." Sulzer, *Allgemeine Theorie,* II: 53.

24. "Sie haben vielleicht diejenige Stelle im zweyten Theil des ersten *Allegro* nicht schön gefunden, wo die Modulation ins As moll, Fes dur, und von da auf eine etwas harte Art wieder zurück ins F moll geht. Ich muß gestehen, daß ich sie, außer ihrer Verbindung mit dem Ganzen betrachtet, eben so wenig schön gefunden habe. Aber wer findet auch wohl die harten, rauhen und heftigen Aeußerungen eines zornigen und unwilligen Menschen schön? Ich bin sehr geneigt zu glauben,

EXAMPLE 1.1   C. P. E. Bach, Sonata in F minor, H 173 (Wq 57/6), first movement.

Bülow, Baumgart, Bitter, Riemann, and Schenker all had a shot at it[25]—but in one sense, his is the most valuable, in that it conveys a contemporary perception of rare insight: the passage may be rude and impenetrable, but it is true to the meaning of the piece. More to the point, Forkel allows himself to address this passage in isolation—to speak of it aesthetically as though it were self-contained—only conditionally, "considered quite apart from its connection to the whole." Such passages cannot be understood as though they were not part of something larger, Forkel suggests. The concept of structural dissonance, of the dissonant episode as central to the story of sonata, is strongly implicated.[26]

Sketches and the Improvisatory

Sketches, when they are by the great masters, are often more highly prized than works more completely realized, for all the fire of imagination, often dissipated in the execution of the work, is to be met in them. The *Entwurf* is the product of genius. The working out is primarily the doing of Art and of Taste.[27]

---

daß Bach, dessen Gefühl sonst überall so außerordentlich richtig ist, auch hier von keinem unrichtigen Gefühl geleitet sey, und daß unter solchen Umständen die erwähnte harte Modulation nichts anders ist, als ein getreuer Ausdruck dessen, was hier ausgedrückt werden sollte und mußte." Forkel, "Sendschreiben," 38.

25. Forkel's discussion is reprinted in C. H. Bitter, *Carl Philipp Emanuel und Wilhelm Friedemann Bach und deren Brüder* (Berlin: Verlag von Wilh. Müller, 1868), I: 217–218. Bitter joins Baumgart, whose edition (Breslau: 1863) of the six volumes "für Kenner und Liebhaber" (Breslau, 1863) restores the passages corrupted by von Bülow (Leipzig, 1862). Riemann (Leipzig: Steingräber, n.d.) silently writes B-double-flats in mm. 53–54 [54–55]; Schenker (Vienna: Universal-Edition, 1902) defends this alteration on musical grounds. David Schulenberg, *The Instrumental Music of Carl Philipp Emanuel Bach* (Ann Arbor: UMI Research Press, 1984), 114–117, and footnote 6 (p. 177), smartly reminds us that the enlarged flat symbol shown in the original, both in this passage and before the E in the bass in mm. 57–58 [58–59], was an accepted notation for the double-flat, about which Bach himself wrote in the *Versuch* (II: 18–19). The original edition can be studied in facsimile in *The Collected Works for Solo Keyboard by Carl Philipp Emanuel Bach*, ed. Darrell Berg, 6 vols. (New York and London: Garland, 1985), II: esp. 362.

26. For more on Forkel's attention to this aspect of structural dissonance, see my "The New Modulation of the 1770s: C. P. E. Bach in Theory, Criticism, and Practice," in *Journal of the American Musicological Society*, 38 (1985): 551–592, esp. 573–574.

27. "Entwürfe, wenn sie von grossen Meistern sind, werden oft höher geschätzt, als ausgeführte Arbeiten, weil das ganze Feuer der Einbildungskraft darinn anzutreffen ist, das oft in der Ausführung etwas geschwächt worden. Der Entwurf ist das Werk des Genies; die Ausarbeitung aber ist vornehmlich das Werk der Kunst und des Geschmaks." Johann Georg Sulzer, "Entwurf," in *Allgemeine Theorie*, II: 80; for another translation, see Christensen, "Selected Articles," 65–66.

Thus, Johann Georg Sulzer invites us to the window of the artist's soul. If it is graphic art, principally, that Sulzer entertains, music might lay equal claim to this understanding of the matter. At another place, a similar thought evokes these lines: "Like the first sketches of the draftsman, the fantasies of great masters, and especially those that are performed out of a certain abundance of feeling and in the fire of inspiration, are often works of an exceptional power and beauty that could not have been composed in a reflective state of mind."[28] The idea of sketch is intimately bound in with the notion of *Begeisterung* (inspiration), a topic that inspired Sulzer to an inquiry into the physiological root of it all.

For Sulzer, the sketch itself acquires value as the rare evidence of a mysterious process: a glimpse of the artistic mind in the act of creation. His notion of the sketch, a hieroglyph of artistic meaning, resonates with Hamann's view of the origins of language. For both Sulzer and Hamann, meaning and expression, in some sense synonymous, are to be found in the utterance—unmediated, unreasoned, inspired. Inspiration (*Begeisterung*) was understood as a powerful and indispensable state of mind from which would emanate the utterance—as sketch, as fragment, improvisatory and unfinished: the beginnings of works whose refinement and completion, invoking later waves of inspiration, would depend on more reflective, less impassioned states of mind.

Sulzer was preceded in these thoughts by Denis Diderot, writing of some sketches by Greuze in the *Salons* of 1765. "Sketches commonly have a fire that the painting does not," he begins. "This is the moment when the artist is full of fervor, pure inspiration, without any of the careful detail born of reflection; it's the painter's soul spread freely over the canvas. A poet's pen, the skillful draftsman's pencil seem to frolic and amuse themselves. A rapid thought finds expression in a single stroke."[29] For Diderot, the appeal is much tied in with the critical enter-

28. "Die Fantasien von grossen Meistern, besonders die, welche aus einer gewissen Fülle der Empfindung und in dem Feuer der Begeisterung gespielt werden, sind oft, wie die ersten Entwürfe der Zeichner, Werke von ausnehmender Kraft und Schönheit, die bey einer gelassenen Gemüthslage nicht so könnten verfertiget werden." Sulzer, "Fantasiren; Fantasie," in *Allgemeine Theorie*, II: 205. On the authorship of the music articles in the encyclopedia, see Christensen, "Selected Articles," 14 and 23.

29. "Les esquisses ont communément un feu que le tableau n'a pas. C'est le moment de chaleur de l'artiste, la verve pure, sans aucun mélange de l'apprêt que la réflexion met à tout; c'est l'ame du peintre qui se répand librement sur la toile. La plume du poète, le crayon du dessinateur habile, ont l'air de courir et de se jouer. La pensée rapide caractérise d'un trait." Denis Diderot, *Salons*, II: Salon de 1765 (London: Oxford University Press, 2nd ed., 1979), 153, 154. I borrow from two translations: Denis Diderot, *Selected Writings on Art and Literature*, tr. Geoffrey Bremner (London: Penguin Books, 1994), 244; and *Diderot on Art*, tr. John Goodman, with an Introduction by Thomas Crow, I (New Haven and London: Yale University Press, 1995), 104.

prise: "the more expression in the arts is ill-defined, the more the [critic's] imagination is at ease."[30] If there is some confusion here between the unmediated inspiration of the creative act and the task of the critic to read meaning in these inchoate signs, Diderot compounds it in the following lines, where the specificity of meaning in vocal music is set alongside music without text: "I can make a well-constructed symphony say almost anything I like."[31] Diderot's "anything" naively disables the elocutionary specificity of music to say precisely what it means.

Sulzer's idealized *Entwurf* and Diderot's sketch are graphic artifacts. The artist's vision is recorded directly through the drawing hand. For the composer, the utterance is expressed less directly. The *Entwurf* has something to do with performance. The vision is realized in an imagined performance, then immobilized in a notation that may specify too much, or not enough. The writing hand serves the composer not quite so truly as the drawing hand the artist. If the composer's sketch does not speak as eloquently as the draftsman's, that is because sketches only stand for an imagined performance, at another remove from the inspired utterance.

The hand then becomes the medium, as the conduit that guides performance (even as it appropriates the physiological grain of the voice), and as writer. We scrutinize the autograph—the *Handschrift*—for these obscure signs of transference, signs that the *writing* of music, no longer a mechanical act of translation, actualizes the bringing to life of an imagined utterance. In the sketch notation of a Beethoven, the evidence of such transference needs no lengthy argument. The signs are there to be deciphered.

The sketch, as it partakes of this quality of utterance, has something to do with what musicians call improvisation. The Romantics sought in their music to convey the suggestion of the improvisatory. Work as sketch. The sketchlike as work. Sulzer's model is turned on its head. Beethoven had more than a little to do with the reversal: the opening of the Piano Sonata, Opus 101, made to sound as if we were witness to the spontaneous creation of ephemera; the feigned innocence of the search for a fugue subject after the Adagio in Opus 106;[32] the deep C♯ and the arpeggiation that unfolds above it at the outset of Opus 31, no. 2 (a topic to itself in chapter 8); an arpeggiation of another kind at the Adagio espressivo in the first

30. "Or, plus l'expression des arts est vague, plus l'imagination est à l'aise." Diderot, *Selected Writings*, 244; *Diderot on Art*, I: 104.

31. "Il faut entendre dans la musique vocale ce qu'elle exprime. Je fair dire à une symphonie bien faite, presque ce qu'il me plaît." Diderot, *Selected Writings*, 244; *Diderot on Art*, I: 104–105.

32. "The improvisatory nature of the scene only contributes to this phenomenon of the piece contemplating its own evolution," I wrote of the passage, in "Between Cavatina and Ouverture: Opus 130 and the Voices of Narrative," in *Beethoven Forum* 1 (1992): 172.

movement of Opus 109 (another topic to itself, in chapter 11)—these each cast the performer (tellingly, always a pianist) in the role of creator, acting out the sense of *Begeisterung* implicit in the idea itself. The composer inscribes himself in the performance. At the end of a laborious creative process, the work pretends to a spontaneous birth.

No wonder that the contributors to Sulzer's encyclopedia were intrigued by reports of a device that could accurately record keyboard improvisations in notation.[33] What might seem a naive quest to locate the source of the improvisatory leads us to a further distinction: formal improvisation as a display in public performance, on the one hand; and the private, inner improvisation that is innate in the act of composition, the indispensable trace that distinguishes the work of genius from hackwork. If this "inner" improvisation resists the kinds of documentation that we routinely demand of empirical evidence, the Beethoven sketches, that fraction of the process that was caught in writing, constitute a precious legacy, for they vividly preserve those compositional improvisations, at once spontaneous and reflective, that a mechanical recording device might well have captured had it been privy to Beethoven's workshop.

This generic distinction is however a vulnerable one, fraught with paradox. One of its aspects, one source of the Romantic inclination toward a state of perpetual improvisation, might again be isolated in the thought of Emanuel Bach, for whom improvisation was at once a practice, a topic of pedagogy, and a compositional genre. And it is precisely in this last sense—improvisation as genre—that the paradox is engaged. This is perhaps nowhere more eloquently observed than in the final pages of Bach's *Versuch über die wahre Art das Clavier zu spielen,* in the chapter titled "Von der freyen Fantasie" (to which I shall return more than once in the studies that follow).[34] Here, Bach makes a categorical dis-

---

33. Much of the article "Fantasiren; Fantasie" is given over to a report from London in the annals of the Royal Society of Science for 1747 of a design for a machine "welche ein Tonstük, indem es gespielt wird, in Noten setzt" (which writes out a piece in notation as it is played), and to another from Berlin in 1749 of work progressing on "einem Clavier . . . das die Fantasien in Noten setzen könne" (a keyboard that is able to capture improvisation in notation); see Sulzer, *Allgemeine Theorie,* II: 205. Charles Burney, too, was intrigued by it; see *An Eighteenth-Century Musical Tour in Central Europe and the Netherlands,* ed. Percy A. Scholes (London: Oxford University Press, 1959), 201–203.

34. Carl Philipp Emanuel Bach, *Versuch über die wahre Art das Clavier zu spielen ,* II (Berlin: George Ludewig Winter, 1762), 340–341. The chapter was the subject of a searching analytical study by Heinrich Schenker, as "Die Kunst der Improvisation," in *Das Meisterwerk in der Musik* (Munich, Vienna and Berlin: Drei Masken Verlag, 1925), now translated, with commentary, by Richard Kramer in Schenker, *The Masterwork in Music,* ed. William Drabkin, I (Cambridge and New York: Cambridge University Press, 1994), 2–19.

tinction, represented in two depictions of a Fantasy in D major: a *Gerippe*—a skeleton—in which the bass, with its intervalic figures, is written out in the text of the final paragraph, in note values whose relationship to one another means to guide the larger rhythms of what Bach calls the *Ausführung,* which is engraved on a separate plate and tipped into the text (both are shown in fig. 5.1). Clearly, the *Gerippe* is premeditated, reasoned, planned. The *Ausführung* is not—or rather, is meant to suggest that it is not. The word is itself suggestive of that which is performed, even if its meaning is not limited to the English "performance"; it is the word that Sulzer, in the epigraph above, opposes to *Entwurf.* The paradox resides precisely here, in the writing out, in elaborate detail, of this "freye Fantasie." Decidedly *not* improvised, the degree of premeditation attending its creation is perhaps even greater than that of the *Gerippe* from which it is meant to be adduced. If Forkel's *Anordnung* and *Begeisterung* are at play here, it is not in simple equation with *Gerippe* and *Ausführung,* but enmeshed in a rather more convoluted dialogue.

Genre intrudes here as well. The Fantasy is of a kind meant to sound as though improvised. In the act of true improvisation, the composer and the performer are one, and the troubled relationship between composition and performance dissolves. When improvisation is feigned, the relationship is problematized. The performer wears the composer's mask. The composer, free now to invent the signs of the improvisatory, is driven back to first things, to that state of mind that would capture the "Feuer der Einbildungskraft"—the fire of imagination—that Sulzer perceives in the sketches of the great masters. The conventions of formal composition are suspended. The music means to suggest a purity of idea—idea removed from the constraints that such formal limitations as sonata, dance, fugue impose. In the theater in which Berlin's "origins of modern irrationalism" are played out, the figure of Emanuel Bach comes alive.

The "freye" fantasy, as Bach named it, acquired its own set of conventions: one can easily enough identify such a work from the symptoms of its discourse, symptoms that all such works seem to share. In a sense, the failure of the fantasy as a self-perpetuating genre is precisely in the exposure of its illusory game, in which the more serious enterprise of sonata (and all the permutations that take its formal imperatives as a given) is challenged by that which pretends to the profundities of original creation, but which too often suggests only the contrivance of improvisation. In the late eighteenth century, the test of genius lay in the ability to improvise—truly to improvise—a sonata, a fugue, variations on a theme given: the categorical distinction between inspiration and reason is here collapsed.

This thin line drawn to distinguish these two senses of improvisation—as a public, performed display of the intuitive, controlled by the clock of "real" time; as composition internalized, where the clock is written into the work—invites its own destruction. As a topic of historical inquiry, the boundaries that separate the two are crossed in perpetual flight from one another. Composition, one might say, is a flight from the anxieties of inspiration; improvisation, from the constraints of convention. Ludwig Tieck, writing of Beethoven in 1812, captures this notion vividly: "he seldom follows through a musical idea or theme, and, never satisfied, leaps through the most violent transitions and, as though in restless battle, seeks to escape from imagination itself."[35] And yet strict composition— "die Kunst des reinen Satzes," in Kirnberger's stern title—seeks the spontaneity of inspiration even as the improvisatory slips unwittingly into its own conventions.

Fragments

> Fragments by classical authors, whatever their species, are priceless. Among musical fragments, those by Mozart certainly deserve full attention and admiration. Had this great master not left behind so many completed works in every species, these magnificent relics alone would constitute an adequate monument to his inexhaustible *Geist*.[36]

Not quite "works," the Mozart fragments have nonetheless found an ear among the devotees of his music, and for several reasons. For one, they have about them the aura of spontaneity, of the immediacy of composition—a proximity to the creative act—even if it is now clear that the works actually completed by Mozart do not differ appreciably in this regard. Pregnant with possibility, they whet the appetite for what might have been, inspiring the author of our epigraph— Constanze Mozart, as it turns out—to endow the fragments with aesthetic value, for it was naturally in her interest to sell the fragments for the highest possible price. "Haven't even the briefest fragments of famous writers—Lessing, for

---

35. The passage is given in Charles Rosen, *The Frontiers of Meaning: Three Informal Lectures on Music* (New York: Hill and Wang, 1994), 52.

36. Wilhelm A. Bauer, Otto Erich Deutsch, and Joseph Heinz Eibl, eds., *Wolfgang Amadeus Mozart: Briefe und Aufzeichnungen. Gesamtausgabe,* 7 vols. (Kassel: Bärenreiter, 1962–1975), IV: 324.

example—been published?" she wrote coyly to Breitkopf in a letter of June 1799. "They ought to be consistently instructive, and the ideas in them could even be used by others and brought to completion."[37]

Surely there can be no argument with the view that Mozart's fragments do not aspire to that condition of fragment so cherished by the Romantics, for whom the completed work, ever contested, is apprehended as unfinished at its core. And yet the Mozart fragments signal aspirations of another kind. Paradoxically, it is precisely in what they portend of a finish forever lost that many of the Mozart fragments stake their claim to aesthetic value. The distance between this portent of profound, unrealized finish and a completion ex post facto in the hands of even the most inspired epigone is simply immeasurable.

Writing in 1799, Constanze's view of the fragment may well have been inspired by the bold ideas of her younger contemporaries. These new sensibilities were sharply etched in Friedrich Schlegel's "Athenäums-Fragmente" (as they came to be known), published in 1798, in among which is this now famous aphorism: "Many works of the ancients have become fragments. Many works of the moderns are fragments at birth."[38] "Irony," writes Schlegel elsewhere, "is the *form* of paradox"—a thought laced with an irony of its own.[39] The irony that charges Schlegel's play on the two conditions of fragment—the one imposed by the accidents of time, the other inherent in the poetic idea—might be extended, with appropriate modulation, to a paradoxical opposition in the fragments of Mozart and Schubert. We call them fragments merely because they have survived in an unfinished state, and yet each has a story to tell, from which might be read the signs that would suggest why they remained unfinished. This is not what Schlegel means by "fragments at birth." The works that he has in mind are complete, even if they simulate the condition of fragment. In the fragments of Mozart and Schubert it is tempting to perceive the converse: the unfinished as a station to-

---

37. *Briefe und Aufzeichnungen*, IV: 250–251.

38. "Viele Werke der Alten sind Fragmente geworden. Viele Werke der Neuern sind es gleich bei der Entstehung." Athenäums-Fragmente, no. 24. The authoritative edition is the *Kritische Friedrich-Schlegel-Ausgabe*, ed. Ernst Behler in collaboration with Jean-Jacques Anstett and Hans Eichner, vol. II, *Charakteristiken und Kritiken I* (1796–1801), ed. Hans Eichner (Munich and Zurich, 1967), 169. The translation is my own. For others, see Friedrich Schlegel, *Dialogue on Poetry and Literary Aphorisms*, ed. and tr. Ernst Behler and Roman Struc (University Park: Pennsylvania State University Press, 1968); and *Friedrich Schlegel's* Lucinde *and the Fragments*, trans. Peter Firchow (Minneapolis, 1971), 164.

39. "Ironie ist die Form des Paradoxen. Paradox ist alles, was zugleich gut und groß ist." Kritische Fragmente, no. 48. *Kritische Friedrich-Schlegel-Ausgabe*, II, 153. See also Firchow, ed., *Schlegel's* Lucinde, p. 148.

ward some imagined and intended completion. Schlegel's aphorism will not hold, and yet it continues to insinuate itself. Are there fragments by Schubert—an avid reader of Schlegel, it will be recalled—of which it might be claimed that their unfinishedness bears the trace of this Romantic disinclination toward finish?

In contending with an "epistemology of fragment" (as I do in chapters 13 and 14), I mean to probe the spaces that separate Mozart from Schubert, from both of whom we have inherited a canonical repertory of unfinished works. For Schubert no less than for Mozart, the fragment captures a moment in the gestation of the work. The fragment has something to do with sketch: neither Mozart nor Schubert routinely sketched in anything resembling the obsessive, repetitive, brutally self-critical acts that constitute the compositional process for Beethoven. For Mozart and Schubert, these fragments put us before the moment at which an imagined music is concretized in written form. Where writing stops, we are witness to a breach in thought. This broken music, echoing into a timeless void, challenges us to imagine the moment where idea and sound collapse—to read the moment for a significance that can never be recovered.

Patrimonies

"He is the father, we are the children," Mozart was said to have exclaimed of Carl Philipp Emanuel Bach. "What he did would be considered old-fashioned now; but the way he did it was unsurpassable."[40] The fanciful invention of the ever-inventive Rochlitz, the exclamation yet lives on, so conveniently does it capture what much other evidence advocates as Bach's patrimonial place at the end of the eighteenth century.

"I have only a few samples of Emanuel Bach's compositions for the clavier," Beethoven wrote to Breitkopf & Härtel on 26 July 1809; "and yet some of them should certainly be in the possession of every true artist, not only for the sake of

---

40. "Er ist der Vater; wir sind die Bub'n. . . . Mit dem, was er macht . . . kämen wir jetzt nicht mehr aus; aber *wie* er's macht—da steht ihm Keiner gleich." See Friedrich Rochlitz, *Für Freunde der Tonkunst* (Leipzig: Carl Cnobloch, 3rd ed., 1868), IV: 202. The context of these lines, in which Rochlitz claims that Mozart, now in Leipzig, had just come from a visit to Bach in Hamburg, is demonstrably false: Mozart visited Leipzig in 1789, a year after Bach's death, and there is no evidence that he ever visited Hamburg. On Rochlitz and the fabrication of anecdotes about Mozart, see Maynard Solomon, "The Rochlitz Anecdotes: Issues of Authenticity in Early Mozart Biography" in *Mozart Studies,* ed. Cliff Eisen (Oxford: Clarendon Press; New York: Oxford University Press, 1991), 1–59.

real enjoyment but also for the purpose of study."[41] The works in question were no doubt the six sets of keyboard works "für Kenner und Liebhaber" (1779–1787) actually printed by J. G. I. Breitkopf for Emanuel Bach, who retained the rights of publication. What was it that Beethoven thought he could learn from this music? And is there any evidence that Bach's music touched Beethoven at this critical juncture in his own work? In asking such questions, I do not mean to set loose a hunt for simple answers, of the kind having to do with influence, with models and borrowings, with veiled intimations of homage.

Beethoven in 1810 is a composer casting about for a new voice. The notorious *Akademie* of 22 December 1808, a marathon retrospective of the grand genres of what has come to be known as Beethoven's heroic phase, gave palpable evidence of the exhaustion of a style.[42] What was exhausted was the vigorous, even belligerent engagement with those genres which collectively formulated a language of classical discourse. The crisis, in its essence, can be reduced to a coming to grips with the figure of Mozart, captured no more vividly than in the driven, manic cadenzas written for Mozart's Concerto in D minor in 1809 (a topic explored in chapter 9).

The Piano Sonata in E minor, Opus 90, composed in 1814, evokes an aesthetic strain that Beethoven might have perceived in certain of the works in these valedictory collections of Bach's keyboard music. "Mit Lebhaftigkeit und durchaus mit Empfindung und Ausdruck": the inscription at the front of the first movement is the first of a new sort in Beethoven's music, escorting the player toward a sensibility of feeling and expression redolent of the *Empfindsamkeit* immanent in the music of Emanuel Bach. Phrasing it in the vernacular—the earliest work of which this is true—gains for Beethoven an immediacy of address which in itself suggests something about the diction of the music.

The opening bars of this sonata emulate no Mozartean prototype. The music gropes for utterance: direct, halting, every note made articulate, without artifice, stripped of the conventional figures of transition. In the midst of these deliberations, the beginnings of a new theme—of something sung—at m. 9 sound sub-

---

41. "Von *Emanuel* Bachs Klavierwerke habe ich nur einige Sachen, und doch müßen einige jedem wahren Künstler gewiß nicht allein zum hohen Genuß sondern auch zum Studium dienen, und mein größtes Vergnügen ist es Werke die ich *nie* oder nur selten gesehn, bey einigen wahren Kunstfreunden zu spielen." *Ludwig van Beethoven: Briefwechsel Gesamtausgabe*, ed. Sieghard Brandenburg (Munich: G. Henle, 1996–), II: 72; Emily Anderson, ed. and tr., *The Letters of Beethoven* (London: Macmillan & Co., 1961), 235.

42. See my "*Gradus ad Parnassum*: Beethoven, Schubert, and the Romance of Counterpoint," in *19th Century Music*, 11 (1987): 112.

limely nonchalant. But beginnings they remain, for the theme dissolves almost as
it is formed. This new quality in Beethoven's music was not lost on the reviewer
for the Leipzig *Allgemeine Musikalische Zeitung,* for whom the first movement
"approaches rather the free fantasy."[43] What I will explore in chapter 10 is something less obvious. Among those works of Emanuel Bach that Beethoven sought
out for purposes of study are several whose traces are evident in the two movements of Opus 90, and in other of Beethoven's later keyboard works as well. In
some sense, it is the *Geist* of Emanuel Bach that hovers in these works, impalpable, and unreceptive to the kinds of documentation that bring reassurance to
the historical enterprise.

Emanuel Bach was himself the child, genetically and artistically, of a father whose
sovereign authority was recognized among a small circle of musicians in the decades after his death, and by everyone else only gradually, following on the publication of Forkel's biography in 1802.[44] The profundity of this relationship of
son to father, and how its repercussions might be heard in the formulating of
Emanuel Bach's idiosyncratic music, is the topic of the chapter that follows.

43. "Er nähert sich mehr der freyen Phantasie." For 24 January 1816, col. 60ff. The review is reprinted
    in *Ludwig van Beethoven. Klaviersonate e-Moll op. 90. Faksimile des Autographs,* ed. with commen-
    tary by Michael Ladenburger (Bonn: Beethoven-Haus, 1993); and in *Ludwig van Beethoven: Die
    Werke im Spiegel seiner Zeit. Gesammelte Konzertberichte und Rezensionen bis 1830,* ed. Stefan
    Kunze, in collaboration with Theodor Schmid, Andreas Taub, and Gerda Burkhard (Laaber:
    Laaber-Verlag, 1987; Sonderausgabe 1996), 266.
44. Johann Nikolaus Forkel, *Ueber Johann Sebastian Bachs Leben, Kunst und Kunstwerke* (Leipzig:
    Hoffmeister und Kühnel, 1802; facs. repr., with commentary by Axel Fischer, Kassel: Bärenreiter,
    1999).

PART II

Emanuel Bach and the Allure of the Irrational

CHAPTER 2

Carl Philipp Emanuel Bach and the Aesthetics of Patricide

We have been taught by history to speak of Emanuel Bach as a function of, an exponent of, the great Bach. The name itself, those four sacred letters enshrined as a topos in the nineteenth century, insists that we do so. It signifies always the great Bach, and always an idealization of only a core of Bach's music that had come to stand for some transcendental power over the notes—a technical, intellectual, and spiritual power that everyone after Bach could only admire and seek to emulate. The weaving of the sacred letters as actual tones into the fabric of some romantic homage—by Beethoven, by Liszt, by Schumann in the Six Fugues "über den Namen Bach" and Schoenberg in the Variations for Orchestra, Opus 31—is only a symptom of this mythic aspect of Bach's preeminence. For old Bach, in his final months, these letters that encode the name of his dynasty also constitute what is arguably his last compositional act—the ultimate "theme" engraved as an emblem into the massive fragment with which the *Art of Fugue* breaks off. It was Emanuel Bach who seemed to testify to the act, in a note inscribed in the manuscript at just that point: "In the midst of this fugue, where the name B A C H is applied in counter-subject, the composer died."[1] "*Seemed* to testify" means to

---

1. "Ueber dieser Fuge, wo der Nahme B A C H im Contrasubject angebracht worden, ist der Verfasser gestorben." For an illustration of the page, see (for one) Christoph Wolff, "Bach's Last Fugue: Unfinished?" in *Bach: Essays on His Life and Music* (Cambridge, Mass., and London: Harvard University Press, 1991), 259. Wolff (261) argues that the page was left unfinished because it had in likelihood been completed elsewhere—in a hypothetical "fragment x" in which Bach would have "worked out, or at least sketched, the combinatorial section of the quadruple fugue in a manuscript that originally belonged together with [the surviving manuscript] but is now lost." Thanks largely to Wolff's researches, we now have reason to believe that the *Art of Fugue* was a work that occupied Bach from as early as 1742; see "The Compositional History of the *Art of Fugue*," in *Bach: Essays*, 265–281. Still, this last fugue is on paper and in a hand that suggested to Wolff that "it is entirely possible that here we are dealing with one of the last documents of Bach's handwriting" (271).

raise the skeptic's flag, for Emanuel had been off in Berlin during Bach's death, and there is now legitimate reason to suppose that this apparent quietus in the manuscript signifies something more complex. Still, Emanuel had much to do with the posthumous publication of the work, and was responsible for the sale of the copper engraving plates in 1756, a few years after the second issue.[2] Perhaps this most oracular of fragments (or what Emanuel believed—or wished us to believe—to be a fragment), and its connection in Emanuel's mind with the rite of passage which he could not witness, intrude subconsciously in a miniature homage to that final fugue that Emanuel composed in the early 1770s as a kind of signature inscribed as a memento for his friends.[3] (This is shown in fig. 2.1.) It is an intense little piece, contorted in all those fugal permutations that we associate with the father, and not with the son. The legacy of the father hangs heavy over its notes, and it is only in the final dissonance, unresolved deep in the bass, that the real C. P. E. signs himself.

What can it have meant to have grown up in Bach's home, to have had Bach both as teacher and father, and at the same time to have been conscious of one's own claims to musical genius? Piecing together the evidence of Emanuel Bach's life, the scholar does not at once turn to the Oedipus myth as a model for illumination into the relationship with the father. By all accounts, his attitude toward the father, and his actions on behalf of the propagation both of Bach's music and the legacy of his teaching, were altogether beyond reproach.[4] But even here, not

---

2. The announcement by Emanuel Bach was printed in Marpurg's *Historisch-Kritische Beyträge zur Aufnahme der Musik*, II (Berlin: Gottlieb August Lange, 1756), 575–76. The passage is reprinted in *Bach-Dokumente III: Dokumente zum Nachwirken Johann Sebastian Bachs, 1750–1800* , ed. Hans-Joachim Schulze (Kassel: Bärenreiter, 1972) 113–114; an English version is given in Hans T. David and Arthur Mendel, eds., *The New Bach Reader: A Life of Johann Sebastian Bach in Letters and Documents*, revised and enlarged by Christoph Wolff (New York: W. W. Norton & Co., 1998), 377–378.

3. Johann Friederich Reichardt, *Briefe eines aufmerksamen Reisenden die Musik betreffend*, II (Frankfurt and Breslau, 1776), 22, at the end of a letter dated "Hamburg, den 12ten Julius, 1774." In precisely this way, Bach entered his signature in the "Stammbuch" of Carl Friedrich Cramer, dated 9 June 1774. The page is shown in *Carl Philipp Emanuel Bach. Musik und Literatur in Norddeutschland* (Heide in Holstein: Boyens & Co., 1988), 97; and in Ernst Suchalla, ed., *Carl Philipp Emanuel Bach: Brief und Dokumente. Kritische Gesamtausgabe* (Göttingen: Vandenhoeck & Ruprecht, 1994), 405. For the facsimile of another, dated 3 November 1775, see Eva Badura-Skoda, "Eine private Briefsammlung," in *Festschrift Otto Erich Deutsch zum 80. Geburtstag am 5. September 1963*, ed. Walter Gestenberg, Jan LaRue and Wolfgang Rehm (Kassel: Bärenreiter, 1963), plate 1 (after p. 288). In a letter dated "Hamburg, den 28. April 84," Bach appended a more elaborate composition in which the letters of his "Vornamen" are woven into the counterpoint. It is printed in C. H. Bitter, *Carl Philipp Emanuel und Wilhelm Friedemann Bach und deren Brüder* (Berlin: Wilh. Müller, 1868), II: 303–304; in Suchalla, *Briefe und Dokumente*, 1009; and in Stephen L. Clark, tr. and ed., *The Letters of C. P. E. Bach* (Oxford: Clarendon Press; New York: Oxford University Press, 1997), 204–205.

4. This is poignantly evident in the letter written by Emanuel Bach in response to the unfavorable comparison with Handel in Charles Burney's *An Account of the Musical Performances in Westminster Abbey in Commemoration of Handel* (London: T. Payne, 1785); Bach's response, published

FIGURE 2.1 From Johann Friederich Reichardt,
*Briefe eines aufmerksamen Reisenden die Musik
betreffend* (Frankfurt and Breslau, 1776), II: 22.

everything is what it seems: beneath this impeccable decorum, one might imagine, is another Bach who had been more happily named anything else.

That there might be something behind the scrim of conventional evidence to wish to investigate seems to me manifest in the facts of the case, and imperative in the very act of biography. Evidence is of many kinds. The most intriguing, the most genuine in its aura of authenticity, is that elusive type that no one knows quite how to "read" as evidence pertinent to a biography. I mean of course the music itself, the most eloquent testimony to the deepest reaches of the mind.

In the 1770s and 80s, it was Carl Philipp Emanuel Bach who was held by his critics to embody all those qualities that, for the philosophers of the Enlightenment, characterize the man of genius. The work of genius embodies, makes articulate, its own law: the creation of the superior mind gripped by some muse of which the mortal man of genius is himself only dimly conscious. Perhaps the telling definition is Immanuel Kant's, in the *Kritik der Urteilskraft* (Berlin, 1790):

> Genius is an *aptitude* to produce something for which no definite rule can be postulated; it is not a capacity or skill for something that can be learnt from some rule

---

anonymously in Friedrich Nicolai's *Allgemeine deutsche Bibliothek,* Vol. 81, Part 1 (1788), 295–303, iterates the very points raised in a letter of 21 January 1786 from Bach to Johann Joachim Eschenburg, who translated Burney's *Account;* see Clark, *Letters,* 243–44. The identification of Bach as the author of the published response to Burney was deduced by Dragan Plamenac in "New Light on the Last Years of Carl Philipp Emanuel Bach," *The Musical Quarterly,* 35 (1949): 565–587, esp. 575–587.

or other. Its prime quality, then, must be *originality*. . . . The aptitude cannot of itself describe how it creates its products, or demonstrate the process theoretically, though it provides the rules by itself being a part of nature. Thus the progenitor of a work of art is indebted to his own genius and he does not himself know how the ideas for it came to him, nor does it lie within his power to calculate them methodically or, should he so wish, to communicate them to others by means of principles that would enable others to create works of equal quality. It is through genius that nature prescribes the rules of art.[5]

The work of art, following its own rule, demands exegesis. This, precisely, is the task that a new criticism in the late eighteenth century set for itself: to develop an apparatus for construing such works. Here is how Carl Friedrich Cramer thought to introduce a long critical piece on a collection of keyboard sonatas, free fantasies and rondos by Bach—the fourth in the famous series "für Kenner und Liebhaber," published in 1783.

About certain men and their works, the judgement of the "Publicum"—that kernel of connoisseurs which unites a natural sensitivity with knowledge, taste and experience—is so well established that a critic, at the appearance of a new product of his genius, has almost nothing more to do than quite simply to indicate that it exists. If this were ever the case with an artist, it is so with Bach. . . . One can continue to apply to him what Herr Forkel, in his excellent review of an earlier collection, with such warm and well-founded enthusiasm, borrowed from Lessing on Shakespeare: "a stamp is imprinted on the tiniest of his beauties which calls forth to the entire world: Ich bin Bachs! and woe to the alien beauty that is inclined to place itself next to him."[6]

---

5. The translation is from Peter le Huray and James Day, eds., *Music and Aesthetics in the Eighteenth and Early-Nineteenth Centuries* (Cambridge: Cambridge University Press, 1981), 228. For the notion of Bach as *Originalgenie*, see Hans-Günter Ottenberg, *C. P. E. Bach* (Oxford: Oxford University Press, 2nd ed., 1991), pp. 1–5, 139–142; and Hans-Günter Klein, *"Er ist Original!": Carl Philipp Emanuel Bach. Sein musikalisches Werk in Autographen und Erstdrucken aus der Musikabteilung der Staatsbibliothek Preußischer Kulturbesitz Berlin* (Wiesbaden: Dr. Ludwig Reichert Verlag, 1988), 11–15.

6. "Ueber gewisse Männer und ihre Werke hat sich nun schon einmal das Urtheil des Publici (. . . den Kern der Kenner, die natürliches Gefühl mit Kenntniß, Geschmack und Erfahrung verbinden) so sehr fixirt, daß ein Recensent, bey der Erscheinung eines neuen Productes ihres Genius, beynahe nichts weiter zu thun hat, als nur ganz einfältiglich anzuzeigen: daß es da ist. . . . War dieß je bey einem Künstler so; so trift es bey Bachen zu. . . . Noch immer kann man das auf ihn anwenden, was Herr Forkel in seiner treflichen Recension einer frühern dieser Sammlungen, mit so warmen und

This "excellent review" by Herr Forkel, a critical account of two collections of accompanied keyboard sonatas—piano trios, we now call them—is in fact very much more than that. It appeared in 1778, in the second volume of Forkel's *Musikalisch-kritische Bibliothek,* and seeks at the outset to take the measure of Bach's genius:

> [T]hose few noble souls who still know how to value and take pleasure in true art repay [Bach] in the approval that the masses cannot give, and his irrepressible inner activity overpowers every obstacle that stands in the way of his creative outburst [*Ausbruch*] and communication. In this way a lively, fiery and active spirit—even in a world which, in relation to him, is hardly better than a desert—is thus in a position to bring forth works of art which carry within them every characteristic of true original genius, and, as fruits of an inner compulsion of doubled strength, are of double worth to those few noble souls who, as Luther says, understand such things a little.

We do not need to determine to what extent this is the case with the famous composer of these sonatas. Not, however, satisfied with that fame long ago established, not satisfied to have created a new taste, and through it, to have widened the musical terrain, he continues to enrich us with the fruits of his inexhaustible genius, and shows us that even in the evening of his life, his imagination is still disposed toward the conception of those noble and stimulating ideas; so that now, as in the noontime of his life, one may say of him what Lessing says of Shakespeare: . . .[7]

What Lessing had to say of Shakespeare is deeply bound up both in his theorizing about German theater and in his own writing for the stage. The passage in question comes from one of the critical pieces published altogether under the title *Hamburgische Dramaturgie* in 1769, and specifically from a review of Christian Felix Weiße's *Richard III,* which Lessing took as a pretext to develop an essay

---

gegründetem Enthusiasmus, Lessingen über Shakespearen aus dem Munde nahm: 'auf die geringste seiner Schönheiten ist ein Stempel gedruckt, welcher gleich der ganzen Welt zuruft: ich bin Bachs! Und wehe der fremden Schönheit, die das Herz hat, sich neben ihr zu stellen!'" Carl Friedrich Cramer, *Magazin der Musik,* I/2(Kiel and Hamburg, 1783; reprint, Hildesheim: Georg Olms, 1971), 1238–1239.

7. "Jedoch, die kleine Anzahl derjenigen Edeln, welche die wahre Kunst noch zu schätzen und zu genießen wissen, halten ihn für den Beyfall des großen Haufens schadlos; und seine innere unaufhaltsame Wirksamkeit überwältigt jede Hinderniß, die seinem Ausbruch oder seiner Mittheilung im Wege steht. Auf diese Weise ist sodann ein lebhafter, feuriger und wirksamer Geist im Stande auch sogar in einer Welt, die in Beziehung auf ihn, beynahe nichts besser als eine Einöde ist, Werke der

on the nature of tragic character and on the issue of imitation and borrowing in literature and the arts.[8] It is well known that Shakespeare figured prominently in the debate, some years earlier, on the purity of classical tragedy. The complexity of Lessing's Shakespeare criticism, of his brilliant and convoluted efforts to reconcile Shakespearean tragedy with the Aristotelian principles of pure classical tragedy, and in opposition to what Lessing held to be a misreading of those principles in the tragedies of Corneille and Racine, need not obscure the intent of those lines quoted by Forkel.[9] But it is in the following lines that Lessing's sense of Shakespeare's creative originality, as a giver of rule, is implicit.

Shakespeare must be studied, and not plundered. If we have genius, then Shakespeare must be to us what the *camera obscura* is to the landscape painter: he looks into it diligently to understand how Nature in all its conditions is projected upon a *single* surface; but he borrows nothing from it.[10]

Kunst hervorzubringen, die jedes Merkmal des wahren Originalgenies an sich tragen, und, als Früchte eines innern Drangs von doppelter Kraft, auch den wenigen Edeln, die, wie Luther sagt, solches ein wenig verstehen, doppelt schätzbar sind. . . . In wiefern dieses der Fall bey dem berühmten Verfasser dieser Sonaten ist, brauchen wir hier wohl nicht zu bestimmen. . . . Aber nicht zufrieden mit seinen längst gegründeten Ruhm, nicht zufrieden, uns einen neuen Geschmack geschaffen, und dadurch die musikalischen Gefilde erweitert zu haben, bereichert er uns noch immer mit den Früchten seines unerschöpflichen Genies, und zeigt uns, daß auch selbst am Abend seines Lebens seine Imagination zur Conception eines jeden edlen und reizenden Bildes noch aufgelegt sey; so, daß man noch jetzt, so gut wie am Mittage seines Lebens, von ihm sagen kann, was Lessing von Shakespear sagt: . . . " Johann Nikolaus Forkel, *Musikalisch-kritische Bibliothek,* 3 vols. (Gotha: C. W. Ettinger, 1778–1779; reprint Hildesheim: Georg Olms, 1964), II: 275–277. For more on Forkel's important review, see my "The New Modulation of the 1770s: C. P. E. Bach in Theory, Criticism, and Practice," *Journal of the American Musicological Society,* 38 (1985): 551–592, esp. 573–574.

8. Lessing's line is "Auf die geringste von seinen Schönheiten ist ein Stempel gedruckt, welcher gleich der ganzen Welt zuruft: ich bin Shakespeares! Und wehe der fremden Schönheit, die das Herz hat, sich neben ihr zu stellen"; it is found in the 73rd number, "den 12. Januar 1768," of *Hamburgische Dramaturgie,* 2 vols. (Hamburg: In Commission bey J. H. Cramer, in Bremen, 1769) accessible in *Gotthold Ephraim Lessings sämtliche Schriften,* ed. Karl Lachmann (Stuttgart: G. J. Göschen'sche Verlagshandlung,3rd ed., 1894; reprint, n.p.:. Walter de Gruyter & Co., 1968), X: 95; and in English in G. E. Lessing, *Hamburg Dramaturgy,* trans. Helen Zimmern, with a new introduction by Victor Lange (New York: Dover Publications, 1962), 173.

9. "In the cult of Shakespeare Göttingen was only a pace behind Strassburg and Frankfurt . . . The Göttingen students imitated the quips, phrases, and mannerisms of Shakespeare in 1772–1778 just as their contemporaries two years before had done in Strassburg," writes Lawrence Marsden Price, *The Reception of English Literature in Germany* (Berkeley: University of California Press, 1932; reprint New York and London: Benjamin Blom, 1968), 34. On the complex topic of Shakespeare reception in Germany among Lessing's contemporaries, see *ibid.,* 269–308. The topic has been addressed more recently in Elaine Sisman, "Haydn, Shakespeare, and the Rules of Originality," in *Haydn and His World,* ed. Elaine Sisman (Princeton: Princeton University Press, 1997), esp. 11–19.

10. "Shakespeare will studiert, nicht geplündert sein. Haben wir Genie, so muß uns Shakespeare das sein, was dem Landschaftsmaler die Camera obscura ist: er sehe fleißig hinein, um zu lernen, wie

The originality of Shakespeare's work allows no imitation, a view consonant with Kant's axiom that "it is through genius that Nature prescribes the rules of art."

That Forkel, in writing about Emanuel Bach, should have reached for this essay is in itself significant, and not, I think, because Forkel intended to force an invidious comparison between Bach's art and Shakespeare's. Rather, the coupling of this eminent critical mind with the idea of Shakespeare conjured the tone that Forkel wished to set in contending with these trios by Bach, suggesting by analogy the relationship between the man of genius and his enlightened critic: Lessing to Shakespeare is as Forkel to Bach. For Forkel, it was Emanuel Bach's music, in its inscrutable originality, that served as a touchstone for the act of criticism. This sense of Bach as law-giver comes through in the *Sendschreiben* (studied earlier, in chapter 1) composed in answer to some putative invitation to divulge the meaning of Bach's Sonata in F minor from the third collection "für Kenner und Liebhaber." Forkel, it will be recalled, turned the opportunity toward nothing less than a disquisition on the concept of sonata. There is talk here about neither thematic idea, nor modulation, nor even harmony—except in some marginal comments that clearly reside outside the main argument. For Forkel, it is only the "*genuine* composer of sonatas [emphasis mine] and the poet of odes" who have the capacity to unite "refined and abstract taste with fiery imagination in bringing regulation and plan in the progression of *Empfindung*," a difficult enterprise that, for Forkel, has always insured that there have been "so few true and genuine composers of sonatas and poets of odes."

> The happy vanquishing of this difficulty is also why I hold the author of our Sonata in F minor for a far greater musical ode-poet than we have ever had.... How precious, then, must be the products of a man who is the only one in his art who unites everything within it that nature and taste can give to the artist, and who among the powerful lords of music stands thus alone in the heights, incomparable. No one can be set at his side, but rather (as Claudius says of Lessing) he sits on his own bench.[11]

---

sich die Natur in allen Fällen auf eine Fläche projektieret; aber er borge nichts daraus." Lessing, *Hamburgische Dramaturgie*, in *Sämtliche Schriften*, X: 95; I have somewhat altered the translation given in *Hamburg Dramaturgy*, 173.

11. "Diese feine Beurtheilung, diesen gebildeten und abgezogenen Geschmack mit der feurigen Einbildungskraft zu verbinden, Ordnung und Plan in den Fortgang der Empfindung zu bringen, ist der Gipfel der Kunst eines ächten Sonatencomponisten und Odendichters, aber auch zugleich, eine Schwierigkeit, welche von jeher verursacht hat, und noch ferner verursachen wird, daß wir so wenig wahre und ächte Odendichter und Sonatencomponisten haben. Die glückliche Ueberwindung dieser Schwierigkeit ist es auch, warum ich den Verfasser unserer Sonate in F moll für einen

Forkel was perhaps best known in the nineteenth century as the author of the first book-length biography of Sebastian Bach, published, finally, in 1802.[12] His work toward that end had begun in the 1770s, and the principal source of his information, both anecdotal and documentary, both archival and in actual musical texts of unknown works, was Carl Philipp Emanuel Bach. Some twenty-six letters from Bach to Forkel, dating from between 1773 and 1778—and a final one from 1786—have survived. Unwittingly, they capture a fundamental opposition in Bach's life: on the one hand, there is a deeply held obligation to the proper dissemination of the father's legacy, and, on the other, the selling of a new aesthetic, one born in antipathy to that legacy. Two passages will convey this double mission, the first from a letter of 7 October 1774:

> In haste, dear friend, I have the satisfaction of sending you the remains of my Sebastianoren: namely, 11 trios, 3 pedal pieces, and Von Himmel Hoch etc. . . . The 6 keyboard trios . . . are among the best works of my dear, late father. They still sound very good, and bring me much satisfaction, even though they are more than 50 years old. There are a few adagios in them which even today could not have been composed in a more vocal style. . . . In the next letter, pure Emanueliana.[13]

---

weit größern musikalischen Odendichter halte, als es je einen gegeben hat. . . . Wie schätzbar müssen uns daher die Producte eines Mannes seyn, der der Einzige in seiner Art ist, der alles in sich vereinigt, was Natur und Geschmack dem Künstler zu geben vermag, der unter dem gewaltigen Heere von Musikern so ganz allein oben an steht, mit keinem verglichen, keinem an die Seite gesetzt werden kann, sondern (wie Claudius von Lessing sagt,) auf seiner eigenen Bank sitzt." [Johann Nikolaus Forkel,] "Ueber eine Sonate . . . Ein Sendschreiben," in *Musikalischer Almanach für Deutschland auf das Jahr 1784* (Leipzig: Schwickert, 1784), 28–29. Forkel is no doubt referring to the witty passage in the "Nachricht von meiner Audienz beim Kaiser von Japan," in Matthias Claudius, *Asmus omnia sua Secum portans, oder Sämmtliche Werke des Wansbecker Bothen,* III (Wandsbeck: Beym Verfasser, 1777). "Der Chan" asks: "Herr Lessing gehört doch auf die Bank der Philosophen?"; to which Asmus replies: "Ich wollte aber doch raten, daß Ew. Majestät ihm lieber seinen eignen Stuhl setzten. Die gewöhnlichen Bänke passen nicht für ihn, oder vielmehr er paßt nicht für die Bänke und sitzt sie alle nieder." (I would rather advise Your Majesty to place him on his own chair. The ordinary benches are not suitable for him, or rather, he is not suitable for them and sits beneath them all.) See, for one, *Matthias Claudius: Werke* (Stuttgart: J. G. Cotta'sche Buchhandlung Nachfolger, [1954]), 166.

12. The work is available in English as Johann Nikolaus Forkel, *Johann Sebastian Bach: His Life, Art, and Work,* trans. with notes and appendices by Charles Sanford Terry (London: Constable & Co., 1920; reprint New York: Vienna House, 1974); and in David and Mendel, eds., rev. Wolff, *New Bach Reader,* 415–482, as "On Johann Sebastian Bach's Life, Genius, Works."

13. "In Eil habe ich das Vergnügen Ihnen, bester Freund, den Rest meiner Sebastianoren zu schicken, nehml. 11 Trii, 3 Pedalstücke u. Vom Himmel hoch p. . . . Die 6 Claviertrio . . . sind von den besten Arbeiten des seel. lieben Vaters. Sie klingen noch jetzt sehr gut, u. machen mir viel Vergnügen, ohngeacht sie über 50 Jahre alt sind. Es sind einige Adagii darin, die man heut zu Tage nicht sang-

The second, from a letter dated 10 February 1775, is three close pages of "pure Emanueliana." The following passage is well-known, but worth retelling:

> Now one would like to have 6 or 12 fantasies from me, like the 18th "Probestück" in C minor. I don't deny that I would love to do something in this genre, and perhaps I am not entirely ungifted in this. Besides, I have a good collection of them which . . . belong to the chapter on free fantasy in the second part of my *Essay [on the True Art of Playing Keyboard Instruments]*. But how many people are there who love this kind of thing, who understand them, and who can play them well?[14]

What kind of music was Bach writing in the 1770s? We know from other letters that Bach made a distinction between music composed for the pleasure of a small circle of connoisseurs—music essentially for himself—and that which was intended for sale to a less endowed public. In the autobiographical notice written in 1773 for the German translation of Charles Burney's travel journals, Bach admitted as much: "Because I have had to compose most of my works for specific individuals and for the public, I have always been more restrained in them than in the few pieces that I have written merely for myself. . . . Among all my works, especially those for clavier, only a few trios, solos and concertos were composed in complete freedom and for my own use."[15]

A sonata composed in 1775, and unpublished until very recently, displays that

---

barer setzen kann. . . . Künftig kommen lauter Emanueliana." Suchalla, *Briefe und Dokumente*, 446–447; my translation. For another, see Clark, *Letters*, 66–67.

14. "Man will jetzt von mir 6 oder 12 Fantasien haben, wie das achtzehnte Probestücke aus dem C-moll ist; ich läugne nicht, dass ich in diesem Fache gern etwas thun mögte, vielleicht wäre ich auch nicht ganz u. gar ungeschickt dazu, überdem habe ich ein Haufen collectanea dazu, welche . . . zu der Abhandlung von der freyen Fantasie meines zweyten Versuchs gehören: allein, wie viele sind derer, die dergleichen lieben, verstehen und gut spielen?" Suchalla, *Briefe und Dokumente*, 486; for another translation, see Clark, *Letters*, 76.

15. "Weil ich meine meisten Arbeiten für gewisse Personen und fürs Publikum habe machen müssen, so bin ich dadurch allezeit mehr gebunden gewesen, als bey den wenigen Stücken, welche ich bloß für mich verfertigt habe. . . . Unter allen meinen Arbeiten, besonders fürs Clavier, sind blos [sic] einige Trios, Solos und Concerte, welche ich mit aller Freyheit und zu meinem eignen Gebrauch gemacht habe." The Autobiography, written for the German translation of Charles Burney's *The Present State of Music in Germany, the Netherlands, and the United Provinces*, II (London: T. Becket, 1773), was published in Burney, *Tagebuch seiner musikalischen Reisen*, 3 vols. trans. C. D. Ebeling and J. J. C. Bode (Hamburg: Bode, 1772–1773), III: 198–209; that portion was reprinted in Carl Philipp Emanuel Bach, *Autobiography. Verzeichniß des musikalischen Nachlasses*, annotations in English and German by William S. Newman (Buren: Frits Knuf, 1991); the passages cited are on pp. 208 and 209. For an English version, see William S. Newman, "Emanuel Bach's Autobiography," *The Musical Quarterly*, 51 (1965): 363–372, esp. 371 and 372.

inimitable originality that had come to be prized as a defining attribute of genius. (Two movements of the sonata are given here as appendix 2A.) It has survived in Bach's autograph and in three contemporary copies, suggesting a wide circulation among the members of Bach's inner circle.[16]

One phrase in particular captures the ear. The most overtly coherent phrase in the piece (the only coherent one, by some measure), it occurs for the first time deep in the interior of the first movement, at mm. 33–37 (first beat), after the first double bar—outside, that is, the formal exposition. The intelligibility of the phrase, the sense that it makes within itself, is only exaggerated through a context that seems intent upon syntactical dislocation. Abruptly abandoned, the phrase suggests no self-evident relation to the immediate surface of the piece. Its significance refuses explanation: reason is not likely to get at the illogical aspect of its place in the course of things, nor to fathom the phrase in its gestural aspect.

This telling phrase returns, and when it does, it engages the narrative of the piece in ways that we could not have predicted. The opening idea, recapitulated at m. 60, is now reset in A♭ major, as though in search of this outcast phrase, and, finding it—see mm. 67–71 (first beat)—draws it into the immediate tonal motion of the piece. Set in the key of the flat submediant, the phrase seems to hover placidly for an instant before the inevitable augmented sixth at the cadence.

"Das Adagio fällt gleich ein," Bach instructs, at the end of the movement: "The Adagio begins straightaway." It is similar in kind, this Adagio, to any number of contemplative intermezzi in Bach's keyboard works that conjure some remote tonal landscape between the outer movements. This one begins its meditation on an isolated D♭. The tone itself, in its naked isolation, establishes a dissonance with the final cadence in the first movement, and therefore suggests a reaching back into the memory of the piece. Again, Bach's "Das Adagio fällt gleich ein" presses the point. Even the disposition of its first harmony is calculated to suggest a Neapolitan sixth in relation to the first movement.

The Adagio, too, has its luminous, telling phrase, and it flowers at just the point where the music begins its descent through the circle of fifths that winds

---

16. *Sonata per il Cembalo solo,* H[elm] 248 (Wq. 65/47), now published in C. Ph. E. Bach, *Klaviersonaten. Auswahl,* ed. Darrell M. Berg, III (Munich: G. Henle, [1989]), 88–95. A facsimile of the autograph is printed in Darrell Berg, ed. *The Collected Works for Solo Keyboard by Carl Philipp Emanuel Bach,* 6 vols. (New York and London: Garland Publishing, 1985), IV: 217–222. Bach himself dated the work "1775" on the autograph, a date iterated in the *Verzeichniß des musikalischen Nachlasses des verstorbenen Capellmeisters Carl Philipp Emanuel Bach* (Hamburg: Gottlieb Friedrich Schniebes, 1790), 22, item 174; reprinted as *The Catalog of Carl Philipp Emanuel Bach's Estate: A Facsimile of the Edition by Schniebes, Hamburg, 1790,* annotated, with a Preface, by Rachel W. Wade (New York and London: Garland Publishing, 1981).

inexorably from D♭ to the half-cadence in C before the final movement. It is precisely at this moment of greatest remove (beginning at m. 10) that a phrase redolent of that expatriate phrase in the first movement is teased out of the narrative. The reciprocity between these moments is not casual, nor is it concrete in the manner of some thematic permutation. Rather, one gropes for the language to convey how they are related: for it is an evocative relationship of just this kind, with all that it suggests of the significatory power of an ambiguous phrase, that cries out for this new mode of criticism that Forkel and his contemporaries were struggling to develop.

On the clavichord, the inclination of those opening D♭s toward some linguistic expression, however dimly felt, is palpable. On any other instrument, this eloquence is missed.[17] The harpsichord, innately antipathetic to such music, would trample on the nuances of what has been called its *"redende"* aspect—music as speech. Because the tangent remains in contact with the string, and establishes one node in the sounding structure, the finger controls the vibrating string as it can at no other keyboard instrument. Like no other keyboard instrument, the clavichord "speaks." And it is further in the nature of the instrument that it speaks directly to the player, and (because one must strain to hear it in all its nuance) only faintly to everyone else. It is the clavichord into which Emanuel Bach withdraws, into its world of near silence, where each tone is an *Empfindung*—expression itself—whose inaudibility only exaggerates its claim to speech. There is no grand splendor in music of this kind, but only a touching of sensibilities.

Less than a year before his own death, in a remarkable review of the first volume of Forkel's *Geschichte der Musik,* Bach affords us a rare insight into his understanding of the nature of musical expression: "Music has long been called a language of feeling, and consequently, the similarities that lie beneath the coherence of its expression and the expression of spoken language have been deeply felt."[18] This "Sprache der Empfindung" (to revive a topic addressed in chapter 1

---

17. In German usage in the late eighteenth century, "Cembalo" is the generic designation for any stringed keyboard instrument. On this point, see, among others, Herbert Grundmann, "Per il Clavicembalo o Piano-Forte," in *Colloquium Amicorum: Joseph Schmidt-Görg zum 70. Geburtstag* (Bonn: Beethovenhaus Bonn, 1967), 100–117.

18. "Man hat die Musik schon lange eine Sprache der Empfindung genannt, folglich die in der Zusammensetzung ihrer und der Zusammensetzung der Sprachausdrücke liegende Aehnlichkeit dunkel gefühlt." The review appeared in the *Hamburgische unpartheyische Correspondent* for 9 January 1788, and is reprinted in Johann Nikolaus Forkel, *Allgemeine Geschichte der Musik,* I (Leipzig: Schwickert, 1788; reprint, ed. Othmar Wessely, Graz: Akademische Druck- u. Verlagsanstalt, 1967), xvii–xviii; and in C. H. Bitter, *Carl Philipp Emanuel Bach und Wilhelm Friedemann Bach und deren Brüder,* II: 109–111.

and anticipate its discussion in chapter 6), and its darkly felt associations with linguistic expression, is at the core of Bach's aesthetic. To hear this music, we need to "feel" with it, to engage in what Herder would famously call *Einfühlung*.[19] The *Empfindungen* somehow conveyed through the syntaxes of this language do not open themselves up to conventional analysis. To seek to explain such music in rational, equation-like syllogism as so many permutations of a *Grundgestalt*, is to miss its point. Analysis of this kind may tell us something about certain aspects of the surface of the music, but it tells us nothing of the essential inner core of it. It is Bach's "dunkel gefühlt" that is suggestive of the critical process that will get us to the essence of the piece.

How might we construe the language of a sonata such as this as testimony of a man whose only teacher, as he himself reverently claimed on more than one occasion, was his father? Where is the patrimony in the sonata? What heritage is this, in which all the old orthodoxies are repudiated? The clichés of music history are not helpful. It will not do to speak of "style change" as though it were some inexorable historical event to which Emanuel Bach's music necessarily contributes. Bach's music sounds like no one else's. It is radical and idiosyncratic beyond anything in the music of even his closest contemporaries. Haydn, Mozart, and Beethoven, however loudly their proclamation of Emanuel Bach as a spiritual father—and there is no reason to doubt them—hardly knew what to make of it. Charles Burney, who spent a good week with Emanuel Bach in 1772, and wrote about it in his travel journals, published the following year, recaptured the special quality of Bach's language in a vivid passage in the fourth volume (1789) of his *General History:* "Emanuel Bach used to be censured for his extraneous modulations, crudities, and difficulties; but, like the hard words of Dr. Johnson, to which the public by degrees became reconciled, every German composer takes the same liberties now as Bach, and every English writer uses Johnson's language with impunity."[20]

---

19. Isaiah Berlin writes of "this contrast between the sense of dialogue, communication, immediate understanding, achieved by what Herder was to call 'feeling into' (Einfühlung) a man, or a style or a period [or, one might add, a musical utterance], with rational, rule-dominated analysis" in *The Magus of the North: J. G. Hamann and the Origins of Modern Irrationalism* (New York: Farrar, Straus and Giroux, 1993), 78–79. See also Berlin's "Herder and the Enlightenment," now reprinted in Berlin, *The Proper Study of Mankind: An Anthology of Essays,* ed. Henry Hardy and Roger Hausheer (New York: Farrar, Straus and Giroux, 1997), 403. Berlin's ideas are drawn primarily from Herder's *Auch eine Philosophie der Geschichte zur Bildung der Menschheit* (1774), reprinted in *Johann Gottfried Herder. Sämtliche Werke,* ed. Bernhard Suphan, 33 vols. (Berlin, 1877–1913; reprint Hildesheim: Georg Olms, 1967), V: 503 in particular.

20. Charles Burney, *A General History of Music,* with Critical and Historical Notes by Frank Mercer, 2 vols. (New York: Dover Publications, 1957), II: 955.

It would be fatuous to suggest that Emanuel Bach's music could have existed without the obscure patrimony to which I referred a moment ago. The figure of Sebastian Bach, totemlike, was ubiquitous. Everywhere, Emanuel felt the need to speak of his father. In his music, he fails to do so. The patrimony is not acknowledged there. And when he speaks about the father's music, it is the astounding technique that is admired, the awesome, powerful control of musical forces— qualities that Emanuel Bach's music does not seek. Even in the most lavish encomium to the father's art—the comparison with Handel, written in 1788, provoked by an essay by Burney, whose bias toward Handel was easily explained (he knew lots of Handel's music, and very little of Sebastian Bach's)—even here, the praise is for Bach as prestidigitator, both as an organist and as a contriver of fugal complexity.[21]

What I mean to suggest is that Emanuel Bach's music tells us something about the relationship of the son to the father, in this complex language of signification, at once abstract and concrete, that is the deepest reflection of feeling. What one reads there hews closely to what one has come to know, through Freud, as an archetype for the ambivalence in the behavior of the son toward the father. A revelatory passage from the third essay in *Moses and Monotheism* from a chapter titled "The Great Man," is very much to the point.

And now it begins to dawn on us that all the features with which we furnish the great man are traits of the father, that in this similarity lies the essence of the great man. The decisiveness of thought, the strength of will, the forcefulness of his deeds, belong to the picture of the father; above all other things, however, the self-reliance and independence of the great man, his divine conviction of doing the right thing, which may pass into ruthlessness. He must be admired, he may be trusted, but one cannot help but fear him as well.[22]

---

21. Plamenac, "New Light," 582–585; and see above, footnote 4.

22. "Und nun mag uns die Erkenntnis dämmern, daß alle Züge, mit denen wir den großen Mann ausstatten, Vaterzüge sind, daß in dieser Übereinstimmung das von uns vergeblich gesuchte Wesen des großen Mannes besteht. Die Entschiedenheit der Gedanken, die Stärke des Willens, die Wucht der Taten gehören dem Vaterbilde zu, vor allem aber die Selbständigkeit und Unabhängigkeit des großen Mannes, seine göttliche Unbekümmertheit, die sich zur Rücksichtslosigkeit steigern darf. Man muß ihn bewundern, darf ihm vertrauen, aber man kann nicht umhin, ihn auch zu fürchten." Sigmund Freud, *Studienausgabe*, 11 vols., ed. Alexander Mitscherlich, Angela Richard, James Strachey, and Ilse Grubrich-Simitis (Frankfurt am Main: S. Fischer Verlag, 1969–1979), IX: 556. *Moses and Monotheism*, tr. Katherine Jones (New York: Vintage Books, n.d.), 140. I have modified the translation slightly.

Freud imagines Moses as a "tremendous father imago" to his people. "And when they killed this great man they only repeated an evil deed which in primeval times had been a law directed against the divine king, and which, as we know, derives from a still older prototype"—a reference to totemism among aboriginal tribes.[23]

Freud's own obsession with Moses is a topic to itself. The famous 1914 essay on the Moses of Michelangelo is rich in evidence for this, even in its misreadings. But it is also rich in what it suggests about the power of psychoanalytic scrutiny for the interpretation of art, for it forces us to separate out an analysis of the work, and the play of psyche within it, from an investigation of what Freud openly refers to as "the artist's intention." Freud's strategy calls for no such separating out, as I think is clear from a passage early on in the Michelangelo essay. "It can only be the artist's *intention*," he writes, "in so far as he has succeeded in expressing it in his work and in conveying it to us, that grips us so powerfully. . . . It cannot be merely a matter of *intellectual* comprehension; what he aims at is to awaken in us the same emotional attitude, the same mental constellation as that which in him produced the impetus to create."[24]

But the impetus to create and the text of what is created are two very different phenomena, deeply related as they may be. This impetus, which the artist may sense only vaguely, does not readily translate into the substance of the work. How to read a psychoanalytic print of the author in the text, how the text itself constitutes evidence for such a reading, is a critical enterprise of a certain legitimacy. Its converse—how a psychoanalytic reading of the author might tell us of motives

---

23. "Und wenn sie dann einmal diesen ihren großen Mann erschlugen, so wiederholten sie nur eine Untat, die sich in Urzeiten als Gesetz gegen den göttlichen König gerichtet hatte und die, wie wir wissen, auf ein noch älteres Vorbild zurückging." Freud, *Studienausgabe*, IX: 556. Translation from Freud, *Moses and Monotheism*, 140–141. For a discussion of a variant of just this sentence, see Ilse Grubrich-Simitis, *Back to Freud's Texts: Making Silent Documents Speak*, tr. Philip Slotkin (New Haven and London: Yale University Press, 1996), 174.

24. "Was uns so mächtig packt, kann nach meiner Auffassung doch nur die Absicht des Künstlers sein, insofern es ihm gelungen ist, sie in dem Werke auszudrücken und von uns erfassen zu lassen. Ich weiß, daß es sich um kein bloß verständnismäßiges Erfassen handeln kann; es soll die Affektlage, die psychische Konstellation, welche beim Künstler die Triebkraft zur Schöpffung abgab, bei uns wieder hervorgerufen werden." Freud, *Studienausgabe*, X: 198. Sigmund Freud, "The Moses of Michelangelo" (1914), in *The Standard Edition of the Complete Psychological Works of Sigmund Freud,* tr. and ed. James Strachey, in collaboration with Anna Freud, assisted by Alix Strachey and Alan Tyson, 24 vols. (London: The Hogarth Press and the Institute of Psycho-Analysis, 1953–1974), XIII: 212; emphases in the original. I follow the phrasing in the translation of Joan Riviere, as reprinted in Sigmund Freud, *On Creativity and the Unconscious: Papers on the Psychology of Art, Literature, Love, Religion,* selected, with introduction and annotations, by Benjamin Nelson (New York: Harper & Brothers, 1958), 12. For a fascinating account of Freud's encounter with the *Moses* of Michelangelo, see Peter Gay, *Freud: A Life for Our Time* (New York and London: W. W. Norton & Co., 1988), 314–317.

in the work—cannot lay claim to similar legitimacy: the work and the life are not interchangeable, are not the terms of a simple equation. In its unhinged, neurotic, fitful acts at speech, this isolated Sonata from 1775—he did not again write a sonata for keyboard alone until 1780—tells us something of Emanuel Bach's cast of mind, of an aesthetics born in some internalized revolt, in a playing out of a family romance, just as its inner coherence, however "darkly felt," speaks to that power of law-giving that Forkel senses in his lengthy communication on the Sonata in F minor. That nostalgic phrase in the Adagio, for all its self-referentiality within the interiors of the piece, yet suggests something about its author. Recourse to a family romance can offer no more than the sketch of some internalized drama against which such a phrase might have been conceived. In the end, the piece must remain its own singular testimony to its meaning.

Sebastian Bach as Moses? In precisely how it has been made to signify in these past two hundred years, no repertory of music more nearly approaches the commandments engraved in those tablets that Moses holds than Bach's. There is a temptation to extend the simile to those "hundred-weight" copper plates—the tablets on which is engraved the "Art of Fugue"—which Emanuel Bach sold off after public advertisement, six years after his father's death.[25] *Kunst der Fuge*: the title itself has a scriptural ring to it, some sort of cabbalah in search of the hermeneut. From a purely pragmatic point of view, Bach's decision to rid himself of these tablets seems entirely justifiable—and it must be said that the autograph score remained in his possession. But the ambivalent undercurrent in the act, its veiled suggestion of some public renunciation, has its place in the story as well.

A word about Bach's mother. If history tends to obliterate this aspect of the lineage, Emanuel Bach makes certain that she has her place. The opening lines of his autobiographical notice are unequivocal about that: "I, Carl Philip Emanuel Bach, was born in Weimar, March 1714. My late father was Johann Sebastian, Kapellmeister at several courts and ultimately music director in Leipzig. My mother was Maria Barbara Bach, youngest daughter of Johann Michael Bach, a solidly founded composer."[26]

If we are too ready to attribute Bach's musical gifts unconditionally to the father's side, the son corrects us. The mother died in July 1720. Sebastian Bach,

---

25. See above, footnote 2.

26. "Ich, Carl Philip Emanuel Bach, bin 1714 im März, in Weimar gebohren. Mein seliger Vater war Johann Sebastian, Kapellmeister einiger Höfe, und zuletzt Musikdirektor in Leipzig. Meine Mutter war Maria Barbara Bachin, jüngste Tochter, von Johann Michael Bachen, einen gründlichen Komponisten." Burney, *Tagebuch*, III: 199; Newman, "Autobiography," 366.

knowing nothing of this, returned from a trip to Carlsbad to discover that her body had been interred. What can it have meant to a six-year-old to have been witness to that? Perhaps it is to the point to remind ourselves that Maria Barbara and Sebastian were related before marriage. Her father and Bach's father were first cousins. In this sense, too, the line between father's side and mother's side is blurred.

It was Forkel who, in the final lines of his biography of Sebastian Bach, established an hegemony of the father that necessarily set in subordination the works of his progeny—indeed, of all who were to follow. Forkel's mantic words have an evangelical ring: "And this man, the greatest musical poet and the greatest musical orator that ever existed, and probably ever will exist, was a German. Be proud of him, fatherland! Be proud of him, but worthy of him as well!"[27]

There was an agenda for the nineteenth century. In effect the discovery and resurrection of Bach's music was an obsession with its own ambivalences. The appropriation of Bach as the original Romantic—the *Ur-Romantiker*—by composers as disparate as Beethoven, Schumann, Mendelssohn, Wagner, Brahms, and Schoenberg coincided with a stripping away of all such extravagant excess, in the endeavor to discover and scrape clean that enormous repertory whose magnitude Forkel could only vaguely surmise. It is not an exaggeration to say that the invention of a *Musikwissenschaft* at mid-century, along with a scholarly apparatus that vibrates sympathetically with all those other monumental achievements of the industrial revolution, was born of this moral necessity that Forkel preached: to be worthy of Bach. The *Gesamtausgabe* produced by the editorial staff of the Bach Gesellschaft was an enterprise that consumed a half century, from its founding on the centennial of Bach's death to its completion in 1899.[28]

In the 1770s, seeking a critical language adequate to convey Emanuel Bach's music to his contemporaries, Forkel thought to invoke Lessing on Shakespeare, at a time when the call to write a biography of Sebastian Bach seemed driven more by historical curiosity than of a profound passion for the music. Thirty years later, this assessment of their music would be turned on its head. Along with

---

27. "Und dieser Mann—der größte musikalische Dichter und der größte musikalische Declamator, den es je gegeben hat, und den es wahrscheinlich je geben wird—war ein Deutscher. Sey stolz auf ihn, Vaterland; sey auf ihn stolz, aber, sey auch seiner werth!" Johann Nikolaus Forkel, *Ueber Johann Sebastian Bachs Leben, Kunst und Kunstwerke. Für patriotische Verehrer echter musikalischer Kunst* (Leipzig: Hoffmeister & Kühnel, 1802; reprint, Kassel: Bärenreiter, 1999), 69. The translation is from David and Mendel, eds., rev. Wolff, *New Bach Reader*, 479.

28. The final volume appeared, appropriately, in 1900. See David and Mendel, eds., rev. Wolff, *New Bach Reader*, 504.

the clavichord, Emanuel Bach's music vanished.[29] How indeed could the imperious political and aesthetic agendas of the nineteenth century find a place for this idiosyncratic, heretical music that, when it can be heard at all, speaks out so eloquently against all such monument making? Its eccentricities touch the mind and the soul, and bring us close to the human condition in a way that Bach the father would not have wished to understand.

---

29. If a serious restoration of Emanuel Bach's reputation, founded upon the recent publication of the voluminous documents central to his life and career, has had to wait until the final decades of the twentieth century, the restoration of the music remains a work in progress. The first half-dozen volumes of the newly inaugurated *Carl Philipp Emanuel Bach: The Complete Works* (Los Altos, California: The Packard Humanities Institute, in cooperation with the Bach-Archiv Leipzig, the Sächsische Akademie der Wissenschaften zu Leipzig, and Harvard University, 2005–), soundly edited and handsomely produced, herald the solid textual foundation that will inspire a newly focused view of this extraordinary repertory.

APPENDIX 2A C. P. E. Bach, Sonata per il cembalo solo, H 248 (1775), first and second movements

From Carl Philipp Emanuel Bach, *Klaviersonaten: Auswahl,* ed. Darrell M. Berg, 3 vols. (Munich: G. Henle, 1986–1989), III:88–92. Used by permission.

(continued)

APPENDIX 2A *(continued)*

Das Adagio fällt
gleich ein

(continued)

APPENDIX 2A *(continued)*

CHAPTER 3

The Ends of *Veränderung*

I

"While composing these Sonatas I thought especially of beginners and of those amateurs who, on account of their years or of other business, have neither patience nor time enough to practice much," writes Bach toward the end of the famous preface to the publication of his *Sechs Sonaten fürs Clavier mit veränderten Reprisen* (Berlin: George Ludewig Winter, 1760). "Apart from giving them something easy I wanted to provide them with the pleasure of performing alterations [*Veränderungen*] without having to resort either to inventing them themselves or to getting someone else to write them and then memorizing them with much difficulty."[1]

But the argument put forward in its opening paragraph is of a different kind. Concerned less with the pragmatics of the thing than its theoretical underlay, it interrogates current practice, and unwittingly sets a mirror to the relationship between composer and performer. Here is the full text of that familiar paragraph:

It is indispensable nowadays to alter repeats. One expects it of every performer. A friend of mine goes to endless trouble to play a piece as it is written, flawlessly and in accordance with the rules of good performance; how can one not applaud him? Another, often pressed by necessity, makes up by his audacity in alteration for the

---

1. A facsimile of the preface in the French imprint of the first edition (Berlin: George Ludewig Winter, 1760), together with the original German text and an English translation, are given in *Carl Philipp Emanuel Bach. Sechs Sonaten mit veränderten Reprisen (1760)*, ed. Etienne Darbellay (Winterthur: Amadeus Verlag, 1976), xii–xiii.

lack of expression he shows in the performance of the written notes; the public nevertheless extols him above the former. Almost every thought is expected to be altered in the repeat, irrespective of whether the arrangement of the piece or the capacity of the performer permits it. But then it is just this altering which makes most hearers cry *Bravo*, especially when it is accompanied by a long and at times exaggeratedly ornate cadenza. This leads to much abuse of those two true ornaments of performance! Such players have not even the patience to play the notes as written the first time; the overlong delay of Bravo is unendurable. These untimely alterations, an annoyance to most composers, are often quite contrary to the grammer, contrary to the affect and contrary to the relation of one thought to another. Even granting that the performer has all the qualities required for altering a piece as it should be done, will he also at all times be so disposed? Will not unknown pieces present him with new difficulties? Is not the main purpose of alterations to reflect honorably on both the performer and the piece? Should he not therefore produce ideas at least as good the second time? Despite these difficulties and the abuses mentioned, good alterations keep their value always. For the rest, I refer the reader to what I said on this subject at the end of the first part of my *Versuch* [*über die wahrer Art das Clavier zu spielen*].[2]

Often reprinted and commonly cited, Bach's preface is itself an indispensable document, both for what it tells us about the composition of these sonatas as a

---

2. "Das Verändern beym Wiederholen ist heut zu Tage unentbehrlich. Man erwartet solches von jedem Ausführer. Einer meiner Freunde giebt sich alle mögliche Mühe, ein Stück, so wie es gesetzt ist, rein und den Regeln des guten Vortrags gemäß herauszubringen; solte man ihm wol den Beyfall versagen können? Ein anderer, oft aus Noth gedrungen, ersetzt durch seine Kühnheit im Verändern, das, was ihm am Ausdruck der vorgeschriebenen Noten fehlt; nichts destoweniger erhebt ihn das Publicum vor jenem. Man will beynahe jeden Gedanken in der Wiederholung verändert wissen, ohne allezeit zu untersuchen, ob solches die Einrichtung des Stücks, und die Fähigkeit des Ausführers erlaubt. Bloß dieses Verändern, wenn es zumal mit einer langen und zuweilen gar zu sonderbar verzierten Cadenz begleitet ist, preßt oft den meisten Zuhörern das BRAVO aus. Was entsteht nicht daher für ein Mißbrauch dieser zwo wirklichen Zierden der Ausführung! Man hat nicht mehr die Gedult, beym erstenmahle die vorgeschriebenen Noten zu spielen; das zu lange Ausbleiben des BRAVO wird unerträglich. Oft sind diese unzeitigen Veränderungen wider den Satz, wider den Affect und wider das Verhältniß der Gedanken unter sich; eine unangenehme Sache für manchen Componisten. Gesetzt aber, der Ausführer hat alle nöthige Eigenschaften, ein Stück so, wie es seyn soll, zu verändern: ist er auch allezeit dazu aufgelegt? Ereignen sich nicht bey unbekannten Sachen deswegen neue Schwierigkeiten? Ist nicht die Hauptabsicht beym Verändern diese: daß der Ausführer sich und zugleich dem Stücke Ehre mache? Muß er nicht folglich beym zweytenmale wenigstens eben so gute Gedanken vorbringen? Jedoch dieser Schwierigkeiten und des Mißbrauchs ohngeachtet, behalten die guten Veränderungen allezeit ihren Werth. Ich beziehe mich übrigens auf das, was ich am Ende des *ersten Theils meines Versuchs* hiervon angeführt habe." *Ibid.*, xiii. I have altered the translation in several places.

response to praxis and, much to my purpose here, for what it suggests of a dialectic of sonata in 1760, wherein the act of composition is itself to be understood as a kind of performance: composer and performer as *Doppelgänger,* the composer as player, the performer as composer. A dialectic of composition and improvisation is embedded here as well. However we think to read Bach's text, it cannot be dismissed as a plain and easy caveat to the performer. There is something deeper in it.

For one, there is the question of improvisation. What, precisely, is meant by it? If the answer seems self-evident at the outset, by the end of Bach's preface the distinction between the "composed" piece and these *Veränderungen* that the performer improvises has been narrowed appreciably. "Oft sind diese unzeitigen Veränderungen wider den Satz, wider den Affect und wider das Verhältniss der Gedanken unter sich," Bach writes, exposing the composer's abiding fear of misreading in the hands of the performer. What is at stake here are the actual notes, the substance, the guts of the work, and more, for Bach worries about the disposition of the performer, who must somehow manage to affect—to wear, as though in mask—the temperament of the composer in the act of composing this music: "Gesetzt aber, der Ausführer hat alle nöthige Eigenschaften, ein Stück so, wie es seyn soll, zu verändern: ist er auch allezeit dazu aufgelegt?" Here, the boundary between composition and performance is imperceptible. Performance in its deepest sense is understood not as an imitation of the creative act or as a recreation, but as creation itself. In Bach's account, the act of *Veränderung* is an extension of the primary act of composition. Indeed, there is a permanence to these alterations— "good alterations keep their value always"—that elevates them to a sphere beyond the ephemeral, and suggests that they belong now to the work in a defining, textual sense.

There is of course another issue here, having to do with the friction between the rituals of what is commonly called "performance practice" and the epistemology of a new rhetoric of sonata. When Bach writes "wider den Satz, wider den Affect und wider das Verhältniss der Gedanken unter sich," he is protecting the integrity of the work. More than that, these sonatas—each in its own way— explore how the imperatives of large-scale binary form, historically ingrained, in which the two divisions of the work are to be repeated literally, might be deployed in the service of this new rhetoric. The idea of development, of narrative unfolded in a sequence of events, abhors literal repetition, and yet the historical legacy of such repetition is powerfully inscribed as an axiom of instrumental form. There is a conflict, then, between these axiomatic repetitions and the scripting of a new narrativity that together forge in sonata a genre that will dominate music through the death of Schubert.

How, then, can these varied reprises be said to be indispensable (*unentbehrlich*)? Written into the text of the music, they are made so by the act itself. And if in some instances one wants to speak of "variation" in the commonplace sense as mere decorative cover, the cumulative function of these variants is of greater substance. The drama of sonata engages the imperative of repetition. The variant is made an event of significance.

II

These issues are played out with microcosmic intensity in Bach's *Kurze und leichte Klavierstücke mit veränderten Reprisen,* first published in two sets in 1766 and 1768.[3] In the "Andantino e grazioso" from the second set, the subtle unfolding of its thematics is made to depend upon *Veränderungen* of high sophistication. (The complete piece is shown in ex. 3.1.)

The compression of form in the Andantino intensifies the affect of the *Veränderungen,* which consequently come to stand for something more than the embellishment of thematic archetypes. Heard in retrospect through the prism of the *Veränderung* starting at m. 13, the very opening of the piece seems distracted, so many wisps of phrase in search of a theme. At m. 13, the incise that marks this first repetition, a true theme comes. The music originally in the treble is rendered subordinate. The repetition of mm. 9–10, whose harmony is a first inversion triad, is bolder still. Here, at m. 21, the striking intervallic figure is intensified, isolated in a momentary flare of imitation. But there is more to this salient gesture, for the figure has been anticipated in the thematic continuation of the *verändert* opening phrase: the phrase at m. 17, analogous to m.5, recollects the figure first heard at m. 9. And so the music of m. 21 is significant both as an intensification of its analogue at m. 9 and as an echo, formally misplaced, at m. 17. Finally, the figure is embedded in the continuation of the phrase in m. 22, forcing a change of harmony on the third beat, itself an alteration of a higher order.

---

3. *Kurze und leichte Clavierstücke mit veränderten Reprisen und beygefügter Fingersetzung für Anfänger von C. P. E. Bach* (Berlin: George Ludewig Winter, 1766);—*Zweyte Sammlung* (1768); available in a volume "edited from manuscript copies and first editions by Oswald Jonas" ([Vienna:] Universal Edition, [1961]); a "Revisionsbericht," bound separately, contains a rich analytical commentary on the music. The authoritative text of these pieces is now Carl Philipp Emanuel Bach, *Miscellaneous Keyboard Works* I, ed. Peter Wollny, in Carl Philipp Emanuel Bach, *The Complete Works,* Series I, Volume 8.1 (Los Altos: The Packard Humanities Institute, 2006).

EXAMPLE 3.1 C. P. E. Bach, *Kurze und leichte Klavierstücke mit veränderten Reprisen*, II (1768), no. 2 (H 229).

(continued)

EXAMPLE 3.1 *(continued)*

A recapitulation of sorts begins at m. 33, where a sense of return, tentative and fragmentary, is suggested in the motivic detritus of the opening bars, as though to point up the fragility with which the piece begins. And just as the varied reprise at m. 13 formulates something of thematic substance from the barren opening bars, so, too, does the music at m. 49, the analogue to m. 33, play upon this process. The figure isolated and made prominent in m. 21 now becomes the principal thematic agent. Finally, its telling interval is expanded to a diminished seventh and augmented in its temporal dimension in the bass at mm. 53–55: *verändert* to conspicuous purpose.

Picture for a moment how the piece would go if written in the conventional mode, with double bars and repeat marks. By the assumptions set forth in Bach's preface to the sonatas of 1760, this unvaried form and the published version with its *Veränderungen* are two versions of a single piece. The variants written out here, exemplary though they may be, constitute but one permutation of a staggering number of possible alternatives. Apprehended minimally as *Veränderungen,* we have then to contend with the composer, through whose agency these varied reprises—and none of the imaginary alternatives—have purpose. The very meaning of the piece hinges upon a process of thematic discovery—of revelation. There is a continuity in the process of the piece. Return the piece to its state of innocence before the *Veränderungen,* and we feel ourselves in the presence of a draft, an *Entwurf,* of a design yet incomplete.

III

The exercise of *Veränderung* in the Sonatas of 1760 is rigorous and complex, and from it emerges an idea of sonata whose essence will survive the specificity of 1760. Whatever else we might learn from these sonatas, the actual practice of varying the reprise of the exposition—the playing through of Bach's reprise— induces the expectancy that the second half will of necessity be subject to the same mode of *Veränderung.* This is not a question of symmetry, but again of thematic engagement, of process. Not that each and every *Veränderung* in all six sonatas is of a quality and import to bolster a claim for indispensability, for the teleology of narrative, for the celebration of event. Some are merely decorative, perhaps even didactic. They do not evidently contribute to the work as Sonata in the new sense in which it was coming to be defined.

Others do, insinuating themselves into the fiber of the piece, now subtly and imperceptibly, now aflame in the rhetoric of the form. In Sonata VI (H 140)—a

EXAMPLE 3.2 C. P. E. Bach, Sonata in C minor, H 140.

single movement of the "double variation" type (tonic minor, tonic major)—
these distinctions are exhibited in sharp clarity. *Veränderungen,* by formal definition, are deployed at three levels: in the internal phrase structure of the theme
itself; in the conventional bipartite repetitions of the closed formal "frames" of
the theme; and in the subsequent repetitions of the entire theme. There is a sense
in which the return of the opening theme in C minor, following upon the new
music in C major, is made to feel like the da capo after the trio, this in turn followed by a reprise of the trio (and the da capo) a second time. Unlike the seriate
process of the conventional "tema con variazione," the sonata movement puts
great emphasis on the recall of event and the signals of closure.[4]

The most emphatic of these signals comes, logically, at the very end (see ex.
3.2). A newly inflected harmony at the third beat of m. 228—a diminished seventh that signals a dominant ninth on C—sets things off. Struck *fortissimo,* its
tones gripped in two hands (the only such éclat in the piece), the music erupts for
an instant, violating the formal constraints of *Veränderung.* The descending
sixths and the solitary B♮ in the bass play on this moment in the theme itself (see
ex. 3.3). By simple parsing, mm. 230 and 231 are interpolations. The form is perfectly respected when they are omitted. But that is not how the passage is heard.
Rather, the B♮ in m. 230 fails to move as all its predecessors have moved. Its repetition at the lower octave in m. 231 is the lowest note in the piece, and very nearly

4. Elaine Sisman claims the work to have been "[t]he most important predecessor for Haydn's alter-
nating [variation] procedures." See her *Haydn and the Classical Variation* (Cambridge, Mass., and
London: Harvard University Press, 1993), 153–154.

EXAMPLE 3.3 C. P. E. Bach, Sonata in C minor, H 140.

in the entire set. In somber isolation, sounded just this once, it invites all the burr and *Bebung* that Bach's clavichord would bring to it. Too soon (as Bach shrewdly calculated) the right hand breaks in, peremptorily striking the highest note in the piece, from which the figure in big intervals descends.

The second part of Theme II trades in similar intensifications. The deployment of the figures, the spacing of the intervals, is suggestive even in the first instance (mm. 64–72; ex. 3.4A). At the repetition of these bars (mm. 78–86; ex. 3.4B) expression is wrung out of each interval: the drooping third is inverted to a vaunting sixth, and the lower register is more firmly delineated in the process; in the answering dyads, diminished sevenths are now formed, with implications as dominant ninths. The sheer tactile pleasures of the music are exploited in a dizzying counterpoint of displaced accents. At the first iteration in the da capo (mm. 156–164; ex. 3.4C), each alteration touches the music in minimalist gestures that again exercise the physical act of performing. The registral reversal in the answering phrase is "felt" in the echoing dyad at the precise middle of m. 159, where the two hands argue against the slur. Stunningly, the three diminished intervals earlier sounded at the expiration of a slur are here articulated in distinct isolation, each now inflected with the flatted ninths that imply roots even as they displace them in affective dissonance, now in three real voices, and *fortissimo*.

IV

The rhetorical incision of *Veränderung* speaks out in the first movement of Sonata I (H 136; Wq 50/1). This is perhaps most evident in its final bars, one of those characteristic passages in Bach's sonatas that negotiates between one movement and the next. It is worth noting how the music at the close of the movement dissolves (see ex. 3.5). This bare fifth, faintly sounded at the downbeat of m. 47, has to do with liquidation. It is an effect of paradox and deception. All good sense

EXAMPLE 3.4 C. P. E. Bach, Sonata in C minor, H 140.

EXAMPLE 3.5 C. P. E. Bach, Sonata in F major, H 136, first movement.

grasps the simple harmonic facts here: the E is *not* the harmonic fifth above a root A, but rather, an appoggiatura that displaces the F above it, while the A must be understood as the third degree, here inverted beneath the displaced root. And yet the disposition of these tones deep in the bass repudiates this commonsense view, for the emptiness of the harmony incites a purely intervallic hearing, and so, too, does the motion of the bass to the lower F, suggesting a brief patch of austere counterpoint in pure intervals.

The moment is further striking because it grows directly out of the music of mm. 44–45—is more precisely a nearly literal repetition, at a lower octave, of one of the figures embedded in this passage. And even though the interval between the two tones of the fifth at the downbeat of m. 45 is greater by an octave, we emphatically do not hear these tones as anything other than the suggestion of a tonic triad in first inversion.

The figure that guides this passage is itself a *Veränderung* (see ex. 3.6). In relation to its prototype, the figure is incisive, conveying a deliberate intensification of expression. Intervals are widened and hollowed out, the descending seventh an evident commentary on the sixth with which the piece opens. Dissonances are prolonged. A connectedness emerges—nothing more salient, perhaps, than a linking of intervallic peaks in a high register: the high G in mm. 20 and 21 leading the ear to the climactic A at m. 22. By analogue, the *Veränderung* at mm. 44–45 ought to have established a high C at precisely this point, a transposition of the motive at m. 21. The B♭ in its place, as dissonant (implied) seventh, refusing the move up by step to the high D, seems instead to hang suspended. In the continuation of music after the formal cadence in m. 46, we hear why. The B♭ in this highest register now inspires a descent (illustrated in ex. 3.5): not, emphati-

EXAMPLE 3.6 C. P. E. Bach, Sonata in F major, H 136, first movement.

A

B

cally, a descent toward linear closure, but a descent to the F as a dissonance within the augmented sixth at the cadence that opens into the Largo.

Such relationships, born of the practice of *Veränderung*, are about composition in its deepest sense. Without them, the piece is flat, its story untold. It would be a very short story indeed: in its formal brevity, the movement seems to have been conceived so that its thematic fullness is actually dependent on the varied reprises.

V

In among a folder of loose leaves marked on its cover "Veränderungen und Auszierungen über einige meiner Sonaten" is a page in Bach's hand with a set of alterations for the second movement, the Largo, of Sonata I: "Erster Theil der Reprisen Sonaten, ex F, pag. 2," Bach wrote at the top of the page, referring to the pagination in the Winter publication.[5] These are not the only "Veränderungen und Auszierungen" that Bach wrote for the various movements of the sonatas in this

5. Berlin: Staatsbibliothek zu Berlin—Preußischer Kulturbesitz [= SBB], Mus. ms. autogr. Bach P 1135, fol. 2. The page is shown in facsimile in *The Collected Works for Solo Keyboard by Carl Philipp Emanuel Bach*, ed. Darrell Berg, 6 vols. (New York & London: Garland Publishing, 1985), V: 237. The manuscript is discussed in Darrell M. Berg, "C. P. E. Bach's 'Variations' and 'Embellishments' for his Keyboard Sonatas," *Journal of Musicology*, 2 (1983): 151–173.

collection (and, as well, in the two collections called "Fortsetzungen" that Winter published in 1761 and 1762 as sequels to the Reprise Sonatas). For reasons that remain obscure, the variants for the Largo were not entered into the *Handexemplar* (a working copy) of the Winter publication, now at the British Library, into whose margins Bach entered variants for movements from the Sonatas III, IV, and V.[6]

The variants in the *Handexemplar* have recently been the subject of lively dispute. Etienne Darbellay, in his 1976 edition of the Reprise Sonatas, actually incorporated all these *Veränderungen* into the principal text, understanding them precisely as revisions toward a "Fassung letzter Hand."[7] In an inquiry into the entire range of Bach's revisions, Darrell Berg argues from a broader perspective: such *Veränderungen* were meant by Bach "to serve as alternatives rather than replacements."[8] Viewing the matter from another angle, Howard Serwer argues compellingly that the *Veränderungen* in the Reprise Sonatas were motivated by an endeavor to discourage an unauthorized reprint by Johann Karl Friedrich Rellstab.[9]

If true, Serwer's hypothesis might be thought to substantiate Darbellay's claim that these variants were intended by Bach as replacements. Instead, it merely complicates the matter, suggesting as it does that Bach's revisions were motivated not out of a sense that the sonatas of 1760 were, some twenty-five years later, in need of revision, but rather that a new version would legitimate the author's proprietary claims on these works. To have established Bach's motive—if that is what Serwer has done—is to have reasoned only the first cause for having set pen to paper. Such reasoning leaves unexamined Bach's actual engagement with the process of *Veränderung*.

---

6. London: British Library, K.10.a.28. The London *Handexemplar* is reproduced in facsimile in *The Collected Works for Solo Keyboard*, ed. Berg, II: 43–79.

7. In the opening statement of his "Introduction" Darbellay tacitly assumes the marginalia in the London copy to constitute "the version revised by the composer": " . . . the final revision demonstrates quite clearly the critical sense, and the true taste of the composer." See *Carl Philipp Emanuel Bach. Sechs Sonaten mit veränderten Reprisen*, ed. Darbellay, iii. The additional *Veränderungen* in SBB, Bach P 1135 are excluded from Darbellay's edition without comment.

8. Berg, "C. P. E. Bach's 'Variations' and 'Embellishments' for his Keyboard Sonatas," 171.

9. See Howard Serwer, "C. P. E. Bach, J. C. F. Rellstab, and the Sonatas with Varied Reprises," in *C. P. E. Bach Studies*, ed. Stephen L. Clark (Oxford, 1988), 233–243. The unsavory business with Rellstab is described in detail in Bach's long letter of 23 July 1785 to Breitkopf: "Findet sich ein Käufer, u. er hat Lust, so will ich mit dem ersten Theile, Veränderungen oder Vermehrung (ohne die geringste Bezahlung) vornehmen, blos, daß der Nachdruck ersticket wird." (If a buyer is to be found, and if he so wishes, I will undertake alterations or additions to the first volume [without the slightest charge], simply in order to nip [Rellstab's] reprint in the bud.) See Ernst Suchalla, ed., *Carl Philipp Emanuel Bach: Briefe und Dokumente. Kritische Gesamtausgabe* (Göttingen: Vandenhoeck & Ruprecht, 1994), 1081–1085. For a slightly different translation, see Stephen L. Clark, ed., *The Letters of C. P. E. Bach* (Oxford: Clarendon Press; New York: Oxford University Press, 1997), 228–232, esp. 230. Breitkopf did indeed publish a reprint of this first volume, and in 1785, but without Bach's *Veränderungen*; Serwer (242) suggests why that was the case.

The Largo, in its two versions, is a study in the complexity of this dialectic, wherein the plain speech of an original conception defers to an enhanced rhetoric. What is the relationship between them? Is the one demonstrably an improvement upon the other, meant to supersede it in some textual hierarchy? If that were not the intention, we must then ponder whether the *Veränderung* means to gather its meaning *in juxtaposition with* the prototype from which it emanates: to ponder, that is, whether the two constitute a single conception—two alternatives for performance. (The two versions are shown in ex. 3.7.)

There are good grounds for understanding the new music as considerably more than a varied alternative to the original. In its new fluency of diction, the *Veränderung* can be thought to realize the expressive potential of a movement otherwise awkwardly constrained, even mute. Consider, for example, the music at the new incise beginning at m. 14. The iterated Cs, rhythmically enlivened, seem now to probe and to clarify the very similar music beginning at m. 5—whose original rhythm, now complicated in the *Veränderung,* is in a sense reclaimed in the revision at m. 14.

Most impressive of all is the elegance of the new m. 20: how it sweeps up the first three notes of the bar into a rhythmic figure that transforms the rote repetition of the original Lombard rhythm into a moment of pure expression, reaching back to the intervals and the figure of the new mm. 15 and 17, and at the same time, rehearing the new rhythms of mm. 5 and 6. The lithe unfolding of the Neapolitan at the end of the bar, in its simple arpeggiation to the high Db, is very fine.

In that same folder of unpublished "Veränderungen und Auszierungen" is a variant reading of the moving Molto adagio, a soliloquoy in eight ample bars that negotiates between the lean, sinewy outer movement of the Sonata in C minor, H 127 (Wq 51/3). Its opening phrase—a phrase that never returns—sings the plaintive figure of some lonesome cavatina. Precisely its second interval, the fall from the E to the A, is the subject of the second incise, beginning at m. 5. For once in the pages of this folder of "Veränderungen," Bach writes out the entire movement in all its voices. The autograph portrays a confident and supple hand that never once stumbles through its thicket of thirty-second and sixty-fourth notes. (It is reproduced as fig. 3.1.) The chaste opening phrase is made a subject of inquiry, its expressive intervals salted with new dissonance, its rhythms intensified, its harmonies enriched. Even the opening anacrusis, the solitary G whose *gruppetto* launches the phrase, is renotated: the eighth note is replaced by two sixteenths, tied (see ex. 3.8A). If the two versions of the anacrusis will sound imperceptibly the same in performance, the variant nevertheless inspires new thought. How, we ask, are the two sixteenths to be made audible? What nuance of performance can make these two tones distinct? The notation sets us to thinking, and this abstruse process of mind will somehow be conveyed in performance—

EXAMPLE 3.7 C. P. E. Bach, Sonata in F major, H 136, Largo, with *Veränderungen*.

FIGURE 3.1 C. P. E. Bach. *Veränderung* for the Molto adagio from Sonata in C minor, H 127. © Staatsbibliothek zu Berlin–Preußischer Kulturbesitz, Musikabteilung mit Mendelssohn-Archiv. Mus. Ms. Bach P 1135, fol. 9. By kind permission.

even if it is only the solitary performer, alone with his clavichord, who will notice. The striking B♭ in the *Veränderung* that interrupts the clean fifth E—A in the soprano in m. 1 is now invoked at the incise beginning at m. 5, in an arpeggiation that mordantly stresses a dissonant B♮, the A then inflected by B♭ three times, in two registers, before the end of this plenteous measure (ex. 3.8B). Again, the *Veränderung* is no mere embellishment. It speaks to the gist of the music.

VI

This Sonata in C minor, published by George Ludewig Winter in 1761, is the third in a volume titled *Fortsetzung* [continuation] *von Sechs Sonaten fürs Clavier von Carl Philipp Emanuel Bach*—misleadingly titled, one must say, for those anticipating another set of sonatas with varied reprises would have found such

EXAMPLE 3.8 C. P. E. Bach, Sonata in C minor, H 127, Molto adagio.

Veränderungen only in the first movement of the fifth sonata. But the first sonata in the collection—Sonata in C major, Wq 51/1—was subjected to a broader, external process of *Veränderung* in an instance that must be unique in the entire repertory. At some point after its appearance in Winter's print, Bach was inspired to rewrite the entire sonata twice: "2 mal durchaus verändert," Bach notes against its entry in the *Nachlaßverzeichnis*.[10] The manuscript conveying these later variants bears an inscription on its cover in Bach's hand: "die erste Sonata aus der

---

10. See *The Catalog of Carl Philipp Emanuel Bach's Estate. A Facsimile of the Edition of Schniebes, Hamburg, 1790,* annotated, with a Preface, by Rachel W. Wade (New York & London: Garland Publishing, 1981), 16, item 119.

Fortsetzung meiner Reprisen-Sonaten 2mahl durchaus verändert."[11] (For the sake of convenience I speak here of three distinct sonatas, identified by their numbers in the Helm *Thematic Catalogue:* H 150 [= *Fortsetzung*]; H 156, H 157.) These two later versions were not published during Bach's lifetime. Nor can we ascertain with any precision when they were written.[12] Why were they written? Why did Bach single out this sonata for extensive *Veränderung*, and then subject it to the same process a second time? A deeply ingrained pedagogical calling is evident here, and so is the compulsive need to exhaust the resources of *Veränderung*. Are they adequate to an explanation why Bach went to considerable lengths to write out the entire sonata two times, in effect recomposing as he wrote?

Again, we confront an apparent confusion of purpose, the pragmatics of pedagogy faced off against the deeper impulse of *Veränderung* at play in Bach's creative imagination. Perilously difficult to discriminate in this or that instance, the two phenomena seem ever at odds in Bach's decision-making. If by some critical measure we might be inclined to understand either or both of these later versions as recompositions superseding, intentionally or not, the sonata published in 1761, we'd need to remind ourselves that all three sonatas comprise precisely the same number of measures in each of their three movements and in all of their parts. A template of syntactical identity implicates an underlying deep structure, the three sonatas collapsed into a single one.

The locked-tight grip of these constraints must have set loose an impulse to break away, to compose with freer hand. Several passages in particular are worth contemplating in this regard, and will have to stand in for a good many others. The first is the music that negotiates between the end of the first movement and the beginning of the second (see ex. 3.9). A bumpy, baroque-like sequencing and a full stop before the upbeat to the Andante, common to both H. 150 and 156, are refused in H 157. The new music of mm. 50–51, complex in registral layering, now dwells on dominants, picking out its pitches with an ear to nonclosure. The final three notes, no ordinary anacrusis, formulate something motivic, a figure drawn from the complex arpeggiations that precede it. It will imprint itself on the music that follows.

---

11. A facsimile is shown in *The Collected Works for Solo Keyboard*, ed. Berg, IV: 103, and followed by the two new versions. The three versions are given in *C. Ph. E. Bach: Klaviersonaten, Auswahl*, ed. Darrell M. Berg (Munich: Henle Verlag [1989]), III: 1–29.

12. Both manuscripts are in the hand of Michel, Bach's ubiquitous Hamburg copyist. All that this allows us to say is that the copies were made after 1768. See, for one, Rachel Wade, *The Keyboard Concertos of Carl Philipp Emanuel Bach* (Ann Arbor, 1979), 26. On the copies, see *The Collected Works for Solo Keyboard*, ed. Berg, IV: ix, xix, 103–123.

EXAMPLE 3.9 C. P. E. Bach, Sonata in C major, in three versions; final bars of first movement, opening bars of second.

Indeed, the opening bar of the Andante establishes a sense of theme that differs radically from its predecessors. The initial G, a dissonant appoggiatura in H 150 and H 156, is now set loose, responding to the new motivic impetus through which it is prepared. A tempo is established in relation to the Allegro moderato of the first movement, whose final sixteenths fix a kind of tactus that controls the complex new rhythmic contour of the Andante. However one thinks to play those final sixteenths of the first movement, the temptation to crescendo through them to the forte at the downbeat of the Andante is hard to resist. These notes actually play into the Andante, so that the one seems to emerge from the other.[13] Finally, a new thematic figure is established at m. 5 subtly tuned to the shape of those final sixteenths before the Andante. The figure imprints the movement with a bold sense of articulation, its recurrences at mm. 29 and 47 opening up intervallic spaces that simply do not exist in the earlier versions (see ex. 3.10; m. 47 not shown). Its profile is felt even in the exquisite final bars of the movement.

Again in these final bars (shown in ex. 3.11), the sense of the three sonatas as simple variants in synchrony with one another is pointedly challenged. These are the five bars of music with which the Andante avoids its final cadence, moving off to the dominant of C in preparation for the final Allegro. And yet to apprehend the three writings of this passage as a chronicle in which the symptoms of a new attitude are registered, a new style augured, is to conjure an old parable in the historical imagination. How, then, to explain the conceptual leap in H 157: the solitary E♭ in the bass at m. 52; these austere harmonies; the fine voicing of the diminished seventh above the C in m. 54, the *empfindsame* augmented sixth, fortissimo, at the end of m. 53? Perhaps it is in the recognition of something here beyond the expression of words, a music finally in need of interpretation, that we identify in this second *Veränderung* the symptom of a music of another kind.

In her pioneering study of the "Veränderungen und Auszierungen" that is our general topic, Darrell Berg concluded that on the evidence, "Bach intended [the entire corpus of variant versions] to serve as alternatives rather than replacements. . . . Surely, in any case, they were to be applied at the pleasure of the

---

13. Much to the point, the Andante actually begins—is literally inscribed—with the upbeat that is the final eighth note of the first movement, and is so written in the first edition of H 150 and in the Michel copy of H 156. The copy of H 157, however, shows without ambiguity that the new tempo begins at the change of meter: establishes, that is, a relationship between the final notes of the Allegro and the opening notes of the Andante. This distinction, critical in understanding how the movements are differently joined, is lost in the Henle edition, where the upbeats in all three sonatas are written prior to the change in tempo. The incipits in E. Eugene Helm *Thematic Catalogue of the Works of Carl Philipp Emanuel Bach* (New Haven and London: Yale University Press, 1989), 39–40, are similarly misleading, omitting the upbeats in H 150 and H 156 altogether.

EXAMPLE 3.10 C. P. E. Bach, Sonata in C major, from
the Andante.

H 150

H 157

performer and not to be regarded as mandatory alterations."[14] This is a temper-
ate, cautious reading. And yet it leaves unexamined a tension that continues to
sound well beneath the surface of the music, where the composer is glimpsed,
however obscurely, doing battle with himself in an unforgiving process of reflection, of criticism. *Veränderung* and *Auszierung,* we must remind ourselves, are
not synonyms. It is a commonplace to hold that when Bach subjects a piece to
embellishment, he sustains a venerable practice that has more to do with the
ephemera of performance than with the fundamental decision-making of composition, a practice very close to the ancient notion of diminution. But *Verän-*

14. Berg, "C. P. E. Bach's 'Variations' and 'Embellishments' for his Keyboard Sonatas," 171.

EXAMPLE 3.11 C. P. E. Bach, Sonata in C major, in three versions, Andante, final bars.

derung, while it may encompass the practice of *Auszierung,* means something else again. When, in the final bars of the Andante in H 157, the music strips away all diminution to home in on harmonies and inner voices, the process engaged is critical, creative in some higher sense. No handbook of embellishment can contain it. The sense of the passage in H 157 is not heard as a "reading" of the passage in H 150—does not depend on it for its meaning.

To return once again to those unanswerable questions posed earlier, one might venture to think that Bach went to such lengths to write out two completely altered versions of H 150 because publication in Winter's *Fortsetzung* made irrevocably public a work that Bach now felt to be less inspired—less original, less exemplary of an idiosyncratic *Einbildungskraft* (a characteristic imagination) than its companions. To write down the sonata twice more is in a sense to undo the published version. Did Bach intend, by this act, to replace the sonata in some categorical textual sense? The material permanence of the Winter print argues against such a view, even as the evidence marshaled by Howard Serwer regarding a putative revision of the first volume in the Winter series allows that Bach may indeed have contemplated a revised edition of the *Fortsetzung* as well. But then one must ask why Bach admitted all three versions, without further discrimination, into his catalogue as a single sonata "2 mal durchaus verändert."

These are troubling contradictions, but they seem to me perfectly normal ones. "Carl Philipp Emanuel Bach, the Restless Composer": in her provocative title, Rachel Wade hints at some interior compulsion underlying the complex and manifold processes of alteration that Bach imposed upon his works. "Bach was restless because he was a perfectionist," she concludes.[15] Surely, there is ample evidence in support of this view of the man. Perfection, however, is illusory in the arts, an abstraction invoked both as an attribute of the work and, in metaphor, as the critic's yardstick. Wade perhaps means by it nothing more than the modest notion of grammatical correctness. By that measure, one might contend that each of the three versions of the Sonata in C is "perfect" by the criteria implicit in each. But perfection has its discomforting aspect. In the leap from H 150 to H 157, impatient with the limiting "perfection" of the original conception, Bach writes music that now challenges its limits, that strains the very notion of perfection. Certainly, there is a compulsive aspect to Bach's enterprise, situated in this obsessive self-criticism that Wade means to identify, and made manifest across

---

15. Rachel W. Wade, "Carl Philipp Emanuel Bach, the Restless Composer," in *Carl Philipp Emanuel Bach und die europäische Musikkultur des mittleren 18. Jahrhunderts,* ed. Hans Joachim Marx (Göttingen: Vandenhoeck & Ruprecht, 1990), 182.

the wide range of compositional projects that consumed Bach during a very long career.

In these *Veränderungen,* one senses the playing out of some inner crisis, perhaps only vaguely intuited, in the conceptualizing of sonata, bound up with a shift, paradigmatically, in the idea of *Veränderung* itself, from the notion of inexhaustible variation, an aesthetic comfortably at home in the music of an earlier generation, toward a firmer control of diction, of gesture and feeling, and of narrative. The function of variation is redefined. No longer the decorative embellishing of structure, variation now infiltrates to thematic bedrock. When Bach renders an original work in subsequent *Veränderungen,* he puts on public display a process that will have its echo in the private pages of the Beethoven sketchbooks, where a sequence of drafts suggestive of a process at once evolutionary and dialectical enacts a similar rush of decision-making, even while the formal matrix that regulates the process for Bach is now sprung. For Beethoven, the act of *Veränderung* penetrates to form itself, and to the constraints of genre.

CHAPTER 4

Late Works

Kenner und Liebhaber

I

In a letter of 13 May 1780, having sent two sonatas and three rondos to Breitkopf on 21 March, Emanuel Bach now establishes the order of this second volume in the series "für Kenner und Liebhaber," and adds: "since you write that these 5 pieces amount only to something over 7 sheets, I will send you another short sonata in A major in the next mail."[1] The new sonata was sent a week later, on 19 May, with an instructive note: "the entire sonata must be played to the end in the same tempo and without a break; accordingly . . . it is not necessary to indicate any tempo other than Allegretto at the beginning."[2]

An afterthought, one might gather from the correspondence, this "short" sonata has much to tell us about the constructing of a collection. (The complete sonata is shown in appendix 4A.) Its modest opening phrases, without the slightest pretense to that brazen originality commonly sought and found in Bach's music, map out a rudimentary sonata exposition, but an unorthodox one. The dominant is established quickly, D♯ inflecting the music at what begins as a rep-

---

1. "Weil Sie aber schreiben, daß diese 5 Stücke nur etwas über 7 Bogen ausmachen: so werde ich Ihnen mit nächster Post noch eine kurze Sonate aus dem A dur schicken; diese soll alsdenn den Beschluß machen." Ernst Suchalla, ed., *Carl Philipp Emanuel Bach: Briefe und Dokumente. Kritische Gesamtausgabe,* (Göttingen: Vandenhoeck & Ruprecht, 1994), 835; *The Letters of C. P. E. Bach,* tr. and ed. Stephen L. Clark (Oxford: Clarendon Press; New York: Oxford University Press, 1997), 161.

2. " . . . die ganze Sonate in einerley Tempo und ohne Absatz bis zu Ende muß gespielt werden, dahero . . . kein Tempo nöthig ist, darüber zu schreiben, als Allegretto im Anfange." Suchalla, *Briefe und Dokumente,* 838; Clark, *Letters,* 162.

etition of the opening bar. The music closes in the dominant at m. 8, but the D♮ at m. 9 returns the music prematurely to A major. The opening phrase returns literally at m. 11, but continues with a fine variant of m. 2, and for a moment the process of "veränderte Reprise" insinuates itself: in that fleeting moment, we sense a premature repeat of the exposition. But the music veers off to the dominant again, not, however, as firmly as at mm. 5–8. This is an exposition at loose ends, more improvised than plotted: Bach at his keyboard. The music feels a bit too comfortable in the hands. At the double bar, the music takes on some urgency, the placid phrases of the opening bars recast now in B minor. Again, the moment is fleeting, and the music moves off in a chromatic pass through E minor, touching F♯ minor in preparation for a true dominant on E, in the process recalling the phrase at mm. 8 and 9. The tonic is reclaimed, but in the varied form that it took at mm. 11 and 12. Recapitulation, then, begins with the languid extension of the dominant at mm. 9 and 10. The repetition of this second part of the movement, following the double bar, gives on to an eight-bar meditation, a listless, probing music in C major. Bach is often inclined to write something to negotiate between the two principal movements of a sonata: transitional, such passages are commonly named. What must strike us about this music is its sense not of transition, but of a dissolving, a liquidating, of the thematic discourse of the first movement, and of its tonal milieu. Again, the music has an improvisatory feel. It closes resolutely in C major, without the slightest sense of anticipation as to its sequel.[3]

The meter (but not the tempo) changes. What follows, in conventional terms, is a finale. But there is nothing conventional about this movement.[4] Beginning as though in mid-phrase, the music seeks its bearing, circling around B minor not as a defining tonic but rather as a secondary area toward the finding of a strong dominant on E at m. 6. A tonic A major is sounded just barely at m. 10, yet unequivocally as the tonic. The music finds a cadence only at the double bar—but in B minor. In any formulation of sonata procedure around 1780, a cadence in B minor at the end of an exposition in A major would be understood merely as an

---

3. In the Sonata in F (H 269), the other sonata from 1780 published in this collection, the seven bars of music that follow upon the final cadence of the first movement move chromatically through E minor and close in F minor. If, in theoretical terms, the relationship of F minor to the F major of the finale is closer than the relationship of the close in C major to the finale of the A major sonata, in effect it seems even more distracted—a digression with no purpose other than to set the finale in relief.

4. Deprived of an incipit, even its legitimacy as a "movement" is contested in Helm, *Thematic Catalogue*, 61: "1 movt. only," reads the entry against this sonata.

aberration, even a quirky and ironic play on convention.[5] But there is nothing quirky in the effect when the exposition is repeated. That opening harmony, irresolute at the outset, now seems to discover itself, sounding as though it grew naturally out of the cadence in B minor, as though the turn to B minor at the end of the exposition was composed with precisely this staging in mind. In retrospect, the significance of B minor in the first movement, even in the unexpected and unprepared transformation of the opening phrase, now resonates in these turns of event in the finale. As though to play on that earlier transformation, the opening phrase of the finale is now recast in F♯ minor: a resonant, brooding phrase that gives shape to the searching music with which the finale opens.

Having instructed Breitkopf as to the order of the other pieces in the collection, Bach composed this sonata altogether aware that it would follow on the very grand Rondo in A minor (H 262). For Bach, the ordering of such a collection, the sequencing of its keys, its genres, was not a trivial aspect in its production. Still, it is not often that we find evidence of an actual continuity implicit in how one work follows another.[6] Here, at the end of this second collection, we do. The modest opening phrases of this little sonata, in their quaint affirmation of A major, follow strikingly from the closing bars of the rondo, a work given to bold modulatory advances set against the sweeping arpeggiations of its theme: "plaintive and melancholy," wrote the critic for the *Hamburgische unpartheyische Correspondent* of this, his "Favorit-Rondo," adding that he'd "seldom felt the power of harmony in such a degree as when he first heard this rondo played by Bach on the Forte Piano."[7] He singles out the remarkable passage beginning at m. 142 "where the theme begins again pianissimo and proceeds through an indescribably beautiful gradation [*Gradation*] of rise in the discant and fall in the bass, and

5. For Philip Barford, "this kind of device again points to the influence of Haydn. On the other hand, Bach himself had the reputation of being a joker, and it is possible that the influence was reciprocal." See his *The Keyboard Music of C. P. E. Bach* (London: Barrie and Rockliff, 1965), 115–116. Which of Haydn's music Bach can have known in 1780, and how its influence might be perceived, is not offered. And surely there is a distinction to be upheld between the evidence of wit in the music, as an aspect of style, and an allegation as to Bach's social behavior. The turn to B minor here is in any case dead serious.

6. The notable exception is the *Probestücke* published with the first part of the *Versuch* in 1753. How these pieces constitute a collection is taken up in the next chapter.

7. "Das dritte [Rondo] aus A moll ist mehr klagend und melancholisch und das Favorit=Rondo des Recensenten, der selten die Macht der Harmonie in einem solchen Grade empfunden hat, als damals, da er von Bach dieses Rondo zum erstenmal auf dem Forte Piano spielen hörte." *Hamburgische unpartheyische Correspondent*, Nr. 164, with dateline "Am Freitag, den 13. Oktober 1780." Reprinted in Suchalla, *Briefe und Dokumente*, 861.

finally resolves itself again in A minor." (The passage is shown in ex. 4.1.) "We're convinced," he continues," that *Kenner* and *Liebhaber* will linger especially here, and will know, thanks to the composer, that through the application of fermatas, he wishes to leave them time to breathe." And, he adds, "if these rondos, and especially this passage, are to achieve their full effect, they must be played on a good fortepiano on which the resonance of the struck tones will make the effect all the more powerful. . . . These "fermatas [*Aushaltungs-Zeichen*, he now calls them] must be held as long as the instrument will allow."[8] Quite clearly, it is not merely Bach's text that is under scrutiny here, but the manner in which he himself performs it. Bach seems habitually to have introduced new keyboard works, and indeed new publications, to a small circle of Hamburg colleagues both through performance and conversation. This extraordinary enharmonic passage was no doubt the subject of such conversation, and it is tempting to imagine Bach at the keyboard, lingering at the fermatas, exploring the resonance of this instrument for which it is expressly composed.

To argue for a deeper relationship of some kind between the themes of these two works—Rondo in A minor, Sonata in A major—tempting as that may be, is to lose a more immediate sense of connectivity, a tactile and acoustic rapport, even in the hardly perceptible motion from the poco andante of the rondo to the allegretto of the sonata. It would be incautious to insist that Bach intended the two works to be linked in performance. For one, the rondos in these collections were composed explicitly "fürs Forte-Piano," as the title page instructs, whereas the sonatas, and certainly this one, were composed at and for the clavichord, even if one might think that by 1780 the deeper ideological and aesthetic schism provoked by these two instruments had begun to erode. Yet in its composition as a last-minute coda to the collection, in the actual conceiving of the work, Bach seems to have found the lucidity of its opening phrases in the contemplation of what might follow from the bold, labyrinthian closing pages of the rondo,

---

8. "Die Stelle, wo . . . das Thema pianissimo wieder anfängt, das nachher durch eine unbeschreiblich schöne Gradation im Steigen des Discants und Fallen des Basses fortgeht, und sich endlich wieder in A moll auflöset, hat den meisten Effect auf ihn gemacht. Wir sind überzeugt, daß Kenner und Liebhaber bey selbiger vorzüglich verweilen, auch dem Verfasser Dank wissen werden, daß er ihnen durch die angebrachten Fermaten gleichsam Zeit zum Athmen lassen wollen. Doch müssen wir hier bemerken, daß, wenn die Rondos, und besonders die vorgedachte Stelle ihre ganze Wirkung äußern sollten, selbige auf einem guten Fortepiano gespielt werden müssen, wo der Nachklang der angeschlagenen Töne den Effect desto kräftiger macht. Ueberhaupt wollen wir hier noch bemerken, daß alle Aushaltungs=Zeichen in den Rondos so lange ausgehalten werden müssen, als es das Instrument nur immer zulassen will." Suchalla, *Briefe und Dokumente*, 861–862.

EXAMPLE 4.1 C. P. E. Bach, Rondo in A minor, H 262 (*Kenner und Liebhaber*, II, Wq 56/5), mm. 138–157.

grounding its wayward chromaticism, its sustained melancholy, in a plainly spoken prose, and in A major.

II

The *Kenner* and *Liebhaber* invoked in this bit of contemporary criticism, a pairing that we have come to reduce to the schooled adept, the aspiring professional, in vivid contrast to the dilettante, are famously invoked in the titles of these six valedictory collections of Bach's keyboard music. This is not to say that Bach composes now for the one, now for the other, that there is some categorical distinction to be teased out of each of his works. Something else is at play here. That bold chromatic passage in the Rondo in A minor is to the point: both *Kenner* and *Liebhaber* will linger at its *fermate,* writes the critic. Both will enter into its densely chromatic labyrinth, will hear linear vectors and feel the abstruse play of its harmonic roots. They will not *feel* the music differently. "There are passages here and there from which the connoisseurs [*kenner*] alone can derive satisfaction," writes Mozart, of his Piano Concertos, K. 413–415, in a letter of 1782; "but these passages are written in such a way that the less learned [*nicht-kenner*] cannot fail to be pleased, though without knowing why."[9] Frequently cited, Mozart's lines probe this distinction between *Kenner* and *Liebhaber,* and open onto the question of competencies, a matter of degree: less learned, more learned. How, we wonder, did Mozart visualize this difference? At bottom, he is worrying an axiom of Enlightenment aesthetics: the touching of the heart and the exercising of the mind as apparently distinct from one another and yet inseparable. What was it that the *nicht-kenner* did not know? Was it the technical "how" of composition? Or something yet deeper—the "why" (Mozart's "warum") that lies more deeply embedded in the composer's intent? In a superficial sense, it is the former. The latter, that ultimate wisdom to which the Enlightenment sought entry, was accessible to neither *Kenner* nor *Liebhaber,* nor, one suspects, to the composer himself.

How then did Bach now come to envision his work in these terms? Why *Kenner* and *Liebhaber?* An incentive might be located in Forkel's *Ueber die Theorie der Musik insofern sie Liebhabern und Kennern derselben nothwendig und nützlich ist* (Göttingen, 1777), which served Forkel as a curriculum for his lectures at Göttingen in the 1770s.[10] "This learned *Programma,*" as Bach referred to it in a revealing letter to Forkel, is much about the *Liebhaber,* even in a sly addendum in which Bach wonders whether Forkel's *Liebhabern* might be interested in the second volume of his newly published accompanied sonatas (H 531–534).[11] Eventually, the *Programma* served as the basis for the formidable "Einleitung" to Forkel's *Allgemeine Geschichte,* I (1788), a work that Bach himself, in a review that appeared in the *Hamburgische unpartheyische Correspondent* for 9 January 1788, praised for

9. "—hie und da—können auch kenner allein satisfaction erhalten—doch so—daß die nicht=kenner damit zufrieden seyn müssen, ohne zu wissen warum." Wilhelm A. Bauer, Otto Erich Deutsch and Joseph Heinz Eibl, eds., *Mozart:Briefe und Aufzeichnungen. Gesamtausgabe* (Kassel: Bärenreiter, 1962–1975), IV: 245–246. The somewhat constructed translation is from Emily Anderson, tr. and ed. *The Letters of Mozart and his Family* (London: Macmillan; New York: St. Martin's Press, 3rd ed., 1985), 833. The passage is reprinted, with commentary, in Robert L. Marshall, *Mozart Speaks: Views on Music, Musicians, and the World* (New York: Schirmer Books, 1991), 287–288.

10. "Eine Einladungsschrift zu musikalischen Vorlesungen Göttingen," reads its subtitle: an invitation to lectures on music at Göttingen in 1777. A brief summary of its contents is given in Johann Nikolaus Forkel, *Allgemeine Litteratur der Musik* (Leipzig: Schwickert, 1792; reprint Hildesheim: Georg Olms, 1962), 419. The work was reprinted, evidently without permission, in Carl Friedrich Cramer, *Magazin der Musik,* I (1783; reprint Hildesheim: Georg Olms, 1971), 855–912.

11. Suchalla, *Briefe und Dokumente,* 658–659; Clark, *Letters,* 115–116.

the satisfaction that it would bring "not only to every music amateur but to every friend of enlightenment in human knowledge."[12]

And so it makes some sense to understand the six collections "für Kenner und Liebhaber"—published in 1779, 1780, 1781, 1783, 1785, 1787—as a playing-out of the implications in the title of Forkel's treatise, implications which plausibly stirred in Bach's mind amidst strategies for the marketing of new keyboard music.[13] More to the point is what might be called a new conceptualizing of sonata that will speak to both *Kenner* and *Liebhaber,* as distinct from a music intended verifiably for the one or the other. But before we can begin to probe this distinction, it would be good to remind ourselves of what is not often noted about the auspicious first volume in the series: each of its six sonatas was composed no fewer than five years before the publication of the volume in 1779.

III

From its inception, the second volume was envisioned as strikingly new: "The content of these sonatas will be entirely different from all my other works—for everyone, I hope." Bach wrote these bold words in December 1779. He had by then only recently composed the three rondos that would constitute the most striking novelty in the new collection—all three date from 1778, according to entries in the *Nachlaßverzeichnis.* Of the three sonatas in this collection, two date from 1780—one of them, the Sonata in A, would follow only in May—while the third had been composed in 1774. No doubt the sense of this collection as "entirely different" can have referred only to the rondo, whose standing as an independent work on a grand scale, each longer than the three movements of a neighboring sonata, was something of a new concept. The thirteen rondos dispersed over five volumes of these collections for *Kenner* and *Liebhaber* constitute a formidable repertory unique to the genre.

---

12. " . . . nicht nur jeder Musikliebhaber, sondern auch jeder Freund von Aufklärung in den menschlichen Kenntnissen." Reprinted in Suchalla, *Briefe und Dokumente,* 1248–1249; and in Johann Nikolaus Forkel, *Allgemeine Geschichte der Musik,* I (Leipzig: Schwickert, 1788), ed. Othmar Wessely (Graz: Akademische Druck- u. Verlagsanstalt, 1967), xvii–xviii. And finally this "learned *Programma*" served Forkel as the taxonomic scaffold of his monumental *Allgemeine Litteratur der Musik* (see note 10).

13. For an informative study of the publication history of these six volumes, see Peggy Daub, "The Publication Process and Audience for C. P. E. Bach's *Sonaten für Kenner und Liebhaber,*" in *Bach Perspectives,* II: *J. S. Bach, the Breitkopfs, and Eighteenth-Century Music Trade,* ed. George Staufer (Lincoln and London: University of Nebraska Press, 1996), 65–83.

The first volume, however, was conceived differently. "Perhaps I shall soon appear with 6 new sonatas, without accompaniment, [to be offered] by subscription," Bach wrote to Breitkopf on 21 February 1778: "There is a demand for it."[14] Drawing exclusively on earlier work, the project did not progress rapidly, for in a letter of 28 July, Bach again broached the matter somewhat tentatively with Breitkopf: "I would first of all, if it were agreeable to you, come forth with 6 sonatas for keyboard, without accompaniment. I've been asked about this."[15] By 16 September, the project had taken on life: "First of all, I am willing, with your good support, to have my 6 sonatas for keyboard (without accompaniment) 'für Kenner und Liebhaber' printed in two clefs [a certain number printed in violin clef, a certain number in soprano clef] by subscription," with circulation of the published sonatas proposed for the spring book fair.[16]

By 9 October, Bach had set to work in earnest: "Among my sonatas, I've stuck in three shorter ones," he writes to Breitkopf.[17] A manuscript was sent off to Breitkopf with a letter of 13 November: "Herewith, my sonatas. . . . The title is: *Sechs Clavier-Sonaten für Kenner und Liebhaber von Carl Philipp Emanuel Bach, im Verlag des Autors 1779.*"[18] By 20 February 1779, Bach had seen some proof sheets.[19] And on 16 April, Bach asks for a telling alteration: "If the title page of the sonatas should not yet have been printed, please add in the usual place: <u>Erste Samlung</u>. But if the title page has already been printed, this can be omitted, and 'zweyte Sam[m]lung' can be added in the second part."[20] Here, then, is the first hint of a

---

14. "Vielleicht erscheine ich bald mit 6 neuen Sonaten, ohne Begleitung, auf Praenumeration. Man verlangt es." Suchalla, *Briefe und Dokumente,* 679; Clark, *Letters,* 121.

15. "Ich werde zuerst wohl, wenn es Ihnen bequem fällt, mit 6 Sonaten fürs Clavier, ohne Begleitung, herausrücken. Man hat mich hierum ersuchet." Suchalla, *Briefe und Dokumente,* 686–687; Clark, *Letters,* 124.

16. "Fürs erste bin ich Willens, unter Ihren gütigem Beystand, meine 6 Sonaten fürs Clavier (ohne Begleitung) für Kenner und Liebhaber in zweyerley Schlüßel auf Pränumeration drucken zu laßen. . . . Die Ankündigung dieser Sonaten soll bald geschehen, und auf künftige Ostermeße könnte die Auslief[e]rung geschehen." Suchalla, *Briefe und Dokumente,* 693–694; Clark, *Letters,* 125.

17. "Unter meine Sonaten habe ich 3 kurze gesteckt, folgl. werden sie ohngefehr 9 Bogen betragen. Nach der Meße schicke ich das Manuscript." Suchalla, *Briefe und Dokumente,* 698–699; Clark, *Letters,* 126.

18. "Hierbey erhalten Sie meine Sonaten. . . . Der Titel ist: Sechs Clavier-Sonaten für Kenner und Liebhaber von Carl Philipp Emanuel Bach, im Verlag des Autors 1779." Suchalla, *Briefe und Dokumente,* 704–705. Clark, *Letters,* 127. It is not often noted that the designation "fürs Forte-Piano" appears only with volume 2, and in association with the rondos in those subsequent volumes.

19. "I am, dearest friend, very satisfied with your submitted proof sheets [Probe]." Suchalla, *Briefe und Dokumente,* 727; Clark, *Letters,* 134, slightly emended here.

20. Wenn das Titelblat von den Sonaten noch nicht sollte gedruckt seyn: so belieben Sie an den gewöhnlichen Ort zu setzen: <u>Erste Samlung</u>, ist aber der Titel schon gedruckt, so hat es nichts zu

second volume, and it comes even before Bach can have known the critical response to the first volume.

What comes across in the recitation of this correspondence is a halting process in which the idea of a collection of sonatas materializes only gradually, its audience of *Kenner* and *Liebhaber* identified even as the contents of the first volume were being assembled. The process itself invites speculation, for we know that the six sonatas finally chosen for this first volume were drawn from Bach's deep portfolio of unpublished works:

*Date in NV**

Sonata 1. C major.	H 244	1773
Sonata 2. F major.	H 130	1758
Sonata 3. B minor.	H 245	1774
Sonata 4. A major.	H 186	1765
Sonata 5. F major.	H 243	1772
Sonata 6. G major.	H 187	1765

*Date as recorded by Bach in the *Nachlaßverzeichnis*.

None of the six sonatas has survived in an autograph manuscript, and so the inclination to subject these dates to further scrutiny is frustrated. The surviving manuscript copies all transmit texts that agree with the 1779 print.[21] Still, there are hints that Bach himself viewed the collection as comprising two distinct phases. The three sonatas composed in 1772, 1773, and 1774 were among the six most recent sonatas in his portfolio—clearly, the "three shorter ones" to which Bach refers in the letter of 9 October. Of the three older sonatas, two of them were composed in Potsdam in 1765. They are both exceptionally grand. In its display of a symphonic brilliance and proportion otherwise uncharacteristic of Bach, the Sonata in A major remains among the most popular of his sonatas. The Sonata in G major, a bold and ingenious work, exploits the keyboard in other ways, its technical difficulties no doubt prompting its placement at the end of the collection.[22] The first movement of the Sonata in F major (H 130), composed in 1758 in the

---

sagen, u. man kan bey dem 2ten Theil zweyte Samlung hinsetzen." Suchalla, *Briefe und Dokumente*, 747; Clark, *Letters*, 138.

21. This according to the entries for each sonata in Helm, *Thematic Catalogue*.

22. For an appreciation of these two sonatas, see Pamela Fox, "The Stylistic Anomalies of C. P. E. Bach's Nonconstancy," in *C. P. E. Bach Studies*, ed. Stephen L. Clark (Oxford: Oxford University Press, 1988), 106–109. Charles Rosen examines the Sonata in A major in *Sonata Forms* (New York: W. W. Norton, rev. 1988), 178–181.

midst of intensive work on the collection with varied reprises, is all introspection, *Bebung,* nuance, fine shading, and embellishment—all *Empfindsamkeit.*

The three later sonatas are of a different kind. In the toccata-like perpetuum mobile with which it opens, the Sonata in C (1773) seems designed to inaugurate a collection, in emulation of some earlier monument, even while there is no evidence to suggest that Bach had such a collection in view as early as 1773. The apparent modesty and small scale of the sonatas in F major (1772) and B minor (1774), both commonly cited for their beginnings off the tonic, mask a more complex regulation of dissonance over the long haul.

The novelty of the famous opening bars of the Sonata in F (H 243) registered at once. In a piece published in August 1779, the reviewer for the *Hamburgische unpartheyische Correspondent* noted that its first bar "begins in C minor, whose idea will then be repeated in D minor in the second bar, and in the third, will progress to the tonic F."[23] To stress only the unorthodoxy of the gambit, often admired in isolation, is to deflate the eloquent purpose in its phrases, each dissonant with respect to one another, each containing a poignant dissonance within itself. Absorbed in its nuances, the player must yet convey a syntax that binds them to one another while preparing for the shock of a "correct" dominant seventh, struck in a rain of thirty-second notes, *forte,* on the downbeat at m. 3 (see ex. 4.2). The aura is shattered. A proper theme, set squarely on the tonic, emerges finally at the beginning of m. 5.

Precisely how the elements of these half-dozen bars at the outset of the piece are juxtaposed in a scenario of dramatic substance is worth a moment's reflection. In its initial embrace of C minor, in the elliptical space between this phrase and its sequel in D minor, these opening bars posit harmonies that lie outside the immediate orbit of F major: the true tonic cannot be surmised from these opening bars. That in itself tells us something about the profundity of dislocation here. Further, it seems to have gone unnoticed that the phrase, in its rhythmic shape, brazenly contradicts an axiom how sonatas—even those by this iconoclast—are to begin. No earlier sonata by Bach fails to establish a square initial downbeat on the tonic at the outset. The few trivial exceptions only stretch but do not contradict

---

23. "Der erste Satz ist ein Allegro im vierviertel Tact, wo der erste Tact aus C moll anfängt, welcher Gedanke im zweyten aus D moll wiederholt, und im 3ten schon zum Hauptton F dur fortgeschritten wird." The entire review is given in Suchalla, *Briefe und Dokumente,* 762–764. Pamela Fox, "Stylistic Anomalies," 118–119, writes of "expectational defeats" in its first eight measures, and of the "shallow effect" of the opening phrases "which adds to the immediate instability." Charles Rosen, *The Classical Style* (New York: W. W. Norton, 1972), 112–114, observes how "the strange C minor opening and the sequence it initiates continue to disturb the tonal stability as far as their echoes in the sixth and seventh measures."

EXAMPLE 4.2 C. P. E. Bach, Sonata in F major, H 243 (*Kenner und Liebhaber*, I, Wq 55/5), first movement, mm. 1–6.

the axiom. But in this sonata from 1772, its opening phrases each beginning off the beat with a triad in first inversion, the axiom is turned on its head. In performance, the beginning must be made to sound as though the player were caught in the midst of speech. The eloquence of the discourse is tied in with Bach's categorical refusal to explain away—to render conventional—these radical confrontations of affect. The conceptual world of these opening bars is new. An originality that had become the benchmark of Bach's style here opens on to a new level.

In the *Adagio maesto* [*sic*] that follows, the tensions of expression are wound even more tightly.[24] By force of association, its opening bars seem to echo the dissonances of the first movement, whose initial phrases will not recede from memory. Everywhere, the intensity of gesture is felt. Nothing is wasted. No phrase can

24. Bach's (or Breitkopf's) curious "maesto," silently amended to "maestoso" in virtually every subsequent edition and in Helm's *Thematic Catalogue*, may in fact mean what it says. The instances of slow movements marked adagio e mesto, adagio mesto, largo e mesto, and the like are frequent in Bach's works with keyboard instruments. This is music of melancholy, not majesty. I have found only one instance of "maestoso" in any of Bach's slow movements: the Largo maestoso in *Probestücke* IV, in its pointed allusion to the majesty of overture in the French style. In "Beethoven's 'Expressive' Markings," Leo Treitler probes the significance of the "Largo e mesto" inscribed at the head of the second movement of Beethoven's Piano Sonata in D, Opus 10, no. 3; see *Beethoven Forum* 7 (Lincoln & London: University of Nebraska Press, 1999), 89–112, for "mesto" esp. 89–92.

EXAMPLE 4.3
C. P. E. Bach, Sonata in
F major, H 243, second
movement complete,
opening of third
movement.

be attributed to the demands of an imposed convention. The reprise of the two-bar second theme, profoundly conceived in a compressed *Veränderung*, as though the concept itself were under scrutiny, seems to set its sights on the abrupt interruption of the cadence, an isolated and stunning F♮—E♭ in the treble, answered by a deep F♯ (see mm. 9–14 and 23–30 in ex. 4.3). The opening bars of the Allegretto follow with uncanny intimacy, as though hearing the dissonant C♯ left suspended high in register in the final measures of the Adagio. These bars, too, begin off the tonic, in recollection of those riddling phrases of the first movement, as though intuitively to complete—to correct—the syntax of an earlier ellipsis. It is the dissonant gap between the second and third bars in the opening movement that is healed at the opening of the Allegretto. This is a sonata whose three movements need one another—a sonata from beginning to end, in all three of its movements.

IV

The historical place of this sonata is worth contemplating. With the exception of a "Sonate mit veränderten Reprisen" in F major, composed in 1769 and published the following year for the *Musikalisches Vielerley* (Hamburg: M. C. Bock, 1770)—a lesser, conventional work that does not much exercise the mind—it is the first sonata composed by Bach after his arrival in Hamburg in March 1768: indeed, the first since 1766, a watershed year in which, according to the *Nachlaßverzeichnis*, Bach composed no fewer than eleven sonatas, and a good many other works for keyboard.

During those first years in Hamburg, the demands on Bach's time were exceptionally heavy, given not only to the regulation of music for Hamburg's principal churches but to the revival of public concert life in the city. There were teaching duties as well.[25] The new tensions of such a life cannot have been conducive to the introspective peace of mind requisite of the composition of works for solo keyboard, contemplative and introverted in their modes. The return to sonata in 1772 signals a turn inward: a response to, a withdrawal from, the imposing public genres of church and concert hall in which his recent work had of necessity been cast.

---

25. Bach's obligations in Hamburg are described and set in context in Hans-Günter Ottenberg, *C. P. E. Bach*, tr. Philip J. Whitmore (Oxford and New York: Oxford University Press, 1987), 107–117. The formidable classic study is Heinrich Miesner, *Philipp Emanuel Bach in Hamburg: Beiträge zu seiner Biographie und zur Musikgeschichte seiner Zeit* (Leipzig: Breitkopf & Härtel, 1929).

This first decade in Hamburg was a phase of extraordinary ferment in Bach's music. In the background, as yet not perfectly understood in its entirety, was the production of much considerable music for the Church. Passion music was composed (much of it recycled from existing works) and performed every year beginning in 1768.[26] More theatrical, and destined by Bach for greater dissemination through publication, are such works as *Die Israeliten in der Wüste*, composed in 1769 and revised for publication in 1775; the *Passions-Cantate* of 1769; the setting of Ramler's *Auferstehung und Himmelfahrt Jesu*, first performed in 1774 and published in 1787; and the *Heilig, mit zwey Chören und einer Ariette zur Einleitung*, first performed in 1776 and, like the first volume of the sonatas "für Kenner und Liebhaber," published by the author in 1779 through Breitkopf's presses.[27]

Among the notable instrumental projects of these years are the six Symphonies for String Orchestra (H 657–662; Wq 182), composed in 1773 for Gottfried van Swieten, of which Reichardt was to write some years later of their "original, daring flow of ideas, and the great variety and novelty in their forms and modulations";[28] and the four *Orchester-Sinfonien mit zwölf obligaten Stimmen* (H 663–666; Wq 183), composed in 1775–1776 and published in 1780, of which Bach himself wrote: "They are the greatest of this kind that I have composed."[29] And Bach composed keyboard concertos during these years.[30] Six (for harpsi-

---

26. On this topic, see Hans-Joachim Schulze, "Carl Philipp Emanuel Bachs Hamburger Passionsmusiken und ihr gattungsgeschichtlicher Kontext," in *Carl Philipp Emanuel Bach und die europäische Musikkultur des mittleren 18. Jahrhunderts* (Bericht über das Internationale Symposium der Joachim Jungius-Gesellschaft der Wissenschaften Hamburg 29. September–2. Oktober 1988), ed. Hans Joachim Marx (Göttingen: Vandenhoeck & Ruprecht, 1990), 333–343.

27. Details on the dating and publication of both the *Auferstehung* and the *Heilig* are given in my "The New Modulation of the 1770s: C. P. E. Bach in Theory, Criticism, and Practice," *Journal of the American Musicological Society*, 38 (1985), esp. 551–592.

28. " . . . originellen, kühnen Gang der Ideen, und die große Mannigfaltigkeit und Neuheit in den Formen und Ausweichungen." Reichardt's memoir is given in an essay by Wolfgang Gersthofer aptly titled "Große Mannigfaltigkeit und Neuheit in den Formen und Ausweichungen," in *Carl Philipp Emanuel Bach und die europäische Musikkultur des mittleren 18. Jahrhunderts*, 283–306. The symphonies are now published as *Six Symphonies for Baron van Swieten*, ed. Sarah Adams, in Carl Philipp Emanuel Bach, *The Complete Works*, series III, volume 2 (Los Altos: The Packard Humanities Institute, 2006).

29. "Es ist das größte in der Art, was ich gemacht habe." Suchalla, *Briefe und Dokumente*, 712; Clark, *Letters*, 129. The symphonies are now published as *Orchester-Sinfonien mit zwölf obligaten Stimmen*, ed. David Kidger, in Carl Philipp Emanuel Bach, *The Complete Works*, series III, volume 3 (Los Altos: The Packard Humanities Institute, 2005).

30. For a study that takes up matters of provenance, chronology, and compositional process, see Rachel W. Wade, *The Keyboard Concertos of Carl Philipp Emanuel Bach* (Ann Arbor: UMI Research Press, 1981).

chord, H 471–476) were composed in 1771 and published in Hamburg at Bach's expense.[31] Among the chamber works of the 1770s are two sets (three each) of true piano trios—the *Claviersonaten mit einer Violine und einem Violoncell zur Begleitung,* I (Leipzig: 1776) and II (Leipzig: 1777), which provoked Forkel's well-known analytical study of the rondo finale of the second sonata in Book I;[32] and the six "Sonatas for the Harpsichord or Piano-Forte [with the accompaniment of violin and cello]" published in London in 1776.

The range of these new projects, the exhilaration that they display, the enriching of a style responsive to recent developments in theatrical music: all this suggests an escape from the daunting responsibilities that Bach undertook as Kapellmeister and music director of the five principal churches in Hamburg and as Cantor of the Johanneum, responsibilities not unlike those that his father had assumed in Leipzig nearly a half century earlier. His investment in those duties must have been of a rather different kind, for the circle of intellects that surrounded him—Lessing, Klopstock, Gerstenberg, Claudius, Voss, even Diderot (whose overture to Bach during a brief sojourn in Hamburg in 1774 is examined in chapter 6)—spoke to the secular, if not anti-clerical, themes of *Aufklärung.*[33] In his last year, Bach composed twelve "Freymäurer-Lieder" (H 764), and although there is apparently no evidence that Bach was himself a Freemason, many of his friends were active members, and he cannot have been unsympathetic to Masonic ideals.[34] In an earlier age, more secure in its devotions, the apposition of the secular and the sacred was an imperceptible one (witness the many instances of text interchange, of parody, in Bach's cantatas). By the 1770s, the apposition

---

31. Recently published as *Sei concerti per il cembalo concertato,* ed. Douglas A. Lee, in Carl Philipp Emanuel Bach, *The Complete Works,* series III, volume 8 (Los Altos: The Packard Humanities Institute, 2005).

32. In Johann Nikolaus Forkel, *Musikalisch-kritische Bibliothek,* II (Gotha, 1778; repr. Hildesheim: Georg Olms, 1964), 281–293.

33. On Bach's Hamburg circle, see Ottenberg, *C. P. E. Bach,* 142–155. For a rich study, see Ernst Fritz Schmid, *Carl Philipp Emanuel Bach und seine Kammermusik* (Kassel: Bärenreiter, 1931), esp. 38–86.

34. The authorship of these Lieder is established in Gudrun Busch, *C. Ph. E. Bach und seine Lieder* (Regensburg: Gustav Bosse Verlag, 1957), 181–190. For an informative paragraph on these songs, see *Carl Philipp Emanuel Bach: Musik und Literatur in Norddeutschland,* Schriften der Schleswig-Holsteinischen Landesbibliothek, Band 4 (Heide in Holstein: Boyens & Co., 1988), 69. Further of interest in this regard, the *Hamburgische unpartheische Correspondent* for 26 February 1777 reported on the final concert of a "series organized for charity by the city's four united Masonic lodges. . . . Non-Freemasons were also admitted to these concerts, in which Herr Kapellmeister Bach directed some excellent vocal works, chief among them his own *Die Israeliten in der Wüste.*" See Ottenberg, *C. P. E. Bach,* 123, n. 67. See also Miesner, *Philipp Emanuel Bach in Hamburg,* 20.

touched deeper nerves, now evident in the perceived need to invent a "true" music for the church.[35]

It is in this context that these new sonatas of 1772–1774 were conceived. Others have written of the influence of Italian opera on the theatrical religious works from this period, and while Bach pointedly distanced himself from the frivolous world of the new comic opera, it would be naive to think that his music remained untouched by its rhythmic expanse.[36] Hans-Günter Ottenberg suggests that the appointment in 1778 of Georg Benda as Kapellmeister at the Theater am Gänsemarkt may have "brought [Bach] into closer contact with theatrical life in Hamburg."[37] The new modulatory adventures of such works as the *Heilig,* the responses to which were documented with uncommon awareness in contemporary writings;[38] the van Swieten symphonies whose first performance was recalled by Reichardt; the rondo that Forkel analyzed, and the great rondos to follow in volumes 2–6 of the collections "für Kenner und Liebhaber": all are symptomatic of a more theatrical harmonic pacing. The elusive opening phrases of the Sonata in F belong here as well. It cannot be claimed that these phrases capture the staging and timing of opera in any literal sense. But in the anxious silences opened between the phrases, something of the internal clock of opera is suggested. The music breathes new air.

V

In the culling of Bach's portfolio of unpublished works for this first volume, the sonatas *not* chosen are no less provocative in their omission than those with which Bach went to press. Among the *refusées,* two sonatas loom prominently:

---

35. Johann Friedrich Reichardt, reviewing the publication of Bach's *Heilig* (Hamburg, 1779)—in *Musikalisches Kunstmagazin,* I (Berlin, 1782), 84–85—seizes the occasion to proselytize for an "ächten edlen Kirchenmusik." The *Heilig*—and here Reichardt is careful to exclude the introductory Ariette—is exemplary of those qualities that would later inform a theory of a Romantic church music in the writings, preeminently, of E. T. A. Hoffmann. For something on Reichardt's influence on Hoffmann in this matter, see my "In Search of Palestrina: Beethoven in the Archives," in *Haydn, Mozart, and Beethoven: Studies in the Music of the Classical Period,* ed. Sieghard Brandenburg (London and New York: Oxford University Press, 1997), 283–300.

36. Miesner, recognizing that we can know nothing concrete regarding Bach's attitude toward theater in Hamburg, writes an illuminating paragraph on the works, both operatic and theatrical, that crossed the stage in the 1770s. See his *Philipp Emanuel Bach in Hamburg,* 46.

37. Ottenberg, *C. P. E. Bach,* 150. But Benda stayed only a few months. Still, relations between the two composers seem to have been mutually positive.

38. See my "The New Modulation of the 1770s," esp. 565–574.

Sonata in F minor (H 173), composed in 1763, about which Reichardt wrote with unabashed wonder and passion in 1776, and that, on its publication in the third volume "für Kenner und Liebhaber" (1781), would provoke Forkel to his famous *Sendschreiben* on the nature of Sonata.[39] A reviewer for the *Hamburgische unpartheyische Correspondent* for 23 November 1781 described it as one of the best that the composer had ever written, noting that the sonata, "through the circulation of copies which, however, were in part quite corrupt, was already rather well known; and this was the reason why [Bach] was at first unwilling to publish the sonata in this collection." But a number of those who did not yet have the sonata "pleaded with him so urgently that he finally gave in to their entreaties."[40] Bach's decision, finally, to publish it was likely motivated by a wish to establish a clean text; no doubt it was Bach who made the reviewer aware of the state of those copies that were circulating.

Sonata in C major (H 248) from 1775, a radical work whose idiosyncrasies are admired above (see chapter 2): the last sonata to have been composed before Bach went to press with the first volume "für Kenner und Liebhaber," it was the only sonata from the 1770s to have remained unpublished in Bach's lifetime.

Three striking sonatas from 1766—two in B♭ major (H 211 and 212), the third in E major (H 213)—ought to have seemed reasonable candidates as well. We know all three of them in later revision. In its earlier form, the Sonata in B♭ (H 211) is in three movements. In the revision, the first movement is embellished with a complete set of varied reprises, the second movement (Larghetto) is removed, and a new transition of five measures is composed at the end of the first movement in preparation for the final Allegro assai.[41] Similarly, revision subjected the outer movements of the Sonata in E to a full set of varied reprises. Each has survived in a complex tangle of contemporary copies and autographs. Darrell Berg, noting that the handwriting of the manuscript containing the varied reprises displays the telltale tremor evident in Bach's later manuscripts, suggests

---

39. The sonata was evidently alive in Bach's portfolio during these years, for this was the sonata that Reichardt claimed Bach to have played for him during his visit to the composer in July 1774; see Reichardt, *Briefe eines aufmerksamen Reisenden die Musik betreffend*, II: 10–13. Reichardt further claimed that Bach gave him the sonata "in seiner Handschrift für mich allein," but it is not likely that Bach will have parted with the autograph of a sonata not yet published. For more on the sonata, see chapter 1.

40. Suchalla, *Briefe und Dokumente*, 904.

41. The sonata in its revised form is published in C. Ph. E. Bach, *Klaviersonaten. Auswahl*, III, ed. Darrell M. Berg (Munich: G. Henle Verlag, [1989]), 66–76; the deleted Larghetto is printed on 102–104.

that they were prepared "um 1784," the year in which Bach composed the Sonata in
B♭ Major, H 282, whose Largo is a reworking of the Larghetto composed with H
211.[42] But the tremor in Bach's hand is evident in earlier manuscripts as well, and
it is not altogether convincing that the decision to move the Larghetto to a sonata
that Bach was composing in 1784 for the fifth collection "für Kenner und Liebhaber" (1785) was somehow tied in with a decision to enhance the first movements
of the sonatas from 1766 with elaborate *Veränderungen*. Perhaps the Larghetto had
been jettisoned as a part of this reworking of the earlier sonatas—whether in 1784
or earlier—and was thus available for use as Bach set to work on H 282 in 1784. Nor
should we rule out the possibility that these reworkings were undertaken in the preliminary planning of this first volume. *Veränderung*, however, roughly doubles the
printed length of a movement. The first movement of the E major sonata runs to
185 ample measures in three-two meter, and perhaps its length alone acted as a dis-
incentive to the ever frugal Bach, who was now undertaking all fiscal responsibility
in a publishing arrangement with Breitkopf.[43] "The subscribers will probably
have to fork out another 8 gr[oschen] per copy on delivery this time," Bach wrote
on 20 February 1779, as he examined Breitkopf's proof sheets. "The work is turning out longer than I thought. I must guard myself against bankruptcy."[44]

In the effort to put forth a balanced collection, Bach's shrewd reading of the
market is calibrated against those deeper aesthetics that fired his imagination in
the first place. However this may have played itself out in Bach's mind, these five
grand sonatas were kept from a wider public. In the case of the Sonata in F minor,
the rejection was merely temporary.

VI

That the volume published in 1779 set a new kind of sonata in relief against a
backdrop of older sonatas was not lost on the critic for the *Hamburgische un-*

---

42. See Berg, "Carl Philipp Emanuel Bachs Umarbeitungen seiner Claviersonaten," *Bach-Jahrbuch*, 74
(1988): 123–161, esp. 148–149.

43. For an explanation of this arrangement with Breitkopf, see Clark, *Letters*, xxxv–xxxvi; and, more
fully, Clark, "C. P. E. Bach as a Publisher of His Own Works," in *Carl Philipp Emanuel Bach: Musik
für Europa*, ed. Hans-Günter Ottenberg (Frankfurt [Oder]: Konzerthalle "Carl Philipp Emanuel
Bach," 1998), 199–211; and Peggy Daub, "The Publication Process," 71–77.

44. "Die H. Pränumeranten werden diesmahl bey der Ausliefrung wohl noch mit 8 [Groschen] pro
Stück herausrücken müßen. Das Werk wird stärker, als ich dachte. Ich muß meinem Banqverott
vorbiegen." Suchalla, *Briefe und Dokumente*, 727; Clark, *Letters*, 134–135.

partheyische Correspondent for 24 August 1779, who is quick to identify the first, third, and fifth sonatas (those from 1772–1774) as different in tone and manner from the other three:

> The three lighter sonatas in this collection—the first, the third and the fifth—were presumably intended for the *Liebhaber;* indeed, they are easier to perform than the three others. And yet they are so full of Bach's spirit and originality, so full of new ideas and surprising modulations, and at the same time of such engaging melody, that the *Kenner* too will study and play them attentively
>
> We come now to the three sonatas that are somewhat longer than the others, and yet present no great difficulties in performance. These masterpieces are quite similar to those that immortalized the name of Bach during his tenure in Berlin. Similar, we say, with regard to the spirit that on the whole dominates them, but otherwise quite new with regard to idea and execution. It is well known that Herr Bach is one of those rare composers who does not plagiarize. His creative powers appear to be unlimited. Each of his sonatas is newly original, and—apart from the master's general style—quite distinct from all his other sonatas.[45]

To have singled out precisely the sonatas numbered 1, 3, and 5 as "leichter," to have admired their "new ideas and surprising modulations" (neuen Gedanken und überraschenden Ausweichungen), and further to have recognized of the other sonatas a kinship to the Berlin repertory—all this constitutes a criticism of uncanny perspicacity. "And were one to hear these masterpieces performed by Bach himself," the critic closes: "O, there we stand, and know not whether to admire more the player or the composer."[46]

---

45. "Vermuthlich sind die drey leichtern Sonaten in dieser Sammlung, die erste, dritte und fünfte, für die Liebhaber bestimmt, und in der That sind selbige auch leichter vorzutragen, als die drey übrigen. Allein, sie sind dennoch so voll vom Bachischen Geiste und Originalität, so voll von neuen Gedanken und überraschenden Ausweichungen, und dabey doch von so einnehmendem Gesange, daß auch Kenner sie mit Aufmerksamkeit studiren und spielen werden.

   ... Wir kommen nun zu den 3 Sonaten, die etwas länger als die vorigen, aber doch keine große Schwürigkeiten in der Ausführung haben. Diese Meisterstücke sind denen völlig ähnlich, durch welche der Herr Kapellmeister bey seinem Aufenthalt in Berlin seinen Namen verewigt hat. Aehnlich, sagen wir, was den Geist betrifft, der in selbigen im Ganzen herrscht, sonst aber ganz neu, was Gedanken und Ausführung betrifft. Es ist bekannt, daß Herr Bach einer von den seltenen Compositeurs ist, die sich nicht ausschreiben. Seine Erfindungskraft scheint unbegrenzt zu seyn. Jede seiner Sonaten ist ein neues Original, welches, die Manier des Meisters ausgenommen, von allen übrigen seiner eigenen Sonaten gänzlich verschieden ist." The text is reprinted in Suchalla, *Briefe und Dokumente,* 762–764. See also *Carl Philipp Emanuel Bach: Musik und Literatur in Norddeutschland,* 152.

Here again, one must indeed wonder whether the Hamburg reporter profited from a session with Bach, something like a lecture-recital on the contents of the collection, for we know of other instances where Bach's commentary helped to guide the critic's ear.[47] Carl Friedrich Cramer, in a letter to Gerstenberg of 10 January 1779, wrote of a visit to Bach: "The day before yesterday . . . he played to me from his Sonatas 'für Kenner u. Liebhaber,' which are about to appear." Of one movement in particular, Cramer writes "it was a sonata in tempo rubbato [sic], and oh! what a masterwork of modulation, variations of tempo, and expression."[48] What did Cramer mean by "tempo rubbato"? The reviewer for the *Hamburgische unparteyische Correspondent*—Joachim Friedrich Leister, it has been suggested[49]—describing the poco adagio of the Sonata in A, writes: "The tempo rubato with the division into 13 sixteenth notes deserves much study if one wishes to play it the way Bach does. His left hand strikes the notes of the bass according to the most precise measure, while his right hand wanders about in the sixteenths, and at the appointed moment, returns to the bass of the left hand."[50] The passage (shown in ex. 4.4) brings to mind an even more extreme instance of this composed rubato three bars before the recapitulation in the first movement of the Sonata in G (ex. 4.5).

---

46. "Und wenn man nun diese Meisterstücke von Bach selber spielen hört! O da steht man, und weiß nicht, ob man den Spieler oder den Componisten mehr bewundern soll." Suchalla, *Briefe und Dokumente,* 764; and *Musik und Literatur in Norddeutschland,* 152.

47. For evidence of exchanges between Bach and his critics around the first performances of his *Auferstehung und Himmelfahrt Jesu* (H 777) and the *Heilig, mit zwey Chören und einer Ariette zur Einleitung* (H 778), see my "The New Modulation of the 1770s," 551–592. And in a letter of 30 September 1786, about a month before sending off the sixth collection, Bach wrote to Breitkopf: "Meine Freunde wollen durchaus, daß ich mit meiner 6ten Samlung f. K. u. L. herausrücken soll. Sie ist fertig u. ich habe sie ihnen vorgespielt." ("My friends positively want me to come out with my 6th collection *für Kenner und Liebhaber.* It is finished and I have played it for them.") Suchalla, *Briefe und Dokumente,* 1175. Clark, *Letters,* 251.

48. "Vorgestern. . . . Er spielte mir von seinen jetzt herauskommenden Sonaten für Kenner u. Liebhaber vor. . . . Es war eine Sonate in tempo rubbato und o! welch ein Meisterwerk von Modulation, Zeitwendungen u. Ausdruck." The letter, cited only in the fragmentary accounts of two auction catalogs from 1926 in *Briefe und Dokumente,* 723–724, is apparently at the Schleswig-Holsteinische Landesbibliothek, Kiel. See *Carl Philipp Emanuel Bach: Musik und Literatur in Norddeutschland ,*135, for a fuller text.

49. See Ernst Suchalla, "Die *Staats- und Gelehrte Zeitung des Hamburgischen unparteyischen Correspondenten* als unerlässliche Informationsquelle über C. P. E. Bach," in *Carl Philipp Emanuel Bach: Musik für Europa,* 212–220, esp. 214.

50. "Das Tempo rubato mit den 13 Sechszehntheilen kostet viel Studium, wenn man es so, als Herr Bach, spielen will. Seine linke Hand schlägt die Noten des Basses nach dem genauesten Tact an, während daß seine Rechte mit den Sechszehntheilen herumschwärmt, und zur bestimmten Zeit zum Basse der Linken wieder eintritt." Cited from Suchalla, *Briefe und Dokumente,* 763–764.

EXAMPLE 4.4 Sonata in A major, H 186 (*Kenner und Liebhaber*, I, Wq 55/4), second movement, mm. 1–5.

If we can no longer reconstruct the circumstances under which these sonatas were performed for colleague and critic, we can surmise that on the occasion, Bach was not entirely silent on the history of their composition, no doubt pointing up distinctions between the earlier sonatas and the new ones. And from these two accounts of something called "tempo rubato," we might infer that this very passage in the A major sonata inspired some commentary by the composer himself, and that it was his terminology that found its way into Cramer's letter and Leister's review.[51] More provocative still is the notion that in a critical assessment of this music, it was the composer's performance, indelibly inscribed into the notes on the page, that inspired these effusions of admiration. Performance as text.

We return finally to that elusive endeavor to say precisely how these new sonatas would speak to both the *Liebhaber* and the *Kenner*. The perception that *Kenner* and *Liebhaber* embodied two classes of musical literacy, and that they might be reconciled, was what drove the curriculum that Forkel developed in 1777 for his Göttingen lectures. He seems to have sent a copy to Bach, whose reply, in a letter of 15 October 1777, is uncommonly illuminating:

51. And perhaps it is worth contemplating whether it is Cramer's language that we hear in the review in the *Correspondent*. A line like "Und wenn man nun diese Meisterstücke von Bach selbst spielen hört! O da steht man . . ." calls to mind other such expressions in the criticism that would appear in the volumes of his *Magazin der Musik* , published between 1783 and 1787.

EXAMPLE 4.5 Sonata in G major, H 187 (*Kenner und Liebhaber*, I, Wq 55/6), first
movement, mm. 44–50.

To my mind, N[ota] B[ene] in order to educate amateurs, many things may be
omitted that many a musician neither knows nor needs to know. But the most important one—analysis, namely—is missing. One selects true masterpieces from all
kinds of musical works; points out to the amateur the beautiful, the daring, and the
new that is in them; at the same time one shows how insignificant the piece would
be without these things; in addition one points out the mistakes and traps that have
been avoided and, in particular, to what extent one can depart from the ordinary
and venture something daring.[52]

For Bach, as for Mozart, *Wissenschaft* matters less than the acute sensibility of
the *Liebhaber* to recognize, intuitively, the beauty of the thing without knowing

---

52. "Nach meiner Meynung, NB um <u>Liebhaber</u> zu bilden, könnten viele Dinge wegbleiben, die
    mancher <u>Musicus</u> nicht weiß, auch eben nothwendig nicht wißen darf. Das Vornehmste, nehml.
    das analysiren fehlt. Man nehme von aller Art von musicalischen Arbeiten <u>wahrhafte</u> Meister-

how it is achieved. Forkel's goal was more ambitious: "This, then, is the outline of a musical theory through which, to my mind, the *Liebhaber* can be educated to become a true and genuine *Kenner*," he concluded, in the *Einladungsschrift* for his Göttingen lectures.[53] As suggested earlier in this chapter, it is tempting indeed to think that Bach's wording "für Kenner und Liebhaber," first proposed to Breitkopf in the letter of 16 September 1778, owes something to this exchange with Forkel—further, that Bach recognized in Forkel's enterprise the opportunity to exploit a growing market among two classes of the musically literate.[54]

It is commonly assumed that the repertory of the six volumes "für Kenner und Liebhaber" exploits these two faculties: that the new and modish rondos, in the suave profiles of their memorable themes, address the amateur; the bold and introspective modulatory flights of the fantasias, the connoisseur. If there is any truth to this view of the thing, it is complicated by the more profound truth toward which the Hamburg critic points: that these "leichter" sonatas give only the appearance that they are "easy." Both *Kenner* and *Liebhaber* will grasp the profundities hidden beneath simple surfaces and hear the simpler logic implicit in music more overtly complex. These are the classical oppositions that inform style and meaning in the music of the 1770s and 80s. The *Kenner* goes further, probing beneath their surfaces in search of theoretical underpinnings and explanatory models of greater sophistication.

Emanuel Bach remains the supremely enigmatic figure among the composers of the late eighteenth century. The magnitude and range of his output is difficult

---

stücke; zeige den Liebhabern das Schöne, das Gewagte, das Neue darin; man zeige zugleich, wenn dieses alles nicht drinn wäre, wie unbedeutend das Stück seyn würde; ferner weise man die Fehler, die Fallbrücken die vermieden sind; u. besonders in wie fern einer vom ordinären abgehen u. etwas sagen könne ... " Suchalla, *Briefe und Dokumente*, 658–59; Clark, *Letters*, 115–116. The letter is discussed in my "The New Modulation of the 1770s," 590–591.

53. "Dies ist also der Plan einer musikalischen Theorie, durch welche nach meiner Meynung der Liebhaber zu einem wahren und ächten Kenner ausgebildet werden kann." Forkel, *Ueber die Theorie der Musik in so fern sie Liebhabern und Kennern nothwendig und nützlich ist*, in Cramer, *Magazin der Musik*, I (1783), esp. 904. For an argument regarding the intentions of Forkel's Göttingen lectures, see Matthew Riley, "Johann Nikolaus Forkel on the Listening Practices of 'Kenner' and 'Liebhaber,'" *Music & Letters*, 84 (2003): 414–433.

54. In his attack on a dilettantism infecting comic opera, Reichardt drew an instructive "Distinktion" between the *Liebhaber der Musik*—"he who finds satisfaction in the listening to or playing of musical pieces without further troubling himself over the reasons for his pleasure or, more generally, over the rules of art"—and the *Kenner*, "who takes the trouble to study the rules of art insofar as they are necessary to the reasoned criticism of musical works." See his *Ueber die deutsche komische Oper nebst einem Anhange eines freundschaftlichen Briefes über die musikalische Poesie* (Hamburg, 1774); I cite from Johann Friedrich Reichardt, *Briefe, die Musik betreffend: Berichte, Rezensionen, Essays*, ed. Grita Herre and Walther Sigmund-Schultze (Leipzig: Verlag Philipp Reclam jun., 1976), 68–69.

to grasp. His disdain for the popular even as he engages its genres embodies only one of many fruitful contradictions in his work. The sonatas for keyboard alone—some 150 of them, composed between 1731 and 1786—compass fifty-five years of a robust aesthetic history that Bach himself seemed often to dictate. Keenly sizing the marketplace, he cultivates it even as he repudiates it. The marketplace, we must remind ourselves, is no fixed, definable institution even in the circumscribed cultural arena of northern Germany in the 1770s. It is a phenomenon that materializes only in the exchange of ideas: each new idea, and the response elicited by it, alters the marketplace forever.

A Last Sonata

In his final years, Bach continued to compose even as he issued periodic warnings of his determination to stop doing so. "I will finish with the 5th collection [*für Kenner und Liebhaber*]," he wrote on 28 February 1786, "and indeed if there should be thoughts of a 6th, of which still not a note is finished, then nothing can take place before next year."[55] Curiously, the two sonatas finally included in this sixth set were both composed in 1785 according to the *Nachlaßverzeichnis*, though we cannot know whether Bach had yet determined to place them in a projected sixth volume. On 30 September 1786, Bach wrote to Breitkopf of his performance of the set, to the approbation of his friends.[56] The manuscript was dispatched on 26 October.[57] On that very day, he sent Artaria a copy of the announcement of its publication in the *Hamburgische unparteyische Correspondent* for 21 October 1786, noting that this was "to be the last of my printed works for clavier."[58]

It was not however the last of his composed works for keyboard. The great, brooding Fantasy in F# minor (H 300) was composed in 1787, and then arranged for keyboard and violin (H 536), with the famous inscription "C.P.E. Bachs Empfindungen" (a topic to itself in chapter 6). But the purpose of these paragraphs is

---

55. "Mit der 5ten Samlung will ich schließen u. wenn ja an die 6te sollte gedacht werden, davon noch keine Note fertig ist, so kann vor künftiges Jahr nichts werden." Suchalla, *Briefe und Dokumente*, 1142–1144; Clark, *Letters*, 245–247. As Clark explains, the year, missing from the letter, can be inferred from Breitkopf's log.

56. Suchalla, *Briefe und Dokumente*, 1175; Clark, *Letters*, 251.

57. Suchalla, *Briefe und Dokumente*, 1178–79; Clark, *Letters*, 252.

58. "Die hierbey angekündigte 6te Samlung soll die letzte meiner gedruckten Clavierarbeiten seyn." Suchalla, *Briefe und Dokumente*, 1176–1177; Clark, *Letters*, 252.

to contemplate another work, one that seems to have escaped critical scrutiny of any kind since its composition. This is the Sonata in C minor, H 298 (Wq 65/49), entered in the *Nachlaßverzeichnis* as item 205, where its date is given as 1786. Pamela Fox, having a look at its autograph, recognized that the date in the *Verzeichnis* can apply only to the first movement, and that the second and third movements, composed very likely in 1766, belonged originally to another Sonata in C minor, the one that Breitkopf published in 1785 as "Una sonata per il cembalo solo" (H 209, Wq 60).[59] Writing to Breitkopf on 23 September 1785, Bach put it somewhat disingenuously: "It is entirely new, easy, short, and almost without an Adagio, since such a thing is no longer in fashion."[60]

As it turns out, only the second and third movements of this sonata were "entirely new." The first movement was composed nineteen years earlier, in 1766. Fox draws a sensible conclusion from the state in which we find the autograph materials: "In 1786, when Bach was sorting through his stockpile of potential materials, he retrieved the second and third movements from the 1766 sonata and wrote a new first movement."[61] Altogether plausible, Fox's explanation only bears out what we learn from other, similar instances: that Bach abhorred loose ends. The two movements removed from the sonata for Breitkopf needed the grounding of a first movement, and so Bach composed one. (The peregrinations of these six various movements are shown in fig. 4.1.)

It could be left at that, were it not for the burnished luster that this new movement brings to our sense of Bach's final works. In its quiet restraint, in the parsimony of its language and the concision of its thematic play, the music cloaks those subtle intervallic relationships to which we return again and again in an effort to understand why this piece seems to touch those deepest wells of *Empfindsamkeit*. The deployment of pitch and register in the opening phrase, even the isolating of the opening note in each phrase, invites the player to burrow deep into the key. *Ten[uto]*, Bach writes, over the quarter-notes struck at the second half of the measure: five times at the opening, eight times in the reprise, and another five times beginning thirteen bars before the end. In keyboard music, it

59. See Pamela Fox, "Toward a Comprehensive C. P. E. Bach Chronology: Schrift-Chronologie and the Issue of Bach's 'Late Hand'," in *Carl Philipp Emanuel Bach: Musik für Europa*, 306–323, esp. 319–320 and ex. 5A and 5B. The autograph of the sonata—Crakow, Biblioteka Jagiellónska, Mus. ms. Bach P 771—is a fascinating document, for it preserves the final page, crossed through, of the first movement that was sent to Breitkopf. And it preserves as well an actual sketch for the cadenza-like passage five bars before the end.

60. "Sie ist ganz neu, leicht, kurz u. beÿnahe ohne Adagio, weil dies Ding nicht mehr Mode ist." Suchalla, *Briefe und Dokumente*, 1112. Clark, *Letters*, 236.

61. Fox, "Toward a Chronology," 320.

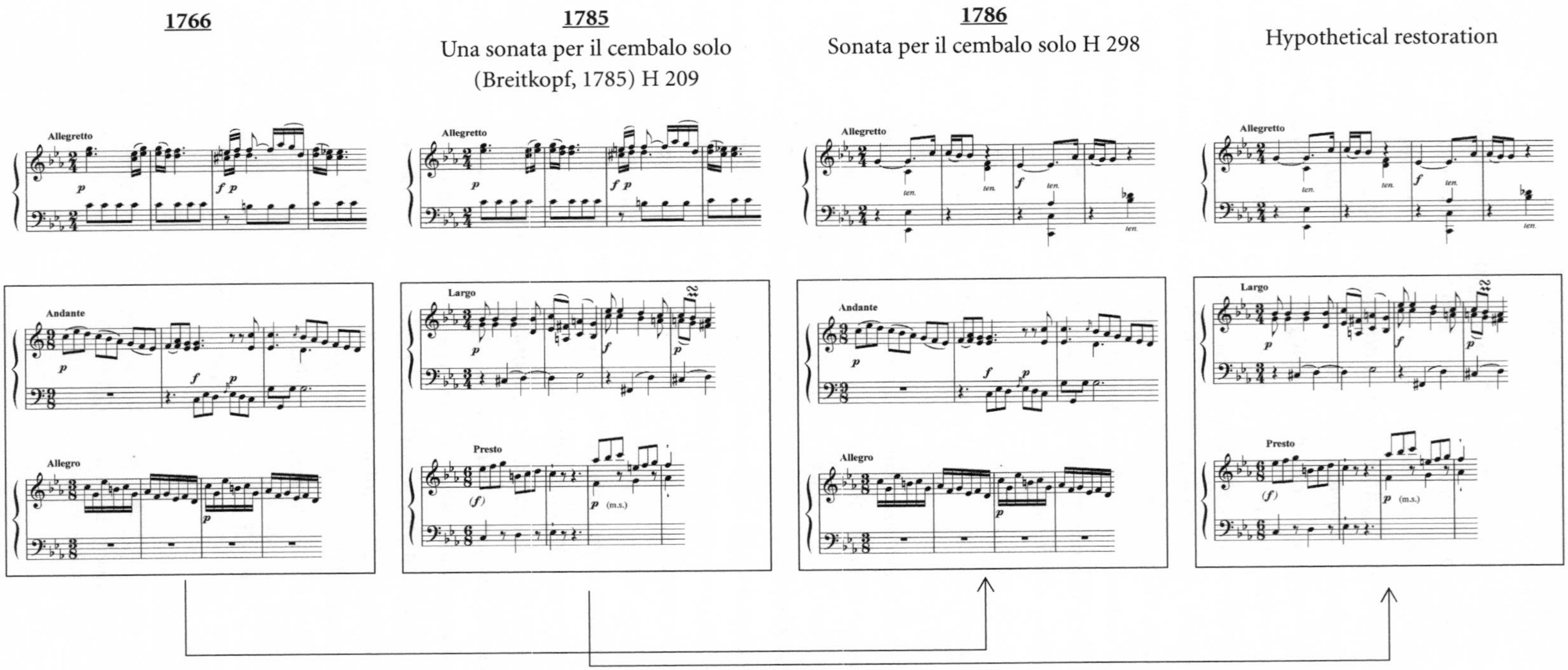
1766
1785
Una sonata per il cembalo solo
(Breitkopf, 1785) H 209
1786
Sonata per il cembalo solo H 298
Hypothetical restoration
Allegretto
Andante
Allegro
Largo
Presto
ten.
(m.s.)

FIGURE 4.1

cannot be a question of notes "sustained at an even volume of tone," as Koch prescribes in his *Lexikon*.[62] Rather, it is the illusion that Bach is after, and a corrective to an inclination to play down these harmonies as somehow less significant than the *Hauptstimme*. In the simulating of the string player's *tenuto*, the keyboard player is forced to think hard about these tones, and in this process, to refuse the conventional notion of "accompaniment." Here, every note matters. (The entire movement is shown as appendix 4B.[63])

It may come as a surprise to discover that in this brief movement the reprises are varied: its eighty bars, that is to say, would be reduced to forty, were the repeats not composed out. And this returns us to the larger issue of *Veränderung*. Why, one must wonder, would it have occurred to Bach to engage the uncompromising process of *Veränderung*–what is there, in this music of gnomic utterance, that would have inspired Bach to vary the reprises? An answer, quite logically, must be sought in the reprises themselves. Consider the opening bars. In the "reprise" sonatas of 1760, it is always the case that the repetitions keep the actual bass intact. However extreme the alteration to the thematic surface, the disposition of the bass with respect to the harmony is invariable. It is striking, then, to hear a radical departure from this practice at the outset of the first reprise in this final sonata. The fragility of its opening bars, the bass staking out a series of harmonies in first inversion, establishes a distinctive quality of voice. At the reprise of these opening bars beginning at m. 17 (see ex. 4.6), the initial octave in the bass, now unequivocally a root, dispels this fragility, taking sharper focus on the appoggiaturas in the upper voice.

And at the end of the recapitulation, the bass is reheard with great purpose. In its first iteration, the harmony shifts somewhat obscurely between mm. 53 and 54 over the sustained F in the bass: the determinants in the treble etch a motion through A♮ and B♮, suggesting that the F is transformed from a root to a seventh at m. 54, where the elaborate diminished seventh implicates a root G. At the reprise of these measures, the harmonic motion is strengthened, the newly voiced bass now articulating a seventh (E♭) at m. 77 that must descend to D in the following bar (the two passages are shown in ex. 4.7). This telling recomposition of the bass has its own thematic significance. At the outset of the second part of the

---

62. Heinrich Christoph Koch, *Musikalisches Lexikon* (Frankfurt am Main: August Hermann dem Jüngern, 1802; reprint Hildesheim: Georg Olms, 1885), col. 1505: "Tenuto . . . wird über diejenigen langen Noten gesetzt, die bey dem Vortrage in gleicher Stärke des Tones ausgehalten werden sollen."

63. A manuscript copy is shown in Berg, ed., *The Collected Works for Solo Keyboard*, IV: 230–235; a page of the autograph is illustrated in Fox, "Toward a Chronology," 322.

EXAMPLE 4.6 Sonata in C minor, H 298, first movement, mm. 1–4, 17–20.

sonata at m. 33–what a later generation would call "development"—the opening is recast with a striking turn of harmony. Restoring the articulative model of the opening bars, the D♭ in the bass (anticipating the seventh in the bass at m. 77) acts as a retrospective inflection of the bass at m. 1, just as *its Veränderung* (m. 57) touches back to the revision at m. 17 (see ex. 4.8).

Veränderung of harmony is pushed to its limit at the passage approaching the recapitulation (see ex. 4.9). The alteration at m. 63 plays hard with the augmented

EXAMPLE 4.7 Sonata in C minor, H 298, first movement, mm. 53–54, 77–78.

EXAMPLE 4.8 Sonata in C minor, H 298, first movement, mm. 33–34, 57–58.

sixth at m. 39, intensifying the waffling between A♮ and A♭. The equivocating is subtle. In the original passage, it has to do with a shift in meaning between a diminished seventh, showing A♮ in harmony with G♭, an appoggiatura that implicates the root F. With the return of A♭ in the bass at m. 39, the G♭ is corrected to F♯. In the *Veränderung,* this ambivalence is made a topic of its own, resolving finally in a fresh harmony: a dominant of the dominant, its root D firmly planted in the bass, coincident with a direct enharmonic shift from G♭ to F♯ in the soprano. On the clavichord, this is a shift of consequence, for the tone can actually be bent here to make the shift audible and touching.[64] Tellingly, it is at the moment just before the recapitulation that this little scene develops. The urgency of resolution is amplified not in some gross display of dissonance and technique, but in a turn inward: a psychological meditation that almost stops the music. The tension is of that special kind

---

64. Leopold Mozart notes that the apparent equivalence of, for example, G-sharp and A-flat, D-flat and C-sharp, F-sharp and G-flat is merely a convenience of "Temperatur" (of equal temperament), but that according to "dem richtigen Verhältnisse" (correct [acoustical] relationships), "all notes lowered by a ♭ are roughly a comma higher than those raised by a ♯. D-flat is higher than C-sharp, for example. . . . Here the good ear must be the judge." See his *Versuch einer gründlichen Violinschule* (Augsburg: Johann Jacob Lotter, 1756), 66–67. The passage is translated somewhat differently in Leopold Mozart, *A Treatise on the Fundamental Principles of Violin Playing,* tr. Editha Knocker (London, New York, Toronto: Oxford University Press, 1951), 70. In practice, the function of the sharped note as leading tone, the flattened note as seventh or ninth, will induce quite the opposite effect, and perhaps it is an inherent tension between the calculus of tempered intervals and the musically functional that magnifies the expressive elocution of such enharmonic relationships.

EXAMPLE 4.9 Sonata in C minor, H 298, first movement, mm. 37–40, 61–64.

intensified in the dynamics of *Veränderung;* what happens here is at once an ex-treme moment in the unfolding of narrative and a synapselike play of analogues.

To experience this sonata at the keyboard, to play it on a good, resonant clavi-chord, is to be taken with music of uncommon subtlety and affect. And yet the modesty of its thematic elocution seems in itself to signal a conscious withdrawal from the public forum. For whatever reasons, the sonata has slipped by unno-ticed. But perhaps there is an explanation for its neglect, and this has to do with the two movements attached to it. It will be recalled that Bach here reinstated the two movements composed in 1766 that were decoupled from that earlier Sonata in C minor during its makeover for Breitkopf in 1785, for which Bach then com-posed a very brief Largo—eight bars to a half cadence—and a splendid new Presto. The earlier movements were rejected for a reason. In its sixty-one tedious bars in 9/8 meter, the Andante in C major is a pale companion to either of these first movements, and so is the routine, work-a-day finale. Seeking to justify the brevity of the Largo to Breitkopf—"almost without an adagio, for such a thing is no longer the fashion" (beÿnahe ohne Adagio, weil dies Ding nicht mehr Mode ist)—Bach's astute sizing of the marketplace is often seen as a capitulation.[65] But perhaps this notion of *Mode* has deeper undercurrents. In often profound mea-sure, his music had undergone an evolution since 1766. The great rondos com-

---

65. For Suchalla, the slow middle movements, no longer wanted, "verkümmern häufig zu kurzen, nichtssagenden Ueberleitungen vom ersten zum dritten Satz" (atrophy often to brief, meaningless transitions from a first movement to a third). "Bach paßt sich hierbei dem Modegeschmack an" (Bach here adapts to fashionable taste). *Briefe und. Dokumente,* 1112.

posed between 1778 and 1786—thirteen of them for the collections "für Kenner und Liebhaber" and the plangent "Abschied von meinem Silbermannischen Claviere in einem Rondo," H 272 (1781)—open a new window of musical space and thematic breadth, just as the six fantasies for the same collections challenge the distant edges of harmonic coherence.

This little imbroglio confronts us with a critical problem that extends beyond the textual residue of these two sonatas, in their incestuous relationship, to the somewhat inscrutable interiors of the creative mind. Bach's final works, those particularly for keyboard alone, seem often to move to that inner space that one associates with lateness. Late style—*Spätstil, Altersstil*—is a concept born of a critical appraisal of the works of Beethoven's final decade, as a way of explaining a music that turns away from artifice, from public display, from the edgy confrontation with novelty: a music that turns inward, that mirrors the isolation of old age.[66] But of course Beethoven was not terribly old at the onset of this late style; he was forty-six years of age in 1816, the year of the Piano Sonata in A major, Opus 101. The question then asks itself whether the concept of "late style" is itself a trope borrowed from some Hegelian construct of historical narrative, an organicist view that models the evolution of art on the scaffold of the Romantic life; or whether there is indeed a quality—an "essence"—in the music that is identifiable with the psychology of old age and lateness, in which, as Georg Simmel put it, "the subject, indifferent to all that is determined and fixed in time and space, has, so to speak, stripped himself of his subjectivity—the gradual withdrawal from appearance, Goethe's definition of old age."[67]

Conundrums of this kind point us toward the imponderable, seeking out that "continually strange newness" that Adorno perceived in the music of *Parsifal*.[68] But the temptation to project a later notion of "late style" on this modest sonata

---

66. A classic, if characteristically difficult, statement is Theodor W. Adorno, "Spätstil Beethovens," reprinted, with "Verfremdetes Hauptwerk: Zur Missa Solemnis," the essay on the Bagatelles, Opus 126, and various notebook entries under the rubrics Spätstil (I), Spätwerk ohne Spätstil, and Spätstil (II) in *Beethoven: Philosophie der Musik*, ed. Rolf Tiedemann (Frankfurt am Main: Suhrkamp Verlag, 2nd ed. 1994), 180–233; English as *Beethoven: the Philosophy of Music*, tr. Edmund Jephcott (Stanford: Stanford University Press, 1998), 123–161. For a fine elaboration on the topic, see Anthony Barone, "Richard Wagner's *Parsifal* and the Theory of Late Style," in *Cambridge Opera Journal*, 7 (1995): 37–54.

67. Georg Simmel, *Goethe* (Leipzig, 1913), 252–253, as translated in Barone, "Wagner's *Parsifal*," 45–46. The Goethe aphorism is from *Maximen und Reflectionen*, item 748, in Johann Wolfgang Goethe, *Werke: Hamburger Ausgabe in 14 Bänden*, XII (Munich: C. H. Beck, "9., neubearbeitete Auflage," 1981), 470.

68. " . . . das stets noch befremdend Neue," as Adorno puts it in his essay "Zur Partitur des '*Parsifal*,'" in Theodor W. Adorno, *Moments musicaux* (Frankfurt am Main: Surhkamp Verlag, 1964), 52.

must confront the chilling circumstances of its completion: the troubling marriage of a first movement that sounds the distant tone of last things, oblivious of
surface display, with two movements composed twenty years earlier for another
sonata entirely. From the patterns discernible in Bach's working habits, we explain the composition of the new first movement of 1786 as a way of bringing
closure to the two movements orphaned in 1785: Bach putting his house in order.
We are left then with an aesthetic problem of a certain gravity. This first movement, articulated in a washed prose that evokes lateness and even exhaustion,
seems remote from the perfunctory stereotypes of those movements from 1766
that are now attached to it.

But what of that other sonata in C minor, the one for Breitkopf? Its two final
movements, composed in 1785 to complete a first movement composed in 1766,
issue from an ear tuned to other sensibilities. In this case, because the first movement constitutes music of some substance, the contradiction is perhaps less conspicuous. That may be, but the result is nonetheless a hybrid whose movements
were composed at different times and in different circumstances. The ethics of
textual scholarship will of course demand that we live with these contradictions:
the author's text, on this account, is inviolate. But it seems to me that a critical inquiry must venture beyond the opaque scrim of such textual stagings. Indeed, the
documents in this case—these six movements patched together for purposes that
we cannot fully explain—powerfully suggest an argument along different lines.
At stake is the viability of the first movement of the later sonata, and its value as
an extreme expression of what might be called Bach's "late style."

It does not take much imagination to recognize that the two movements composed in 1785 for the Breitkopf sonata offer a much better fit with this movement
of 1786, a proposition happily tested in the playing (and called, somewhat coyly,
"hypothetical restoration" in figure 4.1). I am not for a moment suggesting that
we seek justification for this new arrangement in some organicist-inspired hearing of relationships, thematic or otherwise, between these movements. Rather, it
is a more generalized notion of style and voice and even ethos that is acknowledged here. For whatever else one might hear in this newly constructed sonata,
its movements do not violate one another, do not incite a contradiction in style
whose terms cannot be reconciled. The new sonata—two splendid outer movements, tied together in the briefest Largo of intense expression ("vielsagenden,"
pace Suchalla), all of a piece—makes compelling sense, even if we cannot bran-
dish the muted intentions of the composer in its justification.

Intention, however, is a problematical notion in the arts. To invoke it is to
claim privilege of some insight—the author's insight, indeed—into the meaning
of the work that the work itself will not allow, and to admit further that there

might be some discrepancy between what the work says and what the author claims the work to say. Intention, then, seems the wrong word altogether, for what is really at stake is the authority of evidence. In the later years of the Enlightenment, we must often contend with congeries of text whose internal contradictions do not encourage reconciliation of the kind that I wish to propose here. In the rich portfolio left by Emanuel Bach, these contradictions are extreme and unsettling. To contend with them in any reasonable way means to suspend faith in the romance of the masterpiece—an anachronism in any case—even as we labor through the internal crises of style and idea that they trail behind.

Hayden White's reading of the historiographers of the late eighteenth century penetrates with great insight to the core of creative thought in the Enlightenment:

> The *philosophes* needed a theory of human consciousness in which reason was not set over against imagination as the basis of truth against the basis of error, but in which the *continuity* between reason and fantasy was recognized, the mode of their relationship as parts of a more general process of human inquiry into a world incompletely known might be sought, and the process in which fantasy or imagination contributed as much to the discovery of truth as did reason itself might be perceived.[69]

A few pages later, White captures something critical in Kant's perception of this phenomenon. Kant, he claims, "apprehended the historical process less as a development from one stage to another in the life of humanity than as merely a conflict, an *unresolvable* conflict, between *eternally opposed* principles of human nature: rational on the one hand, irrational on the other" (White's emphases).[70] The great philosopher-historians of the Enlightenment, in White's view, understood the world, both its present and past, in ironic terms. Surely, the unresolved contradictions in Bach's manipulation of his portfolio bespeak a certain irony in what might be called his long view of history and his place in it. This we must accept for what it is.

But another distinction suggests itself. The deeper impulses that come into play during the conceiving of the work, and vanish with the ephemera of process, are lost to a later perception of the work, where the perspective is, so to say, constructed and the motives material. At one level, this apparent contradiction

---

69. Hayden White, *Metahistory: The Historical Imagination in Nineteenth-Century Europe* (Baltimore and London: The Johns Hopkins University Press, 1973), 51.

70. White, *Metahistory,* 58.

between reason and imagination, between the rational and the irrational—irrational, only in the sense that such work emanates in the first instance from no consciously rational process of mind—is manifest in the conceptualizing of the creative work. But at another, the author as self-critical historian, the composer as editor, will now figure the work of imagination in the greater theater in which such work is apprehended. The marketplace again intrudes, with all the dialectical uncertainty that such an enterprise will always signal. When Bach composes the Largo and Presto for the Breitkopf sonata, is his ear tuned to the market, as he seems to claim? Or is his reading of the marketplace a projection of some deeper vision of the creative mind? When he composes a new first movement in 1786, is he hearing the subliminal imprint of those two new movements, composed a year earlier for the Breitkopf sonata? If the *Nachlass* will allow no interference in how the documents align themselves, the critical ear yet struggles against what it perceives to be an error in judgment. If we are bound to respect the authority of these two sonatas that Bach cobbled together—and to live with their contradictions—we are no less obliged to understand how they coexist in a complex textual web. Unraveling these knots, the critical mind is left to feel its way through the ironies of Enlightenment thought in pursuit of the elusive music of Bach's last years.

APPENDIX 4A C. P. E. Bach, Sonata in A major, H 270 (*Kenner und Liebhaber* II, Wq 56/6), complete

(continued)

APPENDIX 4A *(continued)*

(continued)

Il Fine

(continued)

CHAPTER 5

Probestück

Probestück: a test-piece, a demonstration of the performer's skill, of the composer's *Kunst*. What the word denotes extends beyond the notion of mere display to the cognitive process of learning—of a skill acquired in the performance of the piece, of idiomatic practices encoded in its notation, and the understanding of the work as an exemplar of composition, of style, of genre. Beyond these more conventional meanings is another, less commonly met, which reveals itself to the critical mind in the presence of a work that probes the frontiers of meaning: *Probestück* as a test of mind, of *Geist*.

Conceived as the final movement of the sixth sonata of the *18 Probestücke* published with the first part of Emanuel Bach's *Versuch über die wahre Art das Clavier zu spielen* (Berlin, 1753), the Fantasia in C minor promptly established itself as a work apart, as though embarrassed by its humble pedagogical origins. Bach himself singled it out in references to the genre, both in the second part of the *Versuch* (1762) and in a well known letter to Forkel.[1] And in 1767, the Fantasia was subjected to a provocative experiment undertaken by the poet Heinrich Wilhelm von Gerstenberg, an experiment much discussed in the contemporary critical press and the focus of several recent studies.[2]

---

1. Carl Philipp Emanuel Bach, *Versuch über die wahre Art das Clavier zu spielen, mit Exempeln und achtzehn Probe-Stücken in sechs Sonaten*. Part I (Berlin: Henning, 1753); Part II (Berlin: Winter, 1762); facsimile reprint, ed. Lothar Hoffmann-Erbrecht (Leipzig: Breitkopf & Härtel, 1969). "Now I have been asked for 6 or 12 fantasies similar to the eighteenth Probestück in C minor," Bach wrote to Forkel, in a letter of 10 February 1775. See chapter 2, note 14. The full text can be found in Ernst Suchalla, ed., *Carl Philipp Emanuel Bach: Briefe und Dokumente. Kritische Gesamtausgabe* (Göttingen: Vandenhoeck & Ruprecht, 1994), 485–486; and *The Letters of C. P. E. Bach*, tr. and ed. Stephen L. Clark (Oxford: Clarendon Press; New York: Oxford University Press, 1997), 75–76.

2. Friedrich Chrysander, "Eine Klavier-Phantasie von Karl Philipp Emanuel Bach mit nachträglich von Gerstenberg eingefügten Gesangsmelodien zu zwei verschiedenen Texten," *Vierteljahresschrift*

I

The brilliant glare of all this admiration seems to have obscured an aspect of the Fantasia that pleads for an understanding of it less as a composition in and of itself than as the third movement of a sonata—more than that, as the final station of a compendious work whose eighteen movements together constitute an essay in its own right: at once an exemplification of and a commentary on genre, and a journal in which these graded steps to keyboard mastery take on a life of their own, in the mode of fictive autobiography, as the *empfindsame Leben*—a life experienced more than reasoned—in which this Fantasia then stands for a state of mind.

Consider how these eighteen pieces comprised in six sonatas plot out a tonal trajectory.[3] It is well known that no single one of the six sonatas sustains its own tonic. Each course of three movements formulates a tonal configuration that wants to be construed syntactically. Trajectories within each sonata plot motion outward, in the manner of a modulation away from an initial tonic—in all but the second sonata, toward its dominant (and in the fifth sonata, to the dominant of its dominant). Without the return to an initial tonic, with conventional closure now in forfeit, the boundaries between sonatas are less clearly drawn. The first movement of the new sonata seems a response to the third movement of its antecedent. As a further consequence, the entire set sketches out a work syntactically coherent in a larger, more complex narrative. Less about some systematic exhaustion of the total chromatic, these eighteen *Probestücke* mean rather to exercise the novice in the incremental difficulties of remote keys, in their tactile and acoustical sense, but also empirically, in the stories that they have to tell. The graphing shown in ex. 5.1A attempts merely a synopsis of the cardinal tonal events in the set. (The contents of the collection are displayed in table 5.1.)

The playing off of sonatas against one another, dialectically (so to say), is ap-

---

für Musikwissenschaft, 7 (1891): 1–25; reprint in *Carl Philipp Emanuel Bach: Beiträge zu Leben und Werk*, ed. Heinrich Poos (Mainz and New York: Schott, 1993), 329–353; Eugene Helm, "The 'Hamlet' Fantasy and the Literary Element in C. P. E. Bach's Music," *The Musical Quarterly*, 58 (1972): 277–296; Tobias Plebuch, "Dark fantasies and the dawn of the self: Gerstenberg's monologues for C. P. E. Bach's C minor Fantasia," in *C. P. E. Bach Studies*, ed. Annette Richards (Cambridge: Cambridge University Press, 2006), 25–66. For an appreciation of another kind, see Annette Richards, *The Free Fantasia and the Musical Picturesque* (Cambridge: Cambridge University Press, 2001), 47–48.

3. We finally have an excellent scholarly edition in *Carl Philipp Emanuel Bach: "Probestücke," "Leichte" and "Damen" Sonatas*, ed. David Schulenberg, in Carl Philipp Emanuel Bach, *The Complete Works*, series I, volume 3 (Los Altos, CA: The Packard Humanities Institute, 2005). The original edition can be studied in facsimile in *The Collected Works for Solo Keyboard by Carl Philipp Emanuel Bach*, ed. Darrell Berg, 6 vols. (New York and London, 1985), I: 39–59.

parent at the outset, where the tonal plot of the second sonata mirrors the first in interval inversion. It is of course not the inversion, for its own sake, that Bach wants us to hear, but, rather, the establishing of two vectors out from a primary C major, one along the sharp side, to the dominant, the other toward the minor subdominant, and what it portends of a "flat" side. The opposition—sharp side/flat side—intensifies as its axes diverge. The distances traversed are dramatized in a schism articulated between the fourth and fifth sonatas: the F♯ minor in which the fourth sonata closes is answered by a volcanic E♭ major, the music erupting, toccata like, from its opening octave in the bass. The vault between F♯ minor and E♭ major, for all its stunning effect, is a characteristic one: an ellipsis, Bach would likely have called it.

Those familiar with the second part of the *Versuch* (1762) may be reminded here of its final paragraph, in the chapter "Von der freyen Fantasie," where a *Gerippe* ("skeleton"), in Bach's vivid metaphor, displays in figured bass notation a fantasy in D major whose "realization" is shown on an engraved plate tipped into the book.[4] (This is shown as fig. 5.1.)

Much has been made of this final and profound illustration, which Bach glosses with a paragraph of analysis that, in its laconic fashion, offers rare insight into Bach's way of conceptualizing the process of composition. At the critical moment in the fantasy—the moment of greatest tonal remove—Bach invokes ellipsis: "The transition [Uebergang] from B with the seventh chord to the following B-flat with the [four-]two chord reveals an ellipsis, for strictly speaking, a six-four chord on B or a root-position triad on C ought to have been interpolated."[5] What I want to suggest is that this notion of a tonal *Gerippe*, static and "rational," in tension with an "*empfindsame*" narrative of experience—a "realization" that moves off into remote regions of dissonance, exacerbating the moment of ellipsis—is a condition manifest as well in the *Probestücke*, taken as a single overarching work. In both, a moment of tonal extremity provokes a crisis in syntax, a breach in which the rule of grammar is taxed. Symptom of reason challenged, the ellipsis is meant to be felt, its narrating agent caught by surprise. And yet the moment must

---

4. Bach, *Versuch*, II: 340–341, and [unpaginated] endplate. For a provocative study of the piece, see Heinrich Schenker, "Die Kunst der Improvisation," in Schenker, *Das Meisterwerk in der Musik*, [I] (Munich, Vienna and Berlin: Drei Masken Verlag, 1925), 9–40; in English as "The Art of Improvisation," tr. Richard Kramer, in *The Masterwork in Music*, ed. William Drabkin, I (Cambridge and New York: Cambridge University Press, 1994), 2–19. See also Annette Richards, *The Free Fantasia and the Musical Picturesque*, 42–43.

5. "Der Uebergang vom h mit dem Septimenaccord, zum nächsten b mit dem secundenaccord verräth eine Ellipsin, weil eigentlich der Sextquartenaccord vom h oder c mit dem Dreyklange hätte vorhergehen sollen." Bach, *Versuch*, II: 340.

EXAMPLE 5.1

A synoptic view of the *18 Probestücke.*

From Sonata IV, Largo, cadenza *a 2.*

indeed respond to analysis—must be shown to have been plotted, a consequence of rational design, even if the effect borders on the irrational. Precisely how the ellipsis between F♯ minor and E♭ major might be explained—better, how dissonance of this magnitude is shown to resonate in the music that follows from it— is an obscure matter to which we shall return.

The setting of an environment in which such crisis can be construed seems clearly the point of the middle movement of the fourth sonata, an exaggerated lesson in the conventions of *ouverture* in French style: *Largo maestoso,* D major, much

A *(continued)*

From Sonata VI, Adagio, cadenza *a 3*.

Sonata VI, Fantasia, opening music.

TABLE 5.1 Contents of *18 Probestücke*.

	1	Allegretto tranquillemente	$\frac{2}{4}$ C major
I	2	Andante mà innocentemente	$\frac{3}{4}$ E minor
	3	Tempo di Minuetto con tenerezza	$\frac{3}{8}$ G major
	4	Allegro con spirito	𝄴 D minor
II	5	Adagio sostenuto	𝄴 B♭ major
	6	Presto	$\frac{12}{8}$ G minor
	7	Poco Allegro mà cantabile	$\frac{3}{4}$ A major
III	8	Andante lusingando	$\frac{9}{8}$ A minor
	9	Allegro	𝄵 E major
	10	Allegretto grazioso	𝄴 B minor
IV	11	Largo maestoso	$\frac{3}{4}$ D major - F♯ minor
	12	Allegro Siciliano e scherzando	$\frac{6}{8}$ F♯ minor
	13	Allegro di molto	$\frac{3}{2}$ E♭ major
V	14	Adagio assai mesto e sostenuto	𝄴 B♭ minor
	15	Allegretto arioso ed amoroso	$\frac{2}{4}$ F major
	16	Allegro di molto	𝄴 F minor
VI	17	Adagio affettuoso e sostenuto	$\frac{3}{8}$ A♭ major
	18	Fantasia: Allegro moderato	𝄴 C minor

overdotting, much embellishment. At m. 23, in a rain of dotted thirty-second notes, *fortissimo,* the music splinters its frame. The B♯ at the end of the bar signals what is about to happen. D, as tonic, is unseated, the tone made dissonant against the B♯. The music settles on C♯, a dominant, isolated in three octaves with great flourish. What ensues is a cadenza in dialogue, deeply felt, trembling in *Bebung*—and in F♯ minor. (See ex. 5.1B.) Bach himself wrote about the intended effect of these two voices engaged in a performance that means to simulate the improvisatory: "The pauses called for at the whole notes occur so that one may imitate the unpremeditated cadenza-making of two or three persons, and at the same time imagine that the one is paying close attention whether the proposition of the other has ended or not."[6]

---

6. "Das bey diesen weissen Noten erforderte Stillehalten geschiehet desswegen, damit man das Cadenzenmachen zweyer oder dreyer Personen, ohne Abrede zu nehmen, nachahme, indem man dadurch gleichsam vorstellet, als wenn eine Person auf die andere genau Achtung gebe, ob deren Proposition zu Ende sey oder nicht." Bach, *Versuch,* I: 132; translation mine. For a different one, see Carl Philipp Emanuel Bach, *Essay on the True Art of Playing Keyboard Instruments,* ed. and tr. William J. Mitchell (New York: W. W. Norton, 1949), 165.

FIGURE 5.1 C. P. E. Bach, *Versuch über die wahre Art das Clavier zu spielen*, II (Berlin, 1762), 341, and unpaginated plate.

In its groping to convey in words what the music does, Bach's language affords one of those rare glimpses into the composer's poetic imagination: what, precisely, these speechlike effusions are saying is of no consequence—are indeed unknowable. What does matter is the "paying close attention" that goes on between and during the cadenza-making, the one hand listening to the other. This, Bach tells us, is what needs to be performed. But what must strike us about this cadenza is its utter incongruity with the music that precedes it, and which it in effect dissolves. In its intimate dialogue, the cadenza seems a colloquy on the *ouverture*—a conversation about it—and by extension, a commentary on a genre, a style. This is not how overtures in the French manner are meant to end. (We return in chapter 9, in quite another context, to the provocations of this remarkable inflection.)

At a telling moment in his *Paradoxe sur le comédien,* Diderot writes: "The man of sensibility obeys natural impulses and expresses nothing but the cry from his heart; as soon as he begins to control or constrain this cry, he's no longer himself, but an actor playing a part."[7] Lifted from its context, Diderot's bold insight (to which we shall return in the next chapter) reflects aptly on an opposition that seems at play in this most contradictory of movements in Bach's *Probestücke.* But the opposition is turned to other ends in Diderot's argument, where the skilled actor is shown to be above sensibility, which he must learn to wear as a mask. To follow Diderot is to ask ourselves whether this schismatic music means, metonymically, to represent a breach in aesthetic: whether, that is, the composer, as playwright, has scripted a narrative for the player; or whether Bach's music, finding its C♯, must be taken as the cry itself, where the notes inscribe an escape from the constraints of the dogmata of another age. Such questions return us to Diderot's *Paradoxe,* where the roles of poet and actor now and again fade into one another. In a sense, Bach's *Probestück* worries this same problem, for the composer is not quite separable from the player, and the player, if he is playing a role, would, at this telling moment where the music unearths its resonant C♯, know what it feels like to *feel* like Bach, to feel empathetically with him.

Ever engaged in role-playing, Bach's keyboard music often voices the player in mask. And then there are those rare, signifying moments when the composer himself seems unmasked. That, I think, is what we hear at this deeply inflected C♯. The mask is lifted. Player and composer are collapsed into one. The music

---

7. Denis Diderot, *Paradoxe sur le comédien,* with preface by Raymond Laubreaux (Paris: [Garnier-] Flammarion, 1981), 151. A translation is published in Denis Diderot, *Selected Writings on Art and Literature,* tr. with an introduction and notes by Geoffrey Bremner (London: Penguin Books, 1994), 124–125.

shifts from the formalities of antique tragedy, distant and impersonal, to a theater of whispered intimacies. The catastrophic collapse into *empfindsame* dialogue as an escape from the overbearing rigor of the *ouverture* has implications that resonate far beyond the modest didactic objectives of the *Probestücke*. One senses here the passing away, the renunciation of *ancien régime*. The stiff mask of the aristocracy and its ceremonial dance are replaced with a music born of sensibility and irony and paradox. For Diderot's actor, the cadenza-in-dialogue is but another mask, another state of mind to be disciplined. And yet this music sings of deeper authenticities, of the composer caught in the act. The quirky *Siciliano* that follows in F♯ minor emanates without pause from the lengthy cadential trills with which the cadenza closes. "Siciliano e scherzando," Bach writes, but the music has its mordant accents (at mm. 41–44, not shown). Again the music seems more a commentary on genre than the thing itself. In its articulation of the form, the music hesitates pensively on octave C♯s, first tonicized (mm. 35–36), then returned as dominant (mm. 39–40), and we are reminded of the signifying C♯ that moves from *ouverture* to cadenza-in-dialogue—reminded, too, of another one: the octave C♯, pianissimo, before the reprise (in E major) of the third movement of Sonata III.

More obliquely, the cadenza on C♯ has an echo in its counterpart at the end of the *Adagio affettuoso e sostenuto* in the Sixth Sonata (see ex. 5.1C). Here, the cadenza splays out in three voices—and finally, to a confusion of voice—again suggestive of intimacies overheard. For the player, certainly, these two passages have much to do with one another. If the earlier cadenza is more effusive, more eccentric, more given to *Bebung*, to dissonance and difficult chromaticism, the cadenza in A♭ explores the *affettuoso e sostenuto* of its source music. Like the earlier cadenza, this one, too, raises expectations. Cadenzas at the close of slow middle movements have a rhetorical mission, for while cadenzas are always about the past—even as the cadenza on C♯ in the Fourth Sonata repudiates its past—they anticipate a future.

It is this sense of expectation that promotes the opening arpeggiation of the Fantasia, whose tones now seem to grow out of the ruminative, cadenza-as-conversation with which this penultimate music closes. Cadenzas, too, are about the improvisatory, and in these written-out instances, exemplify how one goes about the business of spontaneous composition, here constrained by the simple motion between a six-four and its resolution to the dominant. In the Fantasia, there are no such constraints; the very notion of formal convention is itself antagonistic to the idea of fantasy, where perhaps only the diction, the accents, the rhythms of its modulatory tactics might be generalized. The music gives the illusion of spontaneous thought, unrestrained by convention. Capricious wit, at the edge of chaos, plays against the deeper internal laws that govern how the music moves and how it will end. Not the least paradoxical aspect of the fantasy is its enactment, in its own tropelike conventions, of a rite of creation, even as, in the characteristic gestures of fantasy, it renounces the generic and the conventional.

Taking up the conversation of the cadenza, the deep C that sets the Fantasia in motion seems itself an unfolding from those closing imitations, even as this C fixes itself as a new fundamental (see ex. 5.1D). A♭ is now reduced to a dissonant sixth. Indeed, much of the first page of the Fantasia seems aggravated by A♭, at first as a dissonant and prominent upper neighbor (a ninth above the root of the dominant) and then as a root in its own right. As though embedded in these intervallic reverberations, the plangent tones of the Adagio continue to sound.

The ambivalence of the Fantasia as a *third* movement is much to its point. The music has a complicated, even contradictory role to play, for while it serves as a finale, it does not portray the gestures of closure by which finales are ordinarily defined. As Fantasia, it signifies a stage in the education of the musician, the moment at which performer and composer touch, where the act of performance comes closest to emulating the immediacy of creation. This opening arpeggiation, at once mimetic in its envisioning of the growth of Idea from some fundamental tone—as synecdoche, the figure containing within itself the essence of this larger thing that it means to signify—at the same time announces a telling event in a greater narrative of *Bildung*—another untranslatable word that I use here to suggest the maturation, the humanistic coming of age of the inner man through experience and reflection. Here is the moment toward which all this study and practice has been directed. The apprentice, it suggests, is now prepared to improvise, to create from the imagination. For whatever this Fantasia, as the final movement of these eighteen *Probestücke,* might signify of closure, it signifies a commencement as well: here are the beginnings of true invention, of original thought.

II

None of this pedagogical apparatus can have been of much interest to the poet Gerstenberg, a prominent figure in that robust literary circle in northern Germany that included such figures as Friedrich Nicolai, Moses Mendelssohn, Johann Heinrich Voss, Klopstock, Lessing, and Herder (to name only the principal players). A man of considerable musical ability, Gerstenberg took Bach's Fantasia as a *Probestück* in quite another sense, fitting out the music with a rephrasing (more paraphrase than translation) of Hamlet's soliloquy "To be or not to be"— inspired, one might think, by the translation of this much celebrated text in

Moses Mendelssohn's "Observations on the Sublime and the Naive in the Fine Sciences" (1758), then revised, with an entirely different translation, in the *Philosophische Schriften* (1761).[8] Not the least curious aspect of Gerstenberg's experiment was his determination to set Bach's music to yet another text: this time, the final words of Socrates, a fantasy-like invention by Gerstenberg, now perhaps inspired by Mendelssohn's *Phaedon* (published by Nicolai in 1767), which begins as a translation of the Socratic dialogue, but in the end allows *his* Socrates to speak in the accents of a philosopher of the eighteenth century: "meinem Sokrates fast wie einen Weltweisen aus dem achtzehnten Jahrhunderte sprechen lassen," as Mendelssohn puts it in the preface.[9]

Johann Gottfried Herder, warming to his own translation of Hamlet's soliloquy—a version of it was published in 1774—cited Mendelssohn's, which he understood as "more an idealized imitation, as his purposes demanded, than a copy of the melancholy, scornful, bitter tone of the piece"[10]—from which we might gather two things: that Hamlet's soliloquy was something of a classic, a set piece even in these early years of the German Shakespeare obsession; and that the soliloquy served as a kind of barometer of German Enlightenment thought, a touchstone for those practical questions of translation that fed into the deeper problem of language and its origins that intrigued literary thinkers such as Lessing, Herder and Hamann—a barometer as well for the much vexed issue of art as the formal expression of feelings (*Empfindungen*).[11] Mendelssohn's gloss on the monologue is worth having: "Of all the species of the sublime, the sublime of the passions, when the soul is suddenly bewildered by terror, regret, fury and despair,

---

8. "Betrachtungen über das Erhabene und das Naive in den schönen Wissenschaften," in *Bibliothek der schönen Wissenschaften und der freyen Künste*, II, 2tes Stück (Leipzig: Johann Gottfried Dyck, 1758), reprinted in Moses Mendelssohn, *Schriften zur Philosophie und Ästhetik*, I in *Gesammelte Schriften* (Berlin: Akademie-Verlag, 1929), I: 203; *Philosophische Schriften*, I (Berlin: Christian Friedrich Voß, 1761; verbesserte Auflage, 1771), reprinted in *Gesammelte Schriften*, I: 468–469. For a translation of the "verbesserte Auflage" of 1771, see Moses Mendelssohn, *Philosophical Writings*, tr. and ed. Daniel O. Dahlstrom (Cambridge: Cambridge University Press, 1997).

9. Moses Mendelssohn, *Phaedon[,] oder über die Unsterblichkeit der Seele[,] in drey Gesprächen* (Berlin und Stettin: Friedrich Nicolai, 1767), reprinted in *Schriften zur Philosophie und Ästhetik*, III/1, in *Gesammelte Schriften*, III, erster Teil (Berlin: Akademie-Verlag, 1932), 37–128. The connection to Mendelssohn's *Phaedon* owes to Plebuch, "Dark fantasies," esp. 50–54; I am grateful to the author for allowing me access to a typescript of the essay before its publication.

10. "Moses Mendelssohn hat in seinen [Philosophische] Schriften eine Übersetzung geliefert, aber, wie es sein Zweck nur erfoderte, mehr idealisirte Nachahmung, als Kopie im schwermüthig-verachtend-bittern Tone des Stücks." This and a translation that follows are found on some unused leaves published as "[Stücke aus einer Shakespear-Übersetzung]," in *Johann Gottfried Herder: Sämtliche Werke*, ed. Bernhard Suphan (Berlin: Weidmann, 1891; reprint Hildesheim: Georg Olms, 1967), V: 253–256.

11. For a translation in prose by Lessing, see August Fresenius, "Hamlet-Monologe in der Übersetzung von Mendelssohn und Lessing," in *Jahrbuch der Deutschen Shakespeare-Gesellschaft*, 39

demands the most unaffected expression. A mind in anger is preoccupied with its emotion alone, and any thought that would put distance between it and its emotion is a torment. At the moment of a violent emotion, the soul is working under a torrent of images which overtake it. They all press to the point of exploding, and since they cannot all be expressed at the same time, the voice stammers and can scarcely utter the words that first occur to it."[12] In introducing the monologue, Mendelssohn sets the scene—gets into Hamlet's head, so to say—and concludes: "Deep in these despondent thoughts, he steps forward, and reflects: *Seyn,* oder *Nichtseyn;* dieses ist die Frage!"[13]

Mendelssohn, discerning a reflective Hamlet, is contending here with the tension of the reasoning mind "overtaken" by its emotions. It was this very problem that consumed Lessing in his famous *Laokoon* of 1766, provoked in the first instance by the art historian Johann Joachim Winckelmann's analysis of what would become the most widely studied work of sculpture from Greek antiquity. Winckelmann, in his *Reflections on the Imitation of Greek Works in Painting and Sculpture* (1755), understood the muffled control of Laokoon's agony, that "noble simplicity and quiet grandeur," as he memorably phrased it, as a characteristic of the Greek temperament. Lessing understood it rather as a constraint of the plastic arts, over against the literary, the narrative, the dramatic, for in Vergil's *Aeneid,* Laokoon does indeed scream, "sending to heaven his appalling cries like a slashed bull escaping from the altar" (as it goes in Robert Fitzgerald's poetic translation). For Lessing, it is the expressive moment, frozen in time, that is at issue. The ancient painter Timomachus "did not paint Medea at the instant when she was actually murdering her children, but a few moments before, while her motherly love was still struggling with her jealousy. We see the end of the contest before-

---

(1902–1903): 245–246. This was apparently for the Hamburg production of 1776, directed by Friedrich Ludwig Schröder in the translation by Wieland. See also Lawrence Marsden Price, *The Reception of English Literature in Germany* (Berkeley: University of California Press,1932; reprint New York and London: Benjamin Blom, 1968), 282.

12. "Unter allen Gattungen vom Erhabenen, erfordert das Erhabene in den Leidenschaften, wenn die Seele jetzt von Schrecken, Reue, Zorn und Verzweifelung plötzlich betäubt wird, den allerungekünstelsten Ausdruck. Ein aufgebrachtes Gemüth ist einzig und allein mit seinem Affekte beschäftiget, und jeder Begriff der es davon entfernen will, ist ihm eine Marter. Die Seele arbeitet unter der Menge von Vorstellungen, die sie im Augenblicke eines heftigen Affekets übereilen; sie drängen sich alle zum Ausbruche, und da der Mund sie nicht alle zugleich aussprechen kann, so stockt er, und vermag kaum die einzelne Worte zu sagen, die sich ihm am ersten darbieten." Mendelssohn, *Gesammelte Schriften,* I: 469; I have slightly altered the English given in *Philosophical Writings,* 206–207.

13. "Die Ungewißheit stürzt ihn in Verzweifelung, und verleitet ihn fast, sich selbst zu ermorden. Vertieft in diese trübsinnigen Gedanken, tritt er auf, und überlegt: ... " Mendelssohn, *Gesammelte Schriften,* I, 468; *Philosophical Writings,* 205–206.

hand; we tremble in the anticipation of soon recognizing her as simply cruel, and our imagination carries us far beyond anything which the painter could have portrayed in that terrible moment itself."[14]

Lessing's subtitle, "über die Grenzen der Malerie und Poesie"—on the limits of painting and poetry, as it is commonly translated, but with a sense, in "Grenzen," of the porous boundary between them—invites its transliteration to that similarly porous boundary between Shakespeare's monologue and Bach's Fantasia that Gerstenberg explored: "über die Grenzen der Tonkunst und Poesie," he might have been thinking. Contending, in a letter of 1767 to Friedrich Nicolai, that music itself, "without words, conveys only general ideas, ideas which however receive their full definition only with the addition of words," Gerstenberg sought to justify his experiment, noting that it would succeed only "in those works for solo instrument . . . where the expression [Ausdruck] is very clear and speech-like [sprechend]."[15] And yet it cannot have been clarity of expression that drew the poet to Bach's singular work, but, rather, its obverse: a clarity of *diction,* perhaps, that masks the expression of something not at all clear. In his naive way, Gerstenberg touches on a quality in the music that is otherwise difficult to apprehend. If, by certain theoretical lights, music *means* exclusively as syntactical configuration among the notes themselves, this music, beneath the surface of its speechlike accents, yet seeks expression of something more obscure. In an essay titled "On Recitative and Aria in Italian Vocal Music" published in 1770, Gerstenberg wondered "whether it is not in the nature of song that words, which it uses as symbols, are transformed into tone paintings of feeling."[16] That Bach's Fantasia would induce Gerstenberg to seek this transformative act through a coupling

---

14. "Die Medea hatte [Timomachus] nicht in dem Augenblicke genommen, in welchem sie ihre Kinder wirklich ermordet; sondern einige Augenblicke zuvor, da die mütterliche Liebe noch mit der Eifersucht kämpfet. Wir sehen das Ende dieses Kampfes voraus. Wir zittern voraus, nun bald bloss die grausame Medea zu erblicken, und unsere Einbildungskraft gehet weit über alles hinweg, was uns der Maler in diesem schrecklichen Augenblicke zeigen könnte." Gotthold Ephraim Lessing, *Laokoon: oder über die Grenzen der Malerei und Poesie* (Berlin: Christian Friedrich Voß, 1766). I cite from Gotthold Ephraim Lessing, *Werke in drei Bänden,* ed. Herbert G. Göpfert, III (Munich and Vienna: Carl Hanser Verlag, 1982), 9–188, esp. 28; and from *Selected Prose Works of G. E. Lessing,* ed. Edward Bell, tr. E. C. Beasley and Helen Zimmern (London: George Bell and Sons, 1889), 21.

15. "Ich nehme erstlich an, daß die Musik ohne Worte nur allgemeine Ideen vorträgt, die aber durch hinzugefügte Worte ihre völlige Bestimmung erhalten; zweytens geht der Versuch nun bey solchen Instrumentsolos an, wo der Ausdruck sehr deutlich und sprechend ist." Letter from Gerstenberg to Nicolai, Copenhagen, 12 May 1767; text from Suchalla, ed., *Bach: Briefe und Dokumente,* 127.

16. "Ob nicht die Natur des Gesanges darin bestehe daß er die Worte, deren er sich als Zeichen bedient, in Tongemälde der Empfindung verwandelt." In Gerstenberg, *Vermischte Schriften in drei Bänden,* (Altona 1815–1816), III: 353–354; cited in Chrysander, "Eine Klavier-Phantasie von Karl Philipp Emanuel Bach," 24.

with—and a rewriting of—two literary situations of legendary profundity is it-self suggestive of the convolutions of thought and feeling that the music was heard to embody. If Hamlet's actual lines seem, in Stephen Greenblatt's keen ap-praisal, a "formal academic debate on the subject of suicide,"[17] Gerstenberg wants something very different: "To be or not to be: that is the great question. Death! Sleep! Sleep! And dream! Black dream! Dream of death! To dream it, ah! The blissful dream!" The reasoned discourse of debate gives way here to a rush of sen-sibility and *Empfindung.*

What was it, precisely, that provoked Gerstenberg to his experiment? One pas-sage will have to stand for several. In the transition from the end of the Largo to the return of the Allegro moderato, the transformation of B♭ into its enharmonic homonym A♯ presses beyond simple diction. (The passage is shown in ex. 5.2.) The sheer intensity of the tone itself, seems to disgorge the insoluble nut of mu-sical meaning from its midst. In its reach for the distant relationship, the enhar-monic moment strains the process of thought. Inflected by *Bebung,* the single pitch seems in dispute with itself, as though all expression, all meaning, were re-duced to this tremulous focal point.[18] For if we take mimesis in its deeper sense as a representation of human *experience* in the languages of art—not, that is, as an imitation of some material and cognitive *thing*—then the music may be said to represent some unnamed expression, to actualize it, in language that yet had the power to move more deeply than experience itself.[19]

This, it seems to me, is the paradox that Gerstenberg set out to explore: while Bach's music possessed an eloquence of expression—a *Sprache der Empfindungen,* in Forkel's phrase—that was the envy of the poet, what it expressed could not be translated. To endeavor to capture its expression in the literary was to confuse

---

17. *The Norton Shakespeare, Based on the Oxford Edition,* ed. Stephen Greenblatt (New York and Lon-don: W. W. Norton, 1997), 1661.

18. The effect is touchingly conveyed in Burney's memorable description of Bach at the keyboard: "In the pathetic and slow movements, whenever he had a long note to express, he absolutely contrived to produce, from his instrument, a cry of sorrow and complaint, such as can only be effected upon the clavichord; and perhaps by himself." See Charles Burney, *The Present State of Music in Ger-many, the Netherlands, and United Provinces* (London: T. Becket, 1773), revised as *An Eighteenth-Century Musical Tour in Central Europe and the Netherlands* (*Dr. Burney's Musical Tours in Europe,* II), ed. Percy A. Scholes (London: Oxford University Press, 1959), 219.

19. My thoughts here are inspired by Stephen Halliwell's reading of Aristotle's famous invocation of the term in the *Poetics:* "Without ever offering a definition of the term . . . Aristotle employs mimesis as a supple concept of the human propensity to explore an understanding of the world–above all, of human experience–through fictive representation and imaginative 'enact-ment' of experience." Aristotle, *Poetics* (Loeb Classical Library), ed. and tr. Stephen Halliwell (Cambridge, Mass. and London: Harvard University Press, 1995), 8.

EXAMPLE 5.2 Sonata VI, Fantasia, from end of Largo.

means and ends, cause and effect. How, one might ask, could one verify of such a setting that the music was *not* conceived as an expression of Hamlet's soliloquy? If one knew the Fantasia only in the Gerstenberg redaction, wouldn't a post-facto paring away of Gerstenberg's text leave behind a music that now seems unrealized in its expressive mandate? However we manage to explain it, Gerstenberg's cunning experiment stands not least as a probe into the depths of Enlightenment aesthetics.

That Bach's Fantasia induced Gersternberg to find its equivalent in two literary passages that probe a state of mind *in extremis* must tell us something of the expressive power of this music. But it does something else as well. There are really two kinds of music in the Fantasia. Gerstenberg's text is unobjectionable in the Largo, where the music moves in measured song. The diction of the poem is the diction of the music. In the severe aesthetics of Lied—as defined, for one, in the two lengthy essays ("Lied [Dichtkunst]; Lied [Musik]") in Sulzer's *Allgemeine Theorie der schönen Künste*—the music self-effacingly enhances prosody and diction: nothing more. Musical meaning is not in question. But the outer sections are very different in this regard. The music, unmeasured, means to emulate a process of mind in the midst of thought. Here, harmony is everything: not in formally arranged symmetries, but in its reach for the distant relationship. The enharmonic interval (only imagined on the keyboard, and consequently more poignant) strains the process of thought: the single pitch, inflected by its tonal environment, acquires two or more contradictory properties, seeming to carry on a conversation with itself.

Beyond the sense of this passage as expressive in and of itself, it seems as well to reflect upon earlier music in the *Probestücke*. Established as the root of a dominant in E♭ major, B♭ is then extricated, sounded in isolation, *forte,* with much *Bebung*. The new harmony beneath it, a bare octave and fifth on C, further isolates B♭, now a dissonant seventh, in company with E♮, an exposed leading tone. Further transformation is enacted in an extravagant phrase which places A♮ at its peak, rubbing viscerally against A♯: B♭ has been converted enharmonically to a leading tone, its companion E♮ now seated deep in the bass as a seventh. The music is returned to the sharp side, and the extremities of this reversal invoke the two trajectories of the *Probestücke* at the crisis articulated between the fourth and fifth sonatas, exploring the resonant spaces between F♯ minor and E♭ major.

III

Whatever else they might be about, these eighteen pieces document a journey. As protagonist, the player works through the experience of an apprenticeship. If these pieces impart a pedagogical lesson, it is that one learns not through rote imitation of such things as form and style, but rather through the senses: genre is invoked as an adventure of the mind. This way of conceiving the journey will perhaps conjure Laurence Sterne's *Sentimental Journey through France and Italy* (1768), a travel journal in no conventional sense but a record of sensibilities, of encounters of the heart: "a quiet journey of the heart in pursuit of Nature, and those affections which rise out of her." "I have not seen the Palais royal—," confesses Sterne's Yorick, "nor the Luxembourg—nor the Facade of the Louvre—nor have attempted to swell the catalogues we have of pictures, statues, and churches—I conceive every fair being as a temple, and would rather enter in, and see the original drawings and loose sketches hung up in it, than the transfiguration of Raphael itself."[20]

---

20. Laurence Sterne, *A Sentimental Journey through France and Italy by Mr. Yorick* (1768), ed. with introduction by Ian Jack (Oxford and New York: Oxford University Press, 1968), 84. The satirical butt of Sterne's *Journey* was Tobias Smollett's *Travels through France and Italy* (1766), now in a

The heart, this temple of sensibility, houses not the grand work of art, with its pretension to formal perfection and finish, but the sketch, the drawing valued for the spontaneity of the artistic act. Sterne's brilliant conceit takes hold of the process from the inside, where the idea of art is prefigured in the affects of human behavior. Hanging alone in the museum, the work of art is merely a frozen metaphor of living process. This distinction between the finish of art and the allusive traces of ephemeral process—Benjamin's Death Mask, once more—puts us in mind of Goethe's appreciation of the sketch, "those fascinating hieroglyphs," wherein "mind speaks to mind, and the means by which this happens comes to nothing."[21]

Sterne's *Journey* ends in the Savoie, just before the crossing of the Alps into Italy. The expectation of arrival, not least in the sexual sense, is heightened in the erotic final scene: Yorick in bed, almost, with the elegant lady of the Piedmont, as though to suggest that he has indeed found his way to Italy. The book ends in pregnant mid sentence.[22] A sentimental journey of another kind, Bach's *Probestücke* explore a map etched in tonal regions and figured in genre. The peregrinations of Bach's *empfindsame* traveler have an openly pedagogical, less erotic mission. In its poignant coming of age, the Fantasia in C minor signifies the inescapable return home, the impossible return to the place of blissful ignorance. For Bach, three years after the death of his father, the anxieties of this mythic

---

critical edition prepared by Frank Felsenstein (Oxford: Oxford University Press, 1979); see xx. "I must confess, that my appetite for French music was not very keen when I now landed on the continent," begins Charles Burney, on the first page of his second journal, undertaken in 1772—*The Present State of Music in Germany, the Netherlands, and United Provinces* (see above, note 18)— and it is difficult not to think that he is playing here with the famous and riddling opening lines of Sterne's *Journey:* "—They order, said I, this matter better in France—" and its sequel later on the page: "by three I had got sat down to my dinner upon a fricassee'd chicken so incontestably in France . . . " If Burney's "Journal" is avowedly an effort to collect material for *General History of Music*, often enough his encounters are of the sentimental kind, in a prose meant to be savored.

21. Johann Wolfgang von Goethe, "Der Sammler und die Seinigen," Achter Brief, Sechste Abteilung (first published in *Propyläen* II/ 2, 1799), in Goethe, *Werke. Hamburger Ausgabe in 14 Bände,* vol. 12, Schriften zur Kunst, ed. Erich Trunz, commentary by Herbert von Einem (Munich: C. H. Beck, 1981), 94. For different translations, see *Goethe: The Collected Works,* III, *Essays on Art and Literature,* ed. John Gearey, tr. Ellen von Nardroff and Ernest H. Von Nardroff (Princeton: Princeton University Press, 1986), 158; and *Goethe on Art,* ed. and tr. John Gage (Berkeley and Los Angeles: University of California Press, 1980), 70. The passage is discussed more fully in chapter 13 below.

22. Whether or not this famous ending ought to be understood as but an interruption before the serialized publication of a Book III that Sterne never got round to writing—he died only weeks after the publication of Books I and II in February 1768—is a question that leads nowhere. (See chapter 6, note 32.) The breaking-off in mid-sentence, much like the celebrated opening of the book in mid-conversation on matters never explicitly identified: these bold plays with syntax, metonymical journeys of the "sentimental" mind, will have their echoes in the similarly inconclusive closes of some works by Emanuel Bach, taken up in the next chapter.

return must have run deep.[23] That Gerstenberg would hear in the Fantasia evocations of Hamlet contemplating suicide and Socrates about to enact his own may only suggest something of the inner agon played out in this extreme music.

IV

The decision to place the Fantasia at the end, the ultimate *Probestück,* tells us much about its place in Emanuel Bach's aesthetics. Fantasies are similarly placed in the three last collections *für Kenner und Liebhaber* (IV, 1783; V, 1785; VI, 1787). When we encounter fantasies in the music of the earlier eighteenth century, they, too, are about the improvisatory. One thinks, inevitably, of the Chromatic Fantasy of Sebastian Bach. But here, as elsewhere, the fantasy means to exercise the mind, and the fingers, as a preliminary: a tuning up, a gradual coming into focus before the reason of fugue. For Bach the father and Bach the son, the reversal is poignantly evident in how they constructed the repertories of their final years. For the father, the final works are grand summations, compendia of fugal ingenuity. For Emanuel Bach, the final keyboard work in the catalogue is the Fantasia in F♯ minor from 1787—*C.P.E. Bachs Empfindungen,* as he himself inscribed one of its autographs—a plangent fantasy of farewell, riddling and paradoxical, even in the contradictory signals transmitted across the pages of its two autograph redactions. But this is to anticipate the next chapter.

---

23. For Wolfgang Wiemer, following Peter Schleuning, the Fantasy is a lamentation on the death of the father, indeed a "Reminiszenz" of the Chromatic Fantasy. See "Carl Philipp Emanuel Bachs Fantasie in c-Moll—ein Lamento auf den Tod des Vaters?," *Bach-Jahrbuch,* 74 (1988): 163–177.

CHAPTER 6

Diderot's *Paradoxe* and C. P. E. Bach's *Empfindungen*

On his way home to Paris via The Hague, Denis Diderot paused for a few days in Hamburg at the end of March 1774. "I return from St. Petersburg in a housecoat under a fur pelt, and without other clothing, otherwise I should not have missed calling on a man as famous as Emmanuel [*sic*]," he wrote, in the first of two surviving letters to Bach.[1] We know the texts of these letters not from Diderot's autograph, but (tellingly) from their publication in four literary journals within weeks of Diderot's visit—the first of them in Claudius's *Wandsbecker Bothe* for 8 April.[2] The letters are work-a-day: Diderot wants Bach to provide some sonatas for his daughter, and Bach (we must infer from Diderot's second letter) spells out the terms under which he can agree to the request.[3]

That Diderot and Bach never met seems quite clear from the circumstantial evidence. In the continuation on Easter Sunday of a letter dated "Sonnabend vor Ostern, 2 Apr. 1774," the poet Johann Heinrich Voss, describing several visits to Bach during the weekend, adds: "Diderot has traveled through town and written several letters to Bach, asking for the copy of some unpublished sonatas for his daughter,

---

1. *The Letters of C. P. E. Bach*, trans. and ed. Stephen L. Clark (Oxford: Clarendon Press; New York: Oxford University Press, 1997), 50–51, letters 54*a* and 54*b*. Bach's replies to Diderot have not survived.

2. For the text of the letters, as they were published in the *Hamburgische unparteyische Correspondent*, Nro. 57 for the year 1774, "Hamburg, den 8 April," see *Carl Philipp Emanuel Bach im Spiegel seiner Zeit: Die Dokumentensammlung Johann Jacob Heinrich Westphals*, ed. with commentary by Ernst Suchalla (Hildesheim, Zurich, New York: Georg Olms, 1993), 51.

3. "Ma fille, joue a Monsieur cette pièce d'Emmanuel Back [*sic*]," instructs the Philosopher (Diderot, we learn from Diderot's preface) in the Fourth Dialogue of the *Leçons de clavecin et principes d'harmonie*, par Mr Bemetzrieder (Paris: Chez Bluet, 1771). For the complicated issues surrounding the collaboration between Diderot and Bemetzrieder, who indeed taught keyboard and harmony to Diderot's daughter Angélique from as early as 1769, see *Diderot: Musique*, ed. Jean Mayer and Pierre Citron, with Jean Varloot, in *Oeuvres complètes de Diderot* (Paris: Hermann, 1983), XIX: 47–387, esp. 162.

who is an excellent keyboard player."[4] The following day, in a letter to Johann Martin Miller and others of the "Göttingen Grove" poets, Voss writes: "Diderot was here [in Hamburg], but has spoken to no one. He wrote a couple of letters to Bach."[5]

The provocations of this near confrontation of two grand, idiosyncratic minds (theatrically staged, it might be inferred from the alacrity with which Diderot's personal letters were rushed into print) tempts me to juxtapose two of their works: the Fantasia in F♯ minor, composed by Bach in 1787 (six years after the death of Diderot), a work that plays openly with the idea of *Empfindung*;[6] and a dialogue by Diderot that examines with piercing wit the distinction between the man of genuine sensibility, of sensitivity—of *Empfindsamkeit*—and the actor who only stages, enacts, mimics such feeling. Unpublished in his lifetime, Diderot's *Paradoxe sur le comédien (The Paradox of the Actor)* was much on his mind during the months prior to his journey through Hamburg.[7] Had Diderot and Bach actually met, it does not stretch reason to imagine the conversation turning about these ideas that so vigorously probe Enlightenment aesthetic theory.

---

4. "Diderot ist hier durchgereiset, und hat etliche Briefe an Bach geschrieben, worin er um die Abschrift einiger ungedruckten Sonaten für seine Tochter, die eine vortrefliche Klavierspielerin ist, bat." The autograph letter from Voss is at Kiel, Schleswig-Holsteinischen Landesbibliothek. For a fuller discussion of it, see my "The New Modulation of the 1770s: C. P. E. Bach in Theory, Criticism, and Practice," *Journal of the American Musicological Society*, 38 (1985): 579–580. The letter is published in Johann Heinrich Voss, *Briefe von Johann Heinrich Voss nebst erläuternden Beilagen*, ed. Abraham Voss (Halberstadt, 1829; reprint with a foreword by Gerhard Hay, Hildesheim: Georg Olms, 1971), I: 157–162, but omitting without comment the passage on Diderot. The passage is omitted as well in Ernst Suchalla, ed., *Carl Philipp Emanuel Bach: Briefe und Dokumente*. Kritische Gesamtausgabe (Göttingen: Vandenhoeck & Ruprecht, 1994), 381.

5. "Diderot ist hier [in Hamburg] gewesen, hat sich aber nicht sprechen lassen. An Bach hat er ein paar Briefe geschrieben." Cited from Suchalla, *Briefe und Dokumente*, I: 383.

6. "Freie Fantasie fürs Clavier," following the inscription on the autograph, is the title given in E. Eugene Helm, *Thematic Catalogue of the Works of Carl Philipp Emanuel Bach* (New Haven and London: Yale University Press, 1989), 66, item 300. The arrangement for keyboard and violin is called "Clavier-fantasie mit Begleitung einer Violine" in Helm, *ibid.*, 116, item 536, no doubt after the entry in the *Verzeichniß des musikalischen Nachlasses des verstorbenen Capellmeisters Carl Philipp Emanuel Bach* (Hamburg: Schniebes, 1790), p. 41, "No. 46"; the "Verzeichniß" was reprinted as *The Catalog of Carl Philipp Emanuel Bach's Estate: A Facsimile of the Edition of Schniebes, Hamburg, 1790*, ed. Rachel W. Wade (New York and London: Garland Publishing, 1981).

7. Published posthumously in 1830, Diderot's *Paradoxe sur le comédien* was evidently the subject in a letter of August 1773 to Mme d'Epinay, a letter written in the Hague on the eve of his departure for St. Peterburg: "un certain pamphlet sur l'art de l'acteur est presque devenu un ouvrage." See Denis Diderot, *Paradoxe sur le comédien précédé des Entretiens sur le fils naturel*, with a chronology and preface by Raymond Laubreaux (Paris: [Garnier]-Flammarion, 1981), 120. A translation is published in Denis Diderot, *Selected Writings on Art and Literature*, tr. with an introduction and notes by Geoffrey Bremner (London: Penguin Books, 1994), 98–158. These are the texts to which I refer in the following. My own translation is drawn from Bremner and to an extent from a translation by Walter Herries Pollack: Denis Diderot, *The Paradox of Acting*; and William Archer, *Masks or Faces?* (New York: Hill and Wang, 1957), 11–71.

I

I begin by again recalling that frequently invoked insight in Diderot's *Paradoxe:* "The man of sensibility," writes Diderot, "obeys only the impulses of nature, and utters precisely nothing less than the cry of his heart; once he moderates this cry or forces it, he is no longer himself, but an actor in performance."[8] Isolating these lapidary words in his penetrating monograph on Johann Georg Hamann, Isaiah Berlin thought he recognized in Diderot's depiction a sense of self-alienation to which, as he puts it, Rousseau "and much modern psychology have given a central role."[9] For all its insight, Berlin's reading yet slights the paradoxical effect that Diderot is after. Spoken by "the man with the paradox" (as Diderot calls him), this central thesis in the dialogue does not mean to argue for the primacy of nature, but, rather, for a more complex relationship between the man of feeling, the poet, and the actor. Toward the end of the dialogue, when the antagonists have wandered off, absorbed in their own thoughts, the man with the paradox bursts forth with an uncanny fable of human relations. Diderot gives us the sense of a man possessed:

> Here the man with the paradox fell silent. He walked with long strides, not seeing where he went; he would have knocked up against those who met him right and left if they had not got out of his way. Then, suddenly stopping, and catching his antagonist tight by the arm, he said, with a dogmatic and quiet tone: My friend, there are three types—nature's man, the poet's man, the actor's man [l'homme de la nature, l'homme du poet, l'homme de l'acteur]. Nature's is less great than the poet's man, the poet's less great than the great actor's, who is the most exalted of all. This last climbs on the shoulders of the one before him and shuts himself up inside a great basket-work figure of which he is the soul. He moves this figure so as to terrify even the poet, who no longer recognizes himself. He terrifies us . . . just as children frighten each other by tucking up their little skirts and putting them over their heads, shaking themselves about, and imitating as best they can the croaking lugubrious accents of the specter that they counterfeit.[10]

---

8. "L'homme sensible obéit aux impulsions de la nature et ne rend précisément que le cri de son coeur; au moment ou il tempere ou force ce cri, ce n'est plus lui, c'est un comédien qui joue." *Paradoxe,* 151; *Selected Writings,* 124–125.

9. Isaiah Berlin, *The Magus of the North: J. G. Hamann and the Origins of Modern Irrationalism,* ed. Henry Hardy (New York: Farrar, Straus and Giroux, 1993), 83.

10. *Paradoxe,* 186–187; *Selected Writings,* 154.

In this stunning evocation of theater, we are struck by the power ascribed to the actor, who becomes the soul of the figure—the poet's figure—within which he comes to life. In the greater hierarchy of things, the poet's figure must stand above the actor's, but in the end, it is the actor who holds the reins. How, by the way, one might transfer this elaborate construct to the performance of music is not quite so routine as it might at first seem: where the poet and the actor are always discrete and even distant from one another, the composer and the performer often inhabit the same body. And yet even in such cases, the composer as a performer of his own work will play out the tensions immanent in Diderot's subtle conceit.

Diderot's argument has everything to do with an apparently simple observation on the nature of acting, framed in an apothegm early on in the dialogue: "Extreme sensibility," he writes, "makes middling actors; middling sensibility produces the multitude of bad actors; in complete absence of sensibility is the possibility of the sublime actor."[11] For Diderot, the "sorrowful accents" that seem to be drawn from the depth of feeling are, by that measure, evidence not of true feeling but of something planned. They are, he writes:

> part of a system of declamation; in that, raised or lowered by the twentieth part of a quarter of a tone, they would ring false; in that they are in subjection to a law of unity; in that, as in harmony, they are arranged in chords and discords; that laborious study is needed to give them completeness; in that they are the elements necessary to the solving of a given problem; in that, to hit the right mark once, they have been practiced a hundred times; and in that, despite all this practice, they are yet found wanting.[12]

And further to this paradox is an imaginary theater of mirrors and reversals in which Diderot now envisions the world as itself a stage enacting madness, from which the cold eye of the poet constructs its play:

> In the great play, the play of the world, the play to which I am constantly recurring, the stage is held by the fiery souls [that is, by the people governed by their feelings], and the pit is filled with men of genius. The actors are in other words madmen; the spectators, whose business it is to paint their madness, are sages. And it is they who discern with a ready eye the absurdity of the motley crowd, who reproduce it for

---

11. *Paradoxe*, 133; *Selected Writings*, 108.
12. *Paradoxe*, 132; *Selected Writings*, 107.

you, and who make you laugh, both at the unhappy models who have bored you to death, and at yourself.[13]

To question this hierarchy, to suggest that within the bosom of the great actor is some fundamental well of sensibility, that actors and poets are no less capable of true feeling than these primary figures of nature, would be to disable the cunning of Diderot's *Paradoxe*. It has much to tell us of the Enlightenment mind engaged in an inquiry into the nature of thought and idea, and provokes us finally to interrogate this distinction, implicit in the *Paradoxe*, between feeling and expression. What, precisely, is this distinction that Diderot is after between the cry from the heart (surely, this is *expression* of some kind) and the perfectly calibrated gesture of the actor, within whose calculations are choreographed the rhetoric of spontaneity?

Somewhere from within this distinction springs language itself, the origins of which captured the imagination of Enlightenment thinkers: witness Vico's notion of the beginnings of language, where metaphor precedes the literal and song precedes speech;[14] and Rousseau's similar inclination, in the *Essay on the Origin of Languages* (1749).[15] In Herder's *Essay on the Origin of Language* (1770), the dialectical argument leads inexorably to a confrontation of the utterance of passion with a grammar of reason, a confrontation that Bach's Fantasia will bring to life. For Herder, the acquisition of grammar is not without sacrifice: "For as the first vocabulary of the human soul was a living epic of sounding and acting nature, so the first grammar was almost nothing but a philosophical attempt to develop that epic into a more regularized history."[16] The regulation that comes of

---

13. *Paradoxe*, 131,132; *Selected Writings*, 106.

14. See *The New Science of Giambattista Vico*, tr. and ed. Thomas Goddard Bergin and Max Harold Fisch (Ithaca, N.Y., and London: Cornell University Press, 1970), 87–91, on the primacy of metaphor in early speech, and 112–113 on the origins of song.

15. "As man's first motives for speaking were of the passions, his first expressions were Tropes," writes Rousseau. Here Rousseau evidently draws upon Bernard Lamy's *La Rhétorique, ou l'Art de parler* (4th ed., 1701), II: 3: "Tropes are names that are transferred from the thing of which they are the proper name, to apply them to things which they signify only indirectly: thus, all tropes are metaphors, for the word, which is Greek, means translation." Cited from Jean-Jacques Rousseau, *Essay on the Origin of Languages and Writings Related to Music* (The Collected Writings of Rousseau, Vol. 7), tr. and ed. John T. Scott (Hanover, N.H., and London: University Press of New England, 1998), 569, note 27. For another translation, see *On the Origin of Language. Jean-Jacques Rousseau: Essay on the Origin of Languages; Johann Gottfried Herder: Essay on the Origin of Language*, tr. John H. Moran and Alexander Gode (Chicago and London: University of Chicago Press, 1966), 12.

16. "Denn wie das erste Wörterbuch der Menschlichen Seele eine lebendige Epopee der tönenden, handelnden Natur war: so war die erste Grammatik fast nichts, als ein Philosophischer Versuch, diese Epopee zur regelmäßigern Geschichte zu machen." Herder, *Abhandlung über den Ursprung der Sprache* (Berlin: Christian Friedrich Voß, 1772), 132; reprint in Johann Gottfried Herder, *Sämtliche Werke*, V, ed. Bernard Suphan (Berlin: Weidmann, 1891), 84; *On the Origin of Language*, 161.

grammar takes language in its grip: "the more it becomes simplified, the more it declines: the more it turns into grammar–and that is the stepwise progression of the human mind."[17] And yet it is implicit in all this that grammar itself is not arbitrary, but a natural, if reasoned, consequence of speech.

II

> Music has long been called a language of feeling, and consequently, the similarities that lie beneath the coherence of its expression and the expression of spoken language have been deeply felt.[18]

We return yet again to these vivid lines with which Emanuel Bach opened his review of the first volume of Forkel's *Allgemeine Geschichte der Musik* in the *Hamburgische unparteyische Correspondent* for 9 January 1788. In Forkel's view, the efficacy of harmony in the service of a more complex range of expression, only recently achieved, would enable the creation of, as Bach puts it, "einer Musik, die als eine wirklich aneinander hängende Sprache zu unsern Empfindungen reden soll" (of a music that, as a truly coherent language, can speak to our feelings).[19]

This provocative formulation—more Forkel than Bach[20]—only aggravates the paradox which Diderot is at pains to articulate. For if music is a language of *Empfindung*, we want to know with some precision how it negotiates, as language must, among something felt, something thought and something expressed— and, further, whether to identify music as a language of *Empfindung* means to rule out its capacity to embody language in the rational mode of grammar and syntax; or means, rather, to construe *Empfindung* as a more complex phenomenon containing within itself—as Herder seems to have believed—the trace of grammar.

---

17. "Je mehr sie aber erleichtert wird, desto mehr nimmt sie ab; desto mehr wird Grammatik–und das ist Stuffengang des Menschlichen Geistes!" Herder, *Sämtliche Werk*, V: 87; *Origin*, 163.

18. "Man hat die Musik schon lange eine Sprache der Empfindung genannt, folglich die in der Zusammensetzung ihrer und der Zusammensetzung der Sprachausdrücke liegende Aehnlichkeit dunkel gefühlt." *Hamburgische unpartheyische Correspondenten*, 9 January 1788. Reprinted in Johann Nikolaus Forkel, *Allgemeine Geschichte der Music*, I: Leipzig 1788, ed. Othmar Wessely (Graz: Akademische Druck- u. Verlagsanstalt, 1967), xvii.

19. *Ibid.*, xviii.

20. "Aber es lag auch hier, so wie in der Sprache, ein dunkles Gefühl von Harmonie oder musikalischer Logik zum Grunde," writes Forkel, *Allgemeine Geschichte*, I: 24.

The notion of music as modeled on spoken language—even as an intensified instance of it—is often encountered in theoretical discourse in the 1770s. Sulzer, in the article "Gesang" in his *Allgemeine Theorie*, worries the distinction between speech and song. "Human song," he proposes, cannot have arisen through the imitation of something songlike in the natural world (the singing of birds is his example). Rather:

> the individual tones from which song is formed are expressions of animated *Empfindungen*. These tones that are forced from man from the depth of feeling [von der Empfindung dem Menschen gleichsam ausgepresste Töne] we shall call tones of passion [leidenschaftliche Töne]. The elements of song are not so much a discovery of man as they are nature itself. The tones of speech are signifiers [zeichnende Töne] which originally served to awaken images of things that shared the properties of those sounds. Today, the sounds of speech are indifferent or arbitrary in this regard; passionate tones, on the other hand, are natural signs of *Empfindungen*. A sequence of arbitrary tones indicates speech; a sequence of passionate tones, song.[21]

For Sulzer, there is an immediacy of feeling, of *Empfindung*, that characterizes the tones of song. Tones do not depict, but express. They are not reasoned and learned, but of nature itself, even as *Gesang*, like speech, "is the invention of Genius." "The Fine Arts," he writes (in the article "*Empfindung*"), "have two ways of releasing Man's *Empfindungen*. 'If you wish to move me to tears,' says [Sulzer's] Horace, 'then you too must cry.' This is the one way. The other is the animated depiction or performance of those objects which induce *Empfindung*."[22] Often invoked, the passage may be found in the midst of Diderot's lengthy discourse on a painting by Joseph Vernet in the *Salon of 1767:* " . . . but you'll weep all alone . . . if I can't imagine myself in your place." The reader, Diderot continues, has "a double identity": is the actor who shudders and suffers and yet remains himself, experiencing the pleasure of the work.[23] The contradiction in Sulzer's formulation,

21. Johann Georg Sulzer, *Allgemeine Theorie der schönen Künste,* 4 vols. (Leipzig: in der Weidmann-schen Buchhandlung, neue vermehrte, 2. Auflage, 1792–1799), II: 369. The translation is drawn in part from Nancy Kovaleff Baker and Thomas Christensen, eds., *Aesthetics and the Art of Musical composition in the German Enlightenment: Selected Writings of Johann Georg Sulzer and Heinrich Christoph Koch* (Cambridge: Cambridge University Press, 1995), 93.

22. "Wenn du mich willst zum Weinen bewegen, sagt Horaz, so weine du selbst." *Allgemeine Theorie,* II: 57. My translation differs somewhat from Christensen's (*ibid.,* 31). The passage is from Horace, *Ars Poetica,* vv. 103–04: "Si vis me flere, dolendum est / Primum ipsi tibi." ("If you would have me weep, you yourself must first feel grief.")

23. *Diderot on Art, II: The Salon of 1767,* ed. and tr. John Goodman (New Haven and London, 1995), 103.

where *Empfindung* is captured in the creative mind, is played out for Diderot in some amalgam of critical reception and performance—performer and critic as surrogate participants in this act of creation—and reconciled in the mode of paradox.

What, then, can Bach have meant in inscribing "C. P. E. Bachs Empfindungen" above the Fantasia in F♯ minor, purchasing distance from his own feelings through this evocation of himself in the third person? The inscription curiously appears only on the autograph of the version for keyboard and violin (yet another riddle to which we must return).[24] Knowing, as we do, that there can be no verifiably right answer, the call to inquiry and argument is yet implicit in the formulation itself, no doubt heightened in the effort to find a way to put Bach's phrase into English. Even the genitive case needs parsing, for the good grammarians would make a distinction between simple possession ("Bach's *Empfindungen*") and the formality of a title ("The *Empfindungen* of C. P. E. Bach"). And then there is that word itself, which English cannot quite capture: feelings, perceptions, sensibilities, sensitivities, sentiments. If any of these might satisfy the local conditions of translation, they each seem misleadingly specific, overly determined, when perhaps Bach means only to suggest some inscrutable journey of the sensitive soul. When we write about Bach's music, we tend to leave *Empfindung* (and *empfindsam*) untranslated, in the unspoken understanding that we presume to know precisely what is meant, knowing all the while that to say so in actual language is to risk a loss in nuance, if not to betray a more fatal misunderstanding.

One gets some taste for the lexical problem in an extraordinary letter that Lessing wrote in the summer of 1768 to Johann Joachim Christoph Bode, then engaged in the translation of Laurence Sterne's *Sentimental Journey*. Bode had originally thought to render "sentimental" as "sittlich," and then tried out a range of other expressions and *"Umschreibungen."* Admiring Sterne's boldness in creating, out of necessity, a new adjectival form for Sentiment, Lessing urges upon Bode the right of the translator to engage in this same creativity. "The English," he writes, "had no single adjective for Sentiment. For *Empfindung*, we have more than one: *Empfindlich, empfindbar, empfindungsreich:* but they each say something rather different. Give *empfindsam* a try."[25]

---

24. In the *Nachlaßverzeichnis* of 1790, this version is entered under the Trios, where it is identified as "Clavier-Fantasie, mit Begleitung einer Violine; Die 210te Sonate zu einem Trio umgearbeitet." See Wade, *Catalog*, 42. The autograph manuscripts of both versions are in Berlin, Staatsbibliothek zu Berlin—Preußische Kulturbesitz, Mus. ms. Bach P 359, pp. 211–218; and Mus. Ms. Bach P 361. The opening pages of each are shown in facsimile in *"Er ist Original": Carl Philipp Emanuel Bach,* Staatsbibliothek Preußischer Kulturbesitz, Ausstellungskataloge 34 (Wiesbaden: Dr. Ludwig Reichert Verlag, 1988), 88–89.

25. The letter to Bode is given in *Briefe von und an Gotthold Ephraim Lessing* in *Gotthold Ephraim Lessings sämtliche Schriften,* "Dritte, auf's neue durchgesehene u. vermehrte Auflage," ed. Franz

Often enough, *Empfindung* is set in opposition to reasoned thought. Such an opposition is at the seat of Türk's definition of cadenza, in the *Klavierschule* of 1789: "For the cadenza in its entirety ought to resemble a fantasy created from an abundance of feeling more than a properly worked out piece," to which is added a footnote that penetrates to the more obscure relationship between experience and feeling: "Perhaps the cadenza could be compared not inappropriately with a dream. We often dream through in a few minutes, and with the most vivid *Empfindung*,—but without coherence, without clear consciousness—events actually experienced that made an impression on us. So too in a cadenza."[26]

By these lights, spontaneity of intuition "aus der Fülle der Empfindung entstehenden"—indeed an intensified *Empfindung*, "ohne Zusammenhang, ohne deutliches Bewustseyn"—is a defining property of the fantasy, the work conceived in a dreamlike somnambulance. The Fantasia in F♯ minor has, however, plenty of *Zusammenhang*, itself the hardest evidence of "deutliche Bewustseyn." Setting all this against the "regelmässig ausgearbeitete Tonstück" invokes as well one of the grand epistemological problems in Enlightenment aesthetics: how the mind engages in creative thought. Diderot reappears. We are reminded once more of that passage (cited in another context in chapter 1) in the fantasy-like exchange between Diderot and the mathematician D'Alembert. The D'Alembert in the dialogue is having trouble reconciling the actuality of thought—"we can think of only one thing at a time," he says—with the complexity of constructing vast chains of reasoning, or even, as he puts it, "just one simple proposition." Diderot responds in another of his penetrating similes, invoking the phenomenon of strings vibrating sympathetically.

Vibrating strings have yet another property: that of making others vibrate, and it is in this way that one idea calls up a second, and the two together a third, and all three

---

Munchen, Vol. 17, ed. Karl Lachmann (Leipzig: G. J. Göschen'she Verlagshandlung, 1904), 256, letter 201. For more on this, see Harvey Waterman Thayer, *Laurence Sterne in Germany* (New York: Columbia University Press, 1905; reprint New York: AMS Press, 1966), 42–43. It is discussed as well in Darrell Berg, "C. Ph. E. Bach und die 'empfindsame Weise'," in *Carl Philipp Emanuel Bach und die europäische Musikkultur des mittleren 18. Jahrhunderts*, ed. Hans Joachim Marx (Göttingen: Vandenhoeck & Ruprecht, 1990), 93–105, esp. 94.

26. "Denn das Ganze soll mehr einer nur eben aus der Fülle der Empfindung entstehenden Fantasie, als einem regelmässig ausgearbeiteten Tonstücke gleichen." And in a footnote: "Vielleicht liesse sich die Kadenz nicht unschicklich mit einem Traume vergleichen. Man durchträumt oft in wenigen Minuten wirklich erlebte Begebenheiten, die Eindruck auf uns machten, mit der lebhaftesten Empfindung; aber ohne Zusammenhang, ohne deutliches Bewusstseyn—So auch bey der Kadenz." Daniel Gottlob Türk, *Klavierschule oder Anweisung zum Klavierspielen für Lehrer und Lernende* (Leipzig: Schwickert; Halle: Hemmerde und Schwetschke, 1789; facs. reprint ed. Siegbert Rampe, Kassel: Bärenreiter, 1997), 312.

a fourth, and so on. You can't set a limit to the ideas called up and linked together by a philosopher meditating or communing with himself in silence and darkness. This instrument can make astonishing leaps, and one idea called up will sometimes start a harmonic at an incomprehensible interval. If this phenomenon can be observed between resonant strings that are inert and separate, why should it not take place between living and connected points, continuous and sensitive fibres?[27]

Seizing on the image of sympathetic vibration, Diderot conjures the mind of the philosopher enacting complex thought much as vibrating strings induce harmonics. The process, at once intuitive and involuntary, even incomprehensible, is yet grounded in acoustic principle. In this, the foundational relationship between model and process bears an uncanny resemblance to those passages of enharmony in Bach's fantasies which set us to analytical hand-springs: the musical work (as fiction, as narrative) means to invoke this fleet, intuitive process that Diderot describes. The paradox returns, for we are left to wonder whether this journey that the Fantasia depicts is an authentic record of some internal, intuitive process or merely a fictional reconstruction of such a process: whether the *Empfindung* embodied in this or that fantasy is the trace itself—the real thing— or an artifact, an invention.

III

The process is in any case a syntactical one: Diderot's model has more to do with the connections between thoughts—with the grammar of relationships, rather— than with the substance of thought, of idea itself. Even Türk's invocation of dream has to do with the intensification of what might be called explanatory process—how events are recalled (a syntactical concept)—and not with the imaging of the surreal. The aptness of Diderot's conceit to Bach's Fantasia comes vividly clear in several passages upon which the sense of the work seems to turn. The first of them (shown in ex. 6.1) comes at a moment where the music hovers about a first confirmatory cadence in F♯ minor. For all its suggestion as leading tone, the E♯ is led unexpectedly down, through E♭! The D♮ in the bass, primed to

---

27. The translation is taken from Denis Diderot, *Rameau's Nephew and D'Alembert's Dream*, tr. with Introductions by L. W. Tancock (Harmondsworth: Penguin Books, 1966), 156. For the original text, see, for one, Diderot, *Entretien entre D'Alembert et Diderot; le Rêve de d'Alembert; Suite de l'Entretien*, ed. Jacques Roger (Paris: Garnier-Flammarion, 1965), 48–49.

EXAMPLE 6.1 C. P. E. Bach, Freie Fantasie fürs Clavier, H 300.

resolve as ninth to the root C♯, is instead displaced up an octave and made over into a leading tone. As it plays itself out, the music expires weakly in E minor, the subdominant of the subdominant, a few cadences away from the middle section: the Largo, which begins in B minor.

We cut away now to the analogous passage (shown in ex. 6.2), deep in the recapitulation—a recapitulation that begins, by the way, in B minor, a key to which

EXAMPLE 6.2 Freie Fantasie fürs Clavier, H 300.

the music continually retreats. The original syntax is broken. Here, finally, is a true half-cadence in F♯ minor. All the notes are where they belong. But then comes another interruption, and a return to this moment of enharmony, where E minor is now properly established, as though to compensate, retroactively, for the E minor established illicitly, through enharmonic ellipsis, in the exposition. (See ex. 6.3.) The moment is fleeting. E minor dissolves through its own enharmonic game: C in the bass (again, a ninth displacing a root) is again made over as leading tone, now B♯. The music splays hyperbolically out to the registral extremes of the instrument, to (yet again) a dominant of B minor. Obligatory arpeggiations on the way to the final cadence put B minor back in place, as subdominant, breaking off at the augmented sixth before the dominant in F♯ minor. The ear anticipates C♯ in the bass. It does not come. Obscurely, an A is sounded, its sheer depth and isolation seeming to touch the *empfindsamer* core of the work. The player who can resist even the slightest *Bebung* here works against the signifying, gestural sense of the note and its tactile grain. From this A, the music draws forth one last allusion to the Largo theme, grounding it finally in F♯ minor.

And it is from this A, and precisely here, that, in the version for violin and keyboard, the music seems to gather itself for the swerve, the modulation, to the new finale. (It is shown in ex. 6.4.) It is not, of course, called "finale," but that is what it is: a final movement, in sonata form with varied reprises, and in the key of A major: an allegro, a "lieto fine," very much the "regelmässig ausgearbeitete Tonstück," in Türk's phrase. Astonishingly, this is not "new" music at all, but the finale of a sonata in B♭ major (H 212), composed in 1766, a date specified in the *Nachlaßverzeichnis* and inscribed by Bach on the title page of a contemporary

EXAMPLE 6.3
Freie Fantasie fürs
Clavier, H 300.

(continued)

EXAMPLE 6.3 *(continued)*

copy.[28] On that very page, Bach scribbled "hat noch niemand," by which he must have meant that the sonata remained out of circulation, a reassuring memorandum to himself that he could pick this pocket without fear of exposure. It seems reasonable to assume that the inscribing of the title page, the note "hat noch niemand," the autograph of the exceedingly quirky substitute finale (appended to a copy of the sonata now in Cracow), and the arrangement of this old finale as a music with which to close "C. P. E. Bachs Empfindungen" are related acts that date from 1787.

In the duo version, this portentous A is deployed in three octaves, given new timbre, and consequently fixed in time and space: the introverted *Bebung* of the solitary tone, a moment of obscure contemplation, gives way here to an exhortation. Newly inflected, the note will now be heard to announce the coming of a new music in A major. The reversal of function is riddling, for it would be good to remind ourselves that it is only here, on the autograph of the version with accompanying violin, that Bach inscribed "C. P. E. Bachs Empfindungen." Whatever Bach meant by *Empfindungen,* in the sense that it is used here—a question distinct from the one that would probe his intentions in broadcasting the word in this context—I think we might agree that these final measures of the original Fantasia convey a sense of weariness, of exhaustion. The music sinks, and seems to disappear into the wondrous buzzing of the lowest strings in the clavichord, as

---

28. The manuscript is at Cracow, Biblioteka Jagiellónska, Mus. ms. Bach P 771. I am deeply grateful to Darrell Berg for sharing copies. A description of the manuscript sources for this sonata in its two versions is given in *Carl Philipp Emanuel Bach Edition*, series I, vol. 24, Keyboard Sonatas, ed. Claudia Widgery (Oxford: Oxford University Press, 1989), 106. For a better understanding of the new finale and its dating, see Pamela Fox, "Toward a Comprehensive C. P. E. Bach Chronology: *Schrift-Chronologie* and the Issue of Bach's 'Late Hand'," in *Carl Philipp Emanuel Bach: Musik für Europa.* Bericht über das Internationale Symposium, ed. Hans-Günter Ottenberg (Frankfurt an der Oder: Konzerthalle "Carl Philipp Emanuel Bach," 1998), 317–319.

EXAMPLE 6.4 Clavier-Fantasie mit Begleitung einer Violine, "C. P E. Bachs Empfindungen," H 536.

though Bach himself, in a fiction suggestive of autobiography, wished to expire in his music.

Brazenly different in just this respect, the duo puts on a different face. (Its final bars are shown in ex. 6.5.) If these two musics are to be reconciled, it will not help to construct a variorum that postulates a preferred "final version." *Veränderung,* a concept seemingly hard-wired in Bach's musical imagination, seems much to the point here. We are witness to it here on three levels: the Fantasia, as work, is altered; the new finale in A major is a *Veränderung* of the finale of an earlier Sonata in B♭; finally, the reprises in the finale are now written out: *veränderte Reprisen* in the strictest sense. Perhaps one might wish to claim that the two versions play out, and egregiously so, Bach's lifelong ambivalence as to public taste and intellectual privacy. Bach's inscription aggravates this ambivalence, for it is the more public redaction of the work that draws it forth: "C. P. E. Bachs Empfindungen," as though to market these most intimate, confessional thoughts. Here again are the traces of paradox, for it is unclear what it would mean to take Bach's inscription at its face.

EXAMPLE 6.5 Clavier-Fantasie mit Begleitung einer Violine, H 536.

IV

The image of Bach in his final years withdrawing into his clavichord comes clear in another famously private piece: the Rondo in E minor from 1781, the "Abschied von meinem Silbermannischen Claviere, in einem Rondo," as it is called in the *Nachlaßverzeichnis*.[29] The circumstances that brought about this farewell are obscure: Bach seems actually to have given away his fabled instrument to an admiring nobleman, Dietrich Ewald von Grotthuß, attaching to it the Rondo as "proof," he writes to Grotthuß, "that one can also compose plaintive Rondeaux, and that on no other *Clavier* but yours can they be played well."[30]

Even while Bach's instrumentarium retained two other clavichords, the depth of sentiment in the Rondo might suggest of Bach's *Abschied* that it signifies loss in a metonymical sense: the loss of the means to make such music, the passing of the clavichord as an instrument whose intimacies were no longer cherished. Again, a remarkable essay by Diderot springs to mind: in "Regrets sur ma vieille robe de chambre" (published in 1772), the parting with a comfortable old dressing gown worn during the author's less affluent days, stained from the wiping of ink from his pen—"the badge of an author," he writes—unleashes a meditation whose sentiments resonate in sympathy with Bach's "Abschied."[31] But there is a deeper message here: "Listen, and I will tell you what ravages Luxury has made since I gave myself up to the systematic pursuit of it." The gown is only a symptom, in its intimacy the closest to the man himself, of a complete makeover from the honest comforts of poverty to the stiff artificialities of wealth. Pondering the ironic inevitability of the track to success, Diderot yet betrays a flicker of ambivalence: "Fine manners have ruined many a man; the most sublime taste is not exempt from change; change means throwing things away, turning things upside down, building something new. . . . Thus our delicacy produces many fine things,

---

29. See Wade, *Catalog*, 23, item 187.

30. "Sie ist ein Beweis, daß man auch klagende Rondeaux machen könne und kann auf keinem andern Clavier als dem Ihrigen **Gut** gespielt werden." Suchalla, *Briefe und Dokumente*, 891. See Clark, *Letters*, 175–176; and Leonidas Melnikas, "Dietrich Ewald von Grotthus—C. P. E. Bachs Korrespondent in Litauen," in *Carl Philipp Emanuel Bach: Musik für Europa*, 438–442.

31. The original text with commentary is given in *Diderot: Oeuvres complètes*, XVIII: Arts et lettres (1767–1770), ed. Jochen Scholbach with Jeanne Carriat et al. (Paris: Hermann, 1984), 41–60. A translation can be found in Denis Diderot, *Rameau's Nephew and Other Works*, tr. Jacques Barzun and Ralph H. Bowen (Indianapolis, New York, and Kansas City: The Bobbs-Merrill Co., 1964), 309–317. See also Stephen Werner,"Irony and the Essay: Diderot's 'Regrets sur ma vieille robe de chambre,'" in *Diderot: Digression and Dispersion*, ed. Jack Undank and Herbert Josephs (Lexington, Ky.: French Forum, 1984), 269–277.

and at the same time many evils." Bach, of course, does not replace his beloved Silbermann with something new—at least we do not know that he was clearing out space for a forte-piano. But in his parting with it is felt an irrecoverable and inevitable loss.

Bach's inscriptions, I mean to suggest, evoke literary works in more than a superficial sense. As title, "C. P. E. Bachs Empfindungen" conjures *Yoricks empfindsame Reise durch Frankreich und Italien,* as Sterne's *Sentimental Journey* was known in Bode's translation. The bold play of syntax, a reflection of the *empfindsamer* experience, drives the prose of Sterne (and Diderot) in much the way that it drives Bach's music. The famous final line of the *Sentimental Journey* breaks off in flagrant mid-sentence: "So that when I stretch'd out my hand, I caught hold of the Fille de Chambre's———." Abandoned to complete the thought, to imagine how it might be completed, and to wonder why it was not given to Yorick to do so, the reader is made to react empathetically with him: not in the distanced, formal rhetoric with which earlier works would engage their readers, but with a new immediacy and intimacy.[32] The reader, embraced by the work in this way, is less inclined to draw back, to analyze form as distinct from content and "feeling." The relationship between the work and its reader is renegotiated, trafficking now in shared *Empfindungen.*

Calling to mind several instances of such mid-flight endings in Bach's music, this new conceptualizing of syntax works itself deep into the fabric of the musical work (see ex. 6.6, and appendix 10F and G). Admittedly exceptional, these few instances in which Bach's final bars tamper with the protocols of closure may be heard as symptoms of a deeper engagement with a syntactics of *Empfindsamkeit.* The final paragraphs of Bach's "Abschied" Rondo (shown in ex. 6.7) probe the limits of coherence to an extreme. The breaking off at the fermata at m. 68— exceptionally undecorated—will, by simple harmonic parsing, be heard as a Neapolitan-sixth: cadencing must follow. But the rondo theme, in yet another variant, resumes as though nothing had happened, unresponsive to the Neapolitan, whose intervals continue to sound, dissonantly. The theme comes again to its cadence, but closure is again denied, the music moving up in minuscule chromatic increments to that unresolved harmony, no longer a Neapolitan, but a

---

32. For a note on the punctuation of this final line, see Laurence Sterne, *A Sentimental Journey through France and Italy and Continuation of the Bramine's Journal: The Text and Notes,* ed. Melvyn New and W. G. Day, The Florida Edition of the Works of Laurence Sterne, Vol. VI (Gainesville: University Press of Florida, 2002), 383.

EXAMPLE 6.6 C. P. E. Bach, Rondo in C minor, H 283, *Kenner und Liebhaber* V (1784).

dominant seventh in first inversion: the F♮, left hanging in m. 68 as an appoggiatura to E (the fifth of the minor subdominant), is now more powerfully endowed as the root of a seventh chord, finally displaced at the fermata in m. 74 by G♭, a flat ninth above the dominant in the remote key of B♭ minor. The fermate have bonded together. The breach between this fermata and the final iteration of the Rondo theme, still deaf to its antecedent, touches a nerve. Again, the theme will not close, and at m. 79, the dominant on F, now in root position, fortissimo, is given full play, along with its neighboring G♭. Imperceptibly, somewhere between mm. 80 and 81, this G♭, masquerading as a flat six to the dominant in B♭ minor, is reclaimed as F♯: in commonplace language, the root of the dominant of the dominant in E minor. But the effect is not commonplace. As the Rondo vanishes, pianissimo, over a tremulous E alone in the bass, the ear strains to follow. What has it heard? Is this closure, or only an end?

When, at the close of the Rondo—and earlier, of the Fantasia—we are led to ask such questions, we are probing empathetically, with Herder's *Einfühlung*, into the inner workings of the music, seeking sources and roots and the elusive clues

EXAMPLE 6.7 C. P. E. Bach, "Abschied von meinem Silbermannischen Claviere, in einem Rondo," H 272 (1781).

to meaning. That surely is what Bach intends, for his music engages in this probe, even if the *Empfindungen* that reside somewhere in its depths are planted there by the cunning, the craft of the composer.

"But it's getting late," observes Diderot's "man with the paradox" at the end of the day. "Let's go have some supper." We wander off with him, our appetites whetted: for it is in the nature of paradox that it does not choke off thought in self-righteous dogma, but rather excites ever new waves of reflection. And that is why, I think, we are forever returning to Bach's late keyboard music. Riddled in paradox, it drives us back to the condition so wondrously depicted in Diderot's conceit. The actor shutting himself up inside that "great basket-work figure of which he is the soul" is now the player at the keyboard. Reading for the sensibilities of Bach's music, the dispassionate performer must now put on the masks figured in Bach's script—must convince us, then, that we are hearing not the player in mask but rather the beating heart of the music and its living soul.

PART III

Between Enlightenment and Romance

CHAPTER 7

Haydn's *Chaos* and Herder's *Logos*

Die Metapher des Anfangs war Drang zu sprechen.[1]

The itch that provokes the ideas that follow is lodged in some music that trembles between worlds, between aesthetics, balancing at the abyss between reason and the irrational, between chaos and coherence. It is not music that encourages those grand taxonomies from which we historians can't seem ever to shake free. In these two chapters, I revisit three very famous works, composed within five years of one another by two composers—teacher and pupil: privately, and in the public arena of professional interaction—who bring to the problem of improvisation two very different aesthetic attitudes.

I

The Creation, a work that Haydn seems to have held higher than any other in his inexhaustible repertory, moved contemporary audiences to extreme responses even as it remained something of an embarrassment to the critics of the early nineteenth century, in the main for instances of what were viewed as naive picto-

---

1. "The metaphor of the Beginning was the urge to speak." Johann Gottfried Herder, *Abhandlung über den Ursprung der Sprache* (Berlin: Christian Friedrich Voß, 1772), 116; in *Johann Gottfried Herder. Sämtliche Werke* V, ed. Bernhard Suphan (Berlin, 1891; reprint Hildesheim: Georg Olms, 1967), 74; for a translation, see *On the Origin of Language (Jean-Jacques Rousseau, "Essay on the Origin of Languages"; Johann Gottfried Herder, "Essay on the Origin of Language"),* tr. with afterword, by John H. Moran and Alexander Gode (Chicago and London: University of Chicago Press, 1966), 152.

rial illustration. But there is one movement that has always excited the fancy of its critics: the *Vorstellung des Chaos* with which the work unforgettably opens. I retain the librettist van Swieten's German here, because the conventional Englishing of *Vorstellung* as "representation" or even "depiction" is asking for trouble. *Vorstellen* means, in the first instance, the act of imagining, of conjuring in the mind. There is a foundational distinction between an apperception of primordial Chaos as a phenomenon given to tapestry-like depiction, on the one hand, and a conjuring of Chaos as a condition of the *empfindsame* mind offered an opportunity, indeed an imperative, to create, *ex nihilo*.

By 1800, *The Creation* was, in H. C. Robbins Landon's account, "the most discussed musical work in Europe." The title of the fourth volume in his magisterial *Haydn: Chronicle and Works* suggests as much: *The Years of "the Creation": 1796–1800*.[2] Nor has interest in it abated. In the past decade alone, there have been comprehensive handbooks on the work by Nicolas Temperley, Georg Feder, and Bruce MacIntyre.[3] That these compendia have much to say about the composition of Chaos should not surprise us, for it was this music that inspired the most spirited, and indeed diverse, response from Haydn's contemporaries. More recently, it has incited lengthy and probing studies: by A. Peter Brown, who, in a scrutiny of the extraordinary sketches for the work—one of the very few of Haydn's works for which *any* sketches have survived—is led to the notion that the music of Chaos has its prototype both in the archaic *ricercare*, its legacy of rhetorical device extending back some two hundred years, and in the so-called free fantasy as Haydn would have understood it in the music and theoretical writings of Carl Philipp Emanuel Bach;[4] and by Lawrence Kramer, who, in a richly cross-disciplinary study, interrogates the epistemological basis of the idea of "absolute music."[5] Kramer was spurred in his effort by a landmark analysis of the work by Heinrich Schenker, whose lifelong project sought a theoretical framework to account for the great wing-spans of tonal coherence that he believed to be unique to the works of the German masters from Bach through Brahms. Schenker

2. H. C. Robbins Landon, *Haydn: The Years of 'The Creation' 1796–1800*, vol. 4 of *Haydn: Chronicle and Works* (Bloomington and London: Indiana University Press, 1977).

3. Nicholas Temperley, *Haydn: "The Creation"* (Cambridge: Cambridge University Press, 1991); Bruce C. MacIntyre, *Haydn: "The Creation"* (New York: Schirmer Books, 1998); Georg Feder, *Joseph Haydn: Die Schöpfung* (Kassel: Bärenreiter, 1999).

4. A. Peter Brown, "Haydn's Chaos: Genesis and Genre," *The Musical Quarterly*, 73 (1989): 18–59. The sketches can be studied in Robbins-Landon, *Chronicle and Works*, IV: 357–373.

5. Lawrence Kramer, "Haydn's Chaos, Schenker's Order; or, Hermeneutics and Musical Analysis: Can They Mix?" *19th Century Music*, 16 (1992):3–17; the critique of Schenker is put somewhat differently in his "Music and Representation: the Instance of Haydn's *Creation*," in *Music and Text: Critical Inquiries*, ed. Steven Paul Scher (Cambridge: Cambridge University Press, 1992), 139–162.

was consequently concerned less about the "chaotic" in Haydn's *Vorstellung* than with the discovery of some hidden structural "law" that yet makes this music comprehensible.[6]

For Charles Rosen, the "famous depiction of chaos at the opening of the *Creation* is in 'slow-movement sonata form.'"[7] Donald Francis Tovey, many decades earlier, suggested that "the evolution of Cosmos from Chaos might be taken as the 'programme' of a large proportion of Haydn's symphonic introductions."[8] James Webster, contemplating the model from a different perspective, argues that "Haydn's Chaos is not merely a programmatic overture, but an intensification of his last symphonic introductions"—not, that is, sonata-form proper, but an instance of the overture-like music that precedes and yet stands apart from the drama.[9]

In each of these accounts, it is not Haydn's understanding of Chaos, and what it might have meant to "represent" it, either as biblical event or natural phenomenon, that occupies its author, but rather an effort to identify a formal archetype, a convention, a process of music-making that would then, by default, make manifest the paradox of a Chaos apprehended by—conceived in—the rational mind.

In the many rehearsals of the story that this music denotes, the plot is thick with the romance of evolution and its teleologies. The moment of apotheosis comes at the creation of Light, a moment toward which all else ineluctably moves: toward the grand C major at "und es ward Licht." This much celebrated C major chord "resolves" all the dissonance of Chaos, and its seemingly impermeable C minor. Webster puts it this way: "On the threshold of Romanticism stood Haydn's 'Chaos-Light' sequence at the beginning of *The Creation*: a musical progression across three movements from paradoxical disorder to triumphant order."[10] Kramer's account plays off Schenker's: "The 'Chaos' movement famously achieves closure, not through the C-minor cadence that precedes Raphael's recita-

---

6. "Haydn: Die Schöpfung. Die Vorstellung des Chaos," in Heinrich Schenker, *Das Meisterwerk in der Musik*, II (Munich, Vienna, Berlin: Drei Masken Verlag, 1926), 161–170; English, as "The Representation of Chaos from Haydn's *Creation*," tr. William Drabkin, in Heinrich Schenker, *The Masterwork in Music*, ed. William Drabkin, II (Cambridge: Cambridge University Press, 1996), 97–105.

7. Charles Rosen, *The Classical Style: Haydn, Mozart, Beethoven* (New York: W. W. Norton, rev. ed. 1972), 370.

8. Donald Francis Tovey, *Essays in Musical Analysis*, V (London: Oxford University Press, 1937), 114.

9. James Webster, *Haydn's "Farewell" Symphony and the Idea of Classical Style* (Cambridge: Cambridge University Press, 1991), 230–231.

10. Webster, *Haydn's "Farewell" Symphony*, 127. The point is amplified in Webster's "The *Creation*, Haydn's Late Vocal Music, and the Musical Sublime," in *Haydn and His World*, ed. Elaine Sisman (Princeton: Princeton University Press, 1997), 66: "Haydn's blaze of light resolves the disjunction and mystery of the entire Chaos music that has preceded it. The sublime effect depends on his integration of three separate movements . . . into a single progression that moves from paradoxical disorder to triumphant order."

tive, but through the C-major cadence that concludes the setting of the sentence, 'Und es ward Licht' (And there was light)," writes Kramer, and then arrogates Schenker's analysis to this view: "The first C-major chord . . . becomes the fulcrum of an extended foreground arpeggiation of the C-major triad in which, as Schenker observes, 'overtopping the e♭³ of measure 9, the e³ of light lifts itself aloft in measure 89."[11] But the clear objective of Schenker's study is in its circumscribed demonstration that the "Vorstellung des Chaos" runs its course, within itself: "With the arrival of c¹ [at m. 58], all registral tension is released. Chaos has breathed its last; the Light will now appear."[12] For Schenker, these wing-spans of coherence were, by rigorous definition, always contained within the single movement.[13] At the same time, the organicist agenda that underlies Schenker's thought is much in evidence: "Music, as an art that unfolds through time, is well placed to represent Chaos: the first vibrations and movements, the first stirrings of dark forces, the coming into being [das Werden], of giving birth, at last the light, the day, the creation!"[14]

Such blurring of the boundaries between chaos and light ignores a formal distinction between the parts of the work: the *Vorstellung des Chaos,* articulated by a full close in the tonic C minor, was conceived as a prologue, an overture— "*Ouverture,*" as it is even called in van Swieten's autograph libretto.[15] Whatever the settings of its own internal clockwork, this *Vorstellung* sets itself temporally apart from the main narrative of the work, envisioning a world at that unimaginable moment somewhere in the vicinity of the biblical "In the Beginning."

---

11. L. Kramer, "Haydn's Chaos, Schenker's Order," 14–15.

12. " . . . mit c¹ ist nun auch die Spannung der Lage vorüber, das Chaos atmet aus, das Licht erscheint." Schenker, "Haydn: Die Schöpfung," 168; "The Representation of Chaos," 101. Schenker's words might better be understood to say "Chaos breathes its last; light appears," adopting a simple narrative voice, suggesting (in the present indicative) that we are witness to this sequence of events.

13. There seems never to have been the slightest inclination to subsume even the most fragile movements of a single work together under the single arch of tonal continuity, and that, I think, is because for Schenker, the demonstration was always of music as an unbroken syntax that ended with the double bar. In this connection, it is worth mentioning that Haydn did not number the individual movements of the oratorio. An autograph score has not survived. On the numberings adopted in more recent editions, see Feder, *Joseph Haydn: Die Schöpfung,* 30; and, for a description of manuscript and published sources, including sketches, *ibid.,* 241–244.

14. " . . . so ist denn die Musik als eine in der Zeit sich entfaltende Kunst sehr wohl in der Lage, das Chaos wiederzugeben: die ersten Erschütterungen und Bewegungen, das erste Wühlen dunkler Kräfte, das Werden, Gebären, endlich das Licht, den Tag, die Schöpfung!" Schenker, "Haydn: Die Schöpfung," 161; "The Representation of Chaos," 97.

15. See [Joseph Haydn] *The Creation and the Seasons: The complete authentic sources for the Word-Books,* foreword by H. C. Robbins Landon (Cardiff: University College Cardiff Press, 1985), 14, a facsimile of the opening page of van Swieten's autograph.

When, at the outset of Haydn's narrative, Raphael sings "Im Anfange schuf Gott Himmel und Erde," the music means to recapitulate, to remember, as mythic history, that dreamlike condition vividly actualized in the music of Chaos. But of course there is no C major triad in this "Introduction," nor any sign of light. Scripture begins here, before this act that enables life. In Johann Gottfried Herder's *Aelteste Urkunde des Menschengeschlechts* (Earliest Documents of Mankind) of 1774, these words—"In the Beginning God created Heaven and Earth"—were made the topic of a brilliant exercise in hermeneutical problematizing: how are we to imagine this "Beginning"? How to conceptualize the notion "He created"?[16]

The reactions to Haydn's famous music at "Und Gott sprach: Es werde Licht, und es ward Licht" begin with an account of the first rehearsal. The testimony is from the Swedish chargé d'affaires in Vienna, Frederik Samuel Silverstolpe:

> No one, not even Baron van Swieten, had seen the page of the score wherein the birth of light is described. That was the only passage of the work that Haydn had kept hidden. I think I see his face even now, as this part sounded in the orchestra. Haydn had the expression of someone who is thinking of biting his lips, either to hide his embarrassment or to conceal a secret. And in that moment when light broke out for the first time, one would have said that rays darted from the composer's burning eyes. The enchantment of the electrified Viennese was so general that the orchestra could not proceed for some minutes.[17]

With due allowance for inadvertent postfactum embellishment, Silverstolpe's account serves merely to confirm that from the get-go this stunning moment induced hyperbolic responses that obscure what the music actually does. It is now a commonplace to understand the C major triad both as synecdoche for light itself, and, metonymically, in its function as a resolution of the dissonances accrued, literally and figuratively, in all this music of Chaos. But consider again how this passage goes. (It is shown as ex. 7.1.) When God speaks "Let there be light,"

---

16. "Siehe alles was dir auf deine Fragen 'wie ward Anfang? Wie begreif ichs, daß er schuf!' zu Theil wird." Herder, *Aelteste Urkunde des Menschengeschlechts* (Riga: Johann Friedrich Hartknoch, 1774), I: 13–14; Herder, *Sämtliche Werke*, VI (Berlin: Weidmann, 1883; reprint Hildesheim: Georg Olms, 1967), 206.

17. Robbins Landon, *Chronicle and Works*, IV: 318. For the original text, see C.-G. Stellan Mörner, "Haydniana aus Schweden um 1800," *Haydn-Studien*, II/1 (1969):28. It is not commonly noted that Silverstolpe's account, under the title "Die mehrjährige Bekanntschaft eines Schweden mit Joseph Haydn," was first published in 1838—not, evidently, a report from the battlefield, but a memoire.

this first biblical utterance is, in Haydn's instruction, to be sung "sotto voce." In timorous anticipation of the momentous event, a dominant triad is barely sounded in the strings: pizzicato, pianissimo. The simple motion from the one to the other—plucked dominant, blaze of C major—describes neither an act of triumph, of resolution, nor a problem solved through the labors of reason, but rather the happy accident of unexpected discovery—God finds the light switch, as someone once put it. Enlightenment comes through a process of revelation, empirically.

Not everyone thought so. In his reply to the question "What is Enlightenment?" put in a Berlin journal of 1784, Kant opens with the provocation "*Enlightenment is mankind's exit from its self-incurred immaturity,*" which leads then to a manifesto: "*Sapere aude!* Have the courage to use your *own* understanding!" This, claims Kant, must be "the motto of enlightenment."[18] For Kant, Enlightenment is a beginning, not an end. The philosopher guides the immature toward a state of mind that would enable a free, untutored use of reason: *Vernunft.* The word (together with *räsoniren*) aroused Hamann to the churlish "Metacritique on the Purism of Reason," not because Hamann had no faith in reason itself, but because he believed it to be misunderstood in what might be called its empirical dimension, as a constituent in how one goes about the business of thought. "The . . . highest and, as it were, *empirical* purism thus still concerns *language,* the only, first, and last organon and criterion of reason, with no credentials but *tradition* and *usage.*"[19] For Hamann, the entire faculty of thought is founded on language. The knot is tied more tightly here: "language is *also the center of reason's misunderstanding with itself.*"[20] This cryptic "misunderstanding" has something to do with what Hamann identifies as a "partly failed attempt to make reason independent of all tradition and custom and belief," and, in another sentence, "independent from experience and its everyday induction."[21] A few lines down,

---

18. "Beantwortung der Frage: Was ist Aufklärung?" *Berlinische Monatsschrift* 4 (1784): 481–494; reprinted in *Kants Gesammelte Schriften,* Akademie Ausgabe, VIII (Berlin, 1923), 33–42. For one of many translations, see "An Answer to the Question: What Is Enlightenment?" tr. James Schmidt, in *What Is Enlightenment? Eighteenth-Century Answers and Twentieth-Century Questions,* ed. James Schmidt (Berkeley, Los Angeles, London: University of California Press, 1996), 58–64.

19. "Der . . . höchste und gleichsam *empyrische* Purismus betrifft also noch die *Sprache,* das enzige erste u letzte Organon und Kriterion der Vernunft, ohne ein ander Creditiv als *Ueberlieferung* und VSVM [=USUM]" The original text, a draft sent to Herder, can be found in Johann Georg Hamann, *Briefwechsel,* ed. Walther Ziesemer and Arthur Henkel (Wiesbaden and Frankfurt: Insel-Verlag, 1955–1979), V: 210–216. Translated as "Metacritique on the Purism of Reason," tr. Kenneth Haynes, in Schmidt, *What Is Enlightenment?* 154–167, esp. 155.

20. " . . . sondern Sprache ist auch der *Mittelpunct des Misverstandes der Vernunft mit ihr selbt.*"

21. "Die erste Reinigung der Philosophie bestand nemlich in dem theils misverstandenen, theils mislungenen Versuch, die Vernunft von aller Ueberlieferung, Tradition und Glauben daran unabhängig zu machen." Hamann, *Briefwechsel,* V: 211; "Metacritique," 155.

Hamann formulates his bold conceit for the beginning of thought: "The oldest language," he proposes, "was music. . . . The oldest writing was *painting* and *drawing*."[22] Finally, "*sensibility (Sinnlichkeit)* and *understanding (Verstand)* spring as two stems of human knowledge from *One* common root, so that through the former objects are *given* and through the latter *thought:* what is the purpose of such a violent, unjustified, arbitrary divorce of that which nature has joined together!" Here is the crux of Hamann's paradox: reason, in all its apparent purity, is yet unthinkable without language, whose meaning is acquired not *a priori* but through "tradition and usage."

Enlightenment thinkers seem forever disentangling the problem of Word. In another reading of the Beginning, one which ignited much hermeneutical passion in the late eighteenth century, John begins his gospel "In initio erat verbum." And it is precisely these gnostic words that Goethe has Faust pull down from his shelf at the outset of the famous Logos Scene in Faust I. The determination to translate the Bible into Faust's beloved German is what gets the scene underway. "Geschrieben steht: 'Im Anfang war das Wort!'" ("In the Beginning was the Word," it is written), he begins, and at once dismisses "*Wort*" as too heavily invested. He interrogates the alternatives: "*Sinn*"—but is it really the mind that can have set creation in motion? ("Ist es der Sinn der alles wirkt und schafft?"). The inadequacy of "*Kraft*" (Power) strikes him as self-evident. In a moment of bold insight, he finds the word:

Mir hilft der Geist! Auf einmal seh' ich Rat
Und schreibe getrost: Im Anfang war die *Tat!*[23]

A fussy exercise in translation, a parody of Talmudic exegesis, it might at first seem. "Bible-translation: there's the latest fashion in scholarship," wrote Herder in 1774.[24] And yet, beneath Faust's pretext lurks a more serious engagement with language and its place at the beginning of it all—even, on the futility, the impossibility of translation altogether, an idea poignantly conveyed in the suggestive

---

22. "Die älteste Sprache war Musik . . . Die älteste Schrift war *Malerey* und *Zeichung*." Hamann, *Briefwechsel*, V: 213; "Metacritique," 156.

23. "The spirit guides me. I see the wisdom at once, and write with confidence: In the beginning was the *Deed*." These bold lines set the translator an impossible task. *Geist* here means intellect, wit, no less than spirit: the ghost in the machine. *Tat* is often translated as act, but perhaps its linguistic root is closer to deed: *Tat* as that which is *getan; Deed* as that which is *done*. I take the text from Johann Wolfgang von Goethe, *Werke. Hamburger Ausgabe in 14 Bände*, III, Dramatische Dichtungen 1 (Munich: C. H. Beck, 1981), 44.

24. "Bibelübersetzung!—siehe da das neueste Studium der Mode." Herder, *Aelteste Urkunde des Menschengeschlechts*, I: 1; *Sämtliche Werke*, VI: 195.

amplitude of *logos*.[25] This word, not actually named in Faust, resonates under the page (so to say) deep with implications: idea, concept, reason, world-spirit are all aspects of its meaning in ancient Greece, then inflected by the early Christians as divine reason and what Erich Trunz calls "das Schöpfungsprinzip"(the principle of creation).[26] And perhaps Goethe means to conflate the meanings of logos with *davhar*, Hebrew for "word," whose meaning is "at once 'word,' 'thing' and 'act,'" as Harold Bloom reminds us.[27] And I think it is now commonly accepted that Faust, in his worrying of John's meaning, is engaging Herder's richly convoluted gloss on this very phrase, in the *Erläuterungen zum Neuen Testament* (Commentaries on the New Testament) of 1775.[28] In a passage that itself underwent much revision, Herder writes—or rather, stammers in an ecstatic gush—an understanding of "Im Anfang war das Wort":

> And yet the teaching Godhead lowers himself! How to make us worthy of recognizing him as other than Man? In a single image of our images, he chooses the holiest, the most spiritual, the most efficacious, deepest in his creative likeness in our soul: thought [idea]! word! plan! Love! Deed![29]

---

25. Rüdiger Görner even writes of "metatranslation": "Faust nun befaßt sich mit dem Bedeutungsgehalt des *logos,* des Wortes selbst. Er strebt, so gesehen, eine Metaübersetzung an, die zum Ziel hat, das Wort selbst zu übersetzen . . ." (Faust now concerns himself with the significance of logos, of the word itself. He strives, in this view, toward a meta-translation which has as its goal the translation of the word itself . . .) But the impressive achievement of Görner's essay is the exploration in Goethe's thought (within *Faust* and outside it) of what seems an eternal ambivalence in meaning from word—in its origin as tonal speech, and as empty shell without significance—to act, and back again. See "Vom Wort zur Tat in Goethes 'Faust'—Paradigmenwechsel oder Metamorphose?" in *Goethe Jahrbuch,* 106 (1989): 119–132.

26. "Logos . . . war ein Wort, das im Christentum aufgenommen wurde und hier die göttliche Vernunft, das Schöpfungsprinzip und den fleischgewordenen Gott, d. h. Christus bedeutete." (Logos . . . was a word taken up in Christianity, where it signifies divine reason, the principle of creation and God incarnate—that is, Christ.) Goethe, *Werke,* III: 510.

27. "The concept of *davhar* is: speak, act, be. The concept of *logos* is: speak, reckon, think." Harold Bloom, *A Map of Misreading* (Oxford: Oxford University Press, 1975), 42.

28. See Hans Rudolf Schweizer, *Goethe und das Problem der Sprache.* Basler Studien zur Deutschen Sprache und Literatur, Heft 23 (Bern: Francke Verlag, 1959), 67–68, in a chapter titled "Wort und Tat"; and Elizabeth M. Wilkinson, "Faust in der Logosszene–Willkürlicher Übersetzer oder geschulter Exeget?" in *Dichtung. Sprache. Gesellschaft: Akten des IV. Internationalen Germanistenkongresses 1970 in Princeton,* ed. Victor Lange and Hans-Gert Roloff (Frankfurt am Main: Athenäum Verlag, 1971), 116–124.

29. "Und doch ließ sich die erziehende Gottheit hinab! würdigte Uns sich kennbar zu machen, wie anders als Menschen? in Einem Bilde unsrer Bilder; nur wählte sie das Heiligste, Geistigste, Würksamste, Tiefste, ihr schöpferisches Abbild in unsrer Seele: Gedanke! Wort! Entwurf! Liebe! That!" In the final version, the series became "Gedanke! Wort! Wille! That! Liebe!" —Idea, Word, Will, Deed, Love! See Herder, *Erläuterungen zum neuen Testament* (Riga: Johann Friedrich Hartknoch, 1775), reprinted in *Sämtliche Werke,* VII (Berlin, 1884), 356 and note 1.

Faust puts some poetic shape to Herder's effusions, one might say, even as he examines the priority of Word that Herder elaborates in the essay *On the Origin of Language*. That sense of origin, of *Ursprung* (as a leap from something primordial) is ever repeated, if I understand Herder's notion that "parents never teach their children language without the latter, by themselves, inventing language along with them."[30]

In a footnote to his eruption on the opening words of the John Gospel, Herder writes "It is known that *logos* signifies the inner and outer word, *Vorstellung* [imagination] from within and *Darstellung* [representation] from without."[31] This distinction between *Vorstellung* and *Darstellung*, between the inner process of imagination and creation, and the external notion of exhibition and depiction, returns us to the opening music of the Creation. What I am getting at, all too obviously, is the sense in which Haydn's *Vorstellung des Chaos*, whatever else it may be about, is no less an enactment of a quest to discover the beginnings of language, of linguistic utterance, much in tune with these essays by Herder and Hamann. Haydn's scenario further brings to mind a notion attributed to Hamann: that "to understand or think is to participate in the drama that is the creation"[32]—just as for Herder, the genuine learning of language is to engage in creation, again ex nihilo. From which we might infer that to the Enlightenment mind, the idea of The Creation—the engagement, as *Vorstellung*, of the moment between Chaos and Light—is what ought to drive the human enterprise. What is life (Hamann might have asked) if not about this drama of creation?

Haydn's music, then, means less to "depict" chaos than to imagine a process in which the Creator creates: less *Darstellung*, more *Vorstellung*. The music envisions this moment, before language and reason recognize one another; enacts the experiment of the creation of language in the metalanguage of music; and imagines what it might have felt like, as an experience of *Empfindsamkeit* in search of reason, to "create" a world: not a world necessarily of order in any perfect sense, but a world as it would have been understood in the ironical mode of Enlighten-

---

30. "Eltern lehren die Kinder nie Sprache, ohne daß diese nicht immer selbst mit erfänden." *Abhandlung über den Ursprung der Sprache*, in *Sämtliche Werke*, V: 41; Herder, *On the Origin of Language*, 121.

31. "Es ist bekannt, daß λογος das *innere* und *äußere Wort, Vorstellung* von innen und *Darstellung* von außen bedeute." Herder, *Erläuterungen zum neuen Testament, Sämtliche Werke*, VII: 356.

32. This telling phrase is the work of Isaiah Berlin, *The Magus of the North: J. G. Hamann and the Origins of Modern Irrationalism*, ed. Henry Hardy (New York: Farrar, Straus and Giroux, 1993), 5; Berlin refers us to the letter of 26 August 1774 to Herder, though it is unclear to me how Berlin's phrase, for all its aptness to the point at issue, can be distilled from Hamann's letter. See Hamann, *Briefwechsel*, III: 104.

ment thought.[33] The music, as it unfolds, suggests an effort to put notes together, intuitively, guided by some natural sense, and prior to the codification into rules that would govern how notes, under prescribed conditions, must follow one another in works that do not actively engage in Hamann's drama of creation. In its quest for the right notes, for the putting together of phrases, the music registers a journal of the creative act. This seems to me audible at once in the opening bars of Haydn's score (shown in ex. 7.2), where the splaying of notes suggests the play of experiment, of discovery and invention.

When the first violins enter at bar 3, it is an entrance at once tentative and shrewdly provocative. An unprepared dissonance, the F is the missing tone of the diminished seventh at the downbeat of the measure, and so "completes" the harmony—as though the composer, through the players who do his bidding, will discover, intuitively and empirically, the rule by which such dissonances must be prepared, even as this F moves off in the wrong direction. The following F♯ is an implausible passing tone that subverts the main business of the seventh. The empirical adventure continues at bar 6, where the repetition now puts F♯ on the downbeat, reversing the relationship between these two pitches—as though F♯ were being tested as the preparation of the seventh. At bar 8, A♭, first heard as an unprepared flat six at bar 2, is now relocated to the bass, lending support to an emergent augmented sixth seeking the first true dominant, as though A♭ and F♯ had now found their true roles in respect of one another. The flutes, oblivious of this harmonic environment (doubled, comically, by the second trombone several octaves below), exercise a trill on D. By the conventions of the classical phrase, the trill would descend from D above the dominant, embellishing the close on the tonic. For these flutes, the trill is a thing of pleasure, an exercise of the instrument. Ignorant of its normal function as a controlling device, the trill here celebrates an escape to a climactic E♭—blithely contradicting the motion of the bass toward a dominant on G. The aggregate at bar 9 may seem to constitute a triad in first inversion whose root is E♭, but the experience of it suggests something else again:

---

33. I am much indebted in these thoughts to Hayden White, *Metahistory: The Historical Imagination in Nineteenth-Century Europe* (Baltimore and London: The Johns Hopkins University Press, 1973), 45–80, in a chapter called "The Historical Imagination between Metaphor and Irony," and in particular (58) to the notion of the historical process apprehended in the Enlightenment "less as a development from one stage to another in the life of humanity than as merely an . . . *unresolvable* conflict between *eternally opposed* principles of human nature: rational on the one hand, irrational on the other," and consequently, ironically.

(continued)

EXAMPLE 7.2
Haydn, *Die Schöpfung,*
"Einleitung," mm.
1–21.

165

EXAMPLE 7.2 *(continued)*

the C struck by the second violins at the second half of the bar claims the E♭ as a member of a dissonant six-four above G.[34]

In its harmonic trajectories, the music of Haydn's Chaos enacts yet more explicitly this quest for an intuitively coherent language. One passage will have to stand for several. The music wants eventually to move to the key of the relative major, from C minor to E♭ major. Everyone who hears this music will know that such a modulation is imminent. And indeed the music is drawn pointedly in that direction, toward m. 20. Unaccountably, the cadence is interrupted, or better, distracted. In its distraction, the music commits what the ear of 1798 would hear as a solecism: a breach in syntax, even of good grammar. D♭ is struck and ennobled as though it were a tone of significance. And it is uprooted in a blur of diminished seventh chords that finally drives the bass down chromatically, through the defining augmented sixth on C♭ that establishes B♭ as a dominant. E♭ is refound less by design than by accident, intuitively, irrationally. The music teeters on and around its dominant for thirteen bars, and then unwittingly slips back to C minor. There is an exploratory aspect to this music that is much to its point.

Haydn, then, humanizes the act of creation. God is projected in the image of Man. There is nothing heretical in this, and certainly nothing Romantic. It is a hard-nosed, ironical view of the proposition that Enlightenment comes only after a certain mucking about in the empirical forest. C major is the moment of Enlightenment, of *Aufklärung,* and we cannot say that we understand (or that Haydn means for us to believe) that this moment is causally effected by some ineluctable chain of reasoning. In that famous passage from the conversation with d'Alembert, Diderot invents the metaphor of the vibrating string to explain how the mind engages in thought: Vibrating strings have the property "to make others vibrate, and it is in this way that one idea calls up a second, and the two together a third, and all three a fourth, and so on. This instrument can make astonishing leaps, and one idea called up will sometimes start an harmonic at an incomprehensible interval."[35] This is how we think, this is the intuitive process of discovery and creation.

---

34. It is the arrival at this E♭ that Schenker proclaimed to signal the posting of what he calls the structural *Kopfton.* See "The Representation of Chaos," in particular the graph on 102. L. Kramer, "Haydn's Chaos, Schenker's Order," similarly takes the E♭ at m. 9 as a principal structural moment; see his example 3 (p. 12) and the commentary around it. If Schenker is right, then the moment is steeped in irony.

35. Diderot, *Entretien entre d'Alembert et Diderot,* 48–49; "Conversation between D'Alembert and Diderot," in *Rameau's Nephew and D'Alembert's Dream,* 156. See chapter 6 note 27, for fuller reference.

Haydn's *Vorstellung* means *not* to say "this is what Chaos sounds like." Rather, its music enacts, performs, in a *Sprache der Empfindung* (language of sensibility), through the play of syntax, a process of mind inventing speech, probing logos, dialectically, between reason and experience. In a sense, what we hear is not unlike what philosophers like Vico, Herder, and Hamann seem to conjure when they put themselves and their readers before the proposition of a world before language. The effort always to imagine the first word, which, for Hamann, enabled the freeing of the first thought—Herder, viewing the matter with some irony, saw the futility of holding that either reason or language can have preceded the other[36]—is akin to the process in which Haydn imagines the transition from Chaos to Light, even as Goethe, through Faust, tries to understand how logos is the beginning of all things.

To hear in this music the evocation of a Romantic sense of the infinitude of creation, of the sublime, is, to my mind, to mishear it. Haydn's *Vorstellung* enacts the world as syntax and language: an experience of the world is in effect an effort to construe it in linguistic terms. The opening phrases, if they are *about* anything at all, are about the business of creation—the pleasures, divinely endowed, of creating. These musical phrases mean neither to depict nor to represent. Rather, they act out a scenario of creation, set in motion by that inert, ascetic opening octave. Hamann's notion of thinking as a participation, less allegorical than actual, in the "drama that is the creation" resonates with an earlier formulation of the possibilities of artistic creation. Reading Federico Zuccari's "L'Idea de' pittori, scultori ed architetti" of 1607, Erwin Panofsky is led to conclude that "Since the human intellect, by virtue of its participation in God's ideational ability and its similarity to the divine mind as such, can produce in itself the *forme spirituali* of all created things and can transfer these *forme* to matter, there exists, as if by divine predestination, a necessary coincidence between man's procedures in producing a work of art and nature's procedures in producing reality."[37] For Zuccari, "God has one single Design, most perfect in substance . . . ; man, however, forms within himself various designs corresponding to the different things he conceives. Therefore his Design is an accident, and moreover it has a lower origin, namely in the senses."[38] By the end of the eighteenth century, the creative mind

---

36. "Without language man has no reason, and without reason no language." Herder, *On the Origin,* 121. *Abhandlung über den Ursprung der Sprache,* in *Sämtliche Werke,* V: 40.

37. Erwin Panofsky, *Idea: a Concept in Art Theory,* tr. Joseph J. S. Peake (Columbia: University of South Carolina Press, 1968), 89.

38. Panofsky, *Idea,* 88.

could envision a yet bolder congruence between God's Creation and the invention of Art: the magnetic fields are, so to say, reversed, and it is now adduced that what we can know only through empirical experience provides Man the only possible measure of God's Creation. The accident of Design that Zuccari ascribes to human creation is now taken as a model for the Creation itself. Haydn's *Vorstellung* is, to my ears, nothing less than this: God as empiricist, probing infinity for the rules that might impart to it some higher order; God as composer, enacting the original improvisation.

But of course this is no ordinary improvisation. In its personification of the "schöpferische Geist" (to borrow from Herder), the music emulates—enacts, rather—the divine improvisation by which, in Kant's view, the work of genius creates its own rules.[39] We are witness to the mind of Haydn in the act of composition as it conjures in fanciful mimesis the drama that is the Creation. And I do not think that it stretches the idea of composition in the Enlightenment to suggest that in the great works of Emanuel Bach, of Mozart in his maturity, of Haydn, of Beethoven, this drama is each time played out anew: we are meant to feel ourselves in the presence of the adventure of inspired improvisation. The "Ouverture" to Haydn's *Creation* is a meta-improvisation. In its bold imagining of divine exploration, it offers a parable for the creative act as divinely human, a model for the process of enlightened thought.

---

39. "*Genius* is the inborn human aptitude (ingenium) *through which* nature provides art with rules. . . . Genius is the *aptitude* to produce something for which no definite rule can be postulated." Immanuel Kant, *Kritik der Urteilskraft*, Part I, Book 2 (Berlin, 1790), as translated in *Music and Aesthetics in the Eighteenth and Early-Nineteenth Centuries,* ed. Peter le Huray and James Day (Cambridge: Cambridge University Press, 1981), 227–228.

CHAPTER 8

Beethoven and the Romance of Creation

Interior Beethoven: the familiar trope pictures the inner reaches of the creative mind at play—the ultimate creative mind, in a version of the Romantic legend. What can we glean from the disparate, often chaotic evidence that survives of this process? How might the frail and imaginary constructs that we piece together from the traces of this fitful process be heard to imprint themselves as emblems of meaning in the work that finally emerges? With Beethoven, this is not a simple inquiry. The evidence, rich and dauntingly complex, has survived in the voluminous sketches that Beethoven wrote (and, astonishingly, preserved) for seemingly every project that he undertook. Then, for Beethoven the process itself, the act of composing, in its obsessive aspect, seems to infiltrate into the substance of the work in subtle ways that challenge the axiom by which we have come to hold the text of the work inviolable.

I have in mind two congeries of sketches, for movements that have much in common. Both associated in the popular imagination with Shakespeare, both in D minor, they are yet separated from one another by that brief interstice at the turn of the century during which Beethoven sought to reconcile a received, objectifying engagement in classical models with a turning inward toward a newly subjective figuring of the composer's voice—of the composer as protagonist.

Beethoven's Sketches and
Shakespeare's Lovers

The earlier instance has to do with some sketches for the slow movement—Adagio affettuoso ed appassionato—of the quartet in F major, Opus 18 no. 1. The topic is complicated by the survival of a set of parts for the quartet in a version that differs in all four of its movements from the published text. On the outer page of the part marked "Violino I^{mo}" Beethoven inscribed a touching dedication, dated 25 June 1799, to his very close friend, the violinist Karl Amenda, on the occasion of Amenda's departure from Vienna to his native Latvia.[1] Two years later, almost to the day, in a long and deeply moving letter to his now distant friend, he confessed in painful and intimate exclamations to the increased deterioration of his hearing. "I beg you," Beethoven writes toward the end of the letter, "to treat what I have told you about my hearing as a great secret to be entrusted to no one, whoever it may be." And then, in a stunning afterthought, he closes: "Be sure not to hand on to anybody your quartet, in which I have made some drastic alterations. For only now have I learned how to write quartets; and this you will notice straight away when you receive them."[2] He was here referring to the publication of the set of six quartets comprised in Opus 18, which appeared in two installments in the spring and autumn of 1801.[3]

Much has been written about the differences between these two versions of the F-major quartet, and what it was that Beethoven learned in the interval separating them.[4] Mainly, the differences point to a supple, newly gained mastery of the ensemble: an enhanced sensitivity to voicing and balance, and a greater technical control over the densely contrapuntal passages concentrated especially in the outer movements. The main body of surviving sketches is for the earlier, so-called Amenda version, and it is these sketches that will be our concern here.

Indeed, it was Amenda himself who was responsible for a provocative insight of quite another kind into the conceiving of the quartet. Many years after the

---

1. The parts, now at Bonn, Beethoven-Haus, BH 84, may be viewed at the digital website of the Archive. The autograph inscription, often reproduced, may be found in Sieghard Brandenburg, "Beethovens Streichquartette op. 18," in *Beethoven und Böhmen: Beiträge zu Biographie und Wirkungsgeschichte Beethovens,* ed. Sieghard Brandenburg and Martella Gutiérrez-Denhoff (Bonn: Beethoven-Haus, 1988), 271–272.

2. *Ludwig van Beethoven: Briefwechsel Gesamtausgabe,* ed. Sieghard Brandenburg (Munich: Henle Verlag, 1996), I: 84–86. Emily Anderson, ed. and tr., *The Letters of Beethoven* (London: Macmillan, 1961), 63–65.

3. On the details of publication, see Brandenburg, "Beethovens Streichquartette op. 18," 288–297.

4. The Amenda version was first published, with extensive commentary, in Hans Josef Wedig, *Beethovens Streichquartette op. 18 Nr. 1 und seine erste Fassung.* Veröffentlichungen des Beethovenhauses in Bonn, ed. Ludwig Schiedermair, vol. 2 (Bonn: Beethovenhaus, 1922). More recent studies are Janet Levy, *Beethoven's Compositional Choices: The Two Versions of op. 18, no. 1, First Movement* (Philadelphia: University of Pennsylvania Press, 1982); and David H. Smyth, "Beethoven's Revision of the Scherzo of Opus 18, No. 1," in *Beethoven Forum,* 1 (1992): 147–163. See also *Ludwig van Beethoven: A Sketchbook from the Summer of 1800,* ed. Richard Kramer (Bonn: Beethoven-Haus, 1996), II: 19–21.

event, he recounted an exchange with Beethoven that has had consequences for all subsequent readings of the work. Beethoven reportedly played the Adagio for Amenda directly after its composition. Asked what thoughts it aroused in him, Amenda answered: "It depicted for me the parting of two lovers." "*Wohl,*" Beethoven is said to have replied; "I was thinking of the scene in the burial vault in *Romeo and Juliet.*"[5]

There would be every reason to sniff at such evident nonsense were it not for the discovery of some riddling inscriptions among the earliest surviving sketches for this very movement: "il prend le tombeau" (he seizes the grave); "désespoir" (despair); "il se tue" (he kills himself); "les dernier soupirs" (the dying breaths).[6] The temptation to associate these wrought words with the Amenda report on *Romeo and Juliet* is great indeed, and few have resisted it. Owen Jander, in vigorous pursuit of the telltale signs of a *Romeo and Juliet* program embedded in the quartet, was intrigued by the language of these inscriptions. Why French? he asks, and answers that Beethoven's source was not directly Shakespeare, but more likely the opera *Romeo et Juliette* by Daniel Steibelt, first performed in Paris in 1793 and published that same year in full orchestral score. The opera was not performed in Vienna, but (Jander argues) Beethoven would very likely have studied the score.[7]

What, precisely, are these sketchbook hieroglyphs about? (They are shown in ex. 8.1.) How did Beethoven mean to inscribe them in the text of the music? These are not easy questions, and they open on to yet more sinewy ones. From their context in the sketchbook, it is clear that Beethoven is here preoccupied with the closing bars of the quartet. The residue of these fragmentary theatrical effusions continue to sound in the final moments of the completed work (see ex. 8.2).

---

5. Alexander Wheelock Thayer, *Ludwig van Beethovens Leben,* II, ed. Hermann Deiters, rev. Hugo Riemann (Leipzig: Breitkopf & Härtel, 1910), 186; Thayer, *The Life of Ludwig van Beethoven,* ed. and tr. Henry Edward Krehbiel (New York: The Beethoven Association, 1921), I: 272–273; *Thayer's Life of Beethoven,* rev. and ed. Elliot Forbes (Princeton: Princeton University Press, 1967), 261.

6. The sketches, in the sketchbook Berlin: Staatsbibliothek zu Berlin–Preußischer Kulturbesitz, Mus. ms. autogr. Beethoven Grasnick 2, are published in *Beethoven. Ein Skizzenbuch zu Streichquartetten aus Op. 18,* ed. Wilhelm Virneisel, 2 vols. (Bonn: Beethovenhaus, 1972–1974), I (Übertragung), 46–47, II (Faksimile), 8–9. This is the second of a pair of sketchbooks, now commonly known as Grasnick 1 and Grasnick 2, which together comprise a kind of project book for the quartets eventually published as Opus 18 nos. 3, 1, 2 and 5, for which sketches are entered in just that order. For more on the composition history of the quartets, see Brandenburg, "Beethovens Streichquartette op. 18," 268–282.

7. On the version by Steibelt, I am indebted to a fascinating essay, as yet unpublished, by Owen Jander, who graciously allowed me to draw on its ideas and its documentation.

EXAMPLE 8.1 Beethoven, Sketchbook [Berlin: SBB] Mus. ms. autogr. Grasnick 2, pp. 8, 9.

EXAMPLE 8.2 Beethoven, String Quartet in F, Opus 18 no. 1, Adagio affettuoso ed appassionato, mm. 92–106.

(continued)

EXAMPLE 8.2 *(continued)*

Characteristically, Beethoven now proceeds to other projects. He completes the preliminary drafting of the first movement. He works out some ideas for the scherzo and the finale. And he returns then to the Adagio. Several drafts into it, on page 17, we come upon a remarkable entry at staves 7–8, so far as I can tell, altogether unnoticed in the sketch literature. It pertains to the final bars of the exposition, here elaborated in a theme of self-possessed calm whose cadence is made to elide into the brief, highly charged music that will stand between the exposition and its reprise. The theme itself is remarkable in its hymnal decorum, its solving of the dissonances which penetrate the affecting theme with which the movement opens. It is shown (along with a false start) in ex. 8.3. (The full page is shown in facsimile in fig. 8.1.)

Entered at the middle of the page, the new theme (in F major) follows on a draft, occupying staves 1–6, for the final bars of a movement that was to have vanished in a lengthy run of broken sighs in the cello—and in D *major*. It will now have occurred to Beethoven that this pious new theme must sound again at the very end of the movement, and so he returns to the draft at the top of the page and enters the new theme, marked *fine,* evidently coupling its opening F♯ to what was to have been the final chord of the movement, and running its continuation into the margins, for the rest of the page had already been filled (see ex. 8.4). In the manner of a closing benediction, the theme now comes as an afterbeat to the troubled cadencing that precedes it, a palliative to those exaggerated gestures that seemed to fire up the sketching for this extreme movement.

Returning now to the bottom of the page, Beethoven replots the passage, its own cadence now attenuated and elided into the familiar sequence that modulates into G minor and the development, precisely as in the final version. In the draft, however, it is this new theme, and not the opening theme, that will figure

EXAMPLE 8.3 Grasnick 2, page 17, staves 7/8.

prominently here, lending stability to its various tonal outposts. There are two trials at the very end of the page, the one moving toward D minor, the other moving through E♭ (and a new counter theme) toward F minor (see ex. 8.5).

A draft at the top of the next page (18) begins again with the new theme at the end of the exposition. Now a principal player, the new theme again launches a de-

FIGURE 8.1 Beethoven. Page with sketches for String Quartet in F, Opus 18, No. 1, second movement. © Staatsbibliothek zu Berlin—Preußischer Kulturbesitz, Musik-abteilung mit Mendelssohn-Archiv. Mus. ms. autogr. Beethoven Grasnick 2, p. 17. By kind permission.

EXAMPLE 8.4 Grasnick 2, page 17, staves 3/4.

velopment in G minor, and would now bring it to a close in E♭ major (the realm of the Neapolitan), sounding distant and even nostalgic before the inevitable "da capo," as Beethoven routinely labels the moment of reprise. The passage is heavily sketched (ex. 8.6 catches only some of the process), Beethoven listening hard to the silences and inflections that negotiate the return from this fragile E♭ to the grim business of D minor.

At the top of the facing page, the tonal map is rearranged. There are signs that Beethoven seemed now to recognize the extent to which this solemn theme had overplayed its hand, transforming what, in the initial drafting, was to be music of raw, piercing emotion, into something measured and controlled, conciliatory and resolved. The theme makes a final appearance in another draft for the development (19), now in A minor, and is then abandoned, the Adagio evidently replotted yet again—in mind if not on paper, for the sketches in Grasnick 2 trail off here with entries for that difficult patch of music in the coda: again, a listening to silences and inflections.

How might this abandoned theme be understood to play into Beethoven's *Romeo and Juliet?* The question is likely to launch further inquiry into the muddy

---

8. For something on this topic, see chapter 2, note 9.

waters of Shakespeare reception in eighteenth-century Germany.[8] It might, for example, bear on the matter to know that among the most popular settings of *Romeo and Juliet* was a *Singspiel* by Georg Benda composed in 1776, and played with great frequency throughout Germany in the 1780s. It was performed in Bonn in 1782, where Beethoven would have heard it. And so he would have known that in this version, Juliet awakens before Romeo takes the poison. Indeed, both Benda's and Steibelt's operas end happily![9] If this is what Beethoven's conciliatory theme means to emulate, the decision to abandon it might betoken a consequent restoration of an authentic Shakespeare.[10] The vulnerability of such reasoning only points up the fallacy in the argument itself, perched uncomfortably on unprovable suppositions regarding the notion of equivalencies, or identities, or transliterations between the musical work and what is alleged to be its literary or programmatic counterpart. The suppositions become yet more vulnerable when the underlying text adduced is itself a dramatic work, for we might then be inclined to hear the temporal unfolding of the music as coordinate with the actions on the stage—not, of course, in a pedantically literal parsing, but in the alignment of the telling events in the music with those in the drama.[11] And because the work of the stage is manifest in the interaction of its dramatis personae, the musical work must find its own entry into this complex play of voice and body. Does Beethoven's music wrestle with these imponderables? In a purely cognitive sense, we cannot know.

Having now probed a bit into these interiors that put on display some of the process through which the work was conceived, we must now ask where that has gotten us. For Sieghard Brandenburg, it gets to actual meaning. Here is how he put it, in a colloquy on the topic published in 1979:

> Beethoven's well-documented intention of expressing the grave scene of Romeo and Juliet is something that has worked itself into the Gestalt of the movement in a

9. Jander reminds us of the performance of the Benda Singspiel in Bonn. And it is Jander who describes the operatic manipulations of Shakespeare in the versions by Benda and Steibelt. In Jander's programmatic reading, Shakespeare's vault scene is restored.

10. Beethoven's library, as it was inventoried at his death, contained four volumes of Shakespeare, in the Eschenburg translation. The volume containing *Othello* and *Romeo und Julia* dates from 1779, although there is some reason to believe that Beethoven did not acquire it before 1804. See Eveline Bartlitz, *Die Beethoven-Sammlung in der Musikabteilung der Deutschen Staatsbibliothek: Verzeichnis* (Berlin: Deutsche Staatsbibliothek, [1970]), 210–211.

11. Of the many discussions of this perennial topic, one might single out Edward T. Cone's "Beethoven's Orpheus–or Jander's?" *19th Century Music* 8 (1985): 283–286, in reply to Owen Jander, "Beethoven's 'Orpheus in Hades': The *Andante con moto* of the Fourth Piano Concerto," *ibid.,* 195–212.

EXAMPLE 8.5 Grasnick 2, page 17, staves 15/16, 13/14.

180

EXAMPLE 8.6 Grasnick 2, page 18, staves 1–2, 9–11.

way that can be heard. The rather painfully demonstrative character of this *Adagio affettuoso ed appassionato* is to be regarded as the result of his determination to represent extra-musical matters. For these the sketches reveal a concrete program, and even allow us to point to the place where Beethoven realized it, namely the movement's coda.[12]

For Brandenburg, the meaning of the piece is incomplete without these programmatic signs. For although he claims that we can "take in this movement perfectly well without knowing the program," he really intends a distinction between the perceiving of the music as some grammatical construct whose meaning begins and ends in the notes, so to say, and the understanding of what he calls its "concrete program"—those aspects of meaning more explicitly coupled to a dramatic scene.

Here, at this very moment—let us date it 25 June 1799, with the inscription of the Amenda copy—Beethoven touches the nerve of an aesthetic conundrum that would consume all of Romantic music in the century about to follow: how to reconcile the paradox of, on the one hand, music as the language empowered to express the inexpressible, from grand meta-drama with its appeal to the mythic themes of human existence, to the harmonic imaging of the poetic experience; and, on the other, music as a theoretical system that conveys the deep axioms of language—conveys, that is, the grammar and syntax of language, and is about this exclusively.

It touches a few other nerves as well. These intriguing sketches force us to grapple with the thorny problem how, or even whether, such evidence can be permitted into the rigorously circumscribed and much vexed arena of textual authenticity. The sketches, for all that they illuminate of a process of composition, are by definition excluded from the text of the work. We know these sketches only by the sheerest accident: Beethoven happens to have preserved them, guarding them until his death. If we cannot disentangle his deeper motives for doing so, we can surmise with confidence that the sketches were intensely private records that Beethoven kept to himself.[13] What can we possibly know about the obscure deci-

---

12. Sieghard Brandenburg, [reply to Douglas Johnson's] "On Beethoven's Scholars and Beethoven's Sketches," *19th Century Music* 2 (1979): 273.

13. The evidence that Beethoven occasionally gave away a sketch leaf as a memento is tenuous and vague; nowhere is there the slightest hint that his sketchbooks were ever shared with his musical companions. For a lucid and balanced introduction to the study of the sketches, see Douglas Johnson, Alan Tyson, and Robert Winter, *The Beethoven Sketchbooks: History, Reconstruction, Inventory,* ed. Douglas Johnson (Berkeley and Los Angeles: University of California Press, 1985), 3–12.

sion making that would discriminate between the music in the sketches and the music completed for performance and publication? In venturing to say why this pious theme was abandoned, we speculate about the conceiving of the work, but such speculation, critical as it may be to an understanding of the acts of composition, is yet irrelevant to—necessarily locked out of—the discourse of the finished work.

And then there is Beethoven's resolve to exercise, in the physical act of writing, complete control over the process of composition. In that resolve, he challenges the very ground rules by which genius had come to be understood. If, in the Enlightenment, the acts, the labors of creation were shrouded in mysteries having to do with inspiration, of godlike flashes that emanate from the soul of genius—one thinks here of Kant's understanding of the products of genius, and, inevitably, one thinks of Mozart—Beethoven has no tolerance for such distance between the human act and the divine that such a model stipulates. And as a result, these labors of creation become increasingly difficult to separate out from the work itself. The author's imprint is willfully ingrained in the work. These scenes of Romeo in Beethoven's workshop will not go quietly.

Writing of the shift of sensibilities and its effect on the design of the novel of the eighteenth and nineteenth centuries, Milan Kundera explores with uncommon wit the opposition of improvisation and composition:

> The freedom by which Rabelais, Cervantes, Diderot, Sterne enchant us had to do with improvisation. The art of complex and rigorous composition did not become a commanding need until the first half of the nineteenth century. The novel's form as it came into being then, with its action concentrated in a narrow time span, at a crossroads where many stories of many characters intersect, demanded a minutely calculated scheme of the plot lines and scenes: before beginning to write, the novelist therefore drafted and redrafted the scheme of the novel, calculated and recalculated it, designed and redesigned as that had never been done before. One need only leaf through Dostoyevsky's notes for *The Possessed:* in the seven notebooks that take up 400 pages of the Pléiade edition (the novel itself takes up 750), motifs look for characters, characters look for motifs, characters vie for the status of protagonist.[14]

---

14. Milan Kundera, *Testaments Betrayed: An Essay in Nine Parts,* tr. Linda Asher (New York: Harper-Collins Publishers, 1993), 18–19.

The aptness of all this to the compositional plottings encountered among the Beethoven sketches is striking. The game played out in the Dostoyevsky note-books—"motifs look for characters, characters look for motifs, characters vie for the status of protagonist"—seems an evocation of what one finds in these drafts for Beethoven's Adagio. Surely, it helps to explain the comings and goings of this pious theme—a theme that in the end is never heard, for Beethoven expunged it from the final drafts.

Its trace, however, lingers. How that is so can best be apprehended in a con-templation of some final entries for the very end of the movement (shown in ex. 8.7). This new phrase seems a conflation of the opening strain of the pious theme and what is here recognizable as the closing theme in the recapitulation, begin-ning at m. 92 in the final version (shown earlier in ex. 8.2). Further complicating the texture of Beethoven's thought, this familiar closing theme is found early in the sketching. And the pious theme itself is shown to have emerged gradually, in an intriguing entry marked (not altogether legibly) "2da parte" (see ex. 8.8), a designation that for Beethoven normally means "after the first double bar," though must here refer simply to the second group in a sonata exposition. On the facing page—page 17—the new theme is endowed with function and purpose.

These sketchbook calibrations have yet another dimension, not limited to the linear unfoldings of plot and character. If this adagio has anything to do with the vault scene in *Romeo and Juliet,* it is surely not as representation, in some dra-matic or even narrative mode, of the lightning quick sequence of events in Shake-speare's act 5 scene 3, much less an evocation of the brilliance and nuance of lan-guage in which these events are cast. The unfoldings of plot and character in the Adagio—its formal imperatives—are of the purely musical kind that inform all sonata-like music in the late eighteenth century, impossible of congruence with events in the play. The ironic rhythms, the decisive cross-accents of the charac-ters in Shakespeare's scene are not traceable in the music. Action is here reduced to sentiment, tragedy to melodrama.[15] Finally, we are asked to believe that this Adagio, alone in the quartet, refers to Shakespeare's tragedy. But what of the other movements? Is it only the Adagio that shifts into programmatic gear?

Let us concede that the expressive quality of these musical incidents—above

---

15. "What Beethoven's conception of Shakespeare's play might have been, in 1799, rather staggers the imagination," writes Joseph Kerman, *The Beethoven Quartets* (New York: Alfred A. Knopf, 1967), 36. "Something like this quartet movement, only too probably. . . [Beethoven] felt he was traffick-ing with raw exterior emotion here. Emotionality would be the better word; the piece is full of grand melodramatic gestures." "The result," Kerman earlier suggests, "is not sentiment but senti-mentality, or at any rate, one of the things meant by sentimentality."

EXAMPLE 8.7 Grasnick 2, page 19, stave 13.

EXAMPLE 8.8 Grasnick 2, page 16, staves 7–9.

all, those "painfully demonstrative" ones that Brandenburg notices in the coda—might reveal how Beethoven conjured "the parting of two lovers," and that the sketches merely corroborate Amenda's testimony regarding the envisioning of the vault scene in *Romeo and Juliet*. Knowing what we do of Beethoven's sketchbook probes, or even that such conjurings inspired him to music, can we bring such intimate confidences to play in the discourse of the finished Adagio? Or have we then trespassed on the sanctity of the text, and betrayed the testimony of the composer against his work?

Sketching the Improvisatory

Infrequently among the obsessive drafting of expositions, the tinkering with detail, the notating of isolated *Einfälle*, the laboring at contrapuntal fit, there materializes in the sketchbooks an entry so stunning as to suggest that we are witness to some vaulting conceptual leap. The famous draft for the first movement of the Piano Sonata in D minor, Opus 31 no. 2 (shown in ex. 8.9 and fig. 8.2) elicits that sort of response.[16] "A concentrated shorthand wherein the entirety of this music and the particularity of its structure seem already to have been realized," writes Peter Gülke, who is then inspired to wonder about "the relationship of creative process (Entstehungsweise) to composed-out structure" and beyond, "to questions as to the character of a piece that does not, even in its definitive version, lose the improvisatory, draft-like quality that Beethoven so persistently composed against the fixed components of composition."[17]

In the theater of the sketchbook, the entry appears to have been artfully staged, for it occurs in the midst of some eighty-eight pages of compulsive sketching in the spring of 1802 for the three Violin Sonatas that would be pub-

---

16. The draft is to be found in the so-called Kessler Sketchbook, Vienna: Gesellschaft der Musikfreunde, Ms. Beethoven Autogr. 34, and published as *Ludwig van Beethoven. Keßlersches Skizzenbuch*, ed. Sieghard Brandenburg, 2 vols. (Bonn: Beethovenhaus, 1976–1978), I (transcription): 143–144; II (facsimile): fol. 65v.

17. " . . . was nicht nur zu überlegungen zum Verhältnis von Entstehungsweise und auskomponierter Struktur einlädt, sondern darüber hinausgehend zu Fragen an den Werkcharakter eines Stückes, dem auch in der definitiven Fassung das improvisatorisch Entwurfhafte nicht verlorenging, das Beethoven so konsequent gegen die verfestigenden Komponenten des Komponierens komponiert hat . . ."; in a review of *Ludwig van Beethoven. Keßlersches Skizzenbuch*, ed. Sieghard Brandenburg, in *Die Musikforschung* 36 (1983): 101–102.

lished as Opus 30.[18] Barry Cooper, puzzled as well by the curious location of the draft in its isolation at fol. 65v among the sketching for Opus 30, devised an ingenious hypothesis that identifies the draft as a sequel, seemingly written out of turn, to some earlier entries that yet appear fifty pages deeper into the book, at fol. 90v (shown in ex. 8.10).[19] His argument grows from the speculation that the ever frugal Beethoven, having reached the end of the Kessler Sketchbook, now returned to some pages inadvertently left blank and pressed them into service. This is at once compelling as an explanation of the solitary picture of the draft on fol. 65v, and troubling in its contradiction of a practice commonly observed in which new projects are undertaken with a good clutch of blank paper ready at hand.[20] The turning to an isolated page in the midst of a book otherwise entirely filled does not sit comfortably with the challenge to the mind of a gathering of virgin paper ahead. Still, there are exceptions, and this may well have been one of them.

If certainty of order is not a luxury that this scenario enjoys, Cooper yet wishes to hear the two drafts as related in a manner approaching cause and effect. Although the draft on fol. 65v "gives the appearance of being a sudden inspiration—a kind of written-down improvisation that formed [Beethoven's] very first thoughts on the movement," Cooper writes, "careful examination shows that it is simply a *thorough reworking of the material of the synopsis sketch on fo. 90v*" (emphasis added).[21] The earlier draft is perceived to harbor "several inherent weaknesses that led to it being laid aside, but it was now revived in a different shape with the weaknesses eliminated." The published sonata is then understood as "a model of how to solve several conflicting compositional problems without compromising the essence of the original idea."[22]

One such "inherent weakness" in the earlier draft attaches to the new theme, in D major and *dolce,* that responds to the half cadence poised for recapitulation.

---

18. For something on the dating of entries for Opus 30 and Opus 31, see Brandenburg, *Keßlersches Skizzenbuch,* I: 15–16; for further on the relationship of these works in the sketchbook, see my "'Sonate, que me veux-tu?': Opus 30, Opus 31, and the Anxieties of Genre," in *The Beethoven Violin Sonatas: History, Criticism, Performance,* ed. Lewis Lockwood and Mark Kroll (Urbana and Chicago: University of Illinois Press, 2004), 47–60.

19. Barry Cooper, *Beethoven and the Creative Process* (Oxford and New York: Oxford University Press, 1990), 186.

20. Ironically, Cooper (*ibid.,* 186) takes precisely this view in explaining why Beethoven turned a page before beginning work on the finale of Opus 30 no. 2. And Alan Tyson, in his classic study of Mozart's fragments, has Mozart sizing up "a large expanse of unused paper stretching invitingly ahead . . . awaiting the next burst of inspiration." See *Mozart: Studies of the Autograph Scores* (Cambridge, Mass. and London: Harvard University Press, 1987), 150.

21. Cooper, *Creative Process,* 186–187.

22. *Ibid.,* 187.21. Cooper, *Creative Process,* 186–187.

EXAMPLE 8.9 Kessler Sketchbook, Vienna, Gesellschaft der Musikfreunde, Beethoven-Autograph A 34, fol. 65v.

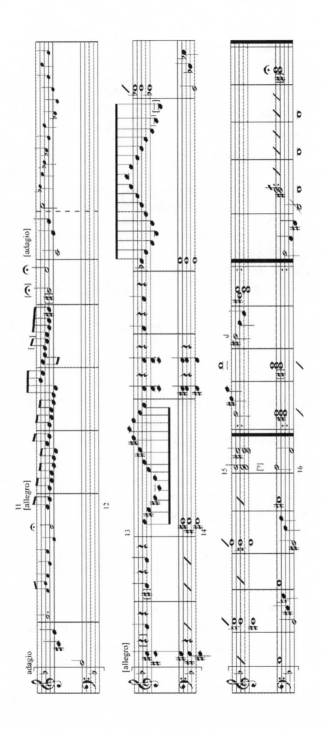

FIGURE 8.2 From the "Kessler" Sketchbook. Vienna: Gesellschaft der Musikfreunde, [Beethoven] A 34, fol. 65v. By kind permission.

We have only an incipit, but its few notes are suggestive of a broadly phrased theme, classically balanced, elegant, courtly. (See ex. 8.11, with a hypothetical bass and continuation.) It cannot go on at great length; the notation in the draft— "e dopo l'allegro di nove"—is clear enough about that. For all its innocence, the theme sets off ominous signals for Cooper: "the slow interruption in D major had to be made more relevant, somehow, to the rest of the movement." Here, following Coooper, is how the problem was solved: "The slow passage at the beginning of the recapitulation in the first sketch could be anticipated, but still appear unexpected, by introducing only a fragment of it at the opening; the problem of key structure could be solved, while keeping the major-key element, by using a dominant chord, A-major, instead of the tonic, for the slow sections."[23] The *dolce* theme, itself incongruent with what was emerging in Beethoven's mind as the main thematic thrust of the movement, is yet salvaged in some of its properties. "Thus," he writes in conclusion, "the sketch on fo. 90v can be seen as the

---

23. *Ibid.*, 187.

EXAMPLE 8.10 Kessler Sketchbook, fol. 90v.

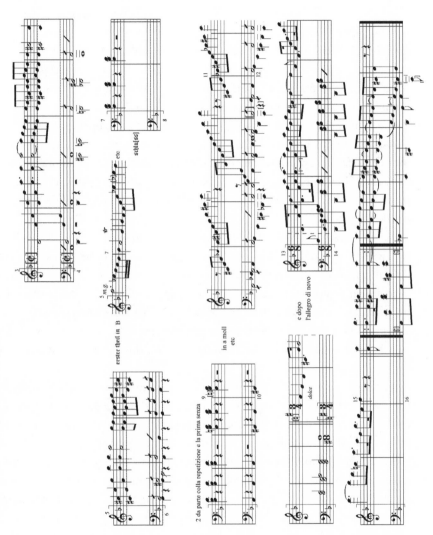

191

main source of the D minor sonata, and the one on fo. 65v as a replacement for it, in which all the compositional problems posed have been resolved."[24]

For all the cunning of Cooper's reasoning from these telegraphic sketches, the stages of thought that he constructs do not take hold. In this view, the *dolce* theme is to be understood as the source from which the opening arpeggiation springs: it is the theme itself (or rather, what Cooper refers to as "the slow passage") that furnishes the basis for this bold gesture "by introducing only a fragment of it at the opening." But the opening of the draft on fol. 65v bears not the slightest resemblance to the motivic substance of the *dolce* theme, nor to its ethos. There is nothing *dolce* about these new opening bars. Then, to hold that the modality of the *dolce* theme (its "majorness") is now transferred to the opening triad in the new draft is to misconstrue the harmonic sense of its gambit. Dominants, major triads by default, stand outside mode. It is dissonance that they are about. To hear in this harmony an evocation of the *dolce* theme is to dismiss as mere contrivance the boldly novel utterance with which the new draft on fol. 65v (and the finished sonata) begins.

Isolated deep in the bass, this solitary C♯ will be understood soon enough as the signifier of radical dissonance. This is not the major third with which the *dolce* theme placates the turbulence of D minor. In the new draft, C♯ is a leading tone, and its position at the bottom of the arpeggio only exacerbates what might be called the structural role of the dissonance. The raised dampers, "se[nza] so[rdini]"—an effect that becomes increasingly thematic in the course of the movement—is inscribed as a grain of its voice, for the arpeggio must be imagined as though in a vault.[25]

Furthermore, to associate the arpeggiated Adagio (Largo, it will become, in the printed version) with what Cooper labels the "slow" theme in D major is to confound the very different temporal functions of these two passages. In stately and measured contrast to the nervous music that it interrupts, the *dolce* theme moves at a new tempo, but it is not demonstrably "slow" in any absolute measure. The opening bars of the draft on fol. 65v are about tempo in a radically different sense. The effect is of a single harmony, reverberating more in space than in time, *senza tempo*. That, surely, is what the fermata signifies and the blurring of raised dampers abets. More than that, the rolling of a dominant in first inversion puts

---

24. *Ibid.*, 187–190.

25. Much on Beethoven's mind in these years, the effect and its technical realization is studied in my "On the Dating of Two Aspects of Beethoven's Notation for Piano," in *Beiträge '76–78: Beethoven-Kolloquium 1977*, ed. Rudolf Klein (Kassel: Bärenreiter Verlag, 1978), 160–173.

EXAMPLE 8.11 Kessler Sketchbook, fol. 90v, st. 11, with hypothetical continuation.

us at once in mind of recitative—an implication of course born out in the recapitulation, in which the fermata is displaced by literal recitative.

The convention itself is worth a moment's thought. In Mozart, the first-inversion triad establishes the new scene, always a shift from the tonal space and formal closure of the scene preceding: Don Giovanni and Zerlina suddenly alone
after Masetto's "Ho capito" in F major—first inversion triad, C♯ in bass; Don
Ottavio and Donna Anna alone in a dark room after the cemetery duet of Don
Giovanni and Leporello in E major—first inversion triad, C♯ in bass; and, most
strikingly, at the aborting of a final cadence in F minor at the conclusion of
the fatal encounters in the *Introduzione*, Don Giovanni and Leporello suddenly
alone—first inversion triad, B♮ in bass. If Beethoven's gambit opens the mind to
recitative and to what it would portend of an imaginary operatic *scena*, it alludes
no less to a music just ended. That is its dramatic function: to clear the stage, to
reset the action.[26] To *begin* a sonata in this way is to evoke the aura of dramatic
action underway. No earlier sonata by Beethoven—and none by Mozart or
Haydn—begins with so radical an opening; the only gambit comparable to it is
Emanuel Bach's Sonata in F, with its fragile opening phrases in C minor and D
minor (see chapter 4).

Perhaps the most intriguing element of Cooper's theory of sketch transference

26. Perhaps the ultimate instance is the striking harmony—again, C♯ in the bass—just before the "Et
incarnatus est" at m. 134 of the Credo in the Missa solemnis, in effect a clearing of the stage before this moment of revelation. For something more on this passage and the sketches for it, see my
"To Edit a Sketchbook," *Beethoven Forum* 12/1 (Spring 2005): 82–96, esp. 87.

is constituted in the sequence of simple chords at the end of the exposition in the draft on fol. 90v, and continuing into the "2da parte." "These repeated-chord figures," Cooper tells us, "anticipate, and help to explain, a similar idea in the recapitulation of the final version (bars 159–168, shown in ex. 8.14). In this final version, the chords seem to have little relevance to the rest of the movement . . . but they can now be seen as a borrowing from this sketch, where, as in the final version, they lead into rapid arpeggios."[27] The ominous, muffled chords beginning at m. 159 are indeed mysterious in origin. Cooper's explanation is of a piece with Brandenburg's notion that the verbal inscriptions among the sketches for the Adagio of Opus 18 no. 2 "reveal a concrete program" otherwise not deducible from the text of the finished work. Wishing us to "understand" these muffled chords as emanating from an earlier sketch, Cooper invokes a field of reference that extends beyond the work to the draft abandoned at fol. 90v. Bearing "little relevance to the rest of the movement," the passage in question evidently gains in "relevance" when its origins in the sketch are recognized. The conceptual provocation of such a view is in its proposal of an epistemological universe in which the internal, self-referential system of the work—in short, its syntax—is disabled. No less provocative, it proposes an integrity of a strange kind: "relevance" is to be sought not in the work itself but in a putative relationship in which the isolated idea, perceived to be irrelevant in the work, is discovered in some inchoate form outside the work. Even if the draft on fol. 90v might be said to figure in some arcane way in the conceptualizing of Opus 31 no. 2, it is the specificity of connection, of the one "anticipating and helping to explain" the other, that should set off alarms. The zealous quest for explanations, as though the *meaning* of such a passage could ever be adduced through arguments laboring toward a proof, is itself suspect.

How, then, might one understand this riddling music at m. 159? Its unique rhythmic cast is only one symptom of what is conveyed at this signal moment in the piece. For one, the moment captures a telling enharmonization in which F minor (toward which the recitative must resolve) is reformulated as a chord of the sixth, a first-inversion dominant whose root is C♯. The trochaic rhythm is heard not as an afterbeat to a final cadence (as in the draft at fol. 90v), but as the beginning of a new paragraph. This is a critical difference in the way these chords are conceived. Surely, the establishing of a root C♯ will resonate profoundly with the very pitch from which the draft on fol. 65v unfolds. These first-inversion tri-

---

27. Cooper, *Creative Process*, 183.

ads, then, invoke the opening arpeggiation of the draft not merely in self-evident reference to dominants in first inversion, but to the deeper implications of a dissonant simultaneity. C♯, invoked now as a root, is thus endowed with hierarchical eminence.

If this way of hearing the music at m. 159 seems a reach, it will be instructive to recall the opening moments of two of Haydn's quartets, both from Opus 33. The Quartet in C major begins with the bare interval of a sixth, soon enough recognized as the outline of a first-inversion tonic in C. And yet it is the grain of dissonance in the interval itself, an E sounding at its bottom, that is of consequence. To begin this way, in the provocation of such ambiguity, is to set a plot in motion. The moment of recapitulation comes at this E with focused intensity: E, pointedly tonicized, sounds its triad only by suggestion, as a naked fifth (see ex. 8.12), then absorbed in the sleight-of-hand return to C major. The opening of the Quartet in B minor, similarly couched in a sixth, F♯ below D, is of course about other things. But again, the telling moment of recapitulation plays upon the dissonance with which the quartet begins. Here, too, the ambivalence of the sixth is exploited: F♯, now unequivocally the root of a dominant, clarifies the dissonance of the opening D, grating now against A♯ as well (see ex. 8.13). There is a new poignance to these bars because the D, no longer construed as harmonically consonant with the F♯, needs resolution to a C-sharp that comes only at the end of the phrase: if the opening teeters between D major and B minor, the recapitulation sharpens the ambivalence, because the new A♯ both strengthens the cause of F♯ as root even as it allows, if fleetingly, the illusion of an augmented fifth, where D poses as the root of a dominant.[28]

In the final version of Opus 31 no. 2, the dominant on C♯ at m. 159 responds as well to another telling moment, this at the outset of the development which, it will be recalled, begins with a sequence of unfolding harmonies, in gestural imitation of the opening measures of the piece. The vehemence of the downbeat at m. 99, where the principal theme is struck, *fortissimo,* in F♯ minor, answers to a six-four arpeggiation above C♯ in the bass. The deliberate impetuosity of the moment causes an ellipsis in which the dominant is short-circuited, setting in relief the temporal relationship established at the opening of the piece. As though impatient with these languid, timeless arpeggiations of harmonies that seem adrift, the theme breaks in prematurely. Sounded deep in the bass, C♯ is again left disso-

---

28. For a different reading of this piquant harmony, see James Webster, *Haydn's "Farewell" Symphony and the Idea of Classical Style* (Cambridge: Cambridge University Press, 1991), 128.

nant, now at the bottom of a six-four that in a sense can be said to resolve only sixty measures later. Marked by a new rhythm, the music at m. 159 plays out in a remote key the implications of the dissonance at the opening of the movement. (Example 8.14 attempts a synoptic view of these cardinal moments.)

We return once again to Cooper's claim for the draft on fol. 65v that while it "gives the appearance of being a sudden inspiration—a kind of written-down improvisation—. . . careful examination shows that it is simply a thorough reworking of the material of the synopsis sketch on fo. 90v." Whether a sketch, in its appearances on the page, can be read to embody the improvisatory is a matter worthy of Cooper's skepticism. The temptation to so read it is encouraged by the improvisatory disposition of the music itself. Its opening idea may mean to signify the improvisatory, and to script a performance that engages in the mannerisms of improvisation, but it does not follow that such an idea was therefore conceived in the spontaneous grip that we come to associate with the improvisatory. And yet another look at this remarkable page puts us in mind of the converse: whether or not the musical idea might *signify* the improvisatory, the conceiving of it must at some point engage that spontaneity of mind through which *idea* is conceived. The sketchbook, for Beethoven, is commonly the site of such improvisations. That is its purpose: to encourage the spontaneity of idea, even on the grandest scale.

"You should have a small table beside the pianoforte," Beethoven instructs his pupil, the Archduke Rudolph, in a well-known letter of 1823. "When sitting at the pianoforte you should jot down your ideas in the form of sketches. In this way not only is one's imagination [*Phantasie*] stimulated but one learns also to pin down immediately the most remote ideas."[29] Often cited for what it tells us about the setup of the workshop, Beethoven's advice yet suggests something about the way in which works are conceived. For Beethoven, composition begins in the quest for the remote idea. Sketching, whatever else it may be about, extends the inner ear in seeking out the inaccessible. The act of writing seeks to ground the idea, to bring it into the cognitive world. And while Beethoven suggests, in the very next sentence, that his pupil "also compose without a pianoforte," there is no question that for Beethoven the piano is at once a sounding-board for these "most remote ideas" and an intermediary between abstract thought and written sign.

---

29. " . . . gleich am Klavier ihre Einfälle flüchtig kurz niederzuschreiben, hiezu gehört ein kleines Tischgen an's Klavier, durch d.g. wird die Phantasie nicht allein gestärkt, sondern man lernt auch die entlegensten Ideen augenblicklich festhalten." *Ludwig van Beethoven: Briefwechsel Gesamtausgabe*, V (Munich: G. Henle Verlag, 1996), 165; Anderson, *Letters of Beethoven*, 1056.

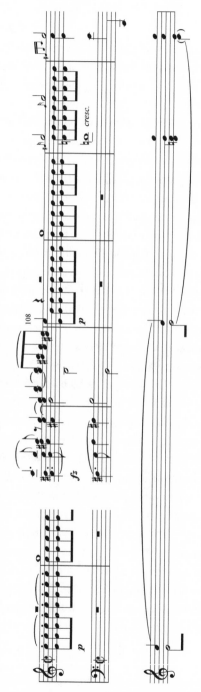

EXAMPLE 8.12 Haydn, String Quartet in C major, Opus 33, No. 3, first movement.

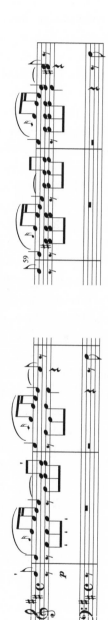

EXAMPLE 8.13 Haydn, String Quartet in B minor, Opus 33, No. 2, first movement.

EXAMPLE 8. 14 Beethoven, Opus 31, no. 2, first movement: a synoptic view.

Indeed, it is difficult to imagine that the draft on fol. 65v did not emerge from an encounter between Beethoven and his instrument—more pointedly, from a testing of this cavernous sonority, knees pressed against the damper mechanism.[30] If the draft was intended as a "thorough reworking" of earlier material, we might reasonably expect to find it littered with the graphic evidence of much alternative thinking, of false starts and puzzling stops. But this draft moves from its incipient C♯ as though in a single breath through to the beginning of the development, with its arpeggiations recharted through alien territory, and on to this most theatrical of recapitulations, in which the cardinal dissonances propounded at the outset are here reengaged.

The feel of the draft depicts a discursive process that is to some extent deceptive. It is not entirely clear whether, for one, the downbeat at the beginning of staves 7–8 was to follow precipitously from the fermata at the end of the previous system. Here, the transcriptions by Brandenburg and Cooper (and even Nottebohm[31]) seem misleadingly coherent. These three arpeggiations entered on staves 5–6, whatever would follow from them, suggest an improvisatory groping toward some undefined tonal outpost. The music breaks off on a six-four on B♭—not, that is, on the telling C♯ of the final version. The draft does not tell us whether Beethoven yet had in his ears the radical ellipsis that would set the development in motion—presumably in E♭ minor, to follow the implications of the six-four on B♭. It does reveal that the powerful connection between the new trochaic phrase at m. 159 and this earlier six-four—the isolation of C♯ in the bass and its further elaboration—would occur to Beethoven only in some subsequent phase in the evolution of the work.

Evidence for these final stages, either in draft or in the autograph score of the finished sonata, has not survived. And so the draft on fol. 65v remains the final

---

30. Owen Jander suggests that the pedal indications in the opening measures constitute Beethoven's "first venture into the realm of composition for a fortepiano with a damper pedal" and further, that "Beethoven's first published specification for the use of the modern damper pedal was at the service of ever-controversial 'musikalische Mahlerei.'" See his "Genius in the Arena of Charlatanry: The First Movement of Beethoven's 'Tempest' Sonata in Cultural Context," in *Musica Franca: Essays in Honor of Frank D'Accone,* ed. Alyson McLamore, Irene Alm, and Colleen Reardon (Stuyvesant, N.Y.: Pendragon Press, 1996), 585–630, esp. 594. But the distinction in terminology is rather more complicated than Jander lets on. Beethoven used "senza/con sordino" in the sketchbooks until the winter of 1803–1804, among sketches for the "Andante favori" (WoO 57) on page 121 of the sketchbook Landsberg 6. See Kramer, "On the Dating of Two Aspects," 164.

31. Gustav Nottebohm, *Ein Skizzenbuch von Beethoven* (Leipzig: Breitkopf und Härtel, [1865]), 27–28.

written witness to the conceiving of a work that is commonly understood to embody a new conceptual mode in Beethoven's thought. If its uncanny isolation in the sketchbook encourages an overly romantic picture of the birth of a bold new concept of sonata, it yet documents that process which Beethoven is at pains to describe to the Archduke, a consequence of Beethoven's efforts to get in writing those aspects of the conception that would come clear only through the visceral act of playing—whether at the keyboard or in the mind. In this view, the act of writing is itself an improvisational reach for the idea that needs to be coaxed from the hidden recesses of the imagination.

How then to explain the lucidity with which those march-like chords beginning at m. 159 are heard and notated in this synopsis? The rhythm of the passage, strikingly unprepared, and without further issue in the sonata, is yet imagined in the draft precisely as it will go in the final version. Its position in the narrative is fixed with chilling exactitude evidently before much of the thematic material had been composed. There is no predicting how things will turn out. Whatever its weight in the dynamics of the finished sonata, this moment of rhythmic counterpoise seems as essential to the conceiving of the sonata as does the C♯ with which it all begins. What matters, of course, is how the passage is to be heard in the sonata, and not how it had been heard to formulate itself in the disarray of the sketchbook. Our sightings in the sketchbooks are as immaterial to an understanding of the work in itself as they are inestimable in the inquiry how this music came to be conceived.

If the appeal of the improvisatory is keenly felt in this sonata, the apparent improvisatory mode of the draft on fol. 65v puts before us the larger question of spontaneity: how to distinguish the symptoms of the improvisatory act—improvisation as a way of bringing thought into the world—from the gestural figures of improvisation that conspire within the substance of the work itself. To come to an understanding how such figures as the opening arpeggio mean to signify improvisation, whatever the premeditations antecedent to their composition, is to get at this distinction. Yet even this apparently simple distinction has its troubling, contradictory aspect. For while the draft might itself seem clear-cut evidence of the power of improvisation in the conceiving of the work—imagine in its place a taped recording of the event—it yet hints strongly of an urge to manipulate a process that is beyond conscious control, even if the immediate intent is to capture in writing the traces of unmediated thought. On the evidence of its fleet, synoptic vision of a complete movement, the draft suggests the power of improvisation—"intoxicated improvisation," Kundera would call it—to generate rich structure. Simultaneously, the opening arpeggio is conceived as a tropological figure that means to represent—to gather within itself, as synecdoche—the idea of the improvisatory. The opening figure signifies the spontaneous process of improvisation. The thematic substance of the work is thus personified, inhabited by the figural spirit of its creator, who insinuates himself into the drama of its conception.

And yet this distinction drawn between the phenomenon of the draft as itself an improvisation and the gestures within it as so many signifiers of an idealized improvisation is continually slipping out of focus. By some understanding, the two phenomena are bound up in one another. The act of writing means to emulate the spontaneity of thought. But the predisposition of Beethoven's mind to think about music in a certain way impedes the kind of spontaneity that Kundera apprehends in the novels of Diderot and Sterne. The improvisatory, now prefigured in the topoi of style, gains in coherence what it forfeits in spontaneity.

The opening bars in the new draft further redefine the relationship between performer and text, and it is worth pondering how that is so. Consider again Emanuel Bach's prescription for the creation of a fantasia in the final paragraph of his *Versuch*. The text of the piece is meant to be exemplary, a final *Probestück* in the advance of the performer to the realm of spontaneously creative thought. Following a script, reading the text of the work, the player impersonates the composer improvising, reenacting the spontaneity of its creation.

On the face of it, there would be no reason to think that in the relationship established between performer and text, Opus 31 no. 2 should differ in this regard. And yet it does. In signifying the moment of its creation, its opening bars ask of the performer that the wonder of *Ursprung* be captured—not, that is, read as a text practiced in the mimesis of improvisation, but performed as though this music were only now conceived, as if it had previously not existed. The imposture is compounded, for the performer must enact whatever is appropriate to this process of "finding" the tone of the work. If Emanuel Bach's fantasies, and Mozart's, begin on tonics and play within the ground rules of genre, Beethoven's sonata begins a step earlier in the process. Genre is reinvented. That is its point.

Somewhere in all of this lies the essential difference between the drafts on fols. 65v and 90v. When Beethoven writes that snippet of phrase marked *dolce,* he is signaling a formal intrusion that brings to mind another passage in D major. In the midst of the development in the first movement of the Symphony in F♯ minor ("Farewell"; Hob. I:45; 1772), Haydn has the music break off on a dominant in B minor, following thirty-five bars of relentless, aggressive attack, all in *fortissimo.* What follows is a new theme, marked *piano*—if *dolce* were in Haydn's lexicon in 1771, here might be the place for it. The tempo is unchanged, but the effect is as if to placate the furies that have been driving this impetuous music.[32] (See ex. 8.15.) The tune circles idly around itself, summoning effort enough to move toward a fragile diminished seventh that denotes a weak dominant ninth in F♯ minor. A solitary D, now dissonant, is left hanging for two bars. The recapitulation begins with a furious downbeat, fortissimo, in F♯ minor.

The placement of Beethoven's *dolce* theme, and his instruction how it will end ("e dopo l'allegro di novo") echos the central episode in Haydn's fractious symphony.[33] The resonance is evident as well in the powerful downbeat arpeggiation with which Haydn's symphony and the draft on fol. 90v begin. If there is some connection here, even if its points of contact are more subliminal than overtly conscious, it is emphatically severed in the draft on fol. 65v. To get at this essential difference from another angle: if the *dolce* theme hints at antecedents and models, and further denotes a strategy for mapping an eccentric, highly charged sonata movement, the draft on fol. 65v, impatient with stratagems, frees itself from any *a priori* plan as to how this will turn out, and pointedly so of the plan at fol. 90v. If any residue of Haydn's symphony survived in the draft on fol. 65v, it might be heard at the outburst of the principal theme in F♯ minor early in the development, as though drawn subconsciously to Haydn's extreme key and the ferocity of the music that it sets loose.[34] Implicitly inscribed in the C♯ with which the draft opens,

---

32. This famous passage and the history of commentary on it are exhaustively studied in James Webster, "The D-Major Interlude in the First Movement of Haydn's "Farewell" Symphony," in *Studies in Musical Sources and Styles: Essays in Honor of Jan LaRue*, ed. Eugene K. Wolf and Edward H. Roesner (Madison: A-R Editions, Inc., 1990), 339–380. See also Webster's *Haydn's "Farewell" Symphony*, esp. 39–45, in a section aptly titled "The D-major interlude and the irony of melody."

33. Webster, "The D-Major Interlude," 380, referring to the "new" theme in E minor in the first movement of the Eroica Symphony, concludes that "although there is no evidence that Beethoven knew the Farewell, the popularity of Haydn's unique work and these striking similarities at least suggest the possibility of actual compositional stimulus." The famous anecdote relating the curious circumstances that motivated the last movement was published in the *Allgemeine Musikalische Zeitung* of 2 October 1799. The symphony was published in score by Le Duc in a collection whose publication was announced in the *Journal Général de la Littérature française* for August/September 1802, and in parts several times in the 1780s. See Anthony van Hoboken, *Joseph Haydn. Thematisch-bibliographisches Werkverzeichnis* (Mainz: B. Schott's Söhne, 1957), I: 52–56. Joseph Kerman suggests that the first movement of Haydn's symphony may have been in Beethoven's ears during the composition of the Piano Quartet in E♭ (WoO 36; 1785), and of the somewhat later draft for a Sinfonia in C minor (Hess 298), which "appears to show clear signs of its impact." See his "Beethoven's Minority," in *Haydn, Mozart, & Beethoven: Studies in the Music of the Classical Period*, ed. Sieghard Brandenburg (Oxford: Clarendon Press, 1998), 151–173, esp. 155.

34. "[T]he Farewell is the only known eighteenth-century symphony in that key," writes Webster, *Haydn's "Farewell" Symphony*, 3. Beethoven never wrote a work in F♯ minor. The only other well-known repertory work in that key is Haydn's String Quartet in F♯ Minor, Opus 50 no. 4. Emanuel

F♯ minor is an ultimate destination, however deeply lodged in the subconscious, and so its coupling with Haydn's symphony is as striking as it is speculative.

This probing of antecedents, of inspirations, returns us to Shakespeare, whose *Tempest* has been invoked in the naming of Beethoven's sonata ever since Anton Schindler recalled for us his conversation with Beethoven on the meaning of Opus 31 no. 2 and Opus 57. "Lesen Sie nur Shakespeare's Sturm," Beethoven is said to have replied—just read Shakespeare's *Tempest*—when Schindler asked after the "meaning" of the two sonatas.[35] Conceding, against all odds, the veracity of Schindler's testimony—allowing that such a conversation actually happened—only brings into focus the deeper aesthetic issues that Beethoven's alleged response would elicit as evidence that might bear on an understanding of Opus 31 no. 2, for without a cross-examination of the circumstances under which Schindler's question was asked and an answer formulated, we are without the slightest clue as to Beethoven's intentions in replying as he did. Was the answer seriously proffered, or pulled out of thin air to rebuff the irritating Schindler? Does it—*could* it—accurately reflect Beethoven's thought during the composition of these sonatas? Beethoven invoked Shakespeare's *Tempest* only after the fact—considerably after, because Schindler seems not to have been on intimate terms with Beethoven until 1822, when entries in his hand first appear in the conversation books.[36] Should we take this, then, as an invention *ex post facto* in recognition of some coincidental similarity of theme, of plot, of temperament? The questioning continues. We can be certain only that answers will not be forthcoming.[37]

Bach's Freie Fantasie fürs Clavier in F♯ minor (1787), in its reworking for keyboard and violin ("C. P. E. Bachs Empfindungen"), remained unpublished until Arnold Schering's edition of 1938 (Leipzig: C. F. Kahnt), the Fantasie in its original version, until Alfred Kreutz's edition of 1950 (Mainz: B. Schott's Söhne; London: Schott & Co.); there is no evidence that Beethoven knew manuscript copies of either work.

35. For a study of the anecdote and its repercussions, see Theodore Albrecht, "Beethoven and Shakespeare's *Tempest:* New Light on an Old Allusion," in *Beethoven Forum* 1 (1992): 81–92. Albrecht then proposes that Beethoven's troubled relationship with his brother Carl around the time of the composition of Opus 31 and "the tempestuous situation in his own life" (91) is mirrored in the relationship between Prospero and his brother Antonio in Shakespeare's play. How is this manifest in the music? We are not told.

36. See, for one, Barry Cooper, ed., *The Beethoven Compendium* (London: Thames and Hudson, 1991), 29, 52.

37. For a richly challenging study that explores "the subjectivity of primitive encounter as one of the horizons of meaning for Beethoven's 'tempestuous' sonatas" (47), see Lawrence Kramer, "Primitive Encounters: Beethoven's 'Tempest' Sonata, Musical Meaning, and Enlightenment Anthropol-

EXAMPLE 8.15 Haydn, Symphony in F# minor, Hob. I:45, first movement, mm. 102–115, 132–145.

205

The Limits of Improvisation

Kundera recalls his first reading of Diderot's *Jacques le fataliste*, "delighted by its boldly heterogeneous richness, where ideas mingle with anecdote, where one story frames another; delighted by a freedom of composition that utterly ignores the rule about unity of action." He ponders again this opposition of improvisation and composition. "Is this magnificent disorder the effect of admirable construction, subtly calculated, or is it due to the euphoria of pure improvisation? Without a doubt, it is improvisation that prevails here," Kundera decides, and in so doing, comes perilously close to confusing the way in which the work was created with the aesthetic mode in which it was conceived. But, he continues, "the question I spontaneously asked showed me that a prodigious architectural potential exists within such intoxicated improvisation, the potential for a complex, rich structure that would also be as perfectly calculated, calibrated, and premeditated as even the most exuberant architectural fantasy of a cathedral was necessarily premeditated."[38] Wrestling with the paradox of "rich structure" as at once "perfectly calculated, calibrated, and premeditated" and yet the product of "such intoxicated improvisation," Kundera seems here to efface the differences between them.

It is a great temptation to invoke Kundera's eloquence against all my circumlocutions around Haydn's *Creation* and Beethoven's Sonata in D minor. And yet it might be claimed that much of Haydn's music, and indeed much of Emanuel Bach's, displays this "magnificent disorder" as a symptom of the improvisational mode that Kundera detects in Diderot and Sterne. In the *Vorstellung des Chaos,* Haydn enacts what I proposed (at the end of chapter 7) as a meta-improvisation: an improvisation that is itself a commentary on the creative act as improvisatory. It is an adventure, a lively engagement with mind and sensibility. The disorder is metaphoric. For the early Romantics—for Beethoven, in the opening bars of Opus 31 no. 2—the improvisatory acquires aesthetic allure: the music simulates what it wishes to imagine as the spontaneity of creation. The creative act, now self-conscious, is sanctified, mystified, romanticized. The "art of complex and

---

ogy," in *Beethoven Forum* 6 (1998): 31–65. Kramer's association of Beethoven's sonata with Joseph Vernet's "Tempête au Clair de Lune" is drawn from Jander's "Genius in the Arena of Charlatanry: The First Movement of Beethoven's 'Tempest' Sonata in Cultural Context," 585–630. Neither Jander nor Kramer attach any credibility to the Schindler anecdote, and yet the generalized idea of "tempest" as an aesthetic trope is central to both essays. Does a hearing of Beethoven's sonata gain from this coupling, for which there is really no external evidence?

38. Kundera, *Testaments Betrayed*, 19–20.

rigorous composition" that Kundera claims for the novel of the nineteenth century is evident here as well. The improvisatory in the sonata is in some sense calculated, even if the written evidence for its calculus survives only in a fugitive draft in a sketchbook.

In his *Creation,* Haydn views the creative act through a piercing lens. Grounded in a profoundly human irony, it looks the Creator straight in the eye, unflinchingly. Haydn takes us by the hand and entrusts to us the courage, and the wit, to *make* something. In 1792, he took Beethoven more literally by the hand, guiding his studies in strict counterpoint and no doubt much else.[39] Decades later, Beethoven will compose a *Vorstellung des Chaos* that would forever alter the moral landscape. The opening pages of the Ninth Symphony play out with uncanny fidelity the romance that Schenker wished too fervently to hear in Haydn's music: "the first vibrations and movements, the first stirrings of dark forces, the coming into being . . . "[40] The bracing wit and optimism of Haydn's Chaos here concedes to the stern purpose of Beethoven's Hegelian heroism, and to the tragic vision that it portends.

Benjamin's death mask returns. The finality of text smothers the enlivening process through which the work is conceived. For the author, the process is charged with a meaning that may be sublimated in the work, or suppressed and denied. That slender vestige of a *dolce* theme, abandoned in the draft for a sonata in D minor, figures here, even in its faint echoing of Haydn's Symphony in F♯ minor. So, too, does that openly devotional theme, newly discovered late in the composition of Adagio of Opus 18 no. 1, worked up to a position of audible prominence in the movement, and abruptly abandoned in the sketchbook. This is a personal matter, internal to the author, and it is the demanding task of criticism to detect the signs of such private dialogue in a text that by aesthetic rule must conceal them. Expeditions such as ours, in search of the merest traces of evidence of the before-the-work, may help to illuminate how it happened that

39. The counterpoint studies with Haydn are reproduced and studied in Alfred Mann, *The Great Composer as Teacher and Student: Theory and Practice of Composition* (New York: Dover Publications, 1994), 65–74, 87–141.

40. Heinrich Schenker, "The Representation of Chaos from Haydn's *Creation,*" 97. In a sense, the opening bars of the Ninth Symphony echo the opening bars of Opus 31 no. 2: the bare fifth on A will be heard soon enough as a dominant, while the conspicuously absent C♯ in the bass will sound only when the passage is recalled at the outset of the finale. On this latter point, see my "Between Cavatina and Ouverture: Opus 130 and the Voices of Narrative," in *Beethoven Forum* 1 (1992): 170.

Beethoven clung with such tenacity to these sketchbooks long after their workaday relevance for the act of composition had past.[41] The sketchbooks belong to the intimate history of the work. They constitute an intensely private journal that Beethoven was at pains to preserve, both as a protection against public scrutiny and as an assurance that this inscrutable history might yet survive.

---

41. "He preserved them with the same obsession that other composers have destroyed theirs, moving them from one apartment to the next over a period of thirty-five years," writes Douglas Johnson in *The Beethoven Sketchbooks* (3). By simple count of the entries in that book, the repertory comprises thirty-three large-format sketchbooks, thirty-seven "pocket" sketchbooks, a very large portfolio of miscellaneous work papers assembled from roughly 1785 until 1798, and in addition, a good many independent sketch leaves and drafts in score.

PART IV

*Beethoven:
Confronting the Past*

CHAPTER 9

Cadenza Contra Text: Mozart in Beethoven's Hands

Mocking the uneasy composure of Mozart's Concerto in D Minor through a diction and a posture alien to Mozart, the cadenza (ex. 9.1) threatens to dismember its host. The tunes are Mozart's, but the touch, the rhetoric, is emphatically Beethoven's. Manifesto-like, these opening measures insinuate themselves into the concerto, infiltrating the text.

Frequently played, Beethoven's cadenzas (there is one for the finale as well) have entered the repertory in their own right. They follow ineluctably from the cadential six-four, feigning continuation of Mozart's text. Critical reception has been ambivalent.[1] To anyone inclined to such thoughts, there is the lingering sense that the cadenza, even in the fact that it exists, poses a threat to the integrity of the concerto. By the conventions that govern practice, we understand that Beethoven can have intended no such malicious tampering with Mozart's text. All the same, the dedicating of the cadenza—of any cadenza—to the permanence of written record, the act of writing it down, constitutes in itself a violation of the rule, for now the cadenza intrudes into the workings of the concerto and assumes a textual presence that the conventions of the genre seem to disallow.

---

1. The estimable Franz Kullak, whose sense for textual integrity and whose profound knowledge of the Beethoven concertos was probably unequaled in the late nineteenth century, tucked the cadenzas away in the *Anhang* to his edition of the Concerto (Leipzig, 1884), favoring cadenzas by Johann Nepomuk Hummel in the text proper. Published as early as 1836 in the *Wiener Zeitschrift für Kunst, Literatur und Mode,* Beethoven's cadenza for the first movement failed to catch public attention until sanctioned in the Breitkopf and Härtel *Gesamtausgabe* in 1864. Friedrich Blume, giving the Beethoven cadenzas in the appendix for the Eulenburg miniature score (1933), praised them as "die meisterhaftesten, die dennoch leider selten benutzt werden"; thirty years later, Hans Engel (Bärenreiter miniature score, 1965; based on the edition of the *Neue Mozart Ausgabe*) more circumspectly wrote of "eine allerdings 'Beethovensche' Kadenz," which he incorrectly believed Beethoven to have written for his own performance.

EXAMPLE 9.1
Beethoven,
Cadenza, WoO
58/1, for Mozart, K
466 mvt. I.

The writing down of cadenzas, whether for didactic purpose or as private *aides mémoires,* is no doubt as old as the convention itself: to write a cadenza is to interpret in some metaphysical sense the call to improvise. The very idea of cadenza is burdened with paradox and enigma. In the syntax of Classical form, the cadenza elaborates an inessential prolongation of the six-four. Ephemeral by nature, its often pronounced imitations of substantive worth—of structural essence—are in the end untenable.

To what ideal should the cadenza reach? Is its improvisatory flight meant to be understood as an integral moment in the text? Could one imagine the perfect cadenza, without which the piece might be said to lose something of its substance and meaning? When Mozart composes the cadenza, must we take it to be expendable in a way that the other composed music in the piece is not? In asking these questions, I want to set aside for the moment the practical concern about cadenzas, and about Mozartean cadenzas in particular, commonly put in some such formulation as: What is the performer to do, two centuries too late, confronting the void after the fermata? This is a question that musicians must ask, but it is here a secondary one.

I

A commentary from without and within, the cadenza, as its name affirms, articulates the structural cadence of greatest weight, and so the music that happens here holds a privileged place. The music seems to stop, but that is illusory. The ultimate dissonance in the work, this quintessential six-four stands for all the others. Its resolution clinches final closure. The cadenza is an instance of shared rhetoric: seeming to part company, the composer and the performer—composition and performance—effect a rapprochement. The inner law that drives the piece and the outer rule that governs performance here move toward reconciliation.[2]

Invoking the embellished cadence at the close, the fermata at the six-four on the dominant signifies a precarious locus at which more is at issue than the com-

---

2. For a recent survey of the prominent theoretical texts on cadenza in the eighteenth century, see Joseph P. Swain, "Form and Function of the Classical Cadenza," *Journal of Musicology* 6 (1988): 27–59. Curiously overlooked here, it was August Friedrich Christoph Kollmann who most clearly abstracted the principles that govern the Classical cadenza, in *An Essay on Practical Musical Composition* (London: "printed for the author," 1799; reprint New York: Da Capo Press, 1973), 22–33 and plates 10 and 11.

petence of the player to enact a role. Oppositions, ambivalent and suppressed, are engaged. That one speaks here of the player and elsewhere of the composer is but one symptom of this ambivalence. It is now the player's piece. The composer puts his music in jeopardy. In the performer, the adrenaline flows faster. Even when the composer and the player are one—Mozart performing his own concerto—the issue is unresolved: the player in the composer is set loose; the composer in the player is seen askance. More abstractly, here is the locus at which the composerly and the performerly (as Wölfflin might have put it) embrace. Engaged in the exercise of textual authenticity, in the quest for the signs of authorship, the cadenza slips away. The piece becomes inscrutable.

Even the earliest of those cadenzas from which Mozart and Beethoven might have drawn a lesson hint at ambivalences in function and significance. Perhaps the extreme case is the cadenza that Emanuel Bach wrote in the Largo of the fourth Sonata contained in the *Probestücke,* discussed in chapter 5 and displayed in ex. 5.1B. It will be good to recall Bach's language here. The player is meant to imitate "the unpremeditated cadenza-making of two or three persons, and at the same time imagine that the one is paying close attention whether the proposition of the other has ended or not. Save for this [unpremeditated quality], cadenzas would lose their distinguishing attribute."[3]

There is a hint, in Bach's gloss, of what might be called a semiotics of cadenza: the music is personified in a mode at odds with the music that precedes it. The cadenza sets itself radically apart from its source. From the shock of the initial C♯ (m. 24), this cadenza in effect rewrites the piece, contradicting and disavowing the obsessive, overture-like music that is its main topic, and defining D major as a tonic no longer. In its ruminating discourse, the cadenza gives the illusion of the improvisatory. And it is precisely this illusory aspect that is itself an obligatory part of the message. The C♯ augurs a bold shift in narrative mode. The cadenza does not partake of the thematic substance of the music to which it pretends a commentary—and that is much to its point. That this cadenza is as well a passage of great poignancy, one of the cherished passages in all of Bach's keyboard music, is perhaps a symptom of how the rhetorical place of the cadenza can be construed—and was so construed—as the occasion for high eloquence.[4]

---

3. " . . . das Cadenzenmachen zweyer oder dreyer Personen, ohne Abrede zu nehmen, nachahme, indem man dadurch gleichsam vorstellet, als wenn eine Person auf die andere genau Achtung gebe, ob deren Proposition zu Ende sey oder nicht. Ausser dem würden die Cadenzen ihre natürliche Eigenschafft verliehren." *Versuch über die wahre Art, das Clavier zu spielen,* I: 132.

4. To my mind, it is a mistake to hold to the categorical distinction between the fermata that stands for an expressive, rhetorical pause and the fermata that stands for embellishment. On the former, Eva and Paul Badura-Skoda, *Interpreting Mozart on the Keyboard,* tr. Leo Black (London: Barrie and

It follows that the cadenza may utter music no less essential and obligatory than what we generally claim for the text proper.[5]

This is a paradox not often perceived. The cadenza, in practice and origin, makes manifest a notion of improvisation. But when the cadenza is composed (no matter to what end), this effectively contradicts a genuine aspect of its improvisatory nature. Its spontaneity is feigned, and so the notion of the spontaneous itself becomes the topic of musical discourse.

II

This obligatory sense of cadenza is now and then manifest in those of Mozart's cadenzas that have survived. Given the fragile nature of the evidence, it would be wise to take the narrowest view of authenticity. Autographs are authentic. Everything else is less good and open to routine suspicion. The famous publications by Artaria and André include cadenzas that have survived in autograph as well, but this must not lead us to suppose that, by extension, each and every cadenza in Artaria and André must have been based, even at some remove, on an autograph text. Conversely, we ought not to assume that the loss of autograph is a sign of inauthenticity.[6]

Rockliff, 1962), 239, remind us of a passage from the article "Fermate" in Georg Sulzer's *Allgemeine Theorie der schönen Künste* (4 vols., Leipzig, "neue vermehrte zweyte Auflage," 1794; reprint Hildesheim: Georg Olms, 1967), II: 226–227(my translation): "The fermata helps to reinforce powerful emotions at points where they reach their climax. . . . It interrupts the melody, just as a man strongly moved may hesitate slightly after an outburst, in order then to proceed yet more passionately." It does not much stretch the imagination to grasp that this explains as well the expressive moment of cadenza, and its cause. In the rhetoric of Classical concerto, the cadenza seems often to respond to just such a moment of climactic interruption.

5. The cadenzas that Bach left for his own concertos rarely touch the profundities of this one. Seventy-five cadenzas survive in a single fascicle, in the hand of the copyist Michel; they are item 264 in E. Eugene Helm, *Thematic Catalogue of the Works of Carl Philipp Emanuel Bach* (New Haven and London: Yale University Press, 1989). Two that come close are again for Adagios, one (H 264/39) for a Concerto in A Minor, rev. 1775 (H 424), another (H 264/42), in A minor, for an unidentified concerto. The elements of dialogue are prominent in both. I am grateful to David Schulenberg for sharing photocopies of these cadenzas.

6. Artaria: *Cadences [sic] Originales se rapportant a ses Concerto pour le Clavecin ou Pianoforte* (Vienna, 1801); André: *Cadence ou points d'orgue* (Offenbach, 1804). For a thoughtful study of the authentic Mozart cadenzas, see Christoph Wolff, "Zur Chronologie der Klavierkonzert-Kadenzen Mozarts," *Mozart-Jahrbuch 1978/79* (1979): 235–246. "So darf mit an Sicherheit grenzender Wahrscheinlichkeit angenommen werden, daß alle in den Frühdrucken überlieferten Kadenzen auf Originalhandschriften Mozarts zurückgehen, auch wenn die Autographe selbst zum Teil nicht mehr erhalten sind" (245). It would perhaps serve us better to take a rather more skeptical view of those instances where the autographs have not survived.

Among those published by André is a cadenza (ex. 9.2) for the slow movement of the Piano Concerto in G Major, K 453, that has survived in no other source. A pensive meditation on its environment, its discourse seems engaged at some intentional remove from the thematics of the piece.[7] Here is a cadenza without the pedigree of an autograph. And yet authorship speaks out from its notes with the composer's eloquence. If the thematic source, rhythmic and intervallic, for this eloquence is simple enough to decipher, it is rather in this suspended quality of discourse disengaged that authenticity is lodged. Seeming to rehear the piece from some privileged authorial outpost, the composer himself assumes a role in the narrative. This is no discourse that even the most adept Mozartean could invent.

In its obsession with certain locutions, pointedly in its plangent central measures (bracketed in the illustration), the cadenza issues an incisive commentary on salient aspects of the principal theme. And then the closing tutti—the telling E♭ in m. 125—seems to echo this very passage: the coda becomes a commentary on the cadenza.[8] Can we justifiably perform the movement without this cadenza, even if the documentary support for its authenticity is weak? To do so would seem to violate an audible grain of integrity in the piece, for the cadenza makes some claim to an obligatory voice in the discourse.[9] Without it, the movement cannot be said to fall apart as though through the excision of some vital structural element. And yet the rhetoric of the piece—a rhetoric innate in the genre—would be palpably diminished. The cadenza seems to take all the license that for-

---

7. K[6] [=Ludwig Ritter von Köchel, *Chronologisch-thematisches Verzeichnis sämtlicher Tonwerke Wolfgang Amadé Mozarts,* ed. Franz Giegling, Alexander Weinmann, and Gerd Sievers (Wiesbaden: Breitkopf & Härtel, 1964)] 626a, no. 50. The authenticity of an alternative cadenza for the slow movement (K[6] 626a, no. 51) is doubted by Eva and Paul Badura-Skoda, the editors of the *Neue Ausgabe sämtlicher Werke,*—Serie V, Werkgruppe 15, vol. 5 (Kassel: Bärenreiter, 1965), ix—although it was published, together with the authentic one, by both Artaria and André.

8. Charles Rosen writes of this final statement of the opening theme: "The initial phrase is used once more with magnificent effect. . . . immediately following the cadenza; until now, each time it appeared it was left . . . not only unresolved, but almost isolated, with a silence that separated it from all that followed. This last time, it melts into the succeeding phrase and is resolved in one of the most expressive, and yet perhaps most conventional, phrases that Mozart could have written" (*The Classical Style: Haydn, Mozart, Beethoven* [New York: W. W. Norton, rev. 1972], 224).

9. Frederick Neumann gets at the issue from another angle: "Mozart's cadenzas, whether written for himself or for others, whether based on his improvisation or independently invented, are often the product of a carefully planned compositional process"; and then, of the cadenza for the first movement of the Concerto in A Major, K 488, written directly into the score: "Strangely, it is the one that sounds most like a spur-of-the-moment improvisation: none of the major themes is cited and the only thematic link occurs at the beginning with a brief quote of a two-measure subordinated motive." Neumann, *Ornamentation and Improvisation in Mozart* (Princeton: Princeton University Press, 1986), 258.

EXAMPLE 9.2 Mozart, K 453, mvt. II, cadenza K.⁶ 626a, no. 50.

mal convention will allow. This friction between the structure of text and the moment of temporal stasis within it is cause for its own eloquence.

By its nature the history of cadenza must be inferred from evidence that is elusive and suggestive—theoretical prescriptions, blurred eyewitness accounts, and an occasional text. That Mozart should have bothered to write out his cadenzas must give us pause. To ask why he did so is to question whether the improvisatory ground rules of cadenza, even in the hands of a composer who would have had supremely little trouble complying with those rules, were perceived as a mask held up at the fermata: a mask that signifies improvisation but conceals composition. The point was not lost on Daniel Gottlob Türk, writing in 1789, who cautions that "a cadenza that has perhaps been learned by heart with great effort or written out beforehand must yet be performed as though hastily sketched, its ideas random and indiscriminate, had only just now occurred to the player."[10] If Türk is here addressing the pragmatics of performance, we might remind ourselves of that earlier paragraph and its footnote (see chapter 6), in which Türk conjures the cadenza as dreamlike: "We often dream through in a few minutes, and with the most vivid *Empfindung*—but without coherence, without clear consciousness—events actually experienced that made an impression on us. So too in a cadenza."[11] If the dream, in its "lebhaftesten Empfindung," stakes its claim to the unconscious, to the irrational, the cadenza, in Türk's provocative metaphor, may be said to capture this quality through mimesis, must feel to the player as though it were dreamed, a state of mind gained only by a certain process of reflection.

Who, one must wonder, is responsible for such eloquent dreaming? The question of agency is worth pondering. In these cadenzas by Mozart, it is the composer who preempts a moment otherwise given to the performer. But there is an

---

10. " . . . eine vielleicht mit noch so vieler Mühe auswendig gelernte oder vorher aufgeschriebene Kadenz doch so ausgeführt werden muß, als wären es blos zufällig und ohne Auswahl hingeworfene Gedanken, welche dem Spieler eben erst einfielen." Daniel Gottlob Türk, *Klavierschule oder Anweisung zum Klavierspielen für Lehrer und Lernende*, (Leipzig: Schwickert; and Halle: Schwetschke, 1789; facs. reprint Kassel: Bärenreiter, 1997), 313; *School of Clavier Playing*, or *Instructions in Playing the Clavier for Teachers & Students*, tr. and ed. Raymond H. Haggh (Lincoln & London: University of Nebraska Press, 1982), 301. The translation here is somewhat modified.

11. "Denn das Ganze soll mehr einer nur eben aus der Fülle der Empfindung entstehenden Fantasie, als einem regelmäßig ausgearbeiteten Tonstücke gleichen." [Footnote:] Vielleicht ließe sich die Kadenz nicht unschicklich mit einem Traume vergleichen. Man durchträumt oft in wenigen Minuten wirklich erlebte Begebenheiten, die Eindruck auf uns machten, mit der lebhaftesten Empfindung; aber ohne Zusammenhang, ohne deutliches Bewustseyn.—So auch bey der Kadenz." Türk, *Klavierschule*, 312; *School of Clavier Playing*, 301 and 498, where again the translation differs somewhat from mine.

unwritten understanding that what he plays here—as *player*—is taken to be improvised. The psychology behind this ambivalence is yet more complex. The concertos, perhaps to a greater extent than any other of Mozart's works, are tied in with a proprietary sense that these things belong to the composer as performer.

How the cadenza might play directly into the larger rhythmic sweep of the piece is keenly felt in the celebrated specimen for the first movement of the Concerto in F, K 459.[12] Its opening measures sustain the thrust of the piano arpeggiations that drive the music hard toward the cadence that signals the end of the exposition and recapitulation (ex. 9.3). The arpeggiations, simple in the body of the concerto, splay out into three real voice parts. The text is subtly engaged. The cadenza, made to seem obligatory, participates in the temporal dynamics of drama.

III

The first three Beethoven concertos, perhaps more so than in other of his works from the 1790s, strain—and in some sense, fail—to measure up to some ideal Mozartean prototype. From the beginning, Beethoven seems to have taken the idea of cadenza as itself a provocation. What we know of the cadenzas that Beethoven had in hand during the 1790s can be only vaguely surmised from the scattered and fragmentary entries in the Kafka Miscellany. The earliest documented cadenza dates from the late 1780s—for a concerto that has not survived.[13]

The cadenzas for Opus 15 and Opus 19, composed a decade and more after the composition of the concertos, violate the formal dimensions and indeed the aesthetics of these earlier works.[14] They range well beyond the limits of the keyboard

---

12. K⁶ 626a, no. 58.

13. *Ludwig van Beethoven: Autograph Miscellany from circa 1786 to 1799, British Museum Additional Manuscript 29801, ff. 39–162* (The 'Kafka Sketchbook'), ed. Joseph Kerman, 2 vols. (London: The Trustees of the British Museum, 1970), I (facs.), fols. 76ᵛ–79ᵛ; II (transcription), 100–101. Intended for the first movement of an unknown concerto in G major, the cadenza moves at once to a statement of a principal theme in the key of E♭ major. The cadenza is written along the bottom of some sheets for the Romance in E Minor, Hess 13, which is in turn implicated as the original slow movement of the missing concerto. On the dating of the Romance, see Hans-Günter Klein and Douglas Johnson, "Autographe Beethovens aus der Bonner Zeit: Handschrift-Probleme und Echtheitsfragen," in *Beiträge zur Beethoven-Bibliographie: Studien und Materialien zum Werkverzeichnis von Kinsky-Halm,* ed. Kurt Dorfmüller (Munich: G. Henle Verlag, 1978), 115–124.

14. These, together with the cadenzas for Opus 58, for the piano transcriptions of the Violin Concerto, Opus 61, and for the two cadenzas for K 466, have been published in facsimile as *Ludwig van Beethoven: Sämtliche Kadenzen. The Complete Cadenzas,* ed. Willy Hess (Adliswil-Zurich: Eulenburg, 1979).

to which the texts of those concertos were bound. To take the most extreme instance, the crabbed, fuguelike vituperations in the cadenza for the first movement of the B♭ Concerto, an exercise in rhythmic obsession that prefigures the finale of the "Hammerklavier" Sonata and even the *Große Fuge,* repudiate the spirit and the substance of the concerto. In the cadenza, Beethoven dissociates himself

EXAMPLE 9.3 Mozart, K 459, mvt. I. (a) Mm. 371–79.

(b) Cadenza, K.⁶ 626a, no. 58, beginning.

from a work, indeed from a style, to which he could no longer subscribe. The cadenza holds no claim to authenticity in the sense that those Mozart cadenzas do. There is no genuine engagement here with the dramaturgy and diction of the concerto. The composer in the cadenza overrides the composer in the concerto.

But the cadenzas for the first and last movements of K 466 (WoO 58) are different, for we must presuppose a reverence for the text that Beethoven might not have felt for a work of his own youth—even if, in the playing out of the cadenzas, some deeper antipathies surface. The circumstances under which they were composed remain a mystery. The manuscripts containing the cadenzas were at some point parted from one another; neither is dated.[15] The cadenza for the first movement has left more of a trail. Its paper, produced by the Kiesling firm, displays a watermark that turns up in a number of manuscripts written by Beethoven no earlier than 1808.[16] The manuscript itself was once in the possession of Ferdinand Ries, and this has led to the notion that the cadenza was written especially for Beethoven's well-regarded pupil. Ries, away from Vienna after 1805, returned in 1808 as a pianist of some acclaim and remained there until 1809.[17] There is a temptation to toss these cadenzas in with those others—virtually all that have survived for the first four published piano concertos and for the transcription of the Violin Concerto—that Beethoven is believed to have composed in 1809. The date itself seems to have sprung up from some general sense about the look of the handwriting in the manuscripts. Whether this in turn engendered the notion that the

---

15. The cadenza for the first movement, once in the possession of Ferdinand Ries, is now at the Beethovenhaus in Bonn; see Hans Schmidt, "Die Beethovenhandschriften des Beethovenhauses in Bonn," *Beethoven-Jahrbuch 7* (1971), item 582, and in the "Addenda and Corrigenda" in *Beethoven-Jahrbuch* 8 (1975), p. 211. The cadenza for the last movement is now at London, British Library, Add. MS. 29803, fols. 1–2b. It was sold to the Library in 1875 by Johann Kafka; see Sieghard Brandenburg, "Die Beethoven-Autographen Johann Nepomuk Kafkas: Ein Beitrag zur Geschichte des Sammelns von Musikhandschriften," in *Divertimento für Hermann J. Abs: Beethoven-Studien dargebracht zu seinem 80. Geburtstag*, ed Martin Staehelin (Bonn: Beethoven-Haus Bonn, 1981), 89–133, esp. 102–103. The supposition that sketches for a "Kadenz zu Mozarts Klavierkonzert (d-moll) KV 466" are to be found in the London sketch miscellany, British Library, Add. MS. 29997, fol. 7—see Hans Schmidt, "Verzeichnis der Skizzen Beethovens," *Beethoven-Jahrbuch* 6 (1969), item 187—is incorrect. When Bathia Churgin, in "Beethoven and Mozart's Requiem: A New Connection," *Journal of Musicology* 5 (1987): 458n, refers to "a sketch for another cadenza to the first movement" of K 466 in the Bodmer Collection at the Beethovenhaus, she no doubt means to refer to the sketch for another cadenza for the first movement of Opus 37.

16. The "rough sketch" of the watermark on the London leaves, shown in Hess, *Sämtliche Kadenzen* [unpag.], suggests the upper edge of the letter K in "Kiesling." The cadenza for the first movement, on twelve-staff paper, shows the watermark "Kiesling" across the middle of the sheet, with the letters "JJ" in a lower corner. On the papers with this mark, see Joseph Schmidt-Görg, "Die Wasserzeichen in Beethovens Notenpapieren," in *Beiträge zur Beethoven-Bibliographie*, 187, watermark 71. Curiously, the cadenza for WoO 58 is listed here erroneously under watermark 60; it was Schmidt-Görg who properly identified its paper in his *Katalog der Handschriften des Beethoven-Hauses und Beethoven-Archivs Bonn* (Bonn: Beethoven-Haus und Beethoven-Archiv Bonn, 1935), item 80. The sketchbook Landsberg 11, with sketches for the incidental music to *Egmont*, is dated "Winter of 1809/1810" in Douglas Johnson, Alan Tyson, and Robert Winter, *The Beethoven Sketchbooks: History, Reconstruction, Inventory*, ed. Douglas Johnson (Berkeley and Los Angeles: University of California Press, 1985), 197; these sketches are partly on paper of Schmidt-Görg's type 71 (although again, not included there).

17. See the article on Ries in *Musik in Geschichte und Gegenwart* (Kassel: Bärenreiter, 1963), XI: cols. 490–494.

cadenzas were composed for the Archduke Rudolph, or whether it went the other way around, the argument in either case was based more on intuition than fact.[18]

As it turns out, the evidence for implicating the Archduke in the early history of these cadenzas had been there all the while. Studying the documents that record the Archduke's *Musikaliensammlung,* Sieghard Brandenburg established that virtually all the cadenzas that have survived for Opera 15, 19, 37, for the piano version of Opus 61, and for K 466 (sixteen cadenzas in all) bear inventory inscriptions either in the Archduke's hand or in the hand of Joseph Anton Ignaz Baumeister (1750–1819), the Archduke's tutor and librarian from as early as 1801.[19]

Content to let facts speak for themselves, Brandenburg does not dwell on the circumstances that would have led Beethoven to furnish the Archduke with cadenzas for all his concertos (excepting of course Opus 73), and for K 466 as well. Although the Archduke did indeed own several Beethoven autographs, the preponderance of Beethoven manuscripts in the so-called *Rudolphinischen Sammlung* are copies, some even with entries and corrections in Beethoven's hand. But the cadenzas, all preserved in Beethoven's autograph, suggest different circumstances. Whether they were composed with some pedagogical mission in mind or to satisfy the Archduke's appetite to control an archive of the "complete" Beethoven, cadenzas and all, we do not know.[20] It must in any case now be acknowledged that the composition of a complete set of cadenzas for the earlier concertos was an ex-

---

18. Much of this owes to Georg Kinsky, *Das Werk Beethovens: Thematische-Bibliographisches Verzeichnis seiner sämtlichen vollendeten Kompositionen,* completed by Hans Halm (Munich-Duisburg: G. Henle Verlag, 1955), 36, in the entry for the cadenzas for Opus 15; and to Max Unger, *Eine Schweizer Beethovensammlung: Katalog* (Zurich: Verlag der Corona, 1939), 124–129.

19. Brandenburg, "Die Beethovenhandschriften in der Musikaliensammlung des Erzherzogs Rudolph," in *Zu Beethoven: Aufsätze und Dokumente,* III, ed. Harry Goldschmidt (Berlin: Verlag Neue Musik, 1988): 141–176, esp. 173–175. The two exceptions are the incomplete cadenza for the first movement of Opus 15 (Beethovenhaus, Bodmer Mh 10, SBH 521), which was evidently acquired by Haslinger directly at the auction of Beethoven's *Nachlass* in November 1827, and a "Kadenz zum Rondo" of the piano transcription of Opus 61, now contained in the sketch miscellany Berlin: Staatsbibliothek zu Berlin—Preußischer Kulturbesitz, Mus. ms. autogr. Beethoven 28, fol. 11. Joseph Fischhof, who once owned the miscellany, had access to the *Rudolphinischen Sammlung,* and (as Brandenburg notes) "was one of the first to prepare a copy of the cadenzas to the piano concertos." Neither of these cadenzas bears the inventory signature that would place it earlier in the Archduke's library.

20. The Archduke owned as well a portfolio of ten cadenzas, now at the Gesellschaft der Musikfreunde in Vienna, said to be for concertos by Joseph Haydn. Anthony van Hoboken, *Joseph Haydn: Thematisch-bibliographisches Werkverzeichnis,* I (Mainz: B. Schott's Söhne, 1957), 814, rules out the possibility that the cadenzas were composed by Haydn. The incipits are shown in *Joseph Haydn: Werke,* series 15, vol. II: *Konzerte für Klavier (Cembalo) und Orchester,* ed. Horst Walter and Bettina Wackernagel (Munich: G. Henle, 1983), 200; see further xii, n. 49. I am grateful to James Webster for bringing this latter to my attention.

ercise that had something to do with Beethoven's relationship to the Archduke, for it seems clear that the terms of this relationship were to some degree refined as a result of the annuity agreement signed in March 1809.

If the cadenzas do date from roughly 1809, it is worth noting that they were written at a time when Beethoven had begun to take seriously his commitment to the instruction of the Archduke.[21] One might go so far as to suggest that in them Beethoven sought to establish a theory of cadenza—that they constitute a repertory of exemplars from which such a theory might be extrapolated. This might explain how it happens that there are three substantial cadenzas for the first movement of Opus 15 (even if one of them is a fragment), all from 1809. But the cadenzas for K 466, even if they belong to this exercise, intimate other motives as well.

IV

Consider once again the opening measures of the cadenza for the first movement. What can they tell us about a theory of cadenza, of concerto? By any definition the construct is unusual. Three fragments extrapolated from the ritornello are reconstituted in a bold new configuration that radically redefines the somber affect of Mozart's shadowy opening measures. The notation specifies no dynamics, no articulation. It hardly matters whether the pianist brutalizes the famous syncopations, *fortissimo,* in disrespect of their uneasy deportment in the concerto itself, or cradles them, *pianissimo,* as though contemplating some revered artifact from another age. In either case, Beethoven's notation suggests an over-articulation. The extreme registral gaps, shifting with each measure, only contribute to a sense of what the theorists—recalling Forkel on Emanuel Bach—call *Zergliederung,* a term not easily rendered in English. "Analysis" belongs in its definition, but in the sense of a breaking down into component parts. That seems very much a part of the process here.

In its tonal spread, the cadenza violates the precepts of Classical decorum. The

---

21. It was Max Unger who suggested a connection between the writing out of these cadenzas and the painstaking preparation of theoretical abstracts for the teaching of the Archduke, enterprises undertaken beginning in May 1809 during those chaotic months of the siege and occupation of Vienna, a period not conducive to the true work of composition. But Beethoven did compose: Opera 73, 73, 78, 81a, 84 (*Egmont*), and 95 all date from 1809–1810. Unger expressed his views in a personal communication to Ludwig Misch, who conveyed them in his *Beethoven Studies* (Norman: University of Oklahoma Press, 1953), 176–177, n. 8.

second theme is given in B major, where it is meant to sound exotic and remote. Is this a quality inherent in the theme itself? Do the parameters of a Classical style, and more narrowly, of the concerto, permit an evocation of the theme reheard as though in historical memory? Mozart's cadenzas rarely, if ever, move beyond what could be understood as an elaboration of the true dominant.[22] Beethoven, even in those earliest cadenzas (and fragments of cadenzas) preserved in the Kafka Miscellany, seems bent on radical tonal deflection.

To justify in some functional agenda the role of B major in the cadenza is a routine exercise. What appears as a simple B-major triad, following upon the six-four on B♭, is in effect the ghost of an augmented-sixth chord: B♮ is C♭. But this common relationship is abandoned. The dwelling on the simple triad itself, prolonged for four full measures (mm. 15–18) in which some meditative process of mind is suggested in a carefully notated vanishing act (*fortissimo* to *pianissimo*), dismisses any vestige of appoggiatura in E♭ minor, and lends to B major this distant sense of itself. The restatement of the theme in B minor, tracking the harmony back toward the actual tonic, serves as well to reinforce the exotic sense of B *major*.

The matter is yet more complex, for B major plays out at another remove the very striking relationship with which the cadenza opens. Established at the outset, E♭ major perhaps means to evoke the Neapolitan sixth struck emphatically in the tutti six measures after the cadenza, in analogue with mm. 49 and 54 in the exposition; E♭ is also a prominent area in the development, at mm. 220–231. But within the cadenza, E♭ is cast rather in terms of its own dominant (see ex. 9.4).

These interiors call vividly to mind another such recess—a *locus classicus*—at the great extremities in the first movement of the *Eroica* (see ex. 9.5). The point to be made here is not that Beethoven means to evoke the symphony in the ca-

---

22. This was well understood by Kollmann (*Essay*, 22–23), whose first rule, under the rubric "The Fancy Cadences," prescribes "no other *harmony*, than what may be introduced as a continued cadence or an Organ Point, between the suspending chord . . . and the leading chord." The rigor of this principle is emphatically not abandoned even in the third rule: "The more *novelty, richness of modulation,* and *variety,* a fancy cadence contains without trespassing against the . . . foregoing rules, or without making it too long, the better it is." This implies a certain desirable tension between the sense of the cadenza as a prolonged cadence and the pull of the harmonies away from the dominant. Kollmann's description of an elaborate cadenza from Clementi's *Musical Characteristics or A Collection of Preludes and Cadences . . . Composed in the Style of Haydn, Kozeluch, Mozart, Sterkel, Vanhal and The Author,* op. 19 (London, 1789) is instructive: "the harmony does not admit of the continuation of the first bass note through the whole cadence, and yet the whole is felt as one continued cadence throughout." See further Eva Badura-Skoda, "Clementi's 'Musical Characteristics' Opus 19," in *Studies in Eighteenth-Century Music: A Tribute to Karl Geiringer on His Seventieth Birthday,* ed. H. C. Robbins Landon and Roger E. Chapman (London: George Allen and Unwin Ltd, 1970), 53–67.

EXAMPLE 9.4 Beethoven, WoO 58/1, mm. 13–16 abstracted.

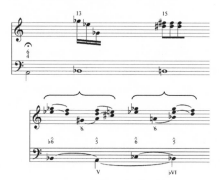

denza, but that the rhetoric of the cadenza revives the tensions normally associated with the extreme dissonance of Beethoven's development. This in turn suggests a misalignment with the place and idea of cadenza in Classical concerto.

It is again to E♭ that the cadenza returns, in a moment of quiet before the rush to the cadential trills. *Zergliederung* is here pressed to an extreme, for this cryptic phrase seems to draw up within itself much of the music of the cadenza in an abstraction meant to stand for the intervallic core of the concerto. Rhythmic displacement only intensifies this sense of the abstract.

And perhaps it is for this reason that the phrase is made to recur at the analogous moment in the cadenza for the finale. The recurrence is no simple echo, even if that were the intention.[23] For it is an axiom of Classical form that the movements of this or that work, no matter how persuasively they may be shown to belong to one another, are by definition self-contained: their "themes" are exclusive of one another; they do not depend on one another for their sense. So that when this phrase, original in the cadenza, is quoted nearly verbatim in the cadenza to the finale, a transgression is committed. Through its repetition in the cadenza for the finale, the phrase is made significant beyond what is permitted in the equation that dictates sense between cadenza and text. Further, the recurrence concretizes the abstruse sense in which the two movements may be said to share thematic substance: the cadenzas make explicit what can only be inferred

---

23. The quotation is ruined in "Kadenzen zu Klavierkonzerten," ed. Joseph Schmidt-Görg, *Beethoven: Werke*, Abteilung VII, Band 7 (Munich-Duisburg: G. Henle, 1967), 47, where the first treble notes in the last quarter of m. 30 are given as a^3 f^3 (middle C = c^1). The autograph has it right, as does the old *Gesamtausgabe*.

EXAMPLE 9.5 Beethoven, Opus 55, mvt. 1, mm. 354–69; winds, brass, and timpani omitted in tutti.

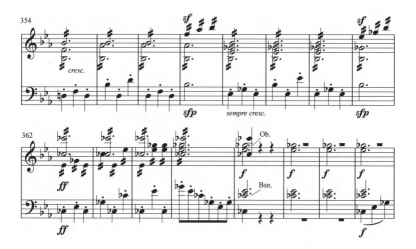

from the text of the work. Through Beethoven's cadenzas, an analytical abstraction is made to work its way into, or just under, the text of Mozart's concerto. Something of the allusive, convoluted process at play here is attempted in ex. 9.6. These intervallic permutations put us in mind of what Carl Dahlhaus, writing of Beethoven's next decade, would call "subthematicism," of a thematic "retreat into latency . . . that can be seen as a sign of a profound change in the concept of 'theme,' which has always been observed in Beethoven's late style."[24] The ramifications of Dahlhaus's insight are pursued in our next chapters, but I want only to suggest that the symptoms of a mode of thematic abstraction are evident in these cadenzas: the Dahlhausian notion of *subthematic*, to the extent that it is manifest here, is all the more provocative in that Beethoven's cadenzas distill from Mozart's concerto, and thereby make explicit in it, a complexity of thematic abstraction that is in some sense foreign to its style.

These, then, are no cadenzas in the Mozartean sense. The continuity of Mozart's discourse is not in question. The music is stopped dead in its tracks. Beethoven contemplates Mozart's text. The process is analytical—a probe into the *Geist* of the concerto. In the cadenza, we hear how the early Romantics might have understood their Mozart, and more pointedly, how this concerto must have reverber-

---

24. Carl Dahlhaus, *Ludwig van Beethoven: Approaches to His Music,* tr. Mary Whitall (Oxford: Oxford University Press, 1991), 204.

EXAMPLE 9.6   Beethoven, WoO 58: some intervallic relationships.

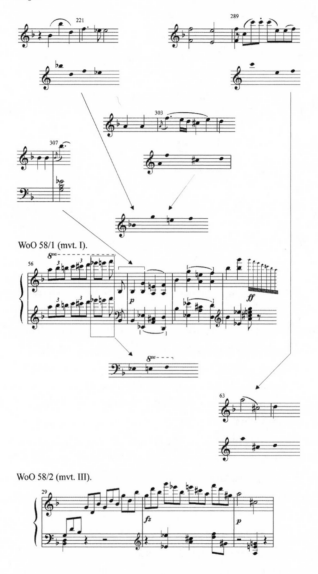

ated in Beethoven: how aspects of Mozart's style, however controlled in the works themselves, exaggerate themselves in Beethoven's mind, and in his fingers. But Beethoven's cadenza is itself no analytical abstraction. It is meant to be played. A performance—the phenomenon of performance, even idealized and imaginary— reifies what otherwise remains abstruse.

V

We shall never have a clear sense how Beethoven, even as late as 1809, reconciled his place in a personal history that may be said to begin agonistically with Mozart. The engagement with Mozart's music is documented as early as 1785, when the violin sonatas published by Artaria in 1781 were taken as working models during the composition of the three Piano Quartets, WoO 36.[25] And it extends to the late music, for we now know that the Kyrie fugue in the Requiem was much on Beethoven's mind during the sketching of the *Missa solemnis* in 1819–1820.[26] In between, Mozart's music—ensemble passages from the great operas, in the main—is copied out in contexts that suggest less a searching for specific models than an exercise meant to establish some deeper accord with Mozartean process.

But the cadenzas are different in this regard. Here, the engagement with Mozart is openly confrontational: Beethoven's notes jostle with Mozart's in this most public of genres. As always, there is a subtext. It cannot be that Beethoven misunderstands Mozart, that he miscalculates the work. Beneath the bluster of Beethoven's attack, one senses the playing out of some deeper antipathy, difficult to define, but surely dyed in this lifelong struggle to conquer the rigorous self-control imposed by Mozartean example. The equilibrium of the concerto—and by extension, the Classical style—is assaulted. Even the conventional signs of Classical cadenza are turned on their heads: the cadenza for the first movement begins with the trill that would signify its close.

It is a simple enough matter to dismiss these cadenzas as an aberration foreign to the style or to celebrate them for their propinquity to the concerto in time and place. But this is to read only the surface of their significance as historical document. We learn from them more of Beethoven's agenda than of Mozart's text—the concerto heard through the afflicted ears of a composer whose style was forged in the aftermath of a Mozartean legacy that had, even in the 1790s, grown to mythic dimensions.

In the end, the cadenza falls away, a foreign agent unacceptable to the host. The text returns to its symbolic fermata, its blank six-four. If these cadenzas do in fact date from 1809, they are coeval with a concerto of Beethoven's own. One might imagine that it was this encounter with the fermata in K 466 that would have led Beethoven to recoil at his own fermata in the "Emperor" Concerto, Opus

---

25. The matter is taken up in chapter 10, footnotes 40 and 41.
26. Churgin, "Beethoven and Mozart's Requiem," 457–459, sketches the evidence for what might be called the Mozart in Beethoven, and provides a useful list of Beethoven's Mozart copies (475–476).

73. "Non si fa una cadenza, ma s'attacca subito il seguente," he instructs the player.[27] "One does not make a cadenza, but attacks the following directly." What the pianist attacks is an obbligato cadenza, conservative to an extreme. The dominant, B♭, is in effect sustained from the beginning of the cadenza, at m. 497 straight through to the tutti at m. 530; there is no moment when B♭ is not literally sounding in some voice.

The retrenchment to a cadenza of Classical scale in the E♭ concerto should not be taken to mean a return of the genre to some classically conceived model. The "Emperor" Concerto is a work on the grandest scale, and the control of its cadenza is only a symptom that the formal tension once resident in the cadential six-four is now to be found elsewhere. Similarly redefined is the dialectic between the composed and the improvisatory. In the grand cadenza-like arpeggiations with which the pianist announces the concerto is hidden an epistemological statement. The verities of Classical form are challenged. Where once the flight of the performer was checked and limited to the single moment where formal syntax can tolerate such indulgence, this social contract is now redrawn.[28] The soloist, now granted the power to engage the process on some new level of narrative discourse, is written into the text as fictional protagonist, a creature of the *composer's* fantasy. What was once a genuine investment in the sensibilities of the performer is sacrificed. The pretense that the performer can be made to sustain the composer's voice is abandoned.

In the cadenza in F♯ minor—the crux, one might say, of the entire set of *Probestücke*—we are drawn intimately into the conceiving of Emanuel Bach's text. To play the cadenza is to live vicariously as *Bach's* ideal player. And this is true of Mozart's cadenzas for K 453 and K 459, where the text is similarly engaged. If we do not in fact improvise, the music yet gives the sense of having been improvised, as though the performer, able to capture the moment of conception, becomes the composer as he himself might have performed the piece. In Beethoven's Opus 73, the game is different. This fictional protagonist assumes a role in

---

27. "Nb. non si deve far una cadenza qui," Beethoven wrote in the autograph, evidently only after a text had been prepared for publication. For an informative note on the two versions of this inscription, see *Beethoven Werke*, Abt. III, Band 3: Klavierkonzerte II, ed. Hans-Werner Küthen, Kritischer Bericht (Munich: G. Henle Verlag, 1996): 50. "Non si fa una cadenza" is the title of a thoughtful essay by Ludwig Misch, *Beethoven Studies*, 171–178. "Thus Beethoven's written cadenzas represent a step forward along the road leading imperceptibly to the abolishment of the cadenza" (176). The idea is explored in greater depth in Paul Mies, *Die Krise der Konzertkadenz bei Beethoven* (Bonn: Bouvier, 1970), which includes a routine synopsis of events in the cadenzas for K 466.

28. The symptom is there as well in the leisurely opening measures of the Concerto in G Major, Op. 58. It is wrong to think that Beethoven engages in such reversals only to shock. Embedded in them is a rethinking of the nature of concerto, and more broadly, of the social dynamics that govern it.

the autobiography of the composer. The cadenza is made prescriptive. In playing it, we enact a script. The player is put at greater remove from the process of the piece, even if the text gives an illusion to the contrary.

To play Beethoven's cadenzas to K 466 is to be enmeshed in a process of quite another kind. The pianist is the player in a bizarre psychodrama. Does he pretend to be Mozart or Beethoven? How does he negotiate between the two? The cadenzas are not conciliatory: to play them is to take up Beethoven's cause. The cadenza dictates how the concerto will go, and not the other way round. In more than a manner of speaking, Mozart's concerto becomes Beethoven's.

Whatever their other virtues, these cadenzas constitute a unique record, embedding as they do the clearest signals how Beethoven construed a Mozartean text, and even how he performed it. Its signals in this regard are not without that ambivalence that is itself a characteristic aspect of the message—a sign, one wants to say, inherent in all notation and in all texts. That Beethoven should have thought that Mozart's suave second theme would sound well in B major is a symptom that hints at performerly decision making. More than that, it is a commentary on the idea of a Classical coherence. In the concerto, B major is an excluded key. In Mozartean cadenza, the tonal spectrum is more exclusive still: B major is an implausible key, and a misplaced locus for any of the principal themes, which in Mozart's cadenzas are relegated to the tonic alone. It is not enough to tolerate B major here on the pretense that Beethovenian cadenza is less restrictive in its tonal play. The cadenza is a function of the concerto. When Beethoven applies the precepts of his own cadenza-making to a concerto that is not his own, he incidentally violates the ground rules of Mozartean cadenza. But the transgression is yet more pernicious, repudiating the Classical notion how a cadenza elaborates a cadence—how, that is, it enhances the structure of the piece.[29]

---

29. Contrast Kollmann's understanding of the structural place of cadenza with a passage from Carl Czerny's *Systematic Introduction to Improvisation on the Pianoforte*, op. 200, ed. and trans. Alice L. Mitchell (New York and London: Longman, 1983), 34–35: "The older concertos (for example, all of Mozart's, most of Beethoven's, etc.) have a prolonged pause towards the close of the last Tutti, after which the performer has to improvise a grand cadenza. These . . . can be extended considerably and the performer can indulge in all conceivable modulations therein. But all interesting subjects from the concerto as well as its most brilliant passages *must* make their appearance here [my emphasis]. These cadenzas can be regarded to some extent as independent fantasies, and . . . the performer can display his artistry here a good deal more than in the concerto itself." In evidence, Czerny gives a cadenza for the first movement of Beethoven's Opus 15. Its 105 measures (counting the actual quantity of the unmeasured measures) violate the spirit and letter of Kollmann's rules. In this it is not unlike the third of Beethoven's cadenzas for the movement, which is yet longer and even bolder in its modulations. While Czerny's Opus 200 seems to have been written in the late 1820s (Mitchell, xii), it may well convey a view of cadenza that was developed during his studies with Beethoven between roughly 1800 and 1803 (Czerny's dates). Czerny actually performed Opus 15 in Vienna in 1806.

Beethoven's cadenzas do not serve the structure of the concerto. They may be *about* structure in some existential sense, and may even enhance it. But they do not partake of that structure, do not participate in its rigorous hierarchical game. Primary evidence of the most vivid kind, they catch Beethoven in a revealing indiscretion. We restore Mozart's text, return it to Mozart. But the cadenzas remain, memorial to an act of artistic impropriety. To those for whom history sails along with the prevailing winds, they are aberrations without consequence, curiosities better left in limbo. To others, they situate a moment in history, a critical one in which the past is caught in Beethoven's lens and a precarious future glimpsed.

CHAPTER 10

Opus 90: In Search of Emanuel Bach

There comes a moment, we would like to believe, when Beethoven turns away from the struggle—for him, the defining struggle—to move beyond Mozart, beyond the dialectics of the Revolutionary years, toward something other. To specify such a moment as a turn, an inflection, in some other direction, seems to me helpful in setting a convincing context for Beethoven's increasingly focused investigations of earlier (and still earlier) music during a relatively silent patch that begins around 1812. The repertory of great final works, beginning with the two monumental ones at the end of the decade—the "Hammerklavier" Sonata and the *Missa solemnis*—invites an historical construct of intentionality, of cause and effect: Beethoven investigates earlier music as a preparation for these final works. To construct a narrative of this kind is to enable the story that *we* want to tell. It is not a story that Beethoven set out consciously to enact. The inquiry into earlier, remote repertories is a complicated business no doubt inspired by inclinations from various sources, but among these the most compelling must have been the urgent need to get on with the business of composing.

I

As Barry Cooper has recently set before us, the 179 settings of "folksongs" in response to the generous terms of George Thomson's continuing invitations, occupied Beethoven from roughly 1810 through 1819.[1] We are coming to realize

---

1. Barry Cooper, *Beethoven's Folksong Settings: Chronology, Sources, Style* (Oxford: Oxford University Press, 1994).

that these settings are of much greater significance, both as works in themselves and as a repertory with its own constraints, than has been acknowledged until quite recently—this, with the help of the exemplary new edition by Petra Weber-Bockholdt for the Bonn *Gesamtausgabe*.[2] The range and variety within this abundant repertory is striking. Alongside occasional instances of the routine are settings of breathtaking originality, passages no less moving, nor less deeply felt than those that we prize in the canonical works: "nowhere else did [Beethoven] transcend the bounds of convention more comprehensively," writes Cooper, and if he overstates the case, it is easy to understand why.[3]

The settings for Thomson constitute a project of a special kind. Content not merely to provide the simple accompaniments for piano, violin and violoncello that Thomson commissioned of him, Beethoven probes the more exotic of these tunes for what they might stimulate of a newly inflected harmonic language. The opening bars of "Save me from the Grave and Wise" (WoO 154/8; shown in ex. 10.1) constitute an extreme case if not an isolated one. The lowered seventh degree, E♭, perched at the upper boundary of the tune, has significance both in its intervallic configuration with G and as a powerful modal determinant. In Beethoven's setting, it is precisely this interval and these pitches that are embraced in the opening measure. The chord of the sixth, its E♭ made at once prominent and ambivalent in its motion to the following triad, cannot really be explained in the conventional grammar of a classical syntax. "Nb: Voila comme on ne doit pas avoir peur pour l'espression les sons le plus etrangers dans melodie, puisque on trouvera surement un harmonie naturell pour cela," Beethoven wrote, at the bottom of the autograph of the song, acknowledging his sense of the exotic in these "foreign sounds" in the tune and the adventure in finding their expression in some "natural harmony."[4] The point is amplified in an entry in the *Tagebuch*, which Beethoven kept between 1812 and 1818: "The Scottish songs show how

---

2. *Beethoven Werke. Gesamtausgabe* . . . ed. Sieghard Brandenburg and Ernst Herttrich im Auftrag des Beethoven-Archivs Bonn, Abt. XI, Bd. 1, Schottische und walisische Lieder, ed. Petra Weber-Bockholdt (Munich: G. Henle, 1999).

3. Cooper, *Beethoven's Folksong Settings*, 210.

4. In rough translation: "Nb: Here is a demonstration that one need not fear for the expression on account of the most exotic tones in the melody, for one will surely find a natural harmony for that." The autograph is at Berlin: Staatsbibliothek zu Berlin—Preußischer Kulturbesitz, Mus. ms. autogr. Beethoven Artaria 190. See Hans-Günter Klein, *Ludwig van Beethoven. Autographe und Abschriften*. Staatsbibliothek Preußisher Kulturbesitz, Katalogue der Musikabteilung, 1. Reihe, Bd. 2 (Berlin: Merseburger, 1975), 178; and Cooper, *Folksong Settings*, 158. The song itself dates from 1812–1813; see Cooper, *ibid.*, 18–21.

EXAMPLE 10.1 Beethoven, *Save me from the Grave and Wise,* from *12 Irische Lieder,* WoO 154/8.

spontaneously even the most irregular melody can be treated by virtue of the harmony."[5]

The engagement with Thomson's repertory gave Beethoven the illusion of a probe into the exotic reaches of a timeless past, even if Thomson's tunes were often merely contemporary approximations of an "authentic" folk music.[6] During these same years, his engagement with a poetics of Greek antiquity similarly sought contact with a remote aesthetic. The *Tagebuch* contains an entry copied from Johann Heinrich Voss's translation of the *Iliad* of Homer in which Beetho-

---

5. "Die Schottischen Lieder zeigen als ungezwungen die unordentlichste Melodie vermöge die Harmonie behandelt werden kann." Maynard Solomon, *Beethovens Tagebuch,* ed. Sieghard Brandenburg (Mainz: v. Hase & Koehler, 1990), 53, item 34. For slightly different translations, see Solomon, "Beethoven's Tagebuch of 1812–1818," in *Beethoven Studies* 3, ed. Alan Tyson (Cambridge: Cambridge University Press, 1982), 227; and Cooper, *Beethoven's Folksong Settings,* 157.

6. On the complex credentials of the tunes that Thomson sent Beethoven, see Cooper, *Beethoven's Folksong Settings,* 58–68.

ven marks off the hexameters with the diacritical accents of poetic scansion.[7] He actually took the pains to set a Homeric verse to music, marked "Hexameter," in the so-called Scheide sketchbook from 1815–1816.[8] The scansion, with its obsessive dactyls, puts us in mind of those poems from Herder's collection *Blumen aus Morgenländischen Dichtern gesammelt* that interested Beethoven at just about the same time. Two of the poems were actually set.[9] One of them–*Der Gesang der Nachtigall,* its autograph dated "3 Juni 1813" —traffics in those complex hexameters that Beethoven was studying in Homer, even as it pursues the *Volkston* immanent in Herder's botanical garden (see ex. 10.2). Herder's trilling nightingale would reappear (now a swallow) a few years later, in the fifth song of the cycle *An die ferne Geliebte* (1816), another song in C major whose prosody is all dactyls and spondees, set in simpler tetrameters. Of the stripped-down harmonies and folklike tunes that characterize both the Herder setting and the Jeitteles cycle as a whole it might be said that Beethoven achieved the studied artlessness, the *Volkston,* that he seemed unable or unwilling to find in the bolder settings of those tunes that Thomson sent him. Paradoxically, the Thomson project inspired a more imaginative investigation into the generating of harmony itself from "foreign" melody, even as it seems to have awakened in Beethoven a new appeal to the essence of a *Volkston* in his original works.

In the context of what might be thought of as a search for a new poetics, it may seem willful to call up the opening phrases of the Piano Sonata in E minor, Opus 90. And yet there is something about these phrases that resonates with those studies in the declamatory, that encourages us to hear the opening phrases as an exploration of a new, narrative mode, not so much songlike in a lyrical sense, but, rather, Lied-like in its diction, and balladlike: *erzählend, sprechend*—speechlike— "im Legendenton," as Schumann would put it in the first movement of the Fantasy some twenty years later. We might then remind ourselves of the similarity between the inscriptions at the top of both movements of Opus 90—"Mit Lebhaftigkeit und durchaus mit Empfindung und Ausdruck" (with liveliness and

---

7. Maynard Solomon, *Beethovens Tagebuch,* 59; for an English text, see Solomon, "Beethoven's Tagebuch of 1812–1818," 232.

8. An entry from the sketchbook is printed in Gustav Nottebohm, *Zweite Beethoveniana. Nachgelassene Aufsätze,* ed. Eusebius Mandyczewski (Leipzig: C. F. Peters, 1887), 328. For more on the sketchbook, see Douglas Johnson, Alan Tyson, and Robert Winter, *The Beethoven Sketchbooks: History, Reconstruction, Inventory,* ed. Douglas Johnson (Berkeley and Los Angeles: University of California Press, 1985), 241–246.

9. Helga Lühning has even suggested that Beethoven may have intended to compose a cycle of songs to Herder texts in 1813. See *Beethoven Werke. Gesamtausgabe,* Abt. XII, Band1, Lieder und Gesänge mit Klavierbegleitung, ed. Helga Lühning, Kritischer Bericht (Munich: G. Henle, 1990), 97.

EXAMPLE 10.2 Beethoven, *Der Gesang der Nachtigall,* WoO 141, mm. 7–12.

throughout with feeling and expression) above the first movement, and "Nicht zu geschwind, und sehr singbar vorzutragen" (not too fast, and to be played *molto cantabile*) above the second—and the inscription, to take but one example, above the song *Resignation,* from 1817: "Mit inniger Empfindung, doch entschlossen, wohl akzentuirt u. sprechend vorgetragen" (to be performed with intimate feeling, yet decisively, well accented and speechlike). In a poetics of *inniger Empfindung* and *Ausdruck,* the porous membrane between song and speech is indispensable. Beethoven's piano, the instrument that seems often a surrogate extension of his being, must simulate a music that captures the essence of both song and speech even as it can neither sing nor speak in any actual sense.

In the bardic opening measures of Opus 90 (shown in appendix 10A) the diction, the accents of the ballad-maker unfold in intentionally repetitive, prosaic iterations. But the prose serves as a backdrop for the ravishingly lyrical phrase that blossoms from the cadence. It is precisely here, in the interstices between these two musics, where speech becomes song, that the singular poetics of Opus 90 resides: the consequences of this concision, its directness of expression, are everywhere manifest in the music that would follow in later years.

II

There seems to me yet another path of inquiry into this music. In January 1812, Beethoven wrote to Breitkopf & Härtel, intensifying his request for the scores of Mozart's Requiem, *Clemenza di Tito, Così, Figaro,* and *Don Giovanni.* "[T]he little [singing] society is beginning again at my home," he writes, and slyly adds: "Surely you could even make me a gift of the things by C. P. Emanuel Bach, for they must be rotting with you."[10] This follows an earlier request, dated 15 October 1810: "In addition, I should like to have all the works of Carl Philipp Emanuel Bach, all of which have of course been published by you."[11] Earlier still, in a letter to Breitkopf of 26 July 1809, the focus on Bach is put sharply:

> I have only a few things from *Emanuel* Bach's keyboard works, and yet some of them should certainly be in the possession of every true artist, not only for the sake of real enjoyment but also for the purpose of study. And my greatest satisfaction is to play at the homes of some true friends of music works which I have never or only seldom seen.[12]

The works in question were no doubt the six *Sammlungen für Kenner und Liebhaber,* published by the author under the auspices of Johann Gottlob Immanuel Breitkopf between 1779 and 1787. Did Breitkopf & Härtel ever comply with Beethoven's request? The inventory of Beethoven's estate, as compiled in an auction catalogue some five months after his death (the *Nachlassverzeichnis,* as it is commonly known), lists each of the Mozart works mentioned in the letter 1812, but there is no sign of any music by Carl Philipp Emanuel Bach.[13] Still, it is hard to imagine that Breitkopf would not have sent the Bach volumes: one must

---

10. "—da meine kleine Gesellschaft bey mir wieder anfängt"; "die *C. p. Emanuel Bachs* sachen, könnten sie mir wohl einmal schenken, sie vermodern ihnen doch." *Ludwig van Beethoven: Briefwechsel Gesamtausgabe,* ed. Sieghard Brandenburg (Munich: G. Henle, 1996) II: 236. See also Emily Anderson, tr. and ed.,*The Letters of Beethoven* (London: Macmillan, 1961), 355.

11. " . . . nebstbey mögte ich alle Werke von Karl Philip *Emanuel* Bach, die ja alle bey ihnen verlegt worden." *Briefwechsel Gesamtausgabe,* II: 163; Anderson, *Letters,* 298–299.

12. "Von *Emanuel* Bachs Klavierwerke habe ich nur einige Sachen, und doch müßen einige jedem wahren Künstler gewiß nicht allein zum hohen Genuß sondern auch zum Studium dienen, und mein größtes Vergnügen ist es Werke die ich <u>nie</u> oder nur selten gesehn, bey einigen wahren Kunstfreunden zu spielen." *Briefwechsel Gesamtausgabe,* II: 72; Anderson, *Letters,* 235.

13. For a study of the various copies of the *Nachlassverzeichnis,* see Johnson, ed., *The Beethoven Sketchbooks,* 567–581, which however lists only sketches. For a relatively complete reprinting of the entire inventory in English translation, see Alexander Wheelock Thayer, *Thayer's Life of Beethoven,* rev. and ed. Elliot Forbes (Princeton: Princeton University Press, 1967), 1061–1076.

assume that there was an ample *Restauflage* sitting on its shelves, for Bach had each volume printed in a run of 1,050 copies.[14] We know with some precision how many were sold ahead of time, for the subscription numbers were published at the front of each volume—and the few stragglers are often identified in Bach's correspondence with Breitkopf. The subscriptions in fact dropped off quite dramatically after the 519 subscriptions to volume 1: for volume 6, there were 290 subscribers. But the numbers in Vienna were fairly constant. Gottfried van Swieten, to whom volume 3 was dedicated, purchased twelve copies of each volume. Artaria purchased twelve copies of the first five volumes, and six of the final one. My point is simply that Breitkopf (as Beethoven shrewdly surmised) will have had copies to spare, even as late as 1812—and that van Swieten, before his death in 1803, might earlier have made copies available to Beethoven.

A sonata in E minor composed in 1785, and published in the final volume—quite possibly the last purely original sonata that Bach composed[15]—has always seemed to me a powerfully suggestive one in the contextual world around Beethoven's Opus 90. In its first movement, terse and *dichterisch,* each of its phrases responds to its antecedent in an overwrought language of *Empfindsamkeit.* (The entire movement is shown in appendix 10B.) The opening phrase seems *about* speech, even as it speaks. The interruption at m. 3, impatient with these measured tones, is abrupt, violent, contrary. In its wake, the measured calm of a new phrase (mm. 5–8), a closed four bars in C major, has an otherworldly quality to it, simulating a new beginning in a remote key, as though oblivious of the outburst that precedes it. The phrase never returns—is not recapitulated—and so the memory of it is yet more poignant than the thing itself. But for all its apparent sense of isolation, a deeper continuity with its environment sounds just beneath the surface. The broken triad at the downbeat of m. 9, not quite the echo of C major that it seems, subtly inflects the harmony. The doubling of E has an acoustical consequence, asserting E as a root in place of C, which sounds now as a dissonant appoggiatura above an implied B. In the devious, chromatic playing out of the exposition, C vanishes altogether, usurped by the close in B minor.

The music that follows the double bar is yet more extreme in its sequence of nonsequiturs: four phrases, each seeming to dwell in its own figural world, with only the most fragile tonal thread tracing the opening in G minor to the half ca-

---

14. See Peggy Daub, the "Publication Process and Audience for C. P. E. Bach's *Sonaten für Kenner und Liebhaber,*" in *Bach Perspectives,* II: *J. S. Bach, the Breitkopfs, and Eighteenth-Century Music Trade,* ed. George B. Stauffer (Lincoln & London: University of Nebraska Press, 1996), 65–83, esp. 75–79.

15. If the first movement of the Sonata in C minor, H 298, may have been composed a bit later, its other movements date from 1766. This and the problem of lateness in Bach is discussed in chapter 4.

dence on the dominant at m. 23. Such music seems intentionally distracted, impatient with the idea of a conventional continuity. With exacting parsimony, Bach picks through his notes as though each were the subject of an intense scrutiny. In bar 15, the isolated B♭, pianissimo, is heavily invested. Its position in the tenor (the only note in the left hand) establishes a second voice against the theme, contradicting the B♮ that is the new tonic in which the exposition closes. Its timing at the last possible moment in the bar enhances its role in the unfolding of this little drama. The B♮, forte, at the outset of the third phrase (m. 19), in turn contradicts the sense of G minor/D minor and its implications of an axis on the flat side of its tonal world, and sets in motion a strange, pointedly archaic two-part invention that gives on to a three-bar phrase of another kind, where the trim clarity of an interval sequence—again, a sharp motivic profile with neither precedent nor consequence—obscures a more complex inner voicing toward the half cadence. In the recapitulation, only the first two bars (excepting a difference in the very first attack) literally repeat music from the exposition. The return of the outburst at mm. 3–4 has an expansiveness to it that passes through C major without the faintest allusion to the phrase at m. 5.

If there is no hard evidence that Beethoven knew this sonata, the opening music of Opus 90, in its open appeal to *Empfindung* and *Ausdruck,* yet resonates suggestively with the sensibilities, the aesthetic world, of Bach's extreme sonata. The elusive trappings of influence in any of its conventional senses are not in evidence, nor is the scent of homage. Rather, one hears in Beethoven's music a subtle trace of the earlier work, of its terse narrative discourse, its disdain for the conventions of form—a disdain not for the overarching principle of sonata form, but for the symptoms that would make of it something conventional. It is this dialectical playing out of a music of sensibility against the formal archetype of sonata that these works share, even if the playing is engaged in very different terms. Beethoven's encounter with Bach is not of the antiquarian sort—a seeking out of the past for the sake of its distance from the present—but rather a meeting of temperaments.

To enumerate all the ways in which Opus 90 differs from Bach's sonata is to differentiate between two styles, two grand and idiosyncratic figures, two epochs. And yet to hear the opening movements of these two sonatas alongside one another is to be struck by evident similarities at the surface of the music and by a deeper affinity, a shared *Geist,* from which they emanate. The brusque juxtaposition of conflicting ideas, the flaring of unexpected, unsustained lyricism, the isolation of gesture, even of tone, sounding the extremes of register, and a coherence that implicates a deeper subjectivity behind the notes: these idiosyncrasies that so mark Bach's music are familiar ones to the students of Beethoven's later style.[16] The "subthematicism" that Carl Dahlhaus would identify as an aspect of Beethoven's late style seems evident as well in Bach's sonata (a work composed in his seventy-first year). For Dahlhaus, it is in the music of this "transitional" period— "the profound caesura that can be sensed in the years around 1816," as Dahlhaus so aptly puts it, even as he problematizes the very notion of a "transitional" phase—that the "lyrical" finds a place outside that "enclave in the classical sonata" to which it had earlier been confined.[17] "A foundational paradox of the late style," this freeing up of the lyrical impulse is coordinate with a "retreat into latency" of actual formal, thematic process: "as the substance underlying the network of relationships grows less distinct, so it retreats from direct perceptibility into the shadows of the 'darkly felt'–as they said in the eighteenth century."[18] *"Dunkel gefühlt"*: these are precisely the words of Emanuel Bach, in his appreciation of the introductory chapter of Forkel's *Allgemeine Geschichte*.[19] Bach meant by them to insinuate the sense that music could convey of and within the grammar and syntax of true language, a sense that is contingent upon the inference of relationships beneath the surface of the music. That Dahlhaus (who does not reveal his sources) might subliminally have associated an idea of the "subthematic" with Bach's efforts to convey the linguistic properties of music is altogether speculative. But it is precisely this kind of association that helps us to enter into the relationship between these two sonatas in E minor. However we think to identify the thematic "process" of Bach's sonata, we are driven to the latency of certain configurations that seem to hover above or beneath the surface of the work, not quite identifiable as intervalic properties, nor predicated on a systematic teleology of formal event. Dahlhaus speaks of a "'subthematic' realm in which threads are tied criss-cross at random, instead of the musical logic manifesting itself as the commanding, goal-directed course of events."[20] If this random tying of threads is only faintly perceptible in Bach's sonata, in Opus 90 the

---

16. Hermann Danuser, in his essay on Opus 90 in the collection, *Beethoven: Interpretationen seiner Werke*, ed. Albrecht Riethmüller, Carl Dahlhaus and Alexander L. Ringer (Laaber: Laaber-Verlag, 1994), II: 26, comprehends the problem under the rubric "Kontrastsukzession und syntaktische Ambiguität."

17. Carl Dahlhaus, *Ludwig van Beethoven: Approaches to his Music*, tr. Mary Whittall (Oxford: Oxford University Press, 1991), p. 203. Carl Dahlhaus, *Gesammelte Schriften in 10 Bänden*, ed. Hermann Danuser, VI: *19. Jahrhundert III* (Laaber: Laaber-Verlag, 2003), 211.

18. Dahlhaus, *Beethoven: Approaches*, 205–206; *Gesammelte Schriften*, VI: 214.

19. See chapter 6, notes 18 and 20.

20. Dahlhaus, *Beethoven*, 204; *Gesammelte Schriften*, VI: 213.

threading is yet more labyrinthian in that certain locutions in Bach's sonata seem to have woven themselves into Beethoven's thought, most obviously in how the opening figures in each sonata suggest inversions of one another. Even the fleeting allusion to C major at mm. 29–32 in Opus 90 seems tied in with that spectral C major early in Bach's sonata. More to the point, in each of these works one senses a coming to terms with the contradiction of the irrational moment—lyrical, eruptive, improvisatory—and the deeper abstraction of musical process.

III

The second movement of Opus 90 is, famously, a rondo. It is not the first rondo that Beethoven composed. Rondo, so named in the score, is inscribed above the finales of ten piano sonatas, from Opus 2 no. 2 through Opus 53, the finales of eleven chamber works, the finales of all five piano concertos (and the Rondo, WoO 6, that was the original finale of Opus 19), the violin concerto and the triple concerto, and in the titles of the two rondos, Opus 51. This is not to speak of a number of rondos from the earliest years, about which more in a moment. The finale of Opus 90 is different. The trappings of rondo are everywhere in the music, but the name itself is withheld. "Nicht zu geschwind, und sehr singbar vorzutragen," Beethoven wrote in the autograph: "Not too fast, and to be played *molto cantabile.*" The sense of the music as a rondo of a certain kind is manifest in the elocution of the theme itself (shown in appendix 10C). Nottebohm, writing of a well-known sketch for the theme, was struck by one deviation in particular: a single note, incomprehensibly missing in the sketch (see ex. 10.3).

> Whoever considers the beautiful melody that emerges as though perfectly formed, and which serves as the basis for the last movement of the Piano Sonata in E minor would be hard pressed to imagine that, as this sketch indicates, the third eighth in the second measure was not originally present. Through the note added to replace the rest, completing the phrase and connecting its subphrases, the melody acquires a feature that significantly contributes to its beauty.[21]

---

21. "Wer die schöne, wie aus einem Guss hervorgegangene Melodie betrachtet, die dem letzten Satz der Claviersonate in E-moll zu Grunde liegt, wird schwerlich vermuthen, dass die Note auf dem 3. Achtel des 2. Taktes ursprünglich, wie diese Skizze zeigt, nicht da war. Durch die an Stelle einer

EXAMPLE 10.3 Beethoven, Opus 90, second movement: sketch, from Nottebohm, *Zweite Beethoveniana,* p. 366.

What is it about this missing note that inspires Nottebohm to such uncharacteristic wonder? If it has in part to do with the notion of *Sangbarkeit* that is at the
core of this music, there is perhaps a purely grammatical reason as well. The G♯
is an unaccented passing tone; to begin a new phrase here, within a tune meant
to evoke simple singing, is inimical to the inner simplicity that the tune means to
embody. More than that, the phrase that is impressed in our minds suggests in its
diction the prosody of verse. Its sequence of dactyls constitutes a full tetrameter.
The missing note in the sketch interrupts the sequence. It is not that the one version is appreciably better than the other, only that the difference is of some consequence in how, in its poetic dimension, the phrase is understood.

If we were casting about for some antecedent to Beethoven's "ultimo pezzo"
(as the sketch is inscribed), seeking not models but rather some earlier work
to which Beethoven's music seems drawn in an affinity of tone and idea, one work
springs to mind, and it is by Emanuel Bach: this is the Rondo in E major (composed in 1779) that opens the third volume *für Kenner und Liebhaber.*[22] (The

---

Pause eingefügte Note, durch Ausfüllung eines Einschnittes und durch Verbindung der Abschnitte
hat die Melodie einen zu ihrer Schönheit wesentlich beitragenden Zug bekommen." Gustav Nottebohm, *Zweite Beethoveniana,* 366–368.

22. Philip Barford, in the course of his fine appreciation of the Rondo in E major, notes "a similarity
of mood between this rondo and the finale of Beethoven's sonata opus 90" in *The Keyboard Music
of C. P. E. Bach* (London: Barrie and Rockliff, 1965), 128, though he does not pursue the matter
beyond this simple observation.

opening is shown as appendix 10D.) In these late collections, the rondo—there are thirteen of them, interspersed in volumes 2–6—achieves a stature and a range of idea and expression incommensurate with the low regard, bordering on contempt, with which the genre was commonly held in northern Germany in the 1770s.

It was the irony of this contradiction that provoked Johann Nikolaus Forkel to sketch a "little theory" of the genre as a preamble to his formidable analysis of the rondo finale of the Piano Trio in G (H 523).[23] For Forkel, the theorizing about genre and the analysis of Bach's rondo are inseparable, for if the theorizing seems merely a ploy to establish the criteria by which such a work might be assessed, it is Bach's music that informs the theory at every stage, and that finally distinguishes the work from all those lesser examples by which the genre had acquired its bad name. The "first rule" for Forkel is that the principal idea ("Hauptgedanke") of the rondo, which is naturally subject to the obligatory repetitions demanded of the form, must possess an inner worth, and because it will be repeated often, "must contain within itself all the properties that would make it worthy of such repetition."[24] Of the first phrase of Bach's rondo, Forkel writes "the theme is so beautiful that we can well imagine that one could hear it without ever tiring of it. It is exceptionally pleasing, simple, clear and comprehensible, without seeming impoverished, and at every repetition one hears it with new satisfaction."[25] Forkel's investment in the quality of the phrase, in its "inner worth," constitutes something of a departure from the normal discourse of music criticism in the eighteenth century, for the talk is not about syntax or form, rhetoric or affect, but about an intangible quality inherent in the idea itself, and it is this quality that presumably distinguishes Bach's rondo from those of the "Modecomponisten" elsewhere disparaged in Forkel's review.

These matters were revived a few years later by Carl Friedrich Cramer in his *Magazin der Musik* for 1783. Writing of the rondos in the fourth of the collections *für Kenner und Liebhaber*, Cramer argues against the notion that Bach can be accused of "condescending" to compose in these "lighter genres" when his music demonstrates by example how even these genres can be enriched and the mind

---

23. Johann Nikolaus Forkel, *Musikalisch-kritische Bibliothek,* II (Gotha: C. W. Ettinger, 1778; reprint Hildesheim: Georg Olms, 1964), 281–93. For an appreciation of Forkel's study, see my "The New Modulation of the 1770s: C. P. E. Bach in Theory, Criticism, and Practice," *Journal of the American Musicological Society* 38 (1985), 551–592, esp. 573–574.

24. " . . . daß er alle Eigenschaften an sich haben müsse, die ihn dieser öftern Wiederholung würdig machen können." Forkel, *Musikalisch-kritische Bibliothek,* II: 282–283.

25. "Wir halten diesen Satz für so schön, daß wir glauben, man könne sich desselben kaum satt hören. Er ist äußerst angenehm, simpel, deutlich und faßlich, ohne arm zu seyn, und bey jeder Wiederholung hört man ihn mit neuem Vergnügen." Forkel, *Musikalisch-kritische Bibliothek,* II: 283–284.

of the *Kenner* satisfied.[26] "No one who brings feeling and insight to their performance, and who at the same time will consult Forkel's analysis of one of the earlier ones, and the very true theory of rondo that he abstracts from it, can doubt that this is the case with Bach's rondos," he writes, and then recounts those qualities that Forkel found immanent in Bach's rondo:

> the indispensable and striking beauty of its theme and its capacity for a breaking up into its components [Zergliederung] and for alteration [Veränderung], the way in which the secondary themes (couplets) would arise from it—how they would paraphrase, confirm, "prove" [their relationship to the them]—how the secondary ideas, variations and transpositions to remote keys will be appropriately applied, and interior modulations and the return to the tonic will be managed with due care.[27]

But when Cramer gets to the actual music, he turns away from the "detail of a sterile ledger of harmonic fine points, of modulations and their paths of return, and the like"—turns away from Forkel's analysis—to an account that "in some measure comes to terms with my *Empfindungen*," as he puts it, "so that I would think of a character that could correspond to a distinguished piece." For Cramer, the theme of the Rondo in A evokes for him "the obstinacy of the most lovely maiden who will quite get her way through her mood and a pleasing persistence." The Rondo in B♭—for Cramer, the most impressive of the entire run—conjures for him "the most youthful, most naive petulance [Muthwill] of a lightly dancing grace! Thalia, it should be inscribed, uniting with this word everything that the Greek thought when he conjured up now the playmate of Venus, the Graces, now that Muse who rules over the comic."[28]

---

26. Carl Friedrich Cramer, *Magazin der Musik*, I/2 (1783): 1241. Hans-Günter Ottenberg, *C. P. E. Bach* (Oxford and New York: Oxford University Press, 1987), 166, claims that Cramer disapproved of Bach's decision, that he "lowered himself to write in that genre." This seems a misreading of Cramer's subtle argument. For Ottenberg's original text, see his *Carl Philipp Emanuel Bach* (Leipzig: Philipp Reclam jun., 1982), 229.

27. "Daß dieses der Fall bey Bachs Rondeaus sey, wird niemand in Zweifel ziehen, der einsichtsvolles Gefühl zum Durchspielen mitbringt, und allenfalls Forkels Analyse eines von den vorigen, und seine daraus abstrahirte sehr richtige Theorie des Rondeaus überhaupt, der dabey nothwendigen auffallenden Schönheit des Thema, seiner Fähigkeit zur Zergliederung und Veränderung, der Art, wie die Zwischensätze oder Couplets, aus demselben entspringen, wie sie paraphrasirt, bestätigt, erwiesen, wie die Nebengedanken, Veränderungen und Versetzungen in entferntere Tonarten gehörig angebracht, Zwischenmodulationen und Rückkehren vorsichtig managirt werden müssen, dabey zu Rathe ziehen will." Cramer, *Magazin*, I/2: 1241–1242.

28. Cramer, *Magazin*, I/2: 1249.

Impatient with the cold analytical strategies of Forkel, Cramer here articulates the beginnings of that eternal divide between the rigorous, hard-boned analysis of music as grammar and syntax and a criticism in pursuit of some meaning beyond the notes. Forkel had of course written brilliantly on the place of *Empfindung* in the music of Emanuel Bach.[29] Feeling, for Forkel, is immanent in the notes. The character of the piece, the embodiment of *Empfindungen*, is itself a subject of analytical scrutiny. For Cramer, the locus of *Empfindung* is shifted. The critic, as sensory organ, registers feeling; it is then the responsibility of criticism to come to terms with those feelings: "von *meinen* Empfindungen Rechenschaft geben können," Cramer proposes [emphasis added].[30] What he writes is an imaginative expression of those *Empfindungen*, its justification the honesty with which he claims to feel.

These passages from Forkel and Cramer convey a sense of witness to something new and unique in Bach's work: for one, the appropriation of genre and its renovation; for another, the contesting of the "popular" in opposition to the learned—the contesting even that there is an opposition here at all; and finally, the sense of a new thematicism—the idea of theme as constituted in expansive, commodious phrases and as subject of further inquiry in the course of the piece. This "inner worth" that Forkel detects is then aligned with the beautiful. Beauty is invoked here not in the general sense of art as "beautiful," but as an identifiable characteristic that would distinguish this theme from its predecessors.

"When did Haydn begin to write 'beautiful' melodies?" asks James Webster, finding an answer finally in the first movement of Haydn's Symphony No. 77 in Bb Major, tellingly composed in 1782, "the first symphony whose second theme seems clearly to adumbrate" a type exemplified in the second theme in the first movement of Mozart's Symphony in G minor (K 550).[31] Haydn's vigorous engagement with the performance and composition of opera at Esterháza quite naturally encourages "the new proximity of symphony and opera" that Webster finds "characteristic of Haydn's music . . . after 1774."[32] Bach's engagement with opera—with the life of the theater—was, on the contrary, distant and passive, even antagonistic, and a matter of much speculation. But the point here is that

---

29. See, for one, the theorizing on sonata in the *Musikalischer Almanach* for 1784. This is discussed at length in chapter 1.

30. Cramer, *Magazin*, I/2: 1243.

31. See *Haydn Studies: Proceedings of the International Haydn Conference, Washington, D. C., 1975*, ed. Jens Peter Larsen, Howard Serwer, James Webster (New York and London: W. W. Norton, 1981), 385–388, esp. 386.

32. Webster, in *Haydn Studies*, 388. See further the discussion following, on the same page.

the kinds of themes that we now find in these late rondos share certain characteristics with the cantabile themes of Haydn and Mozart that begin to emerge around 1780. Webster's question is as pertinent for Bach as it is for Haydn, and the date for which one might claim an answer is pretty much the same.

To suggest that Beethoven, in the finale of Opus 90, means to emulate Bach, to imagine that he would have needed a model, in the mechanical, technical sense, is decidedly not to the point. That these two rondos have something to do with one another, however, is a notion that I wish to pursue as another entry into the vexed topic of Beethoven and his pasts. In their formal mappings, the two are indeed very different. Bach's rondo characteristically sets the theme in remote keys: in F major, in F♯ major (coincident with a change of meter to 12/8), in C major. In none of his rondos is the theme locked into the tonic, as is invariably the case with Beethoven, who in this matter is even more conservative than Mozart.[33] And yet for all its classical poise, Beethoven's theme is pointedly un-Mozartean. The world that it evokes is Emanuel Bach's. Even in its elocution, that *Sangbarkeit* that Beethoven asks of the player, the music reaches back to an earlier generation, retrieving a way of playing that Bach himself described as "das Tragen der Töne," by which he meant a sustaining of the tone from one note to the next, but with a special inflection (*Bebung*-like) within the tone itself: a playing *in* the keys, so to say.[34] Writing in 1753, describing an affect possible only on the clavichord, Bach cannot have had even remotely in mind its eventual applicability to the performance of those rondos of 1779. Still, there is something compelling in the notion that the enactment of this "Tragen der Töne" would, in some compensatory mode of articulation, find its way into these new works "fürs Forte-Piano" (as its title page specifies), even in the elegant fusion of the declamatory and the *singend* that seems central and immanent in the theme of the Rondo in E—an attribute of its inner worth, so to say. It is this quality that Beethoven seeks to capture in the rondo of Opus 90.

---

33. It is precisely this distinction that led Augustus Frederic Christoph[er] Kollmann to speak of "*proper* and *improper* [rondos], of which "the *former* are those, in which the first section always returns in the principal key . . . and the *latter*, those in which the subject or first section also appears in keys to which a digression may be made." As an example of the latter, Kollmann prints the finale of Emanuel Bach's Piano Trio in G (H 523), no doubt inspired by Forkel's study, with running analytical commentary. See *An Essay on Practical Musical Composition* (London: "printed for the author," 1799; reprint, with new introduction by Imogene Horsley, New York: Da Capo Press, 1973), 6 and plates 1–5.

34. Carl Philipp Emanuel Bach, *Versuch über die wahre Art das Clavier zu spielen*, [I]: 126; *Essay on the True Art of Playing Keyboard Instruments*, tr. and ed. William J. Mitchell (New York: W. W. Norton, 1949), 156.

How, then, to understand this enigmatic relationship between works? Harold Bloom, in a well-known passage from *The Anxiety of Influence,* here imagines the return of the dead poet in the work of his successor:

> The later poet, in his own final phase, already burdened by an imaginative solitude that is almost a solipsism, holds his own poem so open again to the precursor's work that at first we might believe the wheel has come full circle, and that we are back in the later poet's flooded apprenticeship, before his strength began to assert itself. . . . But the poem is now *held* open to the precursor, where once it *was* open, and the uncanny effect is that the new poem's achievement makes it seem to us, not as though the precursor were writing it, but as though the later poet himself had written the precursor's characteristic work.[35]

Bloom is helping us to envision the convoluted process of mind in which the later poet in his later years—Beethoven, now feeling the isolation, the "imaginative solitude," at the onset of later middle age—is able to embrace and absorb the work of his precursor (Bach, in this instance) so completely that, for a moment, we are made to feel that Beethoven had gotten himself under the skin of Bach's Rondo. On its face, this is a strange notion: a fantasy in the mind of the beholder. But Bloom's point, in its application to the instance before us, is that there is a deeper struggle here than might be evident from the surface of the music. At the outset of his study, Bloom writes: "Poetic history . . . is held to be indistinguishable from poetic influence, since strong poets make that history by misreading one another, so as to clear imaginative space for themselves."[36] If this "clearing of imaginative space" resonates profoundly in the great creative cycles that characterize Beethoven's lifelong project, the image comes sharply into focus at this critical moment in 1814, where the worn orthodoxies of the past fifteen years are now swept away, and we find ourselves in the presence of Beethoven's "flooded apprenticeship."

Where are the traces of this precursor, and how are they manifest? For Bloom, famously unsympathetic to such questions, the commonplace trappings of influence are the business of "source-hunters and biographers."[37] Rather, it is only in the anxieties with which the late poet confronts his ancestors that meaning can

---

35. Harold Bloom, *The Anxiety of Influence: A Theory of Poetry* (New York and Oxford: Oxford University Press, 2nd ed., 1997), 15–16.

36. Bloom, *Anxiety,* 5.

37. Bloom, *Anxiety,* 71.

be wrung out of the urge to create. "Initial love for the precursor's poetry is transformed rapidly enough into revisionary strife, without which individuation is
not possible."[38] If, in these late works by Bach, there is an immediacy of expression that speaks to Beethoven, a diction that intrigues him, he must now come to
terms with these works in a voice that seeks its own origins. By these lights, the
music of Opus 90 would be heard not as an affectionate evocation of Bach's works,
but as something considerably more obscure: a revision, a correction, a swerve,
as though composition were itself an act of re-composition.

But it is only in the traces of this act that encounters of the Bloomian kind can
be reconstructed in the first place. Such traces are nowhere more evident than in
the closing measures of Opus 90 (shown in appendix 10E). The grand rhetorical
endings, victorious or tragic, of the past decade are deflated in a single dismissive
gesture. This is how Emanuel Bach occasionally closes, memorably so in the
opening sonata (H 281) from the fifth collection "für Kenner und Liebhaber."
The first movement, in E minor, does not end, but moves off to C major, where
eight measures of Adagio, followed by an unmeasured cadenza, ruminate on
some motives that will cohere in the following Andantino, a wispy, fragile rondo
in E *major*, much scaled down from those independent rondos by which the
genre is defined. Its final measures are to the point here (see appendix 10F).[39]
Breaking off as though in mid sentence, the work ends neither with a peremptory,
moralizing statement nor in the grand structural arches that signify closure in a
classical style. It simply vanishes. The final bars of the much grander Rondo in E,
if not quite so radical, have the same effect (see appendix 10G). This way of ending
belongs to the wit of eighteenth-century narrative. In such modest, self-effacing
leave-takings, the work seems to view itself with ironic detachment.

If Bach's voice and manner are evident in the final bars of Opus 90, it will not
do to claim simply that Beethoven has appropriated Bach's keen sense of the
ironic, for to make such a claim would mean to argue for its artificiality. The irony
of Opus 90, no less genuine than Bach's, comes of a complex renunciation of
Beethoven's own earlier music. It seems hardly possible to imagine with any clarity the convoluted figure that Emanuel Bach must have signified for Beethoven
in 1814, seeking to recapture his apprenticeship with Christian Gottlob Neefe
in Bonn, where Emanuel Bach was no remote ancestor, but an aging contemporary whose latest music must have seemed at once inaccessible, profound and
eccentric—seductive, yet without immediate appeal to a teenager whose ears

---

38. Harold Bloom, *A Map of Misreading* (New York: Oxford University Press, 1975), 10.

39. The passage is discussed in another context in chapter 6; see exx. 6.6 and 6.7.

were tuned to Mannheim, to Paris, and to the Vienna of Haydn and Mozart. In his earliest works for keyboard, Beethoven's leanings in those directions—away from Hamburg, Berlin, and Leipzig—are transparent. The two rondos, WoO 48 and 49, published in Bossler's *Blumenlese für Clavierliebhaber* for 1783 and 1784 bear not the slightest trace of the rondos in Bach's collections, nor does the rondo finale of the Piano Sonata in E♭, WoO 47. In these, as in the rondo finales of the Piano Quartets, WoO 36, nos. 2 and 3, from 1785, the themes are oblivious of that "inner worth" that Forkel prized in the themes of Bach's rondos, and refuse the bold modulatory strategies, the improvisatory flights that set these works apart. Beethoven was finding his models elsewhere.

That the Piano Quartet in E♭ Major/Minor (WoO 36, no. 1) was modeled on Mozart's Sonata for Piano and Violin, K 379 has been known ever since Hermann Deiters called attention to it in his revision of the first volume of Thayer's biography.[40] The matter was explored more deeply by Ludwig Schiedermair, and, with considerable insight, Arnold Schmitz.[41] The finale of the Trio in G Major for Keyboard, Flute and Bassoon, WoO 37 (1786), an "andante con variazioni," again draws its inspiration from the finale of Mozart's K 379, while the expansive first movement indulges in the familiar mannerisms of Mozart at the keyboard. Emanuel Bach figures here not at all. Schmitz smartly observed that Beethoven's notion of a contrasting thematic *Ableitung*—by which is meant a derivation of the contrasting element from within the theme itself—was developed early.[42] Writing of the putative relationship between the first movements of Beethoven's Sonata in F minor, Opus 2 no. 1, and Bach's Sonata in F minor (the subject of Forkel's *Sendschreiben,* discussed above in chapter 1), Schmitz concludes that "the concentrated unity in the fashioning of Beethoven's phrase structure indicates the influence of Ph. E. Bach. But Beethoven's technique of contrasting elements is based on other historical foundations."[43] This "concentrated unity" and "a certain tendency toward [thematic] derivation"("eine gewiße Ableitungstendenz") is something that Schmitz finds still earlier, in that Piano Quartet mod-

---

40. Alexander Wheelock Thayer, *Ludwig van Beethovens Leben,* Zweite Auflage, neu bearbeitet und ergänzt von Hermann Deiters, I (Leipzig: Breitkopf & Härtel, 1901), 191–194.

41. Ludwig Schiedermair, *Der junge Beethoven* (Leipzig: Quelle & Meyer, 1925), 286–300; Arnold Schmitz, *Beethovens "Zwei Principe": Ihre Bedeutung für Themen- und Satzbau* (Berlin and Bonn: Ferd. Dümmler, 1923), 20–26. For more on this, see Douglas Johnson, "1794–95: Decisive Years in Beethoven's Early Development," in *Beethoven Studies* 3, ed. Alan Tyson (Cambridge: Cambridge University Press, 1982), 14.

42. Schmitz, *Beethovens "Zwei Principe,"* 96.

43. "Zweifellos deutet gerade die konzentrierte Einheitlichkeit der Beethovenschen Satzgestaltung auf Ph. E. Bachs Einfluß hin. Dagegen beruht Beethovens Konstrastierungstechnik auf anderen historischen Grundlagen." Schmitz, *Beethovens "Zwei Principe,"* 27.

eled on Mozart's K 379. In this view, the eminence of Emanuel Bach makes itself felt in Beethoven's earliest music neither in the articulated surface of the music, nor in the construction of its themes through a simultaneous process of contrast and derivation, nor in the conceiving of large-scale structure, but in something less palpable: in an attitude expressed in the concept of "concentrated unities." The intensity of expression and the high aesthetic purpose of Bach's music (to say nothing of its pedigree) would no doubt have exercised a powerful standard to which Beethoven would in turn have felt a sense of responsibility.

The problem with this view is that it presupposes a familiarity, an intimacy with Bach's music that cannot be verified.[44] In this connection, it is good to remind ourselves that Neefe spent the years from 1776 until his arrival in Bonn in 1779 traveling with the Seyler Theater Company, for whom he acted as music director (in place of Ferdinand Hiller) and composer, and that the engagement with theater continued during his tenure at Bonn. Emanuel Bach, a figure of exceptional stature to Neefe in his apprenticeship, must surely have faded into a more populous background in the 1780s. And yet there can be no question that Bach's *Versuch*, in both its parts, will have served as a pedagogical foundation. This is clearly conveyed in a piece called "Gespräch zwischen einem Kantor und Organist" (Conversation between a Cantor and an Organist) in a collection of poems and miscellaneous pieces brought out by Neefe in 1785. In the "Conversation" (which is dated "1780"), the following lines are given to the Kantor:

[Philipp Emanuel] Bach's Essay on the True Manner of Playing Keyboard Instruments, and his keyboard pieces, are still to be recommended to the advantage of those who aspire to excellence on this instrument, which an impudent rogue has recently and thoughtlessly held against this illustrious man. How then does it come about that the most humble of Bach's students can read off the most difficult things at sight while a keyboard player in the latest style can barely play four measures of a Bach sonata without stumbling? Bach's Allegros demand uncommon dexterity of

---

44. It may be symptomatic of these allegiances that the subscription lists for the six volumes "für Kenner und Liebhaber" include no name from any location in the Rhineland—that Neefe (presumably lacking the means to subscribe) was unable or unwilling to urge a subscription from among the music-loving nobility of Bonn. For the subscription lists, see Ernst Suchalla, ed., *Carl Philipp Emanuel Bach: Briefe und Dokumente. Kritische Gesamtausgabe*, II, (Göttingen: Vandenhoeck & Ruprecht, 1994), 1471–1475, 1491–1496, 1507–1510, 1515–1520. The single work of Emanuel Bach's to have been recorded in Beethoven's *Nachlaß* is the setting of Klopstock's *Morgen-Gesang am Schöpfungsfeste* in a manuscript copy inscribed by Beethoven "Von meinem theuren Vater geschrieben" in a late hand. The work was published in 1784, and it is again the case that Bonn does not appear in the subscription list. The remnants of the manuscript are now at the Beethoven-Haus in Bonn.

the fingers on both hands. The fingers of the left hand must be as capable as the fingers of the right of performing the most varied motions, whereas the arpeggiated basses in the latest fashion require only one kind of motion. The Bach Adagios demand a precise knowledge of the modifications of which the clavichord is capable, if they are to be played from the depths of the soul. And to see through the diverse veilings of his ideas to the design of his works requires more than the usual common sense: it requires study. But one is rewarded for one's labors. He who can play Bach properly can surely play most other composers as well. And he will enjoy a more sustained satisfaction through Bach's work than through the works of many others. . . . I am ashamed for the souls of my countrymen that I must say that I have seen a great region of Germany where one knew no more of Bach than that he is named Karl Philipp Emanuel, that he lives in Hamburg, and that his works are said to be very difficult, and yet not in the current taste. . . .[45]

To imagine Neefe and Beethoven going at some of Emanuel Bach's more recalcitrant works, penetrating those "diverse veilings of his ideas" (*verschiedene Einkleidung seiner Gedanken*) to get at some sense of the larger "plan," is to depict an aspect of Beethoven's formative education that would otherwise remain inscrutable. This little "Gespräch" is something of a polemic in defense of a man whose music Neefe perceived to be no longer in the public consciousness, whose "style" was seen as hopelessly outmoded. For Neefe, Bach's music stood aloof from the pettiness of popular fashion. But there are deeper issues here, for the appeal of a Mozart was clearly the more powerful for Beethoven. The new irony in Opus 90 comes about as a coming to terms with that earlier repudiation of Bach. It is as though Beethoven wished, subconsciously or not, to retrieve the *Geist* of Emanuel Bach, to rewrite in this new work the story of his apprenticeship, and from the perspective of older age.

In 1814, this revisiting of Bonn in the 1780s will have invoked another aspect of Bach's music, for the two works that suggest themselves as precursors stand not only for two distinct genres (Sonata and Rondo) but for two different keyboard instruments. "Fürs Forte-Piano," as Bach's title explicitly puts it, these late rondos exploit the timbre, the resonances of the new instrument.[46] No less ex-

---

45. My translation. From C. G. Neefe, *Dilettanterien* ([n.p.] 1785); the German text is given in Schiedermair, *Der junge Beethoven*, 154.

46. "If these Rondos . . . are to express their full effect, they must be played on a good fortepiano, on which the resonance of the struck tones will make the effect all the more powerful," wrote a reviewer in 1780, the earliest report on the second collection "für Kenner und Liebhaber." For the original text, see Suchalla, *Briefe und Dokumente*, 861–862, and chapter 4, note 8.

plicitly, the first movement of the late Sonata in E minor is music for, and indeed of, the clavichord. In a recent investigation of the matter, Tilman Skowroneck assembles the considerable evidence surrounding the instruments in play during Beethoven's Bonn apprenticeship.[47] That the clavichord figures prominently here will come as no surprise.

In the preface to his *Zwölf Klavier-Sonaten* of 1773, warmly dedicated to Emanuel Bach, Neefe comes directly to the instrument. "These sonatas are for the clavichord," writes Neefe:

> I therefore wished that they be played only on the clavichord, for most of them will have little effect when they are played on the harpsichord or the pianoforte because neither of these instruments is as capable as is the clavichord of producing the cantabile and the divers modifications of tone toward which I guided myself.[48]

Improvements in the fortepiano in the years between 1773 and the early 1780s and greater familiarity with its expressive potential will no doubt have induced Neefe to moderate his thoughts.[49] And yet, his devotion, even in 1785, to the clavichord as an instrument without which the *empfindsame Sprache* of Emanuel Bach could not be conveyed comes clear in that telling line from the "Gespräch": "The Bach Adagios demand a precise knowledge of the modifications of which

---

47. "The Keyboard Instruments of the Young Beethoven," in *Beethoven and His World*, ed. Scott Burnham and Michael P. Steinberg (Princeton and Oxford: Princeton University Press, 2000), 151–192.

48. "Diese Sonaten sind Klavier-Sonaten. Ich wollte daher, daß sie auch nur auf dem Klaviere gespielt würden; denn die meisten werden auf dem Flügel oder Pianoforte wenig Wirkung tun, weil keines von beiden des Kantabeln und der verschiedenen Modifikation des Tons so fähig ist als das Klavier, wonach ich mich doch gerichtet." Christian Gottlob Neefe, *Zwölf Klavier-Sonaten*, (Leipzig: Schwickert, 1773; facsimile reprint, Courlay: Collection Dominantes, 2004). The text of the preface can be found in Irmgard Leux, *Christian Gottlob Neefe (1748–1798)* (Leipzig: Fr. Kistner & C. F. W. Siegel, 1925), 121.

49. We know that Neefe himself "opened an agency for fortepianos and clavichords from the atelier of Friderici . . . and other recognized masters"; see Ludwig Schiedermair, *Der junge Beethoven*, 69. Skowroneck ("The Keyboard Instruments," 161) takes this to suggest that Beethoven's "association with the clavichord became less important rather than being strengthened when Neefe became his teacher, despite Neefe's earlier affinity with this instrument." Surely Beethoven, and everyone else, recognized that the clavichord and the fortepiano occupied two distinct roles in the life of the musician, and this had nothing to do with whatever inclinations Neefe might have continued to hold in the mid-1780s. In this connection, it is instructive to read Cramer's jeremiad against the fortepiano in his account of Bach's rondos *Magazin der Musik*, I/2: 1246–1247), in which Cramer argues that only the clavichord "permits the modifications of tone in every way, opens the widest field to musical expression, and would be quite perfect if it could sustain tone more completely . . . [and] possessed a more penetrating tone."

the clavichord is capable, if they are to be played from the depths of the soul"[50] For Neefe, the two instruments do not stand in some evolutionary succession in which the one supersedes the other. Neefe, I think we must believe, would have instilled in Beethoven the sense of the clavichord as an instrument at the foundation of an aesthetic that would figure prominently in Beethoven's formative *Bildung* as a keyboard player.[51]

We have come to accept without question a teleology that has Beethoven composing for some keyboard instrument whose capacities for extremes of register and sonority had yet to be realized, suggesting that his music seems often intent upon the destruction of the existing prototypes. Even if there is some truth to be teased out of the popular allegory, it would be good to view the matter from the other end of the telescope—from the deeper perspective of a musical sensibility formed in the 1780s. The clavichord has a role to play in this story. How the instrument may be perceived to resonate in Beethoven's final keyboard music is not a phenomenon that we can ever authenticate with the hard evidence that historians want. And yet there seems to me an intuitive truth to be apprehended here: that the clavichord constitutes a fiber in Beethoven's musical sensibility. It is repressed, challenged, superseded—but it is there, just under the skin, acquired like native language, not consciously learned and never entirely displaced. When Beethoven writes the *Bebung*-like passage at the "Recitativo" in Opus 110—the high A♮, dissonant seventh above B, escorted through an expressive gamut: *piano, una corda, crescendo, tutte le corde, diminuendo, ritardando,* again *una corda,* all *sempre tenuto* and with the sustaining pedal—he does not mean to implicate Emanuel Bach in an act of willful historicizing. I should think, rather, that we are here witness to an elocution (call it linguistic) that had once been altogether normal and natural in Beethoven's keyboard playing: an utterance that the much grander instrument of 1820 can only hope to suggest.[52] It is *as though* Beethoven were here

---

50. "Die Bachischen Adagios erfordern eine genaue Bekanntschaft mit der Modification, deren das Klavichord fähig ist, wollen tief aus der Seele vorgetragen seyn." Neefe, *Dilettanterien,* in Schiedermair, *Der junge Beethoven,* 154.

51. For a thorough compilation of the evidence bearing on Beethoven's evolution as a keyboard player, see Th[eodor] von Frimmel, "Der Klavierspieler Beethoven," in *Beethoven-Studien, II: Bausteine zu einer Lebensgeschichte des Meisters* (Munich and Leipzig: Georg Müller, 1906), 201–271. "Without risk," writes Frimmel (211) "we can assume that it was chiefly *the principles of C. Ph. E. Bach's keyboard playing* according to which Neefe instructed the young Beethoven." (The emphasis is Frimmel's.)

52. "There are places in the master's later keyboard works which, unplayable on the *Hammerklavier,* were so notated by Beethoven that one must necessarily think of the old *Bebung,*" writes Frimmel (*ibid.,* 222), citing this famous passage in Opus 110. Schenker observes this as well. See the final entry in his compendious *Beitrag zur Ornamentik* (Vienna: Universal Edition, 1904; rev. 1908), 72;

inventing a notation to capture how he must have performed (for himself and his students) that famous passage from the Fantasy in C minor that is the final number in the *Probestücke* published with Part I of Emanuel Bach's *Versuch*. (The two passages are shown in appendix 10H and I.)

What is played out beneath the notes of Opus 90 is neither an act of simple homage nor a conscious revival of some historical moment, but something more complex. I return to Bloom's *Anxiety of Influence,* to its talk of the "clearing of imaginative space" in the enabling of a first creative act. Without much stretching of Bloom's conceit, one wants to conjure Beethoven finding his way through Thomson's Scottish tunes, reading and parsing Homer in Voss's poetic German, and seeking in Emanuel Bach's late keyboard music a tone and an accent that would help to invigorate a fresh voice, in sympathy with some new impulse in his own thinking. Beethoven is here opening windows to a past, but a past in which a future is envisioned. If Emanuel Bach had in some measure become a "historical" figure for Beethoven, it would seem to me mistaken to argue that what we are observing here is in any sense an instance of historicist thought, a conscious enactment of the past for the sake of its distance from the present. The creative enterprise has always to do with a past, attuned to some earlier work with which the composer is locked in an embrace at once compassionate and antagonistic. It is the internalizing of this engagement that is inscribed in the music. Integral in its text, it will be felt, if not always recognized.

In a certain sense, then, Opus 90 reaches back to a moment somewhere in the early 1780s, a nexus at which the clavichord, in its final lavish exemplars, and the fortepiano, at this critical turn in its development, seem to touch one another for a fleeting, luminous instant, inspiring a strikingly new voice late in Bach's own evolution in these expansive rondo themes in their elegant fusion of a new lyricism with that speech-like elocution deeply ingrained in Bach's style. Opus 90 is of course about other things. It is of and about Beethoven in 1814, and all that this signifies about the complexity of style and genre at a critical juncture in Beethoven's development. Emanuel Bach's legacy lives on here as well, not in open parody or caricature, not in imitation of a style nor in the antiquarian spirit of historical revival, but in the deeper currents of an aesthetic that turned away from all virtuosity and sought in the keyboard an immediacy of the composer's voice.

English as *A Contribution to the Study of Ornamentation,* tr. Hedi Siegel (after Carl Parrish), in *The Music Forum,* IV, ed. Felix Salzer (New York: Columbia University Press, 1976), 139.

APPENDIX 10A
Beethoven, Sonata in
E minor, Opus 90,
first movement,
mm.1–46

APPENDIX 10B
Carl Philipp
Emanuel Bach,
Sonata in E minor,
H 287 (Wq 65/6),
first movement

APPENDIX 10C Beethoven, Sonata in E minor, Opus 90, second movement, mm. 1–29

APPENDIX 10D Carl Philipp Emanuel Bach, Rondo in E major, H 265 (Wq 57/1), mm. 1–14

APPENDIX 10G Carl Philipp Emanuel Bach, Rondo in E major, H 265, mm. 88 to end

APPENDIX 10H Beethoven, Sonata in A♭ major, Opus 110, third movement.

APPENDIX 101 Carl Philipp Emanuel Bach, Fantasia, from *18 Probestücke* (1753), H 75 (Wq 63/6)

CHAPTER 11

Adagio espressivo: Opus 109 as Radical Dialectic

I

In his radically dialectical "Beethoven's Late Style," Theodor W. Adorno corrects what he perceived as the commonplace view of the late works as so many documents in verification of Beethoven's biography—documents, he meant, to an intense subjectivity: "the late work, exiled to the margins of art, approaches the condition of document."[1] Adorno invites us to consider the limits, the "*Grenzlinie*," of such an approach, "beyond which each of Beethoven's conversation books would signify more than the Quartet in C-sharp minor."[2] For Adorno, only a "technical analysis" of the music itself can move toward a revision of this view. He is led at once to the problem of convention—or, as he puts it, to "the role of conventions," in all their particularity—noting the frequency with which the music of Beethoven's last decade draws upon the trappings of classical convention: the trill, the cadenza, the aria (with all its appurtenances), the sixteenth-note figure of the kind

---

1. "Damit wird das Spätwerk an den Rand von Kunst verwiesen und dem Dokument angenähert." Theodor W. Adorno, "Spätstil Beethovens," in Adorno, *Moments musicaux* (Frankfurt am Main: Suhrkamp, 1964), 13; reprinted in Adorno, *Gesammelte Schriften,* ed. Rolf Tiedemann, vol. 17 (Frankfurt am Main: Suhrkamp Verlag, 1982), 13; and in Adorno, *Beethoven: Philosophie der Musik. Fragmente und Texte (Nachgelassene Schriften,* I/1), ed. Rolf Tiedemann (Frankfurt am Main: Suhrkamp Verlag, 1993), 180; English as "Beethoven's Late Style," in Theodor W. Adorno, *Beethoven: The Philosophy of Music.* Fragments and Texts, ed. Rolf Tiedemann, tr. Edmund Jephcott (Stanford: Stanford University Press, 1998), 123. For another translation, see Adorno, *Essays on Music,* selected, with introduction, commentary, and notes by Richard Leppert, tr. Susan H. Gillespie (Berkeley and Los Angeles: University of California Press, 2002), 564–567. Here and elsewhere, my translations draw freely from both Jephcott and Gillespie.

2. " . . . jenseits von welcher dann freilich jedes Konversationsheft Beethovens mehr zu bedeuten hätte als das cis-moll-Quartett." Adorno, "Spätstil," 13; *Beethoven: Philosophie der Musik,* 180; "Late Style," 123–124.

that accompanies the principal theme in the first movement of Opus 110, and so forth. This, it seems to me, implicates by extension genre itself, in all its particularity, as in effect a kind of superspecies of convention: sonata, fugue, variation, motet, dance, song, cavatina, and the rest. "No explanation of Beethoven's late style," continues Adorno, "—indeed, of any late style—is sufficient that construes the ruins of convention in purely psychological terms, indifferent to appearances." Which leads to this insight: "The relationship of conventions to subjectivity itself must be understood as the formal principle from which springs the content of the late works, if they are to signify truly more than sentimental relics."[3]

The dialectics of this uneasy relationship are examined in some final paragraphs that are as renowned for the profundity of their insight as they are for those qualities that Edward Said, writing of Adorno's *Notes to Literature,* described as "eccentric, brilliant, unreadably readable, aphoristic and gnomic in the extreme."[4] Speaking of the fragmented surface that characterizes much of Beethoven's late music, Adorno now invokes "*Prozess.*" The passage needs to be quoted at length:

> Process remains in his late work; not, however, as development, but as kindling between extremes in the strictest technical sense. It is subjectivity which forces together these extremes in an instant, which summons the terse polyphony with its tensions, dispersed in the unison and thence dissipated, leaving behind the bare tone. The flourish sets in as memorial to the past, wherein petrified subjectivity itself decays. But the caesuras, the sudden breaking off that, more than anything else, signifies late Beethoven, are those moments of escape. The work is silent, as though it were abandoned, and turns its hollowness outward. Only then is the next fragment joined to it, the outbreak of subjectivity banned, by command, from its place, and for better or worse renounced.

And all this "illuminates the paradox that the final Beethoven is at once subjective and objective. Objective is the fragmented landscape, subjective, the light that alone glows within it."[5]

---

3. "Keine Auslegung Beethovens und wohl jeglichen Spätstils langt zu, die die Konventionstrümmer nur psychologisch, mit Gleichgültigkeit gegen die Erscheinung motivierte. . . . Das Verhältnis der Konventionen zur Subjektivität selber muss als das Formgesetz verstanden werden, aus welchem der Gehalt der Spätwerke entspringt, wofern sie wahrhaft mehr bedeuten sollen als rührende Reliquien." Adorno, "Spätstil," 15; *Beethoven: Philosophie der Musik,* 182; "Late Style," 125.

4. On the dust jacket to Theodor W. Adorno, *Notes to Literature,* ed. Rolf Tiedemann, tr. Sherry Weber Nicholsen, 2 vols. (New York: Columbia University Press, 1991–1992).

5. "Prozeß bleibt noch sein Spätwerk; aber nicht als Entwicklung, sondern als Zündung zwischen den Extremen, die keine sichere Mitte und Harmonie aus Spontaneität mehr dulden. Zwischen Ex-

The subjective, in Adorno's reading, is constrained—its outbreak *as expression* (but not its essence) is renounced. The power of process lies here, in this constrained subjectivity, and perhaps it is this internalization of the subjective, this impalpable inner light that Adorno believed himself to witness, that does indeed capture something essential in the music of Beethoven's last works.

Seeking answers to the question "What is a Late Work?" Carl Dahlhaus comes at this object/subject opposition as though in dialogue with Adorno, invoking, as he does, a "dialectical antithesis of subject and object," an antithesis which "appears to be resolved in a classic work, but in a late work is a vigorous source of dichotomies."[6] Dahlhaus wishes to understand these antinomies as held, in the late works, in a state of suspension: "the subjective element is no longer 'subsumed' in the objective, and the objective element . . . no longer 'justified' by the subjective—it is no longer the case that either is transformed into the other, but, rather, that they directly confront each other."[7] Dahlhaus hears this confrontation played out in the fugal exposition in the first movement of the Quartet in C♯ minor. Noting that the fugue is directed to be played "molto espressivo," Dahlhaus pits the "schematic and objective facet" (by which he means the mechanics of the exposition and the fixity of the subject and answer) against "an affective and subjective one. The counterpoints of the exposition are not independent voices, each with its own identity, but patchworks of motives that serve no other purpose than to accentuate the expressive quality of the chromatic

---

tremen im genauesten technischen Verstande: hier der Einstimmigkeit, dem Unisono, der bedeutenden Floskel, dort der Polyphonie, die unvermittelt darüber sich erhebt. Subjektivität ist es, welche die Extreme im Augenblick zusammenzwingt, die gedrängte Polyphonie mit ihren Spannungen lädt, im Unisono sie zerschlägt und daraus entweicht, hinter sich lassend den entblößten Ton; die Floskel einsetzt als Denkmal des Gewesenen, worin versteint Subjektivität selber eingeht. Die Zäsuren aber, das jähe Abbrechen, das mehr als alles andere den letzten Beethoven bezeichnet, sind jene Augenblicke des Ausbruchs; das Werk schweigt, wenn es verlassen wird, und kehrt seine Höhlung nach außen. Dann erst fügt das nächste Bruchstück sich an, vom Befehl der ausbrechenden Subjektivität an seine Stelle gebannt und dem voraufgehenden auf Gedeih und Verderb verschworen. . . . Das erhellt den Widersinn, daß der letzte Beethoven zugleich subjektiv und objektiv genannt wird. Objektiv ist die brüchige Landschaft, subjektiv das Licht, darin einzig sie erglüht." Adorno, "Spätstil," 17; *Beethoven: Philosophie der Musik,* 183–184; "Late Style," 126.

6. 1. "Die Subjekt-Objekt-Dialektik, die im klassischen Werk geschlichtet zu sein schien, bricht im Spätwerk in Divergenzen auseinander." *Ludwig van Beethoven und seine Zeit* (Laaber, 1987); reprint in Carl Dahlhaus, *Gesammelte Schriften in 10 Bänden,* ed. Hermann Danuser, VI: *19. Jahrhundert III* (Laaber: Laaber-Verlag, 2003), 227, in a section called "Zum Begriff des 'Spätwerks'." English as *Ludwig van Beethoven: Approaches to his Music,* tr. Mary Whittall (Oxford: Oxford University Press, 1991), 220, where the section is called "What is a Late Work?"

7. "Die Subjektive ist nicht mehr ins Objektive 'aufgehoben' und umgekehrt das Objektive durch das Subjektive 'gerechtfertigt'—das eine 'schlägt' nicht mehr ins andere 'um'—, sondern Subjektives und Objektives stehen sich unvermittelt gegenüber." Dahlhaus, *Gesammelte Schriften,* VI: 227; *Beethoven: Approaches,* 220.

theme. . . . Thus fugal mechanism and motivic expressivity are not sublimated in a 'style d'une teneur' but left to confront each other as discrete attributes."[8]

The positing of these two "discrete attributes" as emblematic of the late style is a bold and challenging notion, even if it is not quite the dialectical condition that Adorno had in mind. To imagine that one could (in any music) identify the actual notes that stand for or indeed embody the subject, as distinct from those that constitute the object—that some notes belong to the formal dimension, others to the expressive—would seem a futile undertaking. And it is now worth asking whether the subjective—or, for that matter, subjectivity itself—need necessarily be linked to the "expressive." In the asking, we are then led to ponder an opposition that has always seemed irrefutably real. The opposition subjective/objective we routinely accept as a condition of artistic experience. But perhaps it is closer to the experience of the thing to suggest that such an opposition is rather a permanent state of mind—in whose mind, precisely, is a problem of another dimension—wherein some shadowy subject written into the work and its performance (in first person, so to say), beats against the objectivity—the object-ness—of the work in all its abstract complexity as structure. To put it more concretely, the *tema* of this fugue in C♯ minor, in the exacting certitude of its twelve notes, is at once object and subject, and the playing out of this opposition is the considerable challenge of contemplation, of analysis, of performance. When Beethoven writes "molto espressivo," the player (real or imaginary) is instructed to get under the skin of the music, to assume the role of the subject as theatrical protagonist, one might say, and therefore to blur the distinction between the material content of the piece and its performance, its expression. Surely, this instruction is not aimed at the counterpoints alone. To imagine a performance in which the *tema* is construed as object to the expressive, subjective business of the counterpoints is to attribute to these qualities a separability, a clarity that they do not possess. "Style d'une teneur"—*Adagio ma non troppo e molto espressivo* is the actual marking—seems precisely to capture the quality of this fugue.

II

An *adagio espressivo* of another kind, the much celebrated disruption at bar 9 of the first movement (Vivace) of the Piano Sonata in E major, Opus 109, has in-

---

8. "Die Kontrapunkte der Exposition sind keine selbständigen, in sich sinnvollen Gegenstimmen, sondern Stückelungen von Motiven, die zu nichts anderem dienen, als die Expressivität des chro-

cited endless theorizing about the extents and limits of sonata form. (The music is shown in appendix 11A.) Everyone who writes about the piece reminds us, as if revealing some arcane secret, that this Adagio, when it first happens, is coordinate with the second tonal phase of a sonata exposition. The pianist Edwin Fischer writes of a movement conceived in "reiner Sonatenform"—pure sonata form–in which "the Adagio espressivo is the second theme."[9] Nicolas Marston, in his exhaustive monograph on the sonata, and in an earlier essay, speaks of this music as "the second group" in the exposition, invoking terminology minted by Donald Francis Tovey a century ago to account for the thematic vicissitudes encountered within sonata-form expositions beginning with Haydn and ending somewhere in the vicinity of Brahms.[10] It is not, however, a term that has much purchase in the first movement of Opus 109. William Kinderman, in several illuminating studies, but most pointedly in an essay called "Thematic contrast and parenthetical enclosure in the piano sonatas, op. 109 and 111," hears this music differently: "In a sense . . . the entire Adagio represents an interpolation, or internal expansion of the music at the moment of the interrupted cadence. Even though the adagio section is much longer than the opening segment of the Vivace, it is parenthetical, and is strictly enclosed within the first two passages in Vivace tempo."[11] If there is any vision in this extreme view, it comes at a price, for it is otherwise blind to the substantive weight of the Adagio as idea itself, and oblivious of a larger rhythmic motion in which these opening bars of the movement are made to seem an extended upbeat to the great downbeat on the diminished seventh chord at m. 9.

These efforts to understand the relationship of the Adagio espressivo to the Vivace betoken a deeply problematic aspect of the piece. Surely, the first move-

---

matischen Themas zu akzentuieren. . . . Fugenmechanik und motivische Expressivität sind also nicht in einem 'style d'une teneur' aufgehoben, sondern stehen sich als getrennte Merkmale gegenüber." Dahlhaus, *Gesammelte Schriften,* VI: 227; *Beethoven: Approaches,* 220–221.

9. "Der Satz ist in reiner Sonatenform gehalten. Das Adagio espressivo ist das zweite Thema." Edwin Fischer, *Ludwig van Beethovens Klaviersonaten* (Wiesbaden: Insel Verlag, 1956), 125.

10. Nicholas Marston, *Beethoven's Piano Sonata in E, Op. 109* (Oxford: Oxford University Press, 1995), 46; "Schenker and Forte Reconsidered: Beethoven's Sketches for the Piano Sonata in E, Op. 109," *19th Century Music* 10 (1986): 24–42, esp 31, which speaks of "the remarkable intrusion of the second group . . . at m. 9."

11. William Kinderman, "Thematic contrast and parenthetical enclosure in the piano sonatas, op. 109 and 111," in *Zu Beethoven: Aufsätze und Dokumente* 3, ed. Harry Goldschmidt (Berlin: Verlag Neue Musik, 1988), 43–59, esp. 46. For Glenn Stanley, resisting Kinderman's hearing, "the dramatic contrasts that the second group presents are all part of the dialogic process." See his "Voices and Their Rhythms in the First Movement of Beethoven's Piano Sonata Op. 109: Some Thoughts on the Performance and Analysis of a Late-Style Work," in *Beethoven and His World,* ed. Scott Burnham and Michael P. Steinberg (Princeton and Oxford: Princeton University Press, 2000), 99.

ment of Opus 109 is radical in its rethinking of the concept Sonata—not merely of the conventions comprised in what we today loosely call sonata form, but of the genre itself. "The first movement is more like a free fantasy, and yet the quite original figure in the Vivace and the principal idea of the soulful Adagio are richly bodied forth in tightly bound alternation," wrote its earliest reviewer (in 1821), groping for language to convey the paradox of a music that, in the alternation of its disparate parts, strives to free itself, fantasy-like, from the formal constraints of sonata even as it pulls the sonata strings more tightly.[12] The estimable A. B. Marx, writing in 1824, hardly knew what to make of the first movement. He could find in it "no leading idea," which, he surmised, "the sublime singer must have dispersed through *Spiel*." Emphasizing the composer's whimsical "play," Marx here plays on the word itself, in its opposition to the immediacy of song, to the clarity with which a leading idea, when it is perceived as song, is made comprehensible.[13] For Marx, the true sonata begins only with the second movement: "But now the true sentiment of the piece rushes forth. A highly charged passion flows with great clarity from a Prestissimo in E minor.... Written in sonata form, it (together with the last movement) constitutes the true sonata."[14] That the first movement would be heard as a music before the main business of the sonata is manifest in Marx's language: "präludierend" (preludizing), he writes of the opening bars, and "Präludien-Form" at the end, no doubt provoked by the join between the first two movements, ensured by Beethoven's instruction to release the final damper pedal only at the opening of the following Prestissimo.[15]

Carl Czerny, writing in 1842, but drawing on a life in Beethoven's company, echoes the language of that earliest review: "More fantasy than sonata. The Vivace

---

12. "Der erste Satz ist mehr einer freien Fantasie ähnlich; doch wird die ganz neue Figur im Vivace und der Haupt-Gedanke des seelenvollen Adagio's in eng verbundenem Wechsel gehaltvoll durchgeführt . . ." *Zeitung für Theater und Musik,* Jg. 1 (1821), 184; reprint in Stefan Kunze, ed., *Ludwig van Beethoven: Die Werke im Spiegel seiner Zeit* (Laaber: Laaber-Verlag, 1987, Sonderausgabe 1996), 357.

13. "Recensent muß aber gestehen, daß er in diesem ganzen ersten Satze keine leitende Idee gefunden hat; sie müßte denn darin bestehen, daß der erhabene Sänger sich durch *Spiel* (es ist in diesem Satze ein sehr angehehmes Klavierspiel) zerstreuen, daß ihm das aber nicht recht gelingen wollte." *Berliner Allgemeine Musikalische Zeitung,* Jg. 1 (1824), 37–38; reprint Kunze, *Beethoven: Die Werke im Spiegel seiner Zeit,* 367.

14. "Jetzt aber stürzt die eigentliche Empfindung hervor. Ein Prestissimo in E moll strömt klar und deutlich eine höchst aufgeregte Leidenschaft aus. Es bildet mit dem letzten Satze die eigentliche Sonate und ist auch in der Sonaten-Form hingeworfen." *Ibid.*

15. Beethoven's ambivalence in the notation of the join between the first and second movements is given intelligent discussion in Marston, *Beethoven's Piano Sonata in E, Op. 109,* 9–10, a commentary on the no less complex reading of it in Heinrich Schenker, *Beethoven, die letzten fünf Sonaten: Sonate E dur Op. 109. Kritische Ausgabe mit Einführung und Erläuterung* (Vienna: Universal-Edition, 1913), and elsewhere in Schenker's papers.

alternates several times with the Adagio. The whole has an extremely noble, calm but dreamy character, and the quick passages in the Adagio must be played very gently, like the figures in a dream, while the Vivace produces its effect only when played molto legato and in a singing manner."[16] Of interest, this is, not least because one might intuitively have put it the other way round: the Vivace "sehr leicht, wie Traumgestalten," the Adagio "sehr legato und gesangvoll." Fischer puts it this way: "The whole must sound as though it is poured out, like an improvisation," and of the Adagio, "Everything is melody, no passage-work."[17]

These hearings of the improvisatory, of the fantasy-like, and indeed of Marx's "präludierend" all resonate with what may be the earliest written sketch for the movement, in the miscellaneous collection known as Berlin Grasnick 20b. The sketch is shown in ex. 11.1. Now, while the actual notes on the page are anything but clear—transcriptions by Marston and Kinderman convey two somewhat different readings—Beethoven's conceptual inscription is highly suggestive: "fällt ein cis moll u. —in einer Fantasie—schließt darin."[18] Each of these terms—"fällt ein"; "cis moll"; "in einer Fantasie"; "schließt darin"—has some bearing on what actually happens in the movement, in its final form. The implications of these words will haunt much of the discussion that follows, even recognizing, as we must, the considerable evidentiary restraints in attributing to the finished work ideas that have survived from some earlier phase of its conception.[19]

"Fällt ein" —*Einfall,* in its sense both of sudden, involuntary idea, and of

---

16. " . . . mehr Fantasie als Sonate. Das *Vivace* wechselt mit dem *Adagio* mehrmal ab. Das Ganze hat einen sehr edlen, ruhigen aber träumerischen *Character,* und die schnellen Passagen im *Adagio* müssen sehr leicht, wie Traumgestalten, vorgetragen werden, so wie das *Vivace* nur sehr *legato* und gesangvoll von Wirkung ist." Czerny, "Über den richtigen Vortrag der sämmtlichen Beethoven'schen Werke für das Piano allein," [chapter 2 of] *Die Kunst des Vortrags der älteren und neueren Klavierkompositionen* (Vienna: A. Diabelli u. Comp., 1842), 67. Reprint as Carl Czerny, *Über den richtigen Vortrag der sämtlichen Beethoven'schen Klavierwerke,* ed. Paul Badura-Skoda (Vienna: Universal Edition, 1963), 59.

17. "Das Ganze muß wie aus einem Guß, einer Improvisation ähnlich, erklingen" —and of the Adagio, "Alles ist Melodie, keine Passagen." Fischer, *Klaviersonaten,* 125.

18. Roughly, "interrupted in C♯ minor and, in a fantasy, closes there." For a facsimile of the page in Grasnick 20b, see Kinderman, "Thematic contrast," unpaginated "Abb. 1."

19. There is reason to believe that in this earlier phase, for a brief moment in the spring of 1820, the movement may have been conceived as one of a group of bagatelles for Friedrich Starke's *Wiener Pianoforteschule.* The evidence is marshaled in *Artaria 195: Beethoven's Sketchbook for the* Missa solemnis *and the Piano Sonata in E Major, Opus 109,* 3 vols., ed. William Kinderman (Urbana and Chicago: University of Illinois Press, 2003), I: 16, 22, 26, 35, 74, 96 and *passim.* If this were the case, then this "kleine neue Stück," as it was called in a conversation book from April 1820, "then assumes a yet more radical role, poised between the increasingly complex rhetoric of sonata as fantasy, on the one hand, and a new aesthetic in which the fragmentary, aphoristic, distracted utterance is much prized," as I wrote in a review of Kinderman's edition; see "To Edit a Sketchbook," in *Beethoven Forum* 12/1 (Spring 2005): 94.

EXAMPLE 11.1 Berlin, SBB, Grasnick 20b, fol. 3r.

interruption–seems perfectly to capture the function, the meaning, the performative act of this diminished seventh chord at m. 9, the *forte* toward which the Vivace aims its long crescendo. Portentous signals of its significance are everywhere, even in its notation. No facile breaking of the chord in the usual shorthand, the arpeggiation is fully notated—made figural, a diminished seventh of thematic substance. The orthography, the graphic expanse of the thing, comes vividly to life in Beethoven's autograph (see fig. 11.1). In another review from 1824, an astute hearing from the irreproachable *Allgemeine musikalische Zeitung* in Leipzig, it is precisely this *Einfall* that is underscored. The movement is heard to break down into two big "chunks" (*Hauptmassen*), and the great moment is depicted in a carefully wrought sentence designed to capture the power of the unexpected: "Following a passage across eight bars of one and the same arpeggiation in a quite natural sequence of harmonies about to arrive at a cadence in the dominant, the diminished seventh chord on B-sharp abruptly interrupts this progression and sweeps the listener away with it in an entirely new direction in the Adagio espressivo in 3/4 time that follows at once."[20]

Adorno has something to say about the diminished seventh chord in late Beethoven. In one of those passages from his notebooks that were collected up in

---

20. "Er zerfällt in zwey Hauptmassen. Nachdem, acht Takte hindurch, eine und dieselbe Akkordbrechung in ganz ungesuchten Harmonieenfolgen, gleichsam bis an die Cadenz der Dominante gelangt ist, tritt plötzlich der verminderte Septimenakkord auf *His* in dem unmittelbar folgenden Adagio espressivo 3/4 Takt diesem Fortschreiten in den Weg und reisst den Zuhörer in ganz neuer Richtung mit sich fort." *Allgemeine musikalische Zeitung* (1824), col. 213–225; reprint Kunze, *Beethoven: Die Werke im Spiegel seiner Zeit,* 360.

FIGURE 11.1 Beethoven, Piano Sonata in E major, Opus 109, first movement, from the autograph score in the Gertrude Clarke Whittall Foundation Collection held at the Library of Congress, Washington, D.C. By kind permission.

Beethoven: Philosophie der Musik, Adorno reminds himself of a curious pronouncement attributed to Beethoven: "Dear boy, the surprising effects which many attribute to the natural genius of the composer alone are often enough achieved quite simply by the correct use and resolution of the diminished seventh chord."[21] Adorno cites Bekker, but the actual passage comes from Theodor von Frimmel, who conducted an interview in 1880 with Carl Friedrich Hirsch, a grandson of Johann Georg Albrechtsberger, who was of course Beethoven's counterpoint teacher from January 1794 till March 1795. Hirsch, then seventy-nine years old, recalled for Frimmel his own studies with Beethoven, which began in the autumn of 1816 and ended in May 1817.[22]

21. "Lieber Junge, die überraschenden Wirkungen, welche viele nur dem Naturgenie der Komponisten zuschreiben, erzielt man oft genug ganz leicht durch richtige Anwendung und Auflösung der verminderten Septimen-akkorde." Adorno, *Beethoven,* German ed., 188; English ed., 129.

22. Th[eodor] von Frimmel, *Bausteine zu einer Lebensgeschichte des Meisters* [= *Beethoven-Studien* II] (Munich and Leipzig: Georg Müller, 1906), 58–59, where the passage goes not quite as Adorno has it: "[Hirsch] recalled that Beethoven lingered for some time at the discussion of the diminished

Quite apart from the obvious questions of veracity elicited in these lines that Hirsch, through Frimmel, attributed to Beethoven some sixty-three years earlier, it is Adorno's gloss on the passage that is interesting. "This statement is very important for Beethoven's procedure," he claims, and then: "The recurrent, idiosyncratic harmonic formulae which *intentionally* suspend the surface clarity include, in particular, the chord of the diminished seventh on the anticipated resolving note in the bass."[23] But the diminished seventh at m. 9 is not quite of this kind, because while the bass note toward which the previous F♯ wants to resolve is indeed B, this note is itself not contained within the diminished seventh. Rather, the chord fleetingly suggests that B ought to be understood in the bass, but as a root made dissonant by the ninth (B♯, heard rather as C♮) sounding above it. That hearing is however contradicted at once, for the actual bass, F♯, sounded at the second eighth, asserts itself as a dissonant seventh beneath an understood G♯, now implicitly the root of this harmony. The inflection is toward C♯ minor— "fällt ein . . . cis moll"—not, to be sure, established as a "new key," but merely as a station toward the tonicization of B major.

Even assuming that Hirsch's memory, reaching back across those sixty-three years, was an exceptionally reliable instrument, it seems odd that Adorno would leap to the conclusion that Beethoven's words should be taken at face value.[24]

---

seventh chord (der 'Dissonanz'). He then said something like the following: 'Lieber Junge, [as in Adorno, until:] erzielt man oft ganz leicht durch richtige Anwendung und Auflösung dieser Akkorde;' whereupon he then demonstrated to the 'Jungen' the several ways of resolving one and the same diminished seventh chord, each according to the key toward which one is drawn." The Pierpont Morgan Library in New York owns a copy of Albrechtsberger's *Gründliche Anweisung zur Composition* (Leipzig: Johann Gottlob Immanuel Breitkopf, 1790) with an inscription, signed by Beethoven: "Februar 1817 | Dem Hirschlein mit | sauberen Ohren u. Pfothen!!!" (For the little Hirsch [= deer] with clean ears and paws).

23. "Dieser Satz ist äußerst wichtig für Beethovens Verfahrensweise." "Zu den durchgehenden, idiosynkratischen harmonischen Formeln, die *absichtsvoll* die Oberflächen-plastik suspendieren, gehört insbesondere der verminderte Septimakkord zum antizipierten Auflösungston im Bass." Adorno, *Beethoven*, 188; English, 129. Adorno refers again to the Hirsch passage in the "Aufzeichnungen zu einer Theorie der musikalischen Reproduktion," in some notes on Rudolph Kolisch's theory of tempo in Beethoven. See Adorno, *Beethoven*, German ed., 356; English ed., 245.

24. Beethoven's words (as Hirsch dictates them) bear an uncanny resemblance to a well-known passage in Carl Philipp Emanuel Bach's *Versuch über die wahre Art das Clavier zu spielen*, II (1762), in the chapter "Von der freyen Fantasie"(§.11), 335: "Auf eine noch kürzere, und dabey angenehm überraschende Art in die entferntesten Tonarten zu kommen, ist kein Accord so bequem und fruchtbar, als der Septimenaccord mit der verminderten Septime und falschen Quinte . . . " (For a yet shorter and agreeably surprising way to move to the most remote keys, no chord is more adept and fruitful than the seventh chord with the diminished seventh and diminished fifth.) Beethoven drew heavily on the earlier chapters of Bach's *Versuch* II in the preparation of teaching materials around 1809 (see Gustav Nottebohm, *Beethoveniana: Aufsätze und Mittheilungen* [Leipzig: C. F. Peters, 1872], 162–170); if the final chapter never appears among Beethoven's excerpts, we

When Beethoven uses the diminished seventh chord, he does so not merely to achieve an "überraschenden Wirkung." Rather, it is the "richtige Anwendung und Auflösung" that must have engaged Beethoven's explanation to Hirsch that day in 1817. And it is precisely this aspect of the thing—the "use" to which it is put, and the disentangling of its ambiguities—that endows the diminished seventh at m. 9 with its special significance. On the face of it, the articulation at m. 9, marked by a change in tempo and meter, and by every other parameter by which we measure things (density of texture, registral disposition, thematic matter and the like) is extreme. And yet the great paradox of m. 9 is that this very act of disruption, in its simple syntax, constitutes a juncture in the course of narrative, as though a sentence had been interrupted in the midst of a thought now deflected in some other direction, very much in the manner suggested by that smart reviewer for the *Allgemeine musikalische Zeitung.* The arpeggiation unfolds at precisely this moment of deflection, and "belongs" as much to the music that precedes it as to the music that issues from it. The theater of classical sonata, its personaggi clearly defined, their entrances choreographed, is here replaced by something else: an internal colloquy, a narrative, by which I mean the act of narrating as distinct from a story told—"ohne Erzähltes erzähle," to borrow again from Adorno[25]—less an enactment of some theatrical script than a journey of the mind, of the *empfind-same Leben.* The figure of Emanuel Bach stirs yet again. To put it differently, when we seek to explain the opposition between Vivace and Adagio espressivo, we are driven to an internal dialectics. And yet it seems to me unhelpful to insist that the Vivace is the thesis in opposition to the antithesis of the Adagio espressivo. Something more radical is at play here: this fantasy-like music that emanates from the diminished seventh chord is richly, broodingly complex, given to stunning outbursts of expression that range over the entire keyboard, as though breaching the tight constraints within which the Vivace is controlled. The distinction of the diminished seventh resides not, as is much claimed for it, in the ease with which it

---

can yet be confident that he knew it well. And it is good to remind ourselves of the primary place of the *Versuch* in the teaching of Beethoven's piano students. "But above all get him Emanuel Bach's 'Lehrbuch über die wahre Art das Clavier zu spielen,' which he must bring with him next time," Beethoven advised Carl Czerny's father at their first meeting in 1800/01. See Carl Czerny, *Erninnerungen aus meinem Leben,* ed. Walter Kolneder (Strasbourg & Baden-Baden: P. H. Heitz, 1968), 15.

25. " . . . narrates without narrative." Theodor W. Adorno, *Mahler: Eine musikalische Physiognomik* (Frankfurt am Main: Suhrkamp, 1960), 106; tr. Edmund Jephcott as *Mahler: A Musical Physiognomy* (Chicago and London: University of Chicago Press, 1992), 76—a passage much admired in Carolyn Abbate, *Unsung Voices: Opera and Musical Narrative in the Nineteenth Century* (Princeton: Princeton University Press, 1991), 27.

can be manipulated to remote ends, but in the complex enharmonic labyrinth that it often engenders.

And that is precisely what happens at the return of the diminished seventh chord at m. 12, setting loose a varied reprise—a *Veränderung* in the most radical sense—of the initial three-bar phrase in the Adagio espressivo: "a sequence of measures that is from all sides and in every respect sorely misunderstood," in Schenker's blunt prelude to his own convoluted explication.[26] These are the tenths between mm. 12 and 13 that come to rest on a D♯ major triad. The similarity in affect with a passage in the first movement of Opus 110, mm. 77–78—indeed, almost the literal pitches (see ex. 11.2)—is striking, and perhaps draws us into some deeper aspect of Beethoven's inner language. The sidestepping of normal root motion, a moment of syntactical inscrutability, might put us again in mind of Emanuel Bach on ellipsis, in explanation of just such a passage in the Fantasy published at the end of the *Versuch*.[27] To explain away the passage in purely contrapuntal terms, as a motion in tenths, is to dismiss its elliptical bending of the "richtige Anwendung und Auflösung" of the diminished seventh. Surely, Beethoven wants us to hear the F-double-sharp in m. 13 as an allusion to the appoggiatura in m. 10, now given a fullness of harmonic weight.

Allusiveness alone, however, fails to account for the slippage felt at just this moment, as though the harmonic underpinnings of the passage had inexplicably shifted. In the diminished seventh that sets off the Adagio, the high A is an appoggiatura to a displaced G♯, the powerfully implicit root of a dominant ninth; the F♯ in the bass is a seventh that resolves inevitably to E. At its repetition at m. 12, the diminished seventh is intensified, the seventh now doubled and sustained, and set in the lowest octave, the A doubled at the highest, isolating these two foundational dissonances. At m. 12, by the rule of *veränderte Reprise*, the ear wants the figure shown in ex. 11.3.

What it gets instead are those riddling tenths that pick up the registral isolation of the deep F♯ and the high A and move them across the grain, so to say, forsaking the original harmonic syntax in favor of something else. It is the F♯ that is made now to function as the appoggiatura-like ninth, moving to a root E♯, whereas the A (to be imagined as G♯♯) is redefined as a third degree of the new triad. It is only in retrospect (a split-second retrospect, as it turns out) that the ear must rethink the original diminished seventh, whose resolution is now made

---

26. "Eine . . . allseits und in jeder Hinsicht schwer verkannte Taktreihe." Heinrich Schenker, *Beethoven: Die letzten Sonaten. Sonate E Dur Op. 109*. Kritische Einführung und Erläuterung, ed. Oswald Jonas (Vienna: Universal Edition, 1971), 8.

27. The passage is discussed in chapter 5; see notes 4 and 5 there.

EXAMPLE 11.2 Opus 110, first movement, mm. 76–79.

deeply problematic. The fleeting tenths at the end of m. 12 are made to bear the considerable weight of this syntactical *Veränderung.* Oblivious of those internal laws that control proper root motion, these extreme tenths that negotiate between mm. 12 and 13 retreat into the abstraction of voice leading, challenging us to hear into the interstices of the ellipsis, into that imaginary silence toward which the diminished seventh makes its *crescendo,* breaking off at, or just before, the sudden *piano* at E♯/G♯. Precisely here, in this imaginary space, something happens. The tenths are uncanny because they proceed as though nothing had happened, but are enabled only because the diminished seventh has been silently

EXAMPLE 11.3 Opus 109, first movement, mm. 12–13, in hypothetical rewriting.

EXAMPLE 11.4 Opus 109, first movement, 12–14, showing root motion

altered at its root. (Aware that Beethoven's notation means precisely what it says, I've yet taken the liberty to notate ex. 11.4 in flats for the visual clarity of the harmony.)

At the recapitulation of the Adagio at m. 58, it is precisely the repetition analogous to mm. 12 and 13 that interrogates the moment of slippage. In the transposition of F♯♯ to the lower fifth, the anticipated B♯ is replaced with its enharmonic equivalent: C♮, now *not* the third degree of a triad, but its root—and all of this enabled because at its repetition, the diminished seventh chord is made to resolve differently (see ex. 11.5).

The challenged relationship between the Vivace and the Adagio espressivo, as two components of a sonata exposition that seem contradictory at their core, where one seems a commentary on the other, recalls once again that remarkable moment in the second movement of the fourth sonata of Emanuel Bach's *Probestücke* (studied in chapter 5) where, in the midst of a solemn Largo maestoso in D major, an exaggerated exercise in the French manner, the music settles unexpectedly on C♯, a dominant, isolated in three octaves with great flourish, triggering a cadenza, an intimate dialogue *a due*, deeply felt—and in F♯ minor, where the movement closes, as though in unabashed contempt of the music that precedes it. The absolute transformation of the piece at a synapse of intense concentration brings to mind Beethoven's "fällt in cis-moll ein u.—in einer Fantasie—schließt darin," and the diminished seventh chord that would set it off. "Fällt in fis-moll ein, u.—in einer Cadenz—schließt darin," Bach may well have been thinking. The sense of interruption in F♯ minor, the closing there in a cadenza, the harmonic quiver that sets it off—all this is suggestive of what will happen in Opus 109. And if there can be no disputing the deep improvisatory impulse immanent

EXAMPLE 11.5 Opus 109, first movement, mm. 61–61, as if transposed from mm. 12–13.

in both cadenza and fantasy in the late eighteenth century, we might wish to remind ourselves that both of these extreme passages are to be found in the midst of sonata movements. In each, the formal constraints, the trappings, of genre are contested, and we are left to wonder whether it is the composer himself who intrudes into the text—a subjectivity in its purest sense—or whether we are witness to the scripting of a masked, figural subjectivity. Perhaps the distinction is itself without merit, the latter merely a disguise for the former.

I cite this earlier example not, emphatically, to enter a brief for influence, however manifest in any of those other acts that specify how composers engage in dialogue with their ancestors, but only to suggest a sense of historical, of aesthetic consciousness, of a touching of musical sensibilities of the kind proposed of Opus 90 in the previous chapter. To hear Opus 109 as a work that embodies its own historical context, reaching into its well of memory as a conscious escape from contemporary convention, is, I think, to apprehend something of the paradox of past and future that so often seems to nourish the formulation—the conceptualizing—of idea in Beethoven's late music.

Dahlhaus, I suspect, was hearing something rather similar when, in his probing study of Opus 109, he alludes to Schering's classic study of Emanuel Bach: "That the 'redende Prinzip' is manifest in the Adagio espressivo, in which the cantabile and the declamatory penetrate one another, is unmistakable."[28] He continues: "The cantabile or speech-like character of the thematic material in Opus 109 . . . indeed poses a threat to the formal coherence of function that, following the criteria of middle-period [Beethoven] in general, legitimates sonata as such in the first place." And then, most provocatively: "it remains . . . for the time being undecided whether it is a question of a movement in sonata-form or of a formulation that will have to be assessed according to some criterion other than the stringency of thematic process."[29] The music beginning at m. 9 is less "second group" than a meditation on the *idea* of a second group.

III

How, then, do we reconcile these extreme views of the movement? For Kinderman and Marston, it is a question of hearing beyond the extravagance of the Adagio espressivo, reductively: what remains are the archetypes of voice-leading and formal convention, the tautology of tonal form. In pursuit of unities, Schenker plays the organicist card: "Beethoven strives to give the internal basis of sonata form its visible embodiment at once in an externally continuous representation of its content, which is to say that he wished the movement to be understood even in its purely external form as a normally unfolding sonata form, according to its

---

28. "Daß sich im Adagio espressivo das 'redende Prinzip' manifestiert, in dem sich Kantabilität und Deklamatorik durchdringen, ist unverkennbar." "Musikalische Gattungsgeschichte als Problemgeschichte. Zu Beethovens Klaviersonaten," in Carl Dahlhaus, *Gesammelte Schriften*, VI: 349. The reference is to Arnold Schering, "C. Ph. E. Bach und das redende Prinzip in der Musik," *Jahrbuch der Musikbibliothek Peters*, 45 (1938), 13–29.

29. "Der kantable oder 'redende' Charakter der Thematik stellt allerdings in op. 109 . . . eine Gefährdung des formalen Funktionszusammenhangs dar, der eine Sonata nach den Kriterien der mittleren Periode überhaupt erst als solche legitimiert. . . . Und es bleibt darum . . . einstweilen unentschieden, ob es sich um einen Satz in Sonatenform oder um ein Gebilde handelt, das nach einem anderen Kriterium als dem der Stringenz des thematischen Prozesses beurteilt werden muß." Dahlhaus, "Musikalische Gattungsgeschichte," 349.

nature."[30] For Dahlhaus, it is this unexplained extravagance of the Adagio espressivo that sets off a challenge to conventional musical coherence, a challenge to those archetypes that are the comfort zones for Schenker and his followers.

To think that they could—these disparate readings—be somehow reconciled is to suggest that diplomacy might stand in for a harder view of the thing. In his lengthy essay on Goethe's *Wahlverwandtschaften* (Elective Affinities)—to which we return in the final chapter—Walter Benjamin takes Goethe's novella as a pretext for an abstruse meditation toward a theory of literary criticism, a theory that begins with a distinction between what Benjamin calls *Sachgehalt* (material content) and, enigmatically, *Wahrheitsgehalt* (truth content). "Criticism," he writes, "seeks the truth content of a work of art; commentary, its material content. The relationship of the two is determined by that fundamental principle of literature according to which the greater the significance of the work, the more inconspicuously and intimately its truth content is bound up with its material content."[31] What, precisely, is this *Wahrheitsgehalt* that Benjamin is so determined to reveal? Can it be grasped? Toward the end of the essay, Benjamin comes round to Ottilie, whose ambivalent "embodiment" figures a central enigma of the novella. For Benjamin, she inspires a quest for the location of the beautiful. "Everything essentially beautiful is always and in its essence bound up, though in infinitely different degrees, with semblance."[32] In what follows, there is tortuous introspection on the nature of beauty, in its essence, as that which is veiled; much is made of the phenomenon of veiling and unveiling, leading to this insight: "The task of art criticism is not to lift the veil but rather, through the most precise knowledge of it as a veil, to raise itself for the first time to the true view of the beautiful . . . to the view of the beautiful as that which is secret." And finally: "Since only the

---

30. " . . . Beethoven den inneren Gründen der Sonatenform zugleich auch in einer äußerlich fortlaufenden Darstellung des Inhaltes ihre sichtbare Verkörperung zu geben sich bestrebte, das heißt, daß er den Satz auch schon rein äußerlich als eine ihrem Wesen nach normal sich abwickelnde Sonatenform angesehen wissen wollte." Schenker, *Sonate E Dur Op. 109,* 5.

31. "Der Kritik sucht den Wahrheitsgehalt eines Kunstwerkes, der Kommentar seinen Sachgehalt. Das Verhältnis der beiden bestimmt jenes Grundgesetz des Schrifttums, demzufolge der Wahrheitsgehalt eines Werkes, je bedeutender es ist, desto unscheinbarer und inniger an seinen Sachgehalt gebunden ist." Walter Benjamin, *Illuminationen: Ausgewählte Schriften,* ed. Siegfried Unseld (Frankfurt am main: Suhrkamp, 1955), 170; and Benjamin, *Gesammelte Schriften,* ed. Rolf Tiedemann and Hermann Schweppenhäuser, in collaboration with Theodor W. Adorno and Gershom Scholem, I/1 (Frankfurt am Main: Suhrkamp, 1974), 123; "Goethe's Elective Affinities," tr. Stanley Corngold, in Benjamin, *Selected Writings,* ed. Marcus Bullock and Michael W. Jennings, I (Cambridge, Mass., and London: Belknap Press of Harvard University Press, 1996), 297. My translation differs slightly.

32. "Alles wesentlich Schöne ist stets und wesenhaft aber in unendlich verschiedenen Graden, dem Schein verbunden." *Gesammelte Schriften,* I/1, 194. *Selected Writings,* I: 350.

beautiful and outside it nothing—veiling or being veiled—can be essential, the divine ground of the being of beauty lies in the secret."[33]

If I understand him, Benjamin is here saying what I suspect we all grasp intuitively: to understand the beautiful, one begins with the assumption that the veil of appearance, of *Schein*, is not separable from some underlying *Wahrheitsgehalt*—some object that this veil means to obscure. In music, the inseparability of the material surface of the piece and this deeper, veiled essence may be said to constitute its beauty, an idea that perhaps drove Schenker to his own theorizing. But if Benjamin is all too aware of the futility of ever unveiling the essence of beauty, Schenker apprehends the abiding relationship of surface and deep structure differently. For Schenker, the veil must be lifted, the mystery revealed, if not solved.

Those of us who continue to ponder the mysteries of Beethoven's late music in the crucible of postmodern discourse might consider Benjamin's words as a provocation for a coming to terms with such enigmas as the diminished seventh chord at m. 9, and all that it suggests of the imponderable motives that underlie the two musics that mark their own worlds on either side of it. We might in this context again consider Adorno's "Objektiv ist die brüchige Landschaft, subjektiv das Licht, darin einzig sie erglüht." Music analysis as technical praxis may help us to find our way in this "fractured landscape." But perhaps it is only in the act of performance (imaginary or actual) that the critical ear can sense the subjective "light" that illuminates the landscape—only the tangible, visceral, improvisatory experience of the work that brings us close to Benjamin's intangible *Wahrheitsgehalt*, where the arcanum of the work is valued above all else. The prizing of the impenetrable moment of beauty, emblem of an early Romantic poetics, is manifest nowhere with such urgency as in the encounter with these late works of Beethoven, where the imaginary membrane between *Sachgehalt* and *Wahrheitsgehalt* drives the task of criticism to its extreme end.

---

33. "Die Kunstkritik hat nicht die Hülle zu heben, vielmehr durch deren genaueste Erkenntnis als Hülle erst zur wahren Anschauung des Schönen sich zu erheben . . . zur Anschauung des Schönen als Geheimnis." "Niemals noch wurde ein wahres Kunstwerk erfaßt, denn wo es unausweichlich als Geheimnis sich darstellte. Weil nur das Schöne und außer ihm nichts verhüllend und verhüllt wesentlich zu sein vermag, liegt im Geheimnis der göttliche Seinsgrund der Schönheit" *Gesammelte Schriften*, I/1: 195. *Selected Writings*, I: 351.

APPENDIX 11A
Beethoven, Opus
109, first movement,
(a) mm. 1–15

(continued)

APPENDIX 11A
(continued)
(b) mm. 45–65

CHAPTER 12

Lisch aus, mein Licht: Song, Fugue, and the Symptoms of a Late Style

I

"Mit inniger Empfindung, doch entschlossen, wohl akzentuirt u. sprechend vor-getr[agen]": with intimate feeling, yet resolutely, well accented, and sung as though spoken. Beethoven inscribed this elaborate instruction on the inside cover of a small notebook—the so-called Boldrini sketchbook—used during the autumn of 1817. Gustav Nottebohm (who described the contents of the book before it vanished shortly after 1890) observed that "inniger" seemed to have been a second thought, added a bit later.[1] Beethoven then either forgot that he'd added it, or thought better of it, for the word does not appear in the published version. It did, however, appear less than a year earlier, in the inscription above the first movement of the Piano Sonata in A, Opus 101: "Etwas lebhaft und mit der in-nigsten Empfindung." A similar instruction, from August 1814, regulates the opening movement of the Piano Sonata in E minor, Opus 90: "Mit Lebhaftigkeit und durchaus mit Empfindung und Ausdruck." Its second movement is inscribed "Nicht zu geschwind und sehr singbar vorzutragen"; in similar mode, the third movement of the Piano Sonata Opus 109, from 1820, is marked "Gesangvoll, mit innigster Empfindung."

The inscription in Boldrini pertains not, however, to some instrumental work that wants to sing, but to a song that wants to speak. *Resignation* (WoO 149), first

---

1. See "Ein Skizzenbuch aus dem Jahre 1817," in Gustav Nottebohm, *Zweite Beethoveniana: Nachge-lassene Aufsätze* (Leipzig: C. F. Peters, 1887), esp. 349–350; and see Douglas Johnson, Alan Tyson, and Robert Winter, *The Beethoven Sketchbooks:* History, Reconstruction, Inventory, ed. Douglas Johnson (Berkeley and Los Angeles: University of California Press, 1985), 347–350.

EXAMPLE 12.1 Boldrini sketchbook (after N II, 352): sketch for *Resignation.*

published in the *Wiener Zeitschrift für Kunst* for 31 March 1818, is a setting of an enigmatic poem by Paul Graf von Haugwitz.[2] (The poem and the song are given as appendix 12A.) Quirky and eccentric, its contradictions are mirrored in Beethoven's fussy guide to its performance. Curiously, the poem has nothing decisive about it, in the affirmative sense conveyed in Beethoven's "doch entschlossen." Tinged in melancholy, Haugwitz's diffident voice phrases a conceit of passion extinguished. If there is a lover concealed here as well, she (or he) is nowhere in evidence, except perhaps in this impalpable, passionless, odorless—yet life endowing—*Luft* of which the flame is deprived. Whether, then, these images mean to signify a love blown away or the creative fire gone cold—or, for that matter, the two together as complicitous in the meaningful life: this is left unsettled.

Beethoven's setting is unsettling in other ways. By way of entry into this riddling song, the ear is drawn to the singular syntactical formulation with which Beethoven conveys Haugwitz's second strophe: a fresh thematic diction that dissolves at "sucht—findet nicht—," turning elliptically back to the opening imperative, "Lisch aus, mein Licht." Exploiting the ambivalence of Haugwitz's neat palindromic device, Beethoven builds in a full reprise of the opening quatrain. The fourth line of the quatrain—"Du musst nun los dich binden," words redolent of the resolve and heroics of an earlier phase in Beethoven's career—is made climactic in the recapitulation. A triumphant moment of *Entschlossenheit* is imposed upon Haugwitz's wistful lyric. Poem and song are not quite about the same sentiments, nor are they formally concordant.

Beethoven evidently notated seven full pages of sketches for the song in Boldrini. Alas, the three very brief entries published by Nottebohm are all that have survived. The third of them (shown in ex. 12.1) is significant. It has a reso-

---

2. The poem was first published in the *Frauentaschenbuch für das Jahr 1817,* which contains several other poems by Haugwitz. For more on this, and for details on the publication of the song, see *Beethoven Werke: Gesamtausgabe,* Abt. XII, Band 1, Lieder und Gesänge mit Klavierbegleitung, Kritischer Bericht, ed. Helga Lühning (Munich: G. Henle Verlag, 1990), 74–75.

EXAMPLE 12.2 British Library, Ms. Add. 29997, fol. 31r: sketches for *Resignation.*

nance in some sketches preserved in the great miscellany now in the British Library (Ms. Add. 29997), a few fleeting entries penciled at the bottom corner of a page evidently a casualty from an autograph of the cantata *Der glorreiche Augenblick* (see ex. 12.2).[3]

These gestures, taken together with that third entry among Nottebohm's Boldrini sketches, hint at some anxiety having to do with the harmonic implications of this much worried phrase at "findet nicht." The chromatics running up to it, at "sucht, sucht," suggest a commonplace cadential sequel: F♯ wants resolution up to G, which in turn wants the support of some harmony rooted to E. How this might go is shown in ex. 12.3. Beethoven's languid phrase—its coupling of F♯ with a discomfiting C♯—constitutes an ellipsis that betrays the harmony powerfully implicated between a dominant seventh on B and the true dominant of return on A. All the orthodoxies that would enact this cadence are here refused.

3. British Library, Add. Ms.29997 (= SV 187), fol. 31. The leaf is of a paper-type that can be dated to 1808 (see Alan Tyson, "The Problem of Beethoven's 'First' Leonore Overture," *Journal of the American Musicological Society,* 28 [1975]: 316). *Der glorreiche Augenblick,* Opus 136, was first performed on 29 November 1814, a date that might serve as nothing more than a terminus post quem for the sketches for *Resignation.* Another brief and isolated entry for the song, on a bifolium (Tours, Conservatoire de Musique, SV 383) that once formed part of a sketchbook from 1814–1815, does indeed seem to date from some years earlier than the Boldrini sketches. The text is clearly "binden lisch aus [—] mein licht!," and the few notes of music suggest something akin to the final bars of a setting. But clef, key, accuracy of pitch and rhythm are difficult to ascertain with any certainty. On this entry, see Johnson, *The Beethoven Sketchbooks,* 239, and *Werke,* XII/1: 74. I am very grateful to Helga Lühning for providing a copy of the Tours leaf.

EXAMPLE 12.3 *Resignation,* hypothetical continuation from m. 26.

II

Thanks to Nottebohm, we have a pretty good sense of the contents of Boldrini. Evidently the largest of the small-format, so-called pocket sketchbooks, it was devoted to work on the first three movements of the Hammerklavier Sonata, Opus 106, the sketches for which occupied most of pages 18 through 128. In their midst—on pages 92 through 109—would be found sketches for the first movement of the Ninth Symphony (rather advanced—"ziemlich vorgerückt"—Nottebohm calls them) and intimations, only, for the remaining movements. But the first sixteen pages of the book are given to other things. Their contents, again according to Nottebohm, are revealing:

Project	*Pages*
Quintet Fugue in D minor, Hess 40: sketches	1, 2 and 7
J. S. Bach. Two passages from the Fugue in B♭ minor, *WTC* I.[4]	4
Entry for setting of Matthisson's "Badelied"	4
Quintet Fugue in D major, Opus 137: last four bars in full score.	5
J. S. Bach. Two passages from the *Kunst der Fuge,* Contrapunct. 4.	7
Marpurg, *Abhandlung von der Fuge,* II, Tab. XVI, figs. 1–6.	8
Setting of Haugwitz's "Resignation": late sketches	10–16

Merely one instance of a consuming inquiry into fugue—the revisiting of the same icons time and again, as though for spiritual sustenance—these sketchbook entries

---

4. Not the fugue in B minor, as given erroneously in Johnson, *The Beethoven Sketchbooks,* 350 (and 598).

take on a special poignancy, lodged at what seems a moment of studious contemplation before the rush of counterpoint and fugal device set loose in Opus 106.

The Fugue for String Quintet, Opus 137, was composed to inaugurate the ambitious *Gesamtausgabe* of Beethoven's works, in clean manuscript copy, undertaken by Tobias Haslinger in 1817.[5] The single entry for it in Boldrini, its final four bars written in quintet score (Nottebohm left no transcription), again implicates sketches in another source. A leaf now bound in with the sketch miscellany Grasnick 20b, and perhaps discarded from a working autograph, again displays the final bars, here entered three times, each in full score: the final seven bars, heavily revised, are followed on a second system by the final four bars, written out twice. No other sketches for Opus 137 are known to have survived.[6]

For Beethoven, fugue is a concept vulnerable to dialectical extremes. It seems to have been so conceived from his earliest music straight through to the final quartets: any assessment of "late style" in Beethoven needs to come to terms with this condition.[7] At the one extreme are those fugues conceived as didactic exercise, responsive to what might be called the constraints of eighteenth-century procedure and modeled on the venerable historical prototypes, as codified in such works as Marpurg's *Abhandlung von der Fuge* (Berlin, 1753–1754) and Albrechtsberger's *Gründliche Anweisung zur Composition* (Leipzig, 1790), both of which served as texts for Beethoven's own lifelong study. At the other extreme are those fugues that were composed against the rules, so to speak: the genre itself reinvented in the service of some poetic, even epic mission. The fugues composed under Albrechtsberger's eye in the mid-1790s are largely of the first kind, the idiosyncratic specimens from the late quartets of the second. Even in these extreme instances, antinomies are played out at one level or another.

Just such dialectical antinomies are audible in the sketches for these troublesome final bars of Opus 137. (A complete score is given in appendix 12B.) For

---

5. For a critical discussion of the so-called Haslinger-Rudolphinische Abschrift, see Sieghard Brandenburg, "Die Beethovenhandschriften in der Musikaliensammlung des Erzherzogs Rudolph," in *Zu Beethoven: Aufsätze und Dokumente* 3 (Berlin: Verlag Neue Musik, 1988), esp. 170–171. In fact, two clean autographs exist. The copy for Haslinger, lacking its first leaf, is now at the Gesellschaft der Musikfreunde in Vienna. The other manuscript is at the Bibliothèque Nationale in Paris.

6. Berlin: Staatsbibliothek zu Berlin—Stiftung Preußischer Kulturbesitz, Mus. ms. Autogr. Beethoven Grasnick 20b, fol. 13r. See also Johnson, *The Beethoven Sketchbooks*, 250.

7. For a conspectus, see my "*Das Organische der Fuge:* On the Autograph of Beethoven's String Quartet in F Major, Opus 59, No. 1," in *The String Quartets of Haydn, Mozart, and Beethoven: Studies of the Autograph Manuscripts,* Isham Library Papers III, ed. Christoph Wolff (Cambridge, Mass.: Harvard University Music Department, 1980), esp. 223–265, and, in the same volume, Robert Winter's "Response," 266–272, and the discussion that follows at 273–277. I take the opportunity to correct two printer's errors that are of some consequence to the arguments set forth below: 228, bottom, item 1, read "Fugue in B♭ minor"; 229, top, item 2, read "Fugue in B minor."

while the opening bars of the fugue expound a subject and answer that hew suspiciously close to some Bach-like paradigm, the final bars probe the harmonic and even the rhythmic implications of the subject—well-concealed implications, one must say—and echo the salient moments of its subsequent elaboration.

The most salient of them comes at the center of the fugue—nearly plumb at its midpoint, at mm. 36–41. A tritone is wrenched, fortissimo, from the open-stringed C in the cello, at the acoustic bottom of the quintet, where it posits a resolution down to an abstract, unplayable B: the root of a dominant ninth theatrically staged but unsounded. Against it, violin 1 and viola 1 strain at the top of their registers. A single diminished seventh chord resonates for fully five bars. D♯ is forged into E♭, and the passage resolves not in E minor, but to the dominant of G major.

This tritone is itself embedded in the subject, but only when the music is cast in B minor, in the entry beginning at m. 30. And this returns us to those troublesome final bars. C♮ is again conspicuous, provoking a series of chromatic descents, and evoking harmonic paths earlier suggested but not taken. In the motion between bars 77 and 78, E♭ is reconverted to D♯ (reversing the enharmonic vector of mm. 36–42): the simultaneity at the downbeat of bar 78 offers up a tripled C—a tripled ninth!—leading to a dominant on B. D♯ is now so prominent as to inscribe itself into the final statement of the subject (at bar 80). The tonic triad that the subject unfolds at its outset is here transformed into an actual dissonance, its opening A now manifestly a seventh, drawn through an imaginary G to the final F♯ with which the subject closes. It is a *harmonic* implication of the subject that is realized here, having driven the fugue through even its most radical episodes. The very last note in the discant, the F♯ is heard finally to respond to the dissonance immanent in the very first note of the fugue.

If these opening pages in Boldrini capture the final stages of work on the fugue for Haslinger, they establish as well the evidence for a puzzling corollary: that Beethoven had now begun to work on a *second* quintet fugue, this one in D *minor*. Yet again, another source is implicated, for the fugal incipit that Nottebohm records from Boldrini—and he records nothing more than that—is precisely what is captured in an autograph manuscript containing a complete prelude in D minor with an elaborate transition to the fugue, of which again only the opening four bars are notated.[8]

---

8. Berlin: Staatsbibliothek zu Berlin—Preußischer Kulturbesitz, Mus. ms. autogr. Beethoven Artaria 185a. The fragment, item 40 in Willy Hess, *Verzeichnis der nicht in der Gesamtausgabe veröffentlichten Werke Ludwig van Beethovens* (Wiesbaden: Breitkopf & Härtel, 1957; rev. as *The New Hess Catalog of Beethoven's Works*, ed. and tr. James F. Green, West Newbury, Vermont: Vance Brook Pub-

Another brief entry for an interior passage in this incomplete D minor fugue has survived in a manuscript now at the Gesellschaft der Musikfreunde in Vienna. Beethoven Ms. Autogr.81 contains a transcription in rough quartet score, in Beethoven's impatient sketch hand, of the fugue in B minor from Book I of Bach's *Well-Tempered Clavier.* Where the fragment breaks off, after bar 32, some blank space at the bottom of the page was used for a hasty, almost illegible penciled entry for an episode from this Quintet Fugue in D minor.[9] The propinquity of these two projects on a single page suggests that the transcription of the Fugue in B minor likely dates from the weeks chronicled in the opening pages of Boldrini. In its watermark, the manuscript at the Gesellschaft is very close to the type prevalent in the sketchbook Beethoven Autogr. 11, fascicle 1 (Staatsbibliothek zu Berlin—Preußischer Kulturbesitz) whose paper was in use between the end of 1816 and the beginning of 1818, and for miscellaneous sketches for Opus 106.[10]

This same watermark has now been identified in a manuscript discovered only very recently, and containing a previously unknown Allegretto in B minor for string quartet.[11] The manuscript bears an inscription in the hand of one Richard Ford: "This quartette was composed for me in my presence by Ludwig v. Beethoven at Vienna Friday 20th November 1817"—precisely the date inscribed by Beethoven on the Paris autograph of Opus 137. In its brusque twenty-three bars, the Allegretto for Ford resonates sympathetically with these other projects. (The piece is shown in its entirety as appendix 12C.) Its opening theme, an offspring (one might think) of the opening of the fugue for Haslinger, is a fugue subject without fugal issue: the 'cello answers at the octave (no hint of an answer at the dominant), but only for a measure. Still, the texture is openly contrapuntal, fuguelike in its intense pursuit of the sharply etched motives of the subject,

---

lishing, 2003), is published in *Beethoven: Supplemente zur Gesamtausgabe,* ed. Willy Hess, VI (Wiesbaden: Breitkopf & Härtel, 1963): 147–149 and 157; and in Beethoven, *Werke,* Abt. VI, vol. 2 (Munich: G. Henle, 1968): 117ff.

9. The manuscript is a full sheet comprising two gathered bifolia, of which only the first three pages contain writing. Fol. 1ʳ contains a passage in quartet score from the finale of Haydn's Symphony No. 99 (see "*Das Organische der Fuge,*" 228–29); fols. 1ᵛ and 2ʳ contain the Bach copy; sketches for the Quintet in D minor are entered at staves 13–14 of fol. 2ʳ. The remaining five pages are blank.

10. This is watermark type 33 in Johnson, *The Beethoven Sketchbooks,* 555; on Autograph 11/1, see 247–252. See also, Joseph Schmidt-Görg, "Die Wasserzeichen in Beethovens Notenpapieren," in *Beiträge zur Beethoven-Bibliographie. Studien und Materialien zum Werkverzeichnis von Kinsky-Halm,* ed. Kurt Dorfmüller (Munich: Henle, 1978), 183, watermark 57.

11. The work came to public notice in the sale of the manuscript at Sotheby's on 8 December 1999, described in *The Pencarrow Collection of Autographs* (London, 1999), lot 189. A facsimile of the autograph, together with a transcription in score, performing parts, a Preface by Martin Bircher and an Introduction by Stephen Roe, is published as *Ludwig van Beethoven: Allegretto in h-Moll/Allegretto in B minor* (Munich: K. G. Saur, Fondation Martin Bodmer Cologny, 2001).

EXAMPLE 12.4 (a) Beethoven, Quartet for Ford; and

(b) J. S. Bach, WTC I, Fugue in B minor, mm.15–16.

overwrought in its picking out of tritones. The return to B minor at m. 16 is co-incident with a restatement of the subject, now tripled at the octave, and with a curious leveling of its second measure, C♯ E G now read as E F♯ G.

The rare value of the piece lies in what it testifies as to Beethoven's state of mind on that Friday in November 1817. For if Ford is accurate in his description of the circumstances of its composition, Beethoven is writing quickly and without premeditation. The autograph is uncommonly clean. A smudged out accidental in the viola at m. 9 hints at an expunged A♯, suggesting an immediate return to B minor and an even shorter piece.[12] If a vagrant sketch might have been found its way into the Boldrini Sketchbook, Nottebohm's selective description of its contents would normally have nothing to say about inconsequential entries for a work that he could not have identified in any case. The manuscript prepared for Ford then documents something of a fugitive thought, free of the kinds of pressures and compulsions that weigh on major projects. The key itself is of interest. B minor, the rarest of keys in Beethoven—"h moll schwarzer Tonart," he scribbled in a sketchbook from 1815[13]—seems an echo of Beethoven's engagement with the transcription of the B-minor Fugue from the *Well-Tempered Clavier*, with which it shares even a turn of phrase (see ex. 12.4). The internal voicings of the quintet fugue for Haslinger echo even more clearly: the Allegretto for Ford takes fugue as a manner of discourse where wit and concision, and the play

---

12. For a thorough discussion of the discovery of the manuscript and its history, and a description of certain aspects of the music, see Barry Cooper, "The Newly Discovered Quartet Movement by Beethoven," *The Beethoven Journal* 15/1 (Summer 2000): 19–24.

13. See Nottebohm, *Zweite Beethoveniana*, 326. The note is to be found among sketches for the finale of the Sonata in D for Piano and Cello, Opus 102 no. 2.

of texture, frees the music from the too familiar temporalities of classical sonata, finding new accents and a new diction even as it challenges the archaic rhetoric of fugal procedure and the hegemony of the Bach fugue. The lifelong engagement with Bach the father is a profoundly dialectical exercise, one without end for Beethoven, and with profound consequences for his late music. The engagement with Emanuel, closer to home, was more fragile, and it is tempting to hear in the music of Beethoven's final decade echoes of the family agon—once more: Bach father, Bach son—even with traces of its redemptive aspects.

III

By the 1770s, Bach's B minor fugue had acquired a reputation. Its harmonies, thought to sound the arcana of an almost biblical profundity, invited exegesis. An invitation was tendered and accepted by Johann Philipp Kirnberger, who, in collaboration with Johann Abraham Peter Schulz, published an analytic display in which a fundamental bass is extrapolated from the first to the very last note of the fugue. The analysis constitutes a magisterial concluding example in Kirnberger's *Die wahren Grundsätze zum Gebrauch der Harmonie*, a book that we know Beethoven to have studied while he was still in Bonn.[14] "This fugue by Joh. Seb. Bach," writes Kirnberger, "which has until today seemed unsolvable by even the great men of our time, is given here with its innate and natural fundamental harmonies, following our precepts, and may serve as a proof of everything stipulated above"—in *Die wahren Grundsätze*, that is. "We believe ourselves to have fathomed the nature of the thing itself when we assert that these fundamental rules of harmony are not only the true, but indeed the only ones according to which this fugue can be explained, and in general all the apparent difficulties in the other works of this greatest harmonist of all times can be elucidated and rendered comprehensible."[15] In fact, the motivation to write *Die wahren Grundsätze* seems

---

14. Johann Philipp Kirnberger, *Die wahren Grundsätze zum Gebrauch der Harmonie, . . . als ein Zusatz zu der Kunst des reinen Satzes in der Musik* (Berlin and Königsberg: G. J. Decker und G. L. Hartung, 1773; reprint Hildesheim and New York: Georg Olms, 1970); the fugue is printed on pp. 55–103. For the arguments that Beethoven knew this work in Bonn, see Gustav Nottebohm, *Beethoven's Studien* (Leipzig and Winterthur: J. Rieter-Biedermann, 1873; reprint Niederwalluf bei Wiesbaden: Sändig, 1971), 6.

15. "Nachstehende Fuge von Joh. Seb. Bach, die bis auf diesen Tag auch großen Männern unserer Zeit unauflöslich geschienen hat, mit denen nach unsern Lehrsätzen daraus natürlich hergeleiteten Grundaccorden, möge als ein Beweis alles dessen dienen, was vorhergegangen ist. Wir glauben uns auf die Natur der Sache selbst zu gründen, wenn wir behaupten, daß diese Grundsätze von der Harmonie nicht allein die wahren, sondern auch die einzigen sind, nach denen diese Fuge erk-

EXAMPLE 12.5 J. S. Bach, WTC I, Fugue in B minor, mm. 12–15.

to have issued from one Herr Hoffmann, organist at the principal church in Breslau. Provoked by a similar analysis in the first part of Kirnberger's *Kunst des
reinen Satzes,* Hoffmann allegedly challenged the theorist "to reduce to its simple
Grundaccorde a certain well-known Bach fugue."[16]

If there is one passage in the fugue that might have quickened Herr Hoffmann's resolve to approach Kirnberger, it would have been the entrance of the
answering voice at bar 13 (shown in ex. 12.5). The tonal answer is of the convoluted, difficult kind engendered when the subject begins on the fifth degree and
moves off to the key of the dominant, for the answer must negotiate a harmonic,
nonsymmetrical return to the tonic while yet preserving what it can of the intervallic integrity of the subject. Bach's answer provoked Marpurg, in his encyclopedic study of fugal answer ("Vom Gefährten") in volume 1 of the *Abhandlung von
der Fuge,* to construct an alternative (shown in ex. 12.6), in which the transposition of the minor second to the minor third is put off till the last moment. "Both
ways are appropriate to the modulations of the subject," Marpurg concludes, fail-
ing to discriminate how Bach's climactic B A♯ G♮ F♯ clinches the return to the
tonic, whereas his modification C♯ B♯ A F♯ only subverts it.[17]

---

läret, und überhaupt alle anscheinende Schwierigkeiten in den übrigen Ausarbeitungen dieses
größten Harmonisten aller Zeiten aufgelöset und verständlich gemacht werden." *Die wahren
Grundsätze,* 53–54 (here and in what follows, my translation, unless otherwise noted).

16. *Ibid.,* "Vorbericht," 3.

17. "Beyde Arten des Gefährten sind den Ausweichungen des Führers gemäß." Friedrich Wilhelm Marpurg, *Abhandlung von der Fuge nach den Grundsätzen und Exempeln der besten deutschen und aus-*

EXAMPLE 12.6 J. S. Bach, WTC I, Fugue in B minor: Marpurg's answer, realized in *Abhandlung,* I, 84.

Tovey, in the preface to his edition of the *Well-Tempered Clavier* (1924), spoke boldly of a "tonal answer . . . almost impossible to harmonise." Taking his cue from a manuscript believed to date from 1722, in the hand of the Bach copyist known latterly as Anon. 5, he believed this tonal answer to have been a later variant. "The autographs," he inaccurately writes, "leave it doubtful whether Bach was really satisfied with his alteration there."[18] And Alfred Dürr, the redoubtable editor of the *Neue Bach Ausgabe,* allows that Bach may well have hesitated over this answer, experimenting with what we might call Tovey's variant (shown in ex. 12.7) before plumping finally for the difficult one.[19]

What, then, does Kirnberger make of this notorious m. 13? His analytical grid of these bars is shown as ex. 12.8. The small F♯ shown in the bass on stave 5 (which gives the fundamental bass with dissonances expressed as figures above the stave) and stave 6 (the fundamental harmony now scraped clean of inessential dissonances) is the critical element. An integral root in the harmonic track, this missing F♯ must be interpolated, even while the sounding surface of the music seals it out. Kirnberger's comment does not trouble over the epistemology of such an interpolation: "In a few places the motion of resolution from a dissonant chord is represented through a small note in the fundamental bass."[20]

Kirnberger's precise language here—"der Uebergang der Resolution eines dissonierenden Accordes"—brings to mind, in yet another context, that well-known passage from the final paragraph in the last chapter of part II of Emanuel Bach's *Versuch* (1762). Here, Bach isolates an elliptical moment in a figured bass that, printed directly in Bach's text, means to lay out the harmonic plan of a "freye Fantasie" fully realized, and engraved on a separate plate. (For an illustration, see

ländischen Meister entworfen, 2 vols. (Berlin: A. Haude and J. C. Spener, 1753–54; reprint Hildesheim and New York: Georg Olms, 1970), I: 84; Bach's configuration is shown in Tab. XXV, fig. 4.

18. J. S. Bach, *Forty-Eight Preludes and Fugues,* ed. Donald Francis Tovey, Preface to Book I (New York: Oxford University Press, 1924), 37.

19. See J. S. Bach, *Neue Ausgabe sämtliche Werke,* Serie V, Band 6.1, Kritischer Bericht von Alfred Dürr (Kassel: Bärenreiter Verlag, 1989), 141–42.

20. "An ein Paar Stellen ist der Uebergang der Resolution eines dissonirenden Accordes durch eine kleine Note im Grundbaß angedeutet." Kirnberger, *Die wahren Grundsätze,* 54.

EXAMPLE 12.7 J. S. Bach, WTC I, Fugue in B
minor: alternative answer, from copy by Joh.
Gottfried Walther (before 1748).

chapter 5, fig. 5.1.) Bach's explanation is worth having: "The transition [der Ue-
bergang] from the seventh chord on B to the following chord of the second on
B♭ constitutes an ellipsis, for really a six-four on B or a triad on C ought to have
been interpolated between them."[21]

The two passages, in fugue and fantasy, differ tellingly from one another. The
rigors of tonal answer and the obligatory counterpoints against it force Bach (the
father) onto a kind of harmonic tightrope. At this signal moment, the constraints
of tonal answer are in conflict with the implacable root motion whose theoretical underpinnings Kirnberger claimed were at the foundation of Bach's music.
But the ellipsis in the fantasy touches at the inner core of meaning. Emanuel
Bach's gloss, characteristically terse, concentrates on the bass alone. Responding
to precisely this gap in the harmony, the realization celebrates a moment of tonal
and metaphorical distance in a convoluted passage of inspired improvisation—
for we are meant to imagine this fantasizing as though witness to the process
through which the music emanates. In setting Bach's fugue against this scrim of
putative roots, Kirnberger unwittingly invokes the rhetorical poetics of the fantasy, while Emanuel Bach, in rendering the diminutions of his fantasy as figured
bass, invokes a venerable model of simple coherence to ground a music embold-
ened by a new poetics of harmonic syntax.

We are returned finally to Beethoven's Haugwitz setting: more precisely, to the

21. "Der Uebergang vom h mit dem Septimenaccord, zum nächsten b mit dem Secundenaccord verräth eine Ellipsin, weil eigentlich der Sextquartenaccord vom h oder c mit dem Dreyklange hätte
vorhergehen sollen." *Versuch über die wahre Art das Clavier zu spielen,* II (1762), 340–341, and engraved plate tipped in. Bach's chapter was the principal text for Heinrich Schenker's "Die Kunst
der Improvisation," in *Das Meisterwerk in der Musik,* I (Munich: Drei Masken Verlag, 1925),
11–40, now translated, with commentary, as "The Art of Improvisation," in *The Masterwork in
Music,* ed. William Drabkin, I (Cambridge and New York: Cambridge University Press, 1994),
2–19 (esp. 8–13).

Uebergang at "findet nicht." In resonance with the fugue for Haslinger, at its dissonant midpoint—in resonance as well with bar 13 of Bach's B-minor fugue; and with the moment of ellipsis in the fantasy by Emanuel Bach—the harmony between "sucht" and "findet" gets caught on the upper intervals of an implied dominant seventh whose root is B. Its resolution elided, the missing root—the E—is sounded finally and with great éclat at a defining moment of *Entschlossenheit:* "*Du* musst nun los dich binden," a phrase sung at first in B minor, sounds forth now triumphantly in the tonic.

The lines of thought laid out in ex. 12.9 mean rather to suggest than to syllogize how it might be that the transcribing of Bach's B-minor fugue will have exercised this concept of ellipsis that I hear both as the gist of Beethoven's song and as a topic of discourse at the center of the fugue for Haslinger; and, further, to suggest how the song and the fugue seem as though two reflections on the common intervallic archetypes of Bach's subject.

IV

What do any of these admittedly modest projects have to do with "lateness"— with a late style, with last works, even with that elusive moment at which the mind begins to picture itself as old? Whatever the explanatory devices with which we come to grips with the music of Beethoven's final decade, these entries in Boldrini have their place.

Fugue and song figure preeminently in Beethoven's last works: not, of course, as genres in the naive sense, but as modes of diction mediating, in their directness of discourse, the stripped-down narratives of sonata, or as dispassionate, fragmentary representations of genre—the ruins of genre, to paraphrase Adorno. The fugue for Haslinger was intended to herald an important issue of Beethoven's collected works. If it does not transcend the conventions of genre, it yet prefigures "late style" in its dead-serious play with the boundaries of fugue—but then, even Beethoven's earliest fugues indulge in such play, and even then, seem to prefigure what we have come to hear as "late" music.

The Haugwitz setting is similarly problematic in this respect. Highly esteemed by Schindler (with whom Thayer, via Deiters and Riemann, for once concurs),[22]

---

22. See Anton Felix Schindler, *Beethoven as I Knew Him*, ed. Donald W. MacArdle, tr. Constance S. Jolly (Chapel Hill and London: The University of North Carolina Press, 1966) 336–337; and Alexander Wheelock Thayer, *Ludwig van Beethovens Leben*, IV, ed. Hugo Riemann (Leipzig: Breitkopf & Härtel, 1907), 76.

EXAMPLE 12.8 Kirnberger [and J. A. P. Schulz], *Die wahren Grundsätze zum Gebrauch der Harmonie*
(Berlin: Decker und Hartung, 1773), pp. 62–63.

EXAMPLE 12.9

and more recently by Ewan West, the song yet seems constrained by the old rules of genre. West, hearing "poetic reinterpretation" in Beethoven's composition, construes this "Neukomposition des Textes" as "Merkmal des romantischen Kunstliedes" which then places the song "klar in einen modernen Kontext."[23] That, I think, gets the matter the wrong way round. For if we are casting about for the "Merkmale des romantischen Kunstliedes" in 1817, *Resignation* seems miscast in the company of Schubert's *Nähe des Geliebten* (1815) or Loewe's *Erlkönig* (1818). Where Beethoven's music "misreads" the poem, the matter hinges upon a point of diction, a turn of phrase. Its marrying of tone to syllable, of harmony to syntax, is fixed in the precepts of the classical Lied. It is precisely the idea of the modern that is challenged in the works of Beethoven's last decade; modernity as a value is questioned, problematized.

Broadly conceived, this fugue and this song are self-evidently "late works" neither in the real time of Beethoven's calendar, nor in spirit, nor even in some metaphorical sense. It is only the occasional gesture that places them for us in 1817: in the song, the iterated C-major triads in root position that erupt from the bare octaves on B, brazenly contradicted; in the fugue, the supreme dexterity of its final bars, an effortless, prismatic mutating of the figures and the rhythms of the subject, a texture luminous in its density. The virtuosity is made to vanish in the sudden *piano* of the last bar. With its final breath, this slightest of gestures, the composer seems to take back the work. Precisely here, in a perceptible shift in voice, we sense the recalibrating of object-subject that Adorno was so at pains to locate in the late works.

This fragile constellation of projects documented in the opening pages of Boldrini situates for us a quiet moment of internal colloquy: a stillness in the autumn of 1817. *Sucht—findet nicht—lisch aus mein Licht:* What was it that Beethoven was seeking? What did he fear not finding? "Man enträthsele—mann wird finden," he scribbled cryptically at the end of a letter to Haslinger in September 1823, as though to set the sullen Haugwitz back on course—roughly: "Unriddle and you shall find." The phrase itself, and its puzzling connection to the substance of the letter, led Hans-Werner Küthen to explore an allusion to the inscription "Quaerendo invenietis" which marks the Canon a 2 in Bach's *Musical Offering*—and to Beethoven's Bach project in general.[24]

---

23. In *Beethoven: Interpretationen seiner Werke,* ed. Albrecht Riethmüller, Carl Dahlhaus, Alexander Ringer (Laaber: Laaber Verlag, 1994), II: 565.

24. Hans-Werner Küthen, "*Quaerendo invenietis.* Die Exegese eines Beethoven-Briefes an Haslinger vom 5. September 1823," in *Musik, Edition, Interpretation: Gedenkschrift Günter Henle,* ed. Martin Bente (Munich: G. Henle, 1980), 282–313.

In the music of Beethoven's final decade, the questioning and the seeking—
the unriddling—exercised to exhaustion, take on a metaphysical tinge. A consuming exhaustion, symptom of a certain aesthetic, a style, a view of a timeless
past, it brings to mind an insight that Christoph Wolff drew from his study of the
canonic appendix to the Goldberg Variations. Did Bach, Wolff asks, finding it
difficult "in his later years to invent new and stimulating musical subject matter,"
choose rather to concentrate "on the contrapuntal elaboration and refinement of
a single musical idea with the aim of exhausting its content?"[25] Bach's consuming project is brought to an almost perfect completion, rational and exhaustive,
in the *Kunst der Fuge.* In Beethoven's last quartets, the exploration is no less consuming, no less exhaustive, even as its fugues avowedly reject—as they must—
Bach's austere, encyclopedic spirit of investigation. And yet it seems to me that
deep in what Dahlhaus would call the "subthematicism" of the late quartets is
embedded a rehearing of Bach's enterprise—a reformulation of this notion of a
final exhaustion. Coupled dialectically in the historical imagination, the phenomena of these two empyreal projects, Beethoven's and Bach's, fuse together
into a generalized language of late style, at once a monument to the exhaustion
of Art and a source of its renewal.

---

25. Christoph Wolff, "Bach's *Handexemplar* of the Goldberg Variations: A New Source," *Journal of the
    American Musicological Society* 29 (1976): 240; reprinted in Christoph Wolff, *Bach: Essays on His
    Life and Music* (Cambridge, Mass., and London: Harvard University Press, 1991), 176.

(continued)

PART V

Fragments

CHAPTER 13

Toward an Epistemology of Fragment

Behind the shameless pretense of its title, the modest intention of this chapter is to come closer to the disorderly notion of fragment, as the term was employed in the decades close on either side of 1800. Any such theorizing would need to reconcile two extreme conditions of fragment: on the one hand, fragment taken to denote the flawed torso of the work left unfinished; on the other, fragment taken to suggest the Romantic condition toward which even the finished works of those volatile years might aspire.

Clearly, when we speak of fragment in this revered aesthetic sense, we mean something quite distinct from those memorably unfinished works that constitute a poignant and cherished repertory in the larger catalogues of the works of, in particular, Mozart and Schubert. (Beethoven figures here as well. Among the thousands of pages of sketches and drafts are now and then embedded the more substantial drafts of works never completed, often obscurely implicated in some larger compositional project, and thus less distinct as self-contained fragments.) The unfinished work is a fragment, even if it can stake no claim to that sublime condition toward which Novalis and Friedrich Schlegel point in any number of well known aphorisms on the subject. Perhaps the most familiar of them is Schlegel's ironic comparison of the works of the ancients that have fallen into the state of fragment with those of the moderns that are made fragmentary in their origins ("bei der Entstehung").[1] Another speaks less to fragment than to

---

1. "Viele Werke der Alten sind Fragmente geworden. Viele Werke der Neuern sind es gleich bei der Entstehung." (Many works of the ancients have become fragments. Many works of the moderns are fragments at birth.) Entry 24 in the so-called Athenäums-Fragmente, in *Kritische Friedrich-Schlegel-Ausgabe,* ed. Ernst Behler et al, II: *Charakteristiken und Kritiken* I (1796–1801) (Munich, Paderborn; Vienna: Ferdinand Schöningh; Zurich: Thomas-Verlag, 1967), 169. For more on this, see chapter 1.

a condition affecting the Romantic work per se, a condition that defines the work as Romantic at its core: "Other poetry is complete, and can thus be thoroughly analyzed. Romantic poetry is still in the process of becoming; indeed that is its characteristic essence, that it forever only becomes, and can never be completed."[2] For Schlegel, the truly Romantic work, ill at ease in the brilliant, classicizing glare of enlightenment, will resist the clarity of cognition that analysis—a concept itself borrowed from the sciences—claims to achieve. To suggest that the finite, completed work is ever in a state of "becoming" is to argue for its condition as permanently unfinished, a condition stubbornly unresponsive to analysis as it is commonly practiced. Romantic art, warns Schlegel, will demand new modes of understanding.

The work unfinished in this Schlegelian sense yet depends paradoxically upon a text that is complete: by all the conventions of art, closed, finished, *vollendet*. The converse makes this clear. If the work is demonstrably incomplete, how can we know that it means to suggest the fragmentary? The power of the text lies in its meaning, but we cannot approach this meaning if we cannot claim to possess the text that would convey it.

These unfinished works by Mozart and Schubert invite us to propose some interpretive construct—theoretical, critical, even metaphysical—that might explain how it comes that the work was not finished. The problem is not of the kind for which we can expect prima facie evidence toward a solution. That the unfinished work is by nature a problem to be solved—that its finish is a puzzle given to solution—is a suspect assumption that asks for trouble. These fragments challenge us to say why we should not value them for what they are, for the immediacy of their expression, unmediated by whatever constraints might be imposed between a conception and its formal perfecting. It is precisely this immediacy that caught the eye (if not the ear) of Goethe in his admiration of the artist's sketch:

> Good sketches by great masters, those enchanting hieroglyphs, are usually the start
> of an enthusiasm for art. Drawing, proportion, form, character, expression, com-
> position, harmony, finish are no longer in question: they are replaced by the illu-
> sion of themselves. Mind speaks to mind.[3]

---

2. "Andre Dichtarten sind fertig und können nun vollständig zergliedert werden. Die romantische Dichtart ist noch im Werden; ja das ist ihr eigentliches Wesen, daß sie ewig nur werden, nie vollendet sein kann." "Athenäums-Fragmente" 116; *Kritische Friedrich-Schlegel-Ausgabe*, II: 183.

3. "Verdienstvolle Skizzen großer Meister, diese bezaubernde Hieroglyphen, veranlassen meist diese Liebhaberei und führen den echten Liebhaber nach und nach an die Schwelle der gesamten Kunst. . . . Hier ist nicht mehr von Zeichnung, von Proportion, von Formen, Charakter, Ausdruck, Zusammenstellung, Übereinstimmung, Ausführung die Rede, sondern ein Schein von allem tritt

The artist's draft that Goethe admires, even in its fragmentary evocation of what is missing, is formally coherent in a way that an unfinished draft by Schubert is not, it is often argued.[4] This distinction is perhaps better understood as one of apprehension, a difference in how we perceive the temporalities of music and the spatial dimensions of graphic art. It is not that the one is demonstrably more complete than the other, but only that the two modes of expression embrace the idea of the work along vectors of different kinds—putting us again in mind of the distinction that drives Lessing's argument in the monograph on the Laokoon: "über die Grenzen der Malerei und Poesie" (on the limits of painting and poetry), as it is subtitled, for which one might here substitute "Malerei und Tonkunst."[5]

The distinction between the work left unfinished, a fragment for no discernible reason, and the work that aspires to the aesthetic condition of fragment, whether or not it has survived complete, ought to be clean and simple. Often it is neither. For while these two conditions of the fragmentary might seem mutually exclusive, they yet invite dialectical inquiry: the unfinished work interrogated for traces in its torso that might suggest why it remains unfinished; these traces further interrogated for evidence of the Schlegelian aspiration toward fragment. To put it differently, we want to know whether the aesthetic pull of the fragmentary is coincident with a music that will not allow of closure.

The problematics of this distinction are exercised in several grand works by Schubert that have entered the repertory in spite of their fragmentary condition. The Symphony in B minor, D 759 (1822) and the Sonata in C, D 840 (1825), both complete in only their first two movements, stake legitimate claim to a place in the performer's repertory. Such a claim is less certain of two sonatas whose first movements have survived only as fragments. The Sonata in F♯ minor, D 571 (July 1817) and the Sonata in F minor, D 625 (summer of 1818) have nonetheless established themselves in the repertory—not as fragments, but as works completed by other hands. In these acts of completion, the work is always debased, deprived

---

an die Stelle. Der Geist spricht zum Geiste . . . " "Der Sammler und die Seinigen," in Johann Wolfgang von Goethe, *Werke. Hamburger Ausgabe in 14 Bände*, XII: Schriften zur Kunst, ed. Erich Trunz, commentary by Herbert von Einem (Munich: C. H. Beck, 9th ed., 1981), 94–95.

4. By Ulrich Konrad, for one: "While the contemplation of unfinished works of architecture, of sculpture torsos, of sketched pictures or the reading of fragmentary [literary] texts can convey characteristic aesthetic experience of some value, the performance of an unfinished composition . . . leaves seldom more than an unsatisfactory impression of a painful confusion, of an aesthetic deficit." See *Wolfgang Amadeus Mozart. Neue Ausgabe sämtlicher Werke* [=NMA], Ser. X, Supplement; Werkgruppe 30, Bd. 4: *Fragmente*, ed. Ulrich Konrad (Kassel: Bärenreiter, 2002), xv (my translation).

5. See above, chapter 5, where Lessing's subtitle is taken as a model for understanding the boundaries (and commonalities) between Gerstenberg's literary fantasy and Emanuel Bach's music.

of its authenticity. The more adept the forgery—for that is what is at issue here—the greater the damage. Indisputably, a unique value of these fragments is in what they record of a process of conceiving. Where the writing stops, we are witness to a moment, captured as though in a snapshot, where the split-second decision making of creation fails. Encrypted evidence revelatory of musical process, the fragmentary autograph documents this failure and invites further investigation into causes and consequences.

Four Mozart Fragments

But the appeal of the fragment has its visceral aspect as well. To read through a fragment by Mozart is to be caught in the vicarious enactment of that chilling moment where the thought is broken and the writing stops. It is to Alan Tyson that we owe a penetrating insight into the complex run of papers comprised in the autographs of several of Mozart's piano concertos, and of other works as well, that led him to suggest that a work may have lain dormant as a "fragment" for a good stretch of time—the autograph may tell us precisely where the writing stopped—until the external incentives to complete it had been internalized with some compelling urgency.[6] But in those cases where only the fragment remains, so, too, does the question whether Mozart intended ever to return to it. And yet the very survival of the fragment may stand as evidence that Mozart had not conclusively given up on it.

1

Consider, for one, the well-known fragment of a String Quartet in G minor, K 587a (Anhang 74), composed, it is now thought, between 1786 and 1789.[7] (It is

6. The concertos are those in B-flat major, K 595, in C major, K 503, A major, K 488, and in E-flat major, K 449. See Alan Tyson, "The Mozart Fragments in the Mozarteum, Salzburg: A Preliminary Study of Their Chronology and Their Significance," in *Journal of the American Musicological Society* 34 (1981): 471–510; reprinted in Alan Tyson, *Mozart: Studies of the Autograph Scores* (Cambridge, Mass., and London: Harvard University Press, 1987), 123–161 esp. 150–153.

7. For a brief synopsis of the history of the dating of this fragment, see my review of *Wolfgang Amadeus Mozart. Skizzen*, ed. Ulrich Konrad (NMA, Ser. X: Supplement; Werkgruppe 30, Bd. 3) in *Notes: Quarterly Journal of the Music Library Association*,57 (September 2000): 189. The fragment can be found in facsimile in NMA, *Fragmente*, Fr 1789i, p. 192; and in NMA, Ser. VIII; Werkgruppe 20, Abteilung 1: *Streichquartette*, Bd. 3 (Kassel: Bärenreiter, 1961), 147–148.

shown as appendix 13A.) In the bold gestures of its fifteen opening bars, its motives formed from the big, expressive intervals in a calculated unfolding of the
total chromatic (only B♮ is missing), the thematic stakes are set very high. The second phrase, at m. 5, is less a consequent of the first than an intense compression
of its last four notes. The process of mind seems so concentrated as to provoke
some theorizing as to the process itself. Are we witness here to a spontaneous flow
of linear speech? Or did Mozart pause after m. 4, uncertain how to continue? If
it is not given to us to know the answer, we may yet sense that this fleeting moment of reflection was of considerable consequence for the future of the work. In
the deep A♭ at m. 11, briefly tonicized, one senses a similar moment of intense reflection, setting forth signals of a complex harmonic unfolding. This is extreme
Mozart.

In apparent retreat from such demanding challenges, the music that follows at
m. 16 is something of a disappointment: eight bars of hard thumping on tonics
and dominants underpinning a conventional flight of sixteenth notes, a deliberate denial of the intense music to which it is an answer. But it is the final wisp
of a phrase with which the music trails off that has something to tell us of its fragmentary condition. The phrase seems a cry of protest, a breaking away from this
incessant harmonic rhythm, a search for something new: a key, a rhythm, a tune,
a fresh voice. Even at the simplest level, it allows for any number of plausible
readings of an underlying harmonic track (see ex. 13.1 for one). Mere conjecture,
they are, for we cannot know precisely what this unfinished phrase wants to say.
Perhaps it spilled from Mozart's pen in a spasm of impatience with the entire
project. It is the kind of phrase that might well have fallen away, had Mozart returned to complete the work. We however must live with it, and with the ambivalent readings that it seems to signify. The inclination to complete this unfinish-
able phrase confronts us with the ultimate riddle of the fragment as a species, for
it assumes access to a process of mind that is unfathomable even within itself.

EXAMPLE 13.1 Mozart, Quartet Movement in G minor, KV 587a: hypothetical
continuation.

It is not the harmonization of the phrase, or even the logical next step in its un-folding, that is at question, but a prior matter having to do with the imponder-ables of the mind that could give us this phrase with one hand and take it back with the other.

2

Mozart did not return to this fragment. We do, and for good reason: the pathos of its opening music is only intensified by the permanence of its fragmentary condition. Another memorable fragment is the remnant of a keyboard fantasy in F minor, K 383C (Anhang 32). Earlier prevarications in regard to the date of the fragment may now be set to rest, for both Alan Tyson and Wolfgang Plath have established that the paper-type and the handwriting of the fragment situate it in 1789, and not—as its Köchel number suggests—in 1782.[8] The music of its open-ing phrases, lavishly complex, reaches hard for the gestures of spontaneity. (The fragment is shown as appendix 13B.)

The hortatory arpeggio, its extension in a more varied arpeggiation (just as Emanuel Bach taught), the speechlike utterance, the sigh, the cutting dissonance, the entwining of chromatically inflected inner voices: the signs of fantasy are pro-fuse in its opening bars. The voicing of the harmonies in m. 2—the unprepared A♭ (and the seventh in which it is compassed), suspended dissonantly above the diminished intervals of a flatted ninth whose implied root is C—is powerful and focused. The concentration of dissonance deployed across the entirety of bar 2, the unfolding of its single harmony, is intense. What appears to be a simple tonic triad at the downbeat of the measure is in effect a dissonant appoggiatura. The bass wants an E♮, in turn implicating a root C. At the second half of the measure, a high A♭ is struck from the seventh below, from a B♭ that is itself a seventh above the root. Against this array, the D♭ in the following chord, a ♭9 above the root, now stirs the memory of that very pitch at the end of m. 1. The pile-up of dissonance in m. 2 has an immediate effect, forcing the bass to take its first step in a chro-

---

8. Konrad, *Fragmente*, Fr 1790b. The fragment, whose autograph is missing, is published in NMA, Ser. IX, Werkgr. 27, Bd. 2: *Einzelstücke für Klavier (Orgel, Orgelwalze, Glasharmonika)*, ed. Wolfgang Plath (Kassel: Bärenreiter, 1982), 152; Plath's commentary is on xxiv–xxv. Written on a leaf whose verso contains sketches for a passage in the second finale of *Cosi fan tutte*—possibly "for a rewrit-ing of the passage," Tyson is led to suggest—on paper otherwise found in the autograph scores of the finales to the String Quartets, K 589 and K 590, the fragment can then be assigned with some confidence to the spring of 1790. See Alan Tyson, "On the Composition of Mozart's *Cosi fan tutte*," in *Mozart: Studies of the Autograph Scores*, 192.

matic descent to the dominant at m. 5. But it is to that dissonant A♭ that the ear returns, and so does the music, which now establishes A♭ as a tonic. At m. 13, A♭ is redefined as a ninth above G and at m. 14 it is returned to the bass as a dissonance of another kind, supporting an augmented sixth, resolving finally to G, now the root of a dominant, as if to respond at last to the unresolved A♭ in bar 2. From its isolation in bar 2 as a "difficult" dissonance with a complex theoretical pedigree, the high A♭ seems to control the discourse of the entire fragment.

"Fantasia," Mozart wrote at the top of the score, and yet the half cadence with which the fragment breaks off signals a second group in the dominant, more sonata than fantasy. (In the labyrinth of its opening pages, the great Fantasy in C minor, K 475, in search of a key, settles gradually onto the dominant of B minor: the true dominant is studiously avoided in the course of its 181 bars.) More problematical, I think, is the new music in A♭ in mm. 7–11: a banal sigh (and its banal answer), a stiffly dotted scale that bumps its way down two octaves, and an inflated operatic cadence that belongs a hundred bars later: *dolce,* twice written, doesn't help. What kind of music might have followed the cadence at m. 14 is anyone's guess, and I suspect that Mozart himself must have felt the impossibility of finding an appropriate tone in the wake of this fitful beginning. If we return again to its probing opening bars, we do so for that shiver of expectation, even to conjure ourselves as witness to the spontaneous moment of Mozart at his keyboard.

3

The opening bars of another unfinished work, a torso in C minor scored for "[cemba]lo" and violin (to judge from the double stops toward the end of the fragment), spring to mind. This is the famous "Fantasia" that everyone knows in Maximilian Stadler's completion as a formidable work for piano alone, published in 1802 as *Fantasie pour le clavecin ou piano-forte,* and registered in the canon as K 396 (K 385f).[9] The fragment, however, breaks off at m. 27 with a cadence in the relative major at a double bar with repeat marks, inscribing the exposition of a sonata movement, written exclusively for keyboard alone until the entry of the violin five measures from the end. The leaf itself is so severely trimmed on all

9. NMA, *Fragmente,* Fr 17821; NMA, Ser. VIII, Werkgr. 23: Sonaten und Variationen für Klavier und Violine, vol. 2, ed. Eduard Reeser (Kassel: Bärenreiter, 1965, rev. 1985), 181–183. The work in Stadler's completion also has its place in the NMA, Ser. IX, Werkgruppe 27, vol. 2: 159–165. The controversy is described on xxv–xxvi.

sides—not, one suspects, the handiwork of Goethe, who acquired the manuscript in 1812—that any trace of title and tempo is cut away.

To contemplate the fragment is to confront riddles at every turn. How Mozart might retrospectively have worked the violin into a texture so otherwise saturated is not at all clear, and perhaps it was this initial miscalculation that led Mozart to stop composing. Was Mozart thinking of something along the lines of the rich, fantasy-like opening of the Sonata for Piano and Violin in G major/minor, K 379 (K 373a)? Whatever he had in mind, we can confidently exclude "fantasia." This is a sonata exposition without question, and Stadler's completion of the fragment, not quite the "Fantasie" that its title claims, does nothing to contradict this fundamental premise. In Stadler's continuation, an overwrought middle section (mm. 33–45) evokes the turbulent passage beginning at m. 84 in the second movement of the Concerto in D minor (K 466) and the great crossing-of-hands passage in the middle of the Adagio e cantabile in Haydn's Sonata in E♭ (Hob. XVI/49), even as it elaborates a more generalized conception of the "fantasy-like" development, inspired, it might seem, by Beethoven's recent music. The date of its publication squares well with what we know of Stadler's engagement with the fragments then in the possession of Constanze Mozart.[10] The date is not trivial, for it sets Stadler's work at a distance of some twenty years from the composition of the fragment.[11] The cataclysmic events of those intervening years would have made the distances seem greater still. To those who had only begun to come to terms with the convulsions of revolutionary Europe, an apprehending of this brave new world would necessarily see the old through a distant focal point. The music of 1782, in the fine, calibrated tension between its passions and its constraints, must have seemed remote in its preoccupations, impossible to recapture in 1802 with any fidelity to its aesthetics.

In Stadler's completion of the fragments, such tensions are no longer so finely calibrated. Even the simple cadence before the double bar in the C minor fragment is the subject of some tinkering (see ex. 13.2). The fine dissonance of Mozart's appoggiatura is neutralized, the deep E♭ removed from a position of metrical weight. More problematic is the very first phrase in Stadler's completion (ex. 13.3). The reformulation of the opening arpeggiation in C major is startling. Stadler was very likely thinking of the opening of the development in the first

---

10. For more on this, see, for one, Alan Tyson, *Mozart: Studies of the Autgraph Scores,* 125–126; Konrad, ed., *Fragmente,* xi–xii; and Ludwig Finscher, "Maximilian Stadler und Mozarts Nachlaß," in *Mozart Jahrbuch* 1960/61 (1961): 168–172.

11. The five fragments written on this paper date from 1781 through 1783. See Konrad, ed., *Fragmente,* 240–241, 283. The paper however recurs in works that can be dated as late as 1787. See Alan Tyson, *Wasserzeichen-Katalog,* NMA, Ser. X, Werkgr. 33, vol. 2, Textband, 26.

EXAMPLE 13.2 Mozart, Sonata Movement in C minor, KV 385f, cadence at end of exposition.

movement of the Sonata in C minor, K 457, a work that he would have had in front of him if, as would make good sense, he was studying that other Fantasy in C minor, K 475, published in a pairing with the sonata in 1785. Are the two passages analogous? In the sonata, C major is at once established as a dominant serving to establish F minor. Its function is never in doubt. In Stadler's Fantasy, the opening phrase undergoes a transformation. The harmonic function of C major, in its motion to an apparent Neapolitan sixth, is unclear; the voicing in the right hand (D♯–C–D♭) is awkward; and the three-note motive at its end seems an immaterial rhythmic distortion of the original motive, the kind of mutation foreign to Mozart's style. There is even a question as to the essential voice leading here: it would appear that Stadler wants a first-inversion triad, with E♮ in the bass moving to the F. But the sounding of the deep root at the outset counteracts that hearing: the E♮ is merely an inner voice.

Problems with the fine-tuning of such voicing is evident as well in Stadler's recapitulation. (The opening bars of Mozart's exposition and of Stadler's recapitulation are shown in appendix 13C). At m. 4, Mozart doubles E♭ in the bass, and redoubles it in the run of sixty-fourth notes up to the extremity of the highest E♭, establishing by implication a simple triad in root position, so that the change

EXAMPLE 13.3 Mozart, Sonata Movement in C minor: Stadler's continuation.

of bass at the very end of the measure has a true harmonic function. The B♭
strongly implicated as the fifth of the triad on E♭ now silently becomes a seventh
above C, resolving to A♭ at m. 5. In the analogous passage (see m. 49), Stadler re-
vises. Without question, the very deep G will be heard as the third of a triad
whose root is E♭—the turn around E♭ in the right hand makes this explicit. And
when the swift run up from the turn finds its target on a high G, the third of the
triad, again heavily accented, is now redoubled in the extreme outer voices. When

the bass moves, the root does not. Mozart's elegant harmonic fluency is replaced with a solecism, a weak transformation of the original.

The move to E♭ major here is itself a bit odd, for the music at once finds its way back to C minor. Finally, a half-cadence in C minor at m. 60 is answered by the second group, now literally transposed to C major. If Stadler were casting about for models from the 1780s of first movements in the minor mode that close in the major, he'd have found plenty.[12] But the issue is not quite that simple. In the first movements of certain kinds of works, Haydn will move to the tonic major at the second group in the recapitulation—a splendid example is the String Quartet in F♯ minor, Opus 50, no. 4—though never in simple transposition. In the sonatas in C minor (XVI:20), B minor (XVI:32), G minor (XVI:44) and C♯ minor (XVI:36) for keyboard alone, all composed in the 1770s, Haydn reformulates the second group in the tonic minor, in each instance with rich alterations. For Mozart, who in such circumstances only rarely closes in the tonic major, the challenge to recompose the music of the second group in the tonic minor, not merely an issue of technique, produces music whose pathos seems the only sensible conclusion of a work conceived in the minor mode. Perhaps the most poignant instance is the close of the Adagio in B minor, K. 540: the second group is recomposed in B minor, the major subdominant in the exposition made over into a breathtaking arpeggiation of the Neapolitan. The minor mode is sustained with an outpouring of chromaticism over a dominant pedal, and it is only at its resolution in the final three bars that Mozart allows D♯ to sound, and the sheer, unexpected beauty of this tone, so long withheld and immaculately prepared, sets loose an exquisite cadencing of complex four-voice part writing in celebration. In contrast, Stadler's shrill E♮ at m. 61, in response to the half cadence in C minor, is altogether unprepared, the brilliance of C major misplaced and jarring. It does not help matters that once again, Stadler writes an awkward cross-relation: E♭–D–E♮.

We cannot of course know how Mozart might have thought to complete this work. Stadler's completion—rather like Süssmayer's completion of the Requiem[13]—has had a long and profitable run of its own. What is at stake here is

---

12. For some data, see R. M. Longyear, "The Minor Mode in Eighteenth-Century Sonata Form," *Journal of Music Theory* 15, nos. 1 and 2 (1971): 182–229.

13. "The question of its authenticity has plagued the Requiem from the first," writes Christoph Wolff: "No wonder, then, that Mozart's Requiem became the first work to be subjected in our modern sense to a most rigorous scrutiny regarding both sources and style." See his review of two facsimile editions of the famous manuscript, *19th Century Music* 15/2 (Fall 1991):162–65, esp. 165, for a succinct summary of the matter. For more, see his subsequent monograph on the work: *Mozart's Requiem: Historical and Analytical Studies, Documents, and Score* (Berkeley: University of California Press, 1994).

not a question of legalities, of intellectual property, but something deeper. Stadler's hearing of the fragment filters out the complex decision making, the obscure, unrecoverable agon inherent in the compositional act. What he composes, putting the best light on it, is a different kind of work, one in which Mozart's music is made over into an imitation of itself. Charles Rosen, identifying a "classicizing" tendency in certain works of Beethoven composed in the late 1790s, writes of a "reproduction of classical forms . . . based upon the exterior models, the results of the classical impulse, and not upon the impulse itself."[14] Stadler, driven by his own impulses, sought to reinvent Mozart. In the end, the music that he wrote plays against the grain of Mozart's voice.

4

Hearing a similar playing against the grain, Ernst Oster, in a probing study of the chromatic Menuetto in D major for keyboard, K 576b [*olim* K 355], was inspired to penetrate the hard shell of a text that has survived only as a completed work to imagine in its place an original fragment completed by another hand.[15] The Menuetto was published in 1801 together with a trio whose author was openly acknowledged to be Maximilian Stadler.[16] Without the testimony of an autograph (whose whereabouts remain unknown), Oster's insight cannot be verified as "fact." That, however, does not lessen its significance for a coming to terms with the elusive evidence—often masquerading in the devilish details—that bears on the hard-wiring of authenticity: how do we *know* that we're in the presence of a Mozart, or, for that matter, of a Stadler?

The gist of Oster's argument resides in a hearing of the recapitulation of the opening music when it returns in the tonic. (The complete piece is shown as appendix 13D.) At the moment of return, the opening bars are reconceived. What follows is mechanical. For Oster, "the most persuasive argument against the authenticity of mm. 33ff lies in their exact transposition, note for note, of mm. 5ff."[17] The rote transposition beginning at m. 33 creates a difficult leap—an

---

14. Charles Rosen, *The Classical Style: Haydn, Mozart, Beethoven,* 381.

15. Ernst Oster's "Schenkerian View" is contained in "Analysis Symposium I: Mozart, Menuetto K.V. 355," in *Journal of Music Theory* 10 (1966): 32–52; reprinted in *Readings in Schenker Analysis and Other Approaches,* ed. Maury Yeston (New Haven and London: Yale University Press, 1977), 121–140.

16. For details, see Mozart, NMA, Ser. IX, Wergr. 27, vol. 2: xviii.

17. Oster, "Schenkerian View," 48–49; *Readings in Schenker Analysis,* 137.

ellipsis, we might generously call it—between the half cadence on the dominant at m. 32 and the simultaneity on the downbeat at m. 33. Oster thinks it "slightly awkward," and explains: "Although contrapuntally correct, d-sharp[1] does not seem to come from anywhere and is weak in comparison to the powerful accented passing tone a-sharp in m. 5."[18]

Is it in fact "contrapuntally correct"? The answer to that question lies somewhere in the bedrock of the passage beginning at m. 33 (and its analogue at m. 5). We understand the D♯ in m. 33, as we do the A♯ in m. 5, as an accented appoggiatura proceeding elliptically from an implicit, understood pure fifth. At m. 5, there is no difficulty in hearing the A which precedes the A♯. It is elegantly prepared, just as the G♮ in the tenor resolves to the F♯ in the soprano. At m. 33, nothing is prepared. We are asked to intuit a direct motion between a triad on A and a triad on G♮: in effect, a direct motion between the dominant and the subdominant, both in root position, that violates a cardinal injunction in harmonic theory and reducible to the stepwise motion between two consecutive major thirds forbidden in pure counterpoint.

In these passages at mm. 5–10 and 33–38, the accented appoggiatura means to establish the sixth, in the usual 5–6 progression. The sixth is then augmented, setting loose a sequence of augmented sixths, in which the bass (D in m. 5, G in m. 33) is made over into the lowered sixth degree leading to the root of a dominant. In the exposition, the sequence is broken at the downbeat in m. 9, where (by the conventions of Mozartean sonata) the music moves toward the key of the dominant. The breach here is a telling one, a syntactical dissonance resolved, we come to expect, only when the passage is "corrected" in the reprise. But that is not what happens in the Menuetto. The breach between mm. 8 and 9 is simply transposed at mm. 37–38: a structural dissonance is compounded at just that point where the music wants not disjunction but resolution, correction, closure. And this, it seems to me, is the strongest evidence for believing the reprise to be inauthentic.

Precisely how the Menuetto might have gone in some version with more convincing claim to authenticity is to invite alternatives shrouded in speculation. The conundrum-like sequence itself suggests why Mozart may at this point have stopped writing. In the spirit of the speculative, consider how this passage might have gone with the "correction" shifted to the breach between mm. 36 and 37— focused, that is, precisely where the exposition established its crux (see appendix 13D and ex. 13.4). The syntax is strengthened, and the unbroken motion in the

---

18. Oster, "Schenkerian View," 48–49; *Readings in Schenker Analysis,* 136–137.

EXAMPLE 13.4 Mozart, Menuetto for Keyboard, KV 576b, voice-leading of recapitulation rewritten, mm. 33–39.

bass suggests an augmentation of the new counterpoint which celebrates the moment of return in mm. 29 and 30—C♯ B, B♭ A—a further iteration of the chromatic descent in the soprano at mm. 17–20. But something is given up as well. The motion of roots in mm. 33–38 in the published version can be heard to put great emphasis on the dominant of the dominant, just as the local dominant on the third beat of m. 36 is heard to shore up the minor subdominant on the second beat of m. 38.

In the end, the proposal to hear the work as incomplete has a certain appeal. The arguments for doing so encourage a yet more radical image of where the writing stops—where, that is, the concentration of thought is broken:

EXAMPLE 13.5 Mozart, Menuetto for Keyboard, KV 576b, imagining where the autograph might have broken off.

To imagine the thought broken precisely here, at the incipit of a recapitulation that would need to come to terms with these bold new counterpoints, is to bring forward an aspect of Mozart's style that is not often discussed. Unlike Haydn, for whom the recapitulation offers the challenge to vast and penetrating recomposition, Mozart seems often disinclined to engage in substantial rethinking at

this stage of the work. These new counterpoints, which deftly compress the harmonic motion at mm. 17–20, might be thought to propose the kind of radical re-
composition that Mozart was reluctant to undertake. And so the work was left
unfinished.

The moral is sobering. The posthumous completion of works left in a fragmentary state is a dangerous game. The inclination to make over the fragment
into an artifact of finish and aesthetic appeal, accessible to the market where art
is consumed, may seem a virtuous one. Such deeds, innocent and high minded
though they may seem, necessarily trample on the integrity of the work, oblivious of the fragile web of decision making that attends the conceiving of the work,
trivializing and obliterating this poignant moment where music is silenced.

A Schubert Fragment

There is perhaps a lesson here for the student of Schubert's fragments as well, for
it would be good to ponder whether these sonata movements from 1817 and
1818 were left unfinished only because the external incentives to complete them
were not immediately envisioned. Schubert did however manage to compose
complete piano sonatas during these years. If, as seems entirely plausible, these
unfinished sonatas were conceived under much the same circumstances that nur-
tured the completion of other works, we are challenged to come to some other
understanding of their fragmentary condition.

Where the ambitious first movement of Schubert's Sonata in F minor breaks
down at the end of a *Durchführung* of unorthodox intensity, the challenge is
keen. (The movement is shown in appendix 13E.) Apart from two initial references to the opening motive, it gets nowhere to seek out thematic "development"
between the double bar and the dissipation of the music at m. 112. The music
strains impetuously, for the remote key, the uncommon harmonic utterance. The
passage at mm. 94–106 is the crisis, probing an aggregate of tones whose bearing
to the tonic is obscure. The harmony at m. 94 is central: the G♯ in the bass, the inflected fifth degree of an augmented triad, is sustained, enharmonically recast,
made the root of a triad on A♭ (major, then minor), returned finally to G♯, now
as the third degree of a triad on E, it, too, inflected as an augmented triad.

What happens next is not immediately intelligible. The bass finds B♮. Augmented sixths establish it as a dominant of significance, the goal of these thirty
bars of incessant motion. As it is scripted for the pianist, the arrival at m. 106 will
sound perilous, if not catastrophic. At the end of m. 105, the left hand is caught

in a difficult trill on A♯ high in the treble. Its *Nachschlag* is made to resolve to an octave B four and five octaves below. This *Luftpause* written into the attack before the downbeat of m. 106 sets the music off on a new trajectory. E major is tonicized but does not sound. The bass descends to a dominant truer to the larger tonality, but it, too, is ambiguous. A hint of the opening motive sounds above a muffled dominant on F. The reprise is prepared, but apparently in the subdominant. The music breaks off altogether.

Why it does so allows no simple explanation. The difficult enharmonic knot of these six bars that negotiate between the attack on B♮ at m. 106 and the arrival at F at m. 112 is embedded in a display of fantasy-like figuration. The liquidation of a sense of E major begins directly with the descent of the bass to A♯, beneath a six-four arpeggiation that suggests a motion toward D♯ minor. Instead, the bass continues to descend, now to A♭, and here precisely is the enharmonic short-circuit that returns us to the pungent harmonies around mm. 94–101, where G♯ undergoes transformation to A♭ and is then restored. The harmony at m. 109 sounds a bit odd—something of a passing harmony that allows for the sounding of the augmented sixth above G♭ at m. 110. For all its resonance with tonal relationships earlier in the movement, in the passage between mm. 106 and 112 an opposition is firmly set between two dominants a tritone apart. The one implicates a tonic on E—a remote "countertonic" a semitone beneath F minor. The other fixes F. When, however, F is struck at m. 112, its function is unequivocally as dominant. Allowed to dissipate, this is no longer the powerful dominant before the recapitulation. In these quiet final measures of the fragment, we are witness to some strange meditation in which a dominant, courting a recapitulation in the subdominant, seems willed into the tonic.[19]

By the lights of what is apparently the most trustworthy of the surviving copies, the iterated E-major triads with which the Scherzo opens would have been the very next music that Schubert composed for this sonata. In the context of the harmonic crisis of strange dominants around m. 106 of the first move-

---

19. The autograph of the sonata is missing, and there is disagreement among the surviving sources as to the precise notes where the autograph broke off. Mandyczewski follows the copy in the Spaun-Witteczek collection, now at the Gesellschaft der Musikfreunde, Vienna; see *Franz Schubert's Werke. Kritisch durchgesehene Gesammtausgabe*, Serie 21, Supplement, Revisionsbericht, ed. Eusebius Mandyczewski (Leipzig: Breitkopf & Härtel, 1897), 2; reprint as *Franz Schubert's Compete Works*, vol. 19 (New York: Dover Publications; Wiesbaden: Breitkopf & Härtel, 1969), 362. The copy is described in *Franz Schubert. Neue Ausgabe sämtlicher Werke*, Serie VIII: Supplement, Band 8, Quellen II: *Franz Schuberts Werke in Abschriften: Liederalben und Sammlungen*, ed. Walther Dürr (Kassel, Basel, Tours, London: Bärenreiter, 1975), 95; see also [Serie VIII: Supplement, Band 4:] Otto Erich Deutsch, *Franz Schubert. Thematisches Verzeichnis seiner Werke in chronologischer Folge* (Kassel: Barenreiter, 1978), 362–363 (D 625).

ment, where E major is proposed as countertonic, the key of the Scherzo rings true. At the crossing of the first double bar in the Scherzo (at m. 49), the music moves from an octave B (established as the key of the dominant) to an octave C, initiating a placid stretch of music in the key of F major (see appendix 13F). The polarity of tonic/countertonic is reversed. The pull of the reversal is especially resonant in the twelve bars (mm. 75–86) that move from the dominant on C back to the dominant on B. This is nettlesome, caustic music. Schubert does not here avail himself of the deft single stroke wherein the dominant on C would become the augmented sixth to a dominant on B. It is obfuscation that he wants.

The return in the Trio is yet more riddling (see appendix 13G). A four-bar phrase, appearing to truncate its six-bar antecedents, outlines a first-inversion triad whose root is E♭ (heard as D♯), its utter simplicity in extreme contrast to much else in this sonata. It simply fails to connect with the return of the opening phrase, on the dominant of A major. Marked pianissimo, the phrase is written at the margins of intelligibility: inaudible, not quite heard.

We return again to the first movement, to the place where writing stops. The completion of a scherzo and trio of bold originality, and of a swift finale as tightly conceived as any from these years (entirely complete in concept, if only in its *Hauptstimme* for mm. 201–270), returns us again to this enigma. Why does the writing stop here? The moment is a familiar one, common to other Schubert fragments, and to Oster's visionary Mozart fragment. This is the moment that defines sonata. It is the moment in the first movement of the Eroica Symphony at which Beethoven's horns are made to personify the dead certainty of a return too long delayed. The manifold ways in which Beethoven contends with this defining moment, even through the last quartets, yet hold this view of the thing in common.

One senses this as well in Forkel's innocent way of getting at the analogous moment in Emanuel Bach's Sonata in F minor, that difficult passage before the recapitulation, discussed in chapter 1 (and shown in ex. 1.1). Forkel here takes up the challenge to elucidate a work that had, even then, come to signify Work as Problem, in need of exegesis. If Forkel's defense of Bach seems vaguely circular, I think that he is yet groping toward something profound, in his awareness of the peril in hearing such a passage "quite apart from its connection to the whole," and further, in his sense that such "difficult modulations" might have something to do with the meaning of the work: that they are true to the character of the work, not aberrations to be explained away, tamed, revised.

These two passages, Bach's and Schubert's, for all their differences (and uncanny similarities) describe a common moment of crisis. Bach reaches (as will Beethoven forty years later) toward the edge of tonal intelligibility that will define the sonata in 1763 and beyond. Schubert, too, makes that reach. But the distance of remote tonal environment, construed in a classical temperament as dissonance to be resolved, is now cultivated in and of itself, in retreat from the intimidating certainties that drive much of Beethoven's music that Schubert will have known during these formative years. This, it seems to me, is the aesthetic crisis upon which Schubert's fragment falters.

It cannot simply be a question whether the moment of recapitulation ought to be established in the tonic or the subdominant—though indecision on this matter is evident in the sonatas, complete and incomplete, from 1817 and 1818. Such indecision is only a symptom of some deeper anxiety about return. Return itself, no longer the signifier of resolution, and the tonic as an emblem of return, is freshly problematized—and problematized again, from a richer perspective, in two works composed seven years later, in the spring of 1825. This is the business of the next chapter.

In its prizing of the remote tonal outpost, in a palpable reluctance to return home—in the Trio, that spectral phrase in E♭, isolated and abandoned before the reprise—Schubert's music enacts a Schlegelian script. Its pull toward fragment in this romanticized sense overwhelms the classical frame within which it is conceived. The frame splinters. A fragment remains. Unlike those neatly preserved relics of broken syntax that Mozart seemed unwilling to repair, this fragment evokes the romance of timeless ruin foretold in Schlegel's disquieting poetics.

APPENDIX 13A Mozart, Quartet Movement in G minor (fragment), K 587a (= Anh. 74)

(continued)

APPENDIX 13A *(continued)*

APPENDIX 13B Mozart, Fantasie for Keyboard (fragment) in F minor, K 383C (= Anh. 32)

APPENDIX 13C Mozart, Sonata Movement in C minor (fragment), K 385f (= 396).

[Stadler] mm. 46–60.

(continued)

APPENDIX 13C *(continued)*

APPENDIX 13D Mozart, Menuetto for Keyboard, K 576b (= 355) . . . with recapitulation rewritten

(continued)

. . . with recapitulation rewritten:

(continued)

(continued)

APPENDIX 13F Schubert, Sonata in F minor, Scherzo, mm. 37 to end

APPENDIX 13G Schubert, Sonata in F minor, Trio, complete

Scherzo da Capo

CHAPTER 14

Reliquie

We return once again to Friedrich Schlegel, whose poetry Schubert much admired, even as it set him daunting aesthetic puzzles that his music could not always solve. Of his writings on literature and art, the most frequently cited are the briefest: the aphorisms contained in the "Athenäums-Fragmente."[1] Taken all together, they adumbrate a theory, not of course in any systematic, expository mode, but in the cumulative experience of the apparently isolated thought, one after another, each brilliantly obscure, and it is only on reflection that Schlegel's journey of the mind unwraps its thematic congeries.[2] These aphorisms, splinters of thought, seem often commentaries upon their own fragmentary condition. A few of them have been appropriated to the arguments of earlier chapters. Another touches on a quality in Schubert's music, and in the man himself, that will be explored in the pages that follow:

> A fragment, like a little work of art, must be quite separated from its surroundings and complete in itself—like a hedgehog.[3]

That a fragment *must*, by Schlegel's lights, be complete in itself is a thought tinged in paradox. It nourishes that other apparent contradiction between fragment by accident and fragment as a quality immanent in Romantic art—"appar-

---

1. Published under the title "Fragmente" in the journal *Athenäum: Eine Zeitschrift von August Wilhelm Schlegel und Friedrich Schlegel,* (vol. I, part 2 (Berlin, 1798). See chapter 1, note 38.

2. Of the 451 fragments in the collection, we know now that 85 were written by August Wilhelm Schlegel, 29 by Schleiermacher, 13 by Novalis, and that 4 were collaborations of one kind or another. Three-hundred twenty, then, were the work of Friedrich Schlegel, who was responsible for the editing of their publication. See *Kritische Friedrich-Schlegel-Ausgabe*, II: 165–265, and xlii–lxxi.

3. "Ein Fragment muss gleich einem kleinen Kunstwerke von der umgebende Welt ganz abgesondert und in sich selbst vollendet sein wie ein Igel." *Kritische Friedrich-Schlegel-Ausgabe*, II: 182–183.

ent," for we are speaking here of two conditions that, in a criticism of art, have only remotely to do with one another. The work left unfinished may, in its substance, powerfully intimate "finish" in some Classical mode. The Romantic fragment may possess all the attributes of the work conventionally "finished," and yet its very meaning conjures those powerful intimations that reside in the "unfinish" of the Classical fragment. The Romantic work reads into the Classical fragment a mystery not intrinsic to its meaning, constructing from its misreading an imaginary condition to which it aspires.

In what follows, I mean to suggest that the fragmentary state of at least one of Schubert's works—the great, if unfinished, Sonata in C major (the so-called Reliquie), D 840—owes its condition, in the actual sense, to this romantic notion of what might be called a conceptual fragment. For while it is commonplace to speak of a canon of unfinished works by Schubert, we might imagine Schlegel taking the adjective "unfinished" to be a condition describing all those works of Schubert worthy of exploration—an unconditional adjective meant to convey that quality in Schubert's music without which the work fails in its claim to the Romantic condition.

I

One senses often enough that this aspect of unfinish, in the Romantic sense, is at odds with some prior commitment to the Classical imperatives. The three versions of *Nähe des Geliebten*, D 162, a setting of a poem by Goethe, convey something of these ambivalencies. (They are shown in ex. 14.1.) The song, universally admired, has been too thoroughly studied to require a lengthy defense of its beauty, or even of its significance in Schubert's evolution.[4] For we must continually remind ourselves that the song was composed in February 1815—129 songs earlier than *Erlkönig*, by simple count in Mandyczewski's chronological edition. It was composed on 27 February, a day on which Schubert evidently set down the song in two versions. The third version, written out in 1816 for the *Liederheft* sent by Spaun to Goethe, was subsequently published as Opus 5 no. 2 by Cappi & Diabelli in 1821.[5]

---

4. These matters are excellently treated by Walter Frisch in "Schubert's *Nähe des Geliebten* (D. 162): Transformation of the *Volkston*," in *Schubert: Critical and Analytical Studies,* ed. Walter Frisch (Lincoln and London: University of Nebraska Press, 1986), 175–199. For a meditation on other aspects of the song, see my *Distant Cycles: Schubert and the Conceiving of Song* (Chicago and London: University of Chicago Press, 1994), 13–16.

5. For the particulars of publication, and on the whereabouts of the three autographs, see Otto Erich Deutsch, *Franz Schubert: Thematische Verzeichnis seiner Werke in chronologischer Folge* (Kassel:

EXAMPLE 14.1 Schubert, *Nähe des Geliebten,* D 162.

A Final version, Cappi & Diabelli, 1821.

(continued)

EXAMPLE 14.1 *(continued)*

B First version, from an autogr. dated 27 February 1815.

C Second version, from another autograph (private collection) dated 27 February 1815.

It is the singer's final note that is troubling. That it troubled Schubert as well is evident in that the three autographs give three different final notes. Surely, the earliest of them is the bravest, the most daring: the singer ends on D♭, the fifth degree of the scale—does not end, that is to suggest. The song is then construed in

Bärenreiter, 1978), 116–117. A facsimile edition of the *Reinschrift* for Goethe, together with a "Beihefte zur Faksimile-Ausgabe" by Peter Hauschild, was published as *Franz Schubert: Sechzehn Goethe-Lieder* (Leipzig: Peters, 1978). The autograph of the second version was sold at auction by Sotheby's, 25 May 2001, lot 186; a facsimile is shown in the catalogue.

two huge phrases. The first of them begins in soaring mid flight, and sketches out a firm sense of cadence. The second at once explores the vacant spaces in that first phrase and probes the implications of those mantic bars with which the piano opens into the song. But here the singer is left hanging.

When, later that day, Schubert wrote out the song a second time, he fixed the meter and reconceived the metrics of the opening bars: the grander 12/8 meter now matches the expanse of the phrase rhythms and translates the distance of the key itself, the exotic G♭. Now the singer ends on B♭. Again unsettling, the B♭ disturbs the tonic in a way that the D♭ does not, and prepares the return of the root position dominant on B♭ with which the song begins, and to which each of the three subsequent strophes returns. This second version moves, we might say, from the naive to the sentimental. The D♭ is perfectly innocent. The B♭ is complicated, even a bit neurotic. In both instances, the voice gives nuance to the subjunctive mood of Goethe's "O, wärst du da!," the haunting final line with which the poem refuses to end.

In the published version, these opening bars are not repeated. The voice now completes its second phrase. The song is "vollendet." Schubert has given it finish. To engage in sterile debate whether we have an aesthetic right to perform one of the settings of 27 February in place of the published version is clearly not to the point here, nor would I want to argue—or even to allow that one *could* argue— that either of the two is "better than" the third. Rather, I want simply to suggest that these earlier versions have a value for us in thinking about the song in its troubling of the concept "finish." Schlegel's notion of the Romantic "Dichtart" as a poetics that by its nature rejects the very idea of completion is here strikingly apropos.[6] And that puts before us an aesthetic conundrum: for while we can speak of the work itself as aspiring to some Hegelian state of "werden"—of perpetual becoming—we must at the same time recognize that we are speaking here of a metaphoric process within the boundaries of the work and a function of its style. Romantic artists do finish their works, do finish even those works whose substance means to suggest that they hadn't quite done so.

II

A sonata that Tovey, among others, held to be among Schubert's loftiest, most subtle works, yet one that Schubert could not bring himself to finish, the

---

6. See chapter 13, note 2.

"reliqued" Sonata in C major of 1825 has been celebrated in the recent publication of a facsimile of those leaves of its autograph that have survived, together with a brace of essays that explore aspects of its paradoxical status.[7]

The two movements that remain unfinished are the Menuetto (but not the Trio) and the finale—and they seem to have been left unfinished for different reasons. In some sense, the less interesting of them is the finale. Paul Badura-Skoda surely goes too far in suggesting of it that "the unfinished last movement cannot rise above a few short-winded and ineffectual flourishes, and was surely abandoned for this reason."[8] Yet there can be no question that in Schubert's major instrumental music from these years, the finale is something of a problem—is perceived, at any rate, to be problematical. Tensions at home in the discourse of sonata are relaxed in the prolixities of the strophic song-miming that often suffuse the finales. In this instance, the music breaks off at measure 272 with the end nowhere in sight: Badura-Skoda's completion for the Henle "Urtext" runs to 556 measures.[9]

The Menuetto is problematical in a different way. Consider how and where it ends (a facsimile of the autograph is shown as fig. 14.1). The rhetoric of recapitulation is strongly felt—fully eighteen bars *on* the dominant, beginning at m. 57 (see ex. 14.2). But the dominant of what? The power of persuasion here is such that Elizabeth McKay, in one of those exploratory essays, was led to write that the opening theme now returns "in the tonic."[10] The Menuetto, however, is in A♭ major, even if its sights are set on A major early on. And so the deeper implication in McKay's formulation is provocative, even for an epistemology of "fragment." Why is the piece unfinished? Why, further, did Schubert write "etc etc" after those few half-hearted bars of reprise—and then, leaving no space for a return to the problem, proceed to write this perfect Trio? Cast in G♯ minor, the Trio dwells on an obsessive D♯ conceivably meant to echo the closing bars of the Menuetto (which of course we do not have), just as the D♯s at its close anticipate the opening notes of the *da capo*.

McKay's harmless oversight yet hints at anxiety around what might be called

7. Franz Schubert, *"Reliquie": Sonata in C für Klavier D 840. Faksimile-Ausgabe nach den Autographen in Cambridge, Paris und Wien*, ed. Hans-Joachim Hinrichsen (Tutzing: Hans Schneider, 1992).

8. Paul Badura-Skoda, "Possibilities and limitations of stylistic criticism in the dating of Schubert's 'Great' C major Symphony," in *Schubert Studies: Problems of Style and Chronology*, ed. Eva Badura-Skoda and Peter Branscombe (Cambridge: Cambridge University Press, 1982), 203.

9. Franz Schubert, *Klaviersonaten*, III, Frühe und unvollendete Sonaten, ed. Paul Badura-Skoda (Munich: G. Henle Verlag [1979]), 219–225.

10. Elizabeth Norman McKay, "Schuberts Klaviersonaten von 1815 bis 1825—dem Jahr der "Reliquie," in *Faksimile-Ausgabe*, 60–61.

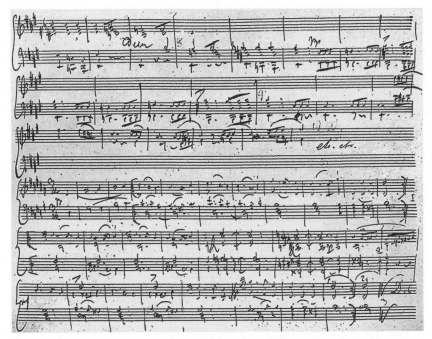

FIGURE 14.1 Schubert, Sonata in C major, D. 840, third movement, page from the autograph score. Vienna: Stadt- und Landesbibliothek (Wienbibliothek im Rathaus), Schubert MH 4125. By kind permission.

the problematizing of tonic in Schubert's music. Is there not something essential in the music to suggest that the truer tonic is *indeed* A major, and that A♭ provides a foil—a conventional frame within which to understand this central and predominant A major? Much to the point is Alfred Brendel's poignant insight: "In his large forms, Schubert is the wanderer. He likes to move at the edge of the precipice. To wander is the Romantic condition."[11]

Certainly, we follow Schubert precipitously close to the edge in this passage— over the edge, perhaps, if that is what its fragmentary condition signifies. In no other menuetto or scherzo—indeed, in no other sonata movement—do we find the music charting its reprise in the flat supertonic. No less radical—differently radical—is the tonality of a scherzo in E major that was evidently intended to follow directly on the first movement, left incomplete, of the Sonata in F minor, D 625 (studied at the end of the last chapter).

11. Alfred Brendel, *Music Sounded Out: Essays, Lectures, Interviews, Afterthoughts* (London: Robson Books; New York: Farrar, Straus and Giroux, 1990), 86.

EXAMPLE 14.2 Schubert, Sonata in C major, D. 840, third movement.

If there is a movement that springs to mind as comparable in its breathtaking challenge to the conventions of reprise, it is the first movement of this Sonata in C major. (The passage is shown as ex. 14.3). Eventually, of course, the music makes its way back to C major. And if one should quibble—as many do—about the precise moment at which "recapitulation" sets in, that would be to quibble about the wrong issue. Rather, one wants to admire the apparent contradiction of a return to C major approached through the back door and the affirmation of B major, with its luminous D♯ sounding the Romantic sixth in ecstatic response to twenty-four big measures on a dominant F♯. The grand gestures of resolution, removed to this exotic key, are tinged in the sublime. The opening theme coalesces into something visionary, a coherent phrase (fusing what, at the opening of the movement, seem four discrete pieces of a puzzle not yet in composite, four phrases in search of a source) now enhanced with a new inner voice that makes audible the silent "innere Stimme" that Schubert's poets are forever invoking. What follows we hear as liquidation of this one signal moment.

These twenty-four measures *on* F♯ are decidedly in B minor, and so the resolution in B *major* is yet another instance of modal inflection in the service of some veiled poetic message—again, the trading in metaphor. Further, the theme, very nearly as it will sound in B major, issues forth in A major at the outset of the development. Andreas Krause, in another of those exploratory essays, speaks here of two dovetailed "fifth-axes": the one, extending from the B minor established early in the exposition, through what he calls F♯ major (those twenty-four bars that must be heard as a dominant), to the B major in what he calls the *Scheinreprise;* the other axis, this A major at the outset of the development and the D major which he understands as the last station before what he identifies as the "return for the first time of the complete and characteristic thematic shape" in the subdominant at mm. 169–176.[12] If the fixity of these tonal axes, embedded as they are in the tonal landscape, is incontestable, one might yet contest their agency to elucidate what the piece is ultimately about. This *Scheinreprise*—the term itself redolent of the illusory, the feigned, the false, thereby diminishing the sense of the moment as epiphanic—seems to me to come in fulfillment of its premonition in A major. The larger step-motion in the course of all this is palpable, suggestive not only of *Stufen,* in the literal sense in which Schenker might have graphed it, but of *Aufhebung,* in all the senses comprised in that Hegelian concept: at once of elevation (even in the mystical sense) and dissolution. Compellingly, Hans-

---

12. Andreas Krause, "Schuberts 'Reliquie,' Beethovens VII. Sinfonie und der 'Weg zur grossen Sinfonie,'" in *Faksimile-Ausgabe,* 75.

EXAMPLE 14.3 Schubert, Sonata in C major, D. 840, first movement, mm. 139–166.

Joachim Hinrichsen speaks of these keys as "Durchführungsränder"—the keys at the margins of the development: A major as "Einsatztonart" and B major "als Punkt der 'Verschmelzung' von Durchführungsende und Reprisenbeginn"—the point of fusion between development and recapitulation.[13]

This moment of *Aufhebung* has its narrative mission, evoking, as it does, an instance of B minor in the interiors of the exposition. No ephemeral passing harmony, B minor in this earlier instance comes in resolution of a memorably enigmatic phrase (shown in ex. 14.4). The simultaneity at the downbeat of m. 51 is less important for what it is—its dissonant tones are quickly enough parsed as so many appoggiaturas to a six-four on F♯—than for what it signifies. Even the sense in which this dissonance translates the dominant seventh in C major in m. 50 to, in retrospect, an augmented sixth in B minor is conventional enough. But the harmony in m. 50 is a dominant *ninth*—and the ninth, as Kirnberger did not fail to remind us, is an inessential dissonance to the essential dissonance of the seventh: its resolution is local, provoking no change of root. But of course this ninth does *not* resolve to G. It *becomes* (in the Schlegelian sense) a very different creature. An essential tone, A♭ is now made over into G♯ above a putative root C♯—all of this sounding somewhere in the crevices between mm. 50 and 51, so that the residue is understood as a suspension of that fifth above C♯.

Do we hear this translation of the dominant ninth as some enharmonic *jeu*—Schubert at play—or as the inevitable next step in the harmonic plotting of the work? The rhythm of the passage is of a piece with the rhythms established in mm. 21–24, prompting the ear to seize the deeper relationship implied here. Even as the music plays out some theoretical imperative in its descent into B minor, a lowering shudder issues from it at m. 51. Here is the crux. The conventional key of the piece is brought into conflict with an unconventional, overwrought B minor. When the gesture returns in the recapitulation (see ex. 14.5), it is purged of all tension, whether one speaks here of resolution or of some quality less teleologically inspired.

More than a point in some axis of tonal relation (though of course it may be understood as that), B minor is fitted out with the rhetoric of poetic conceit. I return again to those twenty-four measures on F♯. Has anyone ever counted the precise number of F♯s struck during this passage? The question was asked—and

---

13. Hans-Joachim Hinrichsen, "Zur Bedeutung des Werks in Schuberts Sonatenschaffen," in *Faksimile-Ausgabe*, 13. "Verschmelzung" is a term borrowed from Armin Knab, "Schuberts unvollendete Klaviersonate in C-Dur und ihre Ergänzung," in Knab, *Denken und Tun. Gesammelte Aufsätze über Musik* (Berlin: Merseburger, 1959), 154.

EXAMPLE 14.4 Schubert, Sonata in C major, D. 840, first movement, mm. 1–26; 48–54.

EXAMPLE 14.5 Schubert, Sonata in C major, D. 840, first movement, mm. 203–214.

answered—of another F♯: the one sounded 536 times in *Die liebe Farbe*.[14] Among pieces in B minor, *Die liebe Farbe* is hardly alone in its fixation on F♯. *Irrlicht* and *Der Leiermann* (from *Winterreise*) belong here, and so does *In der Ferne* (from the Rellstab group), where the turn to B major, an epiphany of another kind, echoes, if faintly, the events of the Sonata.[15] B minor holds a special place in Schubert's tonal lexicon. Consequently, we are driven to ask whether the key itself, as raw poetic substance, means to signify beyond the intervallic relationship that it establishes with the tonic—to signify, that is, in a tonal metaphor that means to conjure poetic image.[16]

Back to Schlegel, and his aphoristic groping for an understanding of Romantic art as fragmentary, as "nie vollendet" in its essence. There seem to me three ways in which the Sonata in C major stakes a claim for this prized condition of unfinish—of fragment. In the most trivial of them, it is of course unfinished in that its two final movements were never completed. In a less trivial sense, the autograph invites us to speculate whether this written record is in the nature of a *Reinschrift* or an *Entwurf*—whether a clean copy meant for other eyes and fur-

---

14. It was Thrasybulos Georgiades who did the counting, in *Schubert: Musik und Lyrik* (Göttingen: Vandenhoeck & Ruprecht, 1967), 283; and we are reminded of it in Arnold Feil's *Franz Schubert: Die schöne Müllerin; Winterreise*, tr. Ann C. Sherwin (Portland, Or.: Amadeus Press, 1988), 75 and 170 n.74.

15. On this matter, see my *Distant Cycles*, 119–120.

16. *Ibid.*, 13 and 165.

ther transmission, or a preliminary draft. If the former, then we cannot speak here of fragment in this elemental sense, for the *Reinschrift* presupposes some earlier iteration in which the work was conceived, was conceptualized, was drafted: the *Reinschrift*, not habitually the locus of such conceptualizing, cannot therefore signal the breaking off of the concept. But Schubert's autographs are frustratingly ambivalent in the signs of their status in this regard. What begins calligraphically with the confidence and good posture of *Reinschrift* is transformed often enough in the course of the piece into the improvisatory: the writing loosens, and we feel ourselves now in the presence of the conceptualizing of the work. Hinrichsen, in that same essay, ponders the paradox of the fragment, broken off in mid-flight, but written in the sure hand of the *Reinschrift*. "'Fragment' ist also nicht gleich 'Fragment,'" he notes, in an aphorism worthy of Schlegel.[17] We are returned to that riddling page from the Menuetto, where the manuscript is ipso facto made over from *Reinschrift* to *Entwurf*.

In its third sense we approach the Schlegelian fragment: fragment as ruin, ruin as evocative of something lost and irretrievable, the finished work as the suggestion of something unfinished. This is the Romantic fragment.[18]

III

Nowhere are the symptoms of such fragment-making more pronounced than around the much vexed problem of reprise—of recapitulation. No moment in the narrative of sonata so unsettled Schubert. Two unfinished sonata movements—the F♯ minor, D 571, from July 1817, and the F minor, D 625, from September 1818, to single out the best known—break off precisely here, where the recapitulation is evidently meant to begin. But even this is ambiguous, for in both cases, the music breaks off on the dominant of the *subdominant*. The claim was put forth

---

17. Hinrichsen, "Zur Bedeutung," 33.

18. In a probing review of John Daverio's *Nineteenth-Century Music and the German Romantic Ideology* (New York: Schirmer Books; Toronto: Maxwell Macmillan Canada; New York: Maxwell Macmillan International, 1993) in *Journal of Music Theory* 40 (1996): 149–160, Kristina Muxfeldt reminds us of the importance of two seminal essays that bear on the idea of fragment: August Wilhelm Schegel's "Ueber Zeichnungen zu Gedichten und John Flaxmans Umrisse," in *Athenäum*, II (1799): 193–246 ("The fragments in the hypothetical new genre Schlegel envisions here are sketches, left as outline drawings so as to stimulate the imagination to make them fully comprehensible," writes Muxfeldt); and Friedrich Schlegel's "Ueber die Unverständlichkeit," in *Athenäum*, III (1800): 337–354.

at the end of the previous chapter that the actuality of their fragmentary condition is bound in with the new problematics of sonata itself, at just this point where the music stops. The two notions of fragment—of work left unfinished; of music that pursues some distant tonal region only vaguely commensurate with its framing tonic—seem to fuse here: the work is unfinished because the concept how it might be "finished" does not come clear.

And then there is the telling example to the contrary. A preliminary *Entwurf* has survived for the first movement of the B major sonata from 1817. It too breaks off at the moment of recapitulation. But whereas the recapitulation in the *final* version begins in—rather, lurches into—the subdominant, the draft is equivocal, suggesting even that the *Scheinreprise* is the one in the tonic (see ex. 14.6).

There are of course commonplace and mechanical explanations for these enigmas, but they cannot be the right ones. To suppose that Schubert in 1817 was oblivious of the dynamics of an inherited Classical sonata—to suppose that the weight of this legacy was not heavy on his mind—is to underestimate him. But by 1825, the insoluble nut of these experimental works of 1817 and 1818—fragments in our first sense—are addressed in two very grand sonatas: the C major fragment, and its companion from the spring of 1825, the Sonata in A minor (D 845), published only months later as *Première grande Sonate . . .* , Opus 42.

In the first movement of Opus 42, the reprise is no less a matter of perplexity. (It is shown in ex. 14.7.) The deep A in the bass at m. 134 establishes a defining dominant in the subdominant, sustained (though embellished) through m. 143. But then the music seems to vanish altogether in a breathtaking, and nearly inaudible, dominant in F♯ minor. The opening theme returns—reluctantly, and in bare, self-reflective counterpoint with itself: first, in F♯ minor, then in A minor (but only in passing, for we have no sense of true tonicity here). A broader continuation is established in C minor. As it is in the first movement of the "Reliquie," the tonic is here established finally at a moment of structural accent well along in the unfolding of the principal theme.

Different as they may be in their local strategies, these two sonatas from the spring of 1825 together convey a profound disquiet at the idea of reprise. One senses a reluctance to return—an unwillingness to celebrate the advance to the tonic, to concede, in the return to the opening music of the sonata, that this music is *about* the tonic. To go at it from another angle, we inevitably measure these moments against the prototype. Whatever Beethovenian example comes to mind—even an abstract conflation of them all—we hear in it the antithesis of this Schubertian hesitation about conquest and triumphant retakings. For Beethoven, the tonic is an article of faith, the implacable doctrine that paradoxically sustains him through all his dialectical efforts to unseat it. How to read Schubert

EXAMPLE 14.6 Schubert, Sonata in B major, D. 575, first movement.
A From an earlier draft (Vienna: Gesellschaft der Musikfreunde).

B The published version (Diabelli, ca. 1844).

in this regard? Brendel, again: "To wander is the Romantic condition." The return home, a return imposed by the deepest theoretical conditions of sonata, is now questioned at its root, probed, problematized.

This ambivalence about recapitulation, I mean to suggest, has something to do with the inclination, in the earlier sonatas, to undermine the act of return. To return in the subdominant is somehow not to return. The subdominant is an evasion: a substitute for the tonic, it has the taste of melancholy. The triumph, the aesthetic satisfaction of return is of another age, another temperament. In the two sonatas from the spring of 1825, this inclination is given mature expression in two passages that capture, as do no other works of Schubert, the pathos of his own agony, in the reconciling of classical orthodoxies with a life at the precipice.

FIGURE 14.2 Pencil drawing by Moritz von Schwind ("Schubert am Klavier"), undated. Vienna: Austrian National Library, Bildarchiv, 460.760-B. By kind permission.

IV

Finally, there is the pencil drawing, recently discovered, of Schubert "Am Klavier" by Moritz von Schwind (see fig. 14.2).[19] It is a sketch, a fragment by the criteria that define the "Reliquie." How might it have been finished, how might Schwind have finished it?[20] The questions are simply wrong. To suggest that one might have the power of imagination to engage in the infinitely complex process of de-

---

19. The undated pencil drawing, formerly in the possession of Wilhelm Kempff, is now in the Bildarchiv of the Austrian National Library, Vienna. For an analysis of the leaf and some speculation as to its date, see Rita Steblin, "Schwinds Porträtskizze 'Schubert am Klavier,'" *Schubert durch die Brille*, Mitteilungen 10 (January 1993): 45–52.

20. The matter is complicated by the relationship of this sketch to the depiction of Schubert in Schwind's famous drawing "Ein Schubert-Abend bei Josef von Spaun" (1868), and the version in oils that Schwind did not live to complete (he died in 1871). Steblin ("Schwinds Porträtskizze," 50) dates the sketch "um 1826" on evidence that is inconclusive. While such a dating would amplify the distance between sketch and "finish" to an implausible forty-two years, I mean here only to suggest that the immediacy of the sketch has a value that even the artist's *Vollendung* cannot efface. For more on the drawings, see Maurice J. E. Brown, "Schwind's 'Schubert-Abend bei Josef von Spaun,'" in Brown, *Essays on Schubert* (London: Macmillan; New York: St Martin's Press, 1966), 155–168.

cision making that would have enabled Schwind to take the next steps is to display an arrogant belief in the infallibility of historical "knowledge."[21]

The Schwind drawing, without much Schlegelian argument, is complete in itself. It is a concept, and a bold one, for it captures a Schubert conveyed in few other authentic representations:[22] the arms in motion, negotiating some *Erlkönig*-like bravura (the invisible "Klavier" is only implied); the face, nearly an expressionistic abstraction of mind and thought, consumed in music-making. The ubiquitous spectacles, fused in the visage, only intensify the concentration: "durch die Brille," to borrow from the title of a Viennese journal of Schubertiana. The central figure in Schwind's "Schubert-Abend" may have more finish, but he is less engaged.

A "Nähe des Geliebten" in which the voice will not bring itself to end; a grand sonata that Schubert cannot bring himself to complete; and Schwind's probing sketch—these artifacts tell us something about Schubert, and I am not sure that what they tell us is of lesser value than what we can learn from those published and public versions of works that lay claim to a more conventional finish. In Schwind's drawing, Schubert is himself without finish—set apart from the "umgebende Welt" (in Schlegel's phrase), beyond the conventions of human context. He does not stop to look at the camera, to set himself in time and place, to acknowledge a world around him. A hedgehog, he is, in the bold Schlegelian sense of the word.[23]

---

21. For a lively inquiry into these problems, see Robert S. Winter, "Of Realizations, Completions, Restorations and Reconstructions: From Bach's *The Art of Fugue* to Beethoven's Tenth Symphony," *Journal of the Royal Musical Association* 116/1 (1991): 96–126.

22. No less provocative is a drawing that depicts Schubert seated at the piano and singing, together with Josephine Fröhlich and Johann Michael Vogl. A facsimile of the original, from a sketchbook of 1827 by Ferdinand Georg Waldmüller, now housed at the Graphische Sammlung Albertina in Vienna, is shown in *Franz Schubert und seine Zeit,* a catalogue prepared by Otto Biba for an exhibition at the Gesellschaft der Musikfreunde (Vienna: Gesellschaft der Musikfreunde in Wien, 1978), 30; and in *Schubert Studies: Problems of Style and Chronology,* 142.

23. What *is* Schlegel's sense of the word? Perhaps he had in mind the famous aphorism attributed to the Greek poet Archilochus, whose work Schlegel elsewhere cites: "The fox knows many things, but the hedgehog knows one big thing." Isaiah Berlin's *The Hedgehog and the Fox: An Essay on Tolstoy's View of History* (London: Weidenfeld & Nicolson; New York: Simon & Schuster, 1953; rev. 1978) opens with a probing meditation on "these dark words" whose authenticity and meaning (to say nothing of a sensible translation) remains unclear. It is, however, their figurative suggestiveness that inspires Berlin.

Charles Rosen, taking the hedgehog as a purely natural conceit, examines the Schlegel fragment in *The Romantic Generation* (Cambridge, Mass.: Harvard University Press, 1995), 48: "Like its definition, the Romantic Fragment is complete (this oxymoron was intended to disturb, as the hedgehog's quills make its enemies uncomfortable): separate from the rest of the universe, the Fragment nevertheless suggests distant perspectives. Its separation, indeed, is aggressive: it projects into the universe precisely by the way it cuts itself off."

PART VI

Death Masks

CHAPTER 15

Walter Benjamin and the Apprehending of Beauty

"Every perfect work is the death mask of its intuition." Returning finally to the epigraph that set this book in motion, we are reminded that Walter Benjamin tried out his lapidary thought in January 1924 in one among several letters on art, history and criticism to his intellectual confidant, Florens Christian Rang. And then, as if to exemplify the wisdom of what he wrote, he cleansed it in revision, making it over into something less daring. "The work is the death mask of conception," he now wrote, as the final entry in "The Writer's Technique in Thirteen Theses," in the miscellany published as *Einbahnstrasse* in 1928.[1] Benjamin draws back now from the extremity of perfection. The mysteries implicit in intuition give place to conception, decidedly less mysterious, more rational.

Characteristically, Benjamin set his sights on a moment that can never click into focus: the unimaginable moment during which idea (and, by extension, art) is imagined—in which the intuitive is transfixed as text. Benjamin's Death Mask invokes the moment at which this elusive, ephemeral, wavelike process of creation is spent: what remains is called the Work. The spontaneity, the play of creation is over. The vitality of making gives way to artifact. The fluidity of composition, the act of creating, is stopped, petrified in the formal construct that more readily responds to cognition and analysis. But this moment at which text is fixed and intuition silenced is a phenomenon fraught with imponderables of its own.

---

1. "Jedes vollkommene Werk ist die Totenmaske seiner Intuition." *Walter Benjamin: Briefe*, I: 327; *The Correspondence of Walter Benjamin, 1910–1940*, 227. "Das Werk ist die Totenmaske der Konzeption." Walter Benjamin, *Gesammelte Schriften* [=GS] IV/1, 538; and Walter Benjamin, *Selected Writings*, I: 459. See Preface, note 1, for fuller citation.

I

It was during these troubled and productive years that Benjamin produced the imposing, often impenetrable essay on Goethe's *Wahlverwandtschaften* (Elective Affinities), the act of reading made into a *Probestück* in search of a genuine criticism over against the literal commentary that conventionally bore the name.[2] If the latter describes the material content of the work, the former goes after its truth content. Having suggested that the history of the work prepares for its critique, and that historical distance consequently increases the power of such critique, Benjamin conjures this extravagant simile: "If one views the growing work as a burning funeral pyre, then the commentator stands before it like a chemist, the critic like an alchemist. Whereas, for the commentator, wood and ash remain the sole objects of his analysis, for the critic the flame itself alone preserves an enigma: that of what is alive. Thus, the critic inquires into the truth, whose living flame continues to burn over the heavy logs of what is past and the light ashes of what has been experienced."[3]

Why *Wahlverwandtschaften?* If one were casting about for a work whose living flame illuminates an enigma, Goethe's riddling novella, in its meshing of timeless parable and contemporary romance, makes the short list. However we think to reconcile the symmetries and alignments of its plot, the invertible counterpoint that its characters perform and the themes of morality and art that control the discourse, there is yet one aspect of the work that remains supremely and intentionally unintelligible, and it has to do with the figure and image of Ottilie, whose obscure, expressionless beauty, somewhere between puberty and maturity, is only affirmed in Goethe's text but never described in conventional literary detail. Her beauty is not of this world. She comes then to signify beauty in some abstract sense, at the margins of experience. Indeed, it is through her eyes that Ottilie is represented in her singular and curious engagement with her environ-

---

2. First published in *Neue Deutsche Beiträge,* 1924–1925. Then, in Walter Benjamin, *Illuminationen: Ausgewählte Schriften,* ed. Siegfried Unseld (Frankfurt am Main: Suhrkamp Verlag, 1955), 70–147; and Benjamin, GS I: 123–201; "Goethe's Elective Affinities," tr. Stanley Corngold, in Benjamin, *Selected Writings,* I: 297–360.

3. "Will man das wachsende Werk als den Scheiterhaufen ansehen, so steht davor der Kommentator wie der Chemiker, der Kritiker gleich dem Alchimisten. Wo jenem Holz und Asche allein die Gegenstände seiner Analyse bleiben, bewahrt für diesen nur die Flamme selbst ein Rätsel: das des Lebendigen. So fragt der Kritiker nach der Wahrheit, deren lebendige Flamme fortbrennt über den schweren Scheiten des Gewesenen und der leichten Asche des Erlebten." *Illuminationen,* 71; GS I: 126; *Selected Writings,* I: 298.

ment. When for the first time she holds the infant son born to Charlotte, her aunt and protectress, she is "startled to see in his open eyes the very image of her own."[4] The curiosity of such a revelation would hint strongly of irony—in the first instance because Ottilie bears only a remote kinship to little Otto, and in the second because the eye, in its optical essence, is not an element of which we are cognizant in our own physical appearance: it is absolutely unrevealing in itself. And yet the meeting of eyes suggests, as does no other human (or even animal) conduct, a deeper contact: an intimacy of inner beings, of souls. There is no irony here. The magnetic, mystical force of Ottilie's eyes are made a pronounced theme. The eye of Ottilie seems to stand for some mystical quest toward the idea of beauty, in the paradox of sensual love and abstract, formal beauty, and finally, in the notion of a pure beauty without expression—indeed, without life. In her gradual withdrawal from the world, Ottilie lapses into utter silence and finally, a self-willed death. On the funeral bier, her beauty takes on an ethereal aspect. In a "state resembling rather sleep than death," as Goethe puts it, her attraction becomes even more magnetic.[5]

Wahlverwandtschaften is about many things, not least about the imponderable mysteries of art and beauty. How does the critical mind come to grips with such a work? This, it seems to me, is the problem that consumed Benjamin. For while his essay, too, is about these other aspects of *Wahlverwandtschaften,* at the end of the day it is about the nature of the beautiful, and the critic's access to such abstractions.

Benjamin makes only the briefest and most riddling references to music, and they seem to stand at the last outpost of the knowable, at the leap into the world beyond cognition. They come toward the end of the essay, the first of them in the midst of a tortuous hunt for the location of beauty in semblance and in essence. "Everything essentially beautiful," he writes, "is always and in its essence bound up, though in infinitely different degrees, with semblance."[6] In the intensity of the

---

4. "Das Gebet war verrichtet, Ottilien das Kind auf die Arme gelegt, und als sie mit Neigung auf das-selbe heruntersah, erschrak sie nicht wenig an seinen offenen Augen; denn sie glaubte in ihre eige-nen zu sehen; eine solche Übereinstimmung hätte jeden überraschen müssen." Johann Wolfgang von Goethe, *Werke. Hamburger Ausgabe* [= HA], VI, Romane und Novellen I, ed. Erich Trunz (Mu-nich: C. H. Beck, 1981), 421. Johann Wolfgang von Goethe, *Elective Affinities,* tr. R. J. Hollingdale (Harmondsworth, Middlesex: Penguin Books, 1971), 221.

5. "Der fortdauernd schöne, mehr schlaf- als todtähnliche Zustand Ottiliens zog mehrere Menschen herbei." HA VI: 488. *Elective Affinities,* 298.

6. "Alles wesentlich Schöne ist stets und wesenhaft, aber in unendlich verschiedenen Graden, dem Schein verbunden." GS I: 194; *Illuminationen,* 140; *Selected Writings,* I:350.

ensuing interrogation of the Platonic idea of the beautiful, semblance and essence, intimately fused in the work of art, are pulled apart:

> Beautiful life, the essentially beautiful, and semblance-like beauty—these three are identical. . . . An element of semblance remains preserved in that which is least alive, if it is essentially beautiful. And this is the case with all works of art, but least among them music. Accordingly, there dwells in all beauty of art that semblance—that is to say, that verging and bordering on life—without which beauty is not possible. The semblance, however, does not comprise the essence of beauty. Rather, the latter points down more deeply to what in the work of art in contrast to the semblance may be characterized as the expressionless; but outside this contrast, it [this essence, he must mean] neither appears in art nor can be unambiguously named.[7]

All of which leads to this ultimate arcanum: "Never has a true work of art been grasped other than where it ineluctably represented itself as a secret. Since only the beautiful and outside it nothing—veiling or being veiled—can be essential, the divine ground of the being of beauty lies in the secret."[8]

This semblance, this expression, which is a necessary veil that obscures the "essentially" beautiful is perceptible even at those extreme points of abstraction—the work stripped down to its core—where nothing seems to reside but the essentially beautiful itself. But these traces of the veil, of life, of expression are least of all present in music. In that sense (if I am grasping the implications of Benjamin's obscure reference), music is the art that comes closest to conveying the purely, the essentially beautiful.

For Benjamin, the deepest expression of the mystery of the novella is couched in that luminous phrase through which Goethe captures the doomed moment of

---

7. "Schönes Leben, Wesentlich-Schönes und scheinhafte Schönheit, diese drei sind identisch. . . . Ein Moment des Scheins jedoch bleibt noch im Unlebendigsten erhalten, für den Fall, dass es wesentlich schön ist. Und dies ist der Fall aller Kunstwerke—unter ihnen am mindesten der Musik. Demnach bleibt in aller Schönheit der Kunst jener Schein, will sagen jenes Streifen und Grenzen ans Leben noch wohnen, und sie ist ohne diese nicht möglich. Nicht aber umfasst derselbe ihr Wesen. Dieses weist vielmehr tiefer hinab auf dasjenige, was am Kunstwerk im Gegensatze zum Schein als das ausdruckslose bezeichnet werden darf, ausserhalb dieses Gegensatzes aber in der Kunst weder vorkommt, noch eindeutig benannt werden kann." GS I: 194; *Illuminationen*, 140; *Selected Writings*, I:350.

8. "Niemals noch wurde ein wahres Kunstwerk erfasst, denn wo es unausweichlich als Geheimnis sich darstellte. Weil nur das Schöne und ausser ihm nichts verhüllend und verhüllt wesentlich zu sein vermag, liegt im Geheimnis der göttliche Seinsgrund der Schönheit." GS I: 195; *Illuminationen*, 141; *Selected Writings*, I:351.

final embrace between Ottilie and Eduard: "Hope soared away above their heads like a star falling from the heavens."[9] And this inspires the apotheosis in Benjamin's critique:

> . . . the symbol of the star falling over the heads of the lovers is the form of expression appropriate to whatever of mystery in the exact sense of the term dwells within the work. The mystery is, on the dramatic level, that moment in which it projects up, out of the domain of its own language into a higher and unattainable one. Therefore, this moment can never be expressed in words but is expressible solely in representation: it is the "dramatic" in the strictest sense. An analogous moment of representation in the *Wahlverwandtschaften* is the falling star. To its epic foundation in the mythic, its lyrical breadth in passion and affect, is joined its dramatic crowning in the mystery of hope. If music encloses genuine mysteries, it remains thus in a mute world from which its reverberations will never sound forth.[10]

In a passage fraught with mysteries of its own, music is invoked as an encrypted language that might yet illuminate something of this leap from the purely linguistic to that other realm, "nicht erreichbaren," this moment—"dramatic in the strictest sense"—that can never be expressed in words. What is it, precisely, that Benjamin attributes to music, in its concealing of mysteries that can never be sounded forth? Perhaps, that in music the representational—the symbolic, in

---

9. "Die Hoffnung fuhr wie ein Stern, der von Himmel fällt, über ihre Häupter weg." HA VI: 456. I have somewhat modified the Hollingdale translation, p. 261. Goethe's line, and Benjamin's gloss on it, inspired Adorno as well. By 1923, Adorno was reading *Die Wahlverwandtschaften* and studying the first draft of Benjamin's essay on it. See Theodor W. Adorno, *Essays on Music*, selected, with Introduction, Commentary, and Notes by Richard Leppert (Berkeley, Los Angeles, London: University of California Press, 2002), 2–3. In *Aesthetic Theory*, he writes, "There are measures in Beethoven's music that sound like that sentence from Goethe's *Elective Affinities:* 'Wie ein Stern fuhr die Hoffnung vom Himmel hernieder.' Adorno, *Gesammelte Schriften 7: Aesthetische Theorie* (Frankfurt am Main: Suhrkamp Verlag, 5th ed., 1990), 280.

10. " . . . das Symbol des über die Liebenden herabfahrenden Sterns ist die gemässe Ausdrucksform dessen, was vom Mysterium im genauen Sinn dem Werke einwohnt. Das Mysterium ist im Dramatischen dasjenige Moment, in dem dieses aus dem Bereiche der ihm eigenen Sprache in einen höheren und ihr nicht erreichbaren hineinragt. Es kann daher niemals in Worten, sondern einzig und allein in der Darstellung zum Ausdruck kommen, es ist das 'Dramatische' im strengsten Verstande. Ein analoges Moment der Darstellung ist in den Wahlverwandtschaften der fallende Sterne. Zu ihrer epischen Grundlage im Mythischen, ihrer lyrischen Breite in Leidenschaft und Neigung, tritt ihre dramatische Krönung im Mysterium der Hoffnung. Schliesst eigentliche Mysterien die Musik, so bleibt dies freilich eine stumme Welt, aus welcher niemals ihr Erklingen steigen wird. GS I: 200–201; *Selected Writings*, I: 355.

Benjamin's highest sense: the extralinguistic—is inseparable from its linguistic basis. Its mysteries remain embedded in the notes.

These days, it might be thought quaint to engage in such talk of essences and Beauty. And yet it seems to me that in these imponderable reflections Benjamin is worrying more than a definition of Beauty: there is a playing out that has to do with the place of works of literature—of Art—in a Europe, in the 1920s, where a concept of beauty as a last frontier of meaning, and therefore of genuine culture, had become estranged from the increasingly politicized banalities of *Kultur.*

II

Not too many years earlier—in 1911—Thomas Mann grappled with this estrangement in the conceiving of *Der Tod in Venedig,* a novella whose mystical quest toward the idea of beauty seems now and again to echo the haunting themes of Goethe's *Wahlverwandtschaften,* a work which Mann himself claimed to have read through no less than five times in the course of his own writing during that Venetian summer.[11] More than that, in its density of thought, the writing often seems to prefigure Benjamin's efforts to get at the nub of Goethe's veiled meaning. Beauty is approached through a vision in which two figures, one elderly and one young, one ugly and one beautiful, turn out to be Socrates and Phaedrus. The famous dialogue is not of course cited in any literal mode, but remembered, half-dreamed, through a distorting lens. These passages are no less about the "essence" of the beautiful than are Benjamin's, though perhaps it might be suggested that Mann and Benjamin begin at different points on the axis and end up again at opposite ends.

The aging Gustav von Aschenbach undertakes his self-willed journey of the soul from a priestly aesthetic station: aloof, distant, classicizing, perceiving beauty in the idealized abstractions of form. His first aperceptions of the Polish adolescent beach boy are as of frozen sculpture, like Winckelmann's views of Greek antiquity. Tadzio is caught in posture—evoking those friezelike tableaux vivants at the outset of Book II of *Wahlverwandtschaften.* Gradually, in a studied

---

11. "What I was after was an equilibrium of sensuality and morality such as I found perfected in the *Elective Affinities,* which I read five times, if I remember rightly, while working on *Death in Venice,*" he wrote, in a letter of 4 July 1920 to Carl Maria Weber; quoted from *Letters of Thomas Mann 1889–1955.* Selected and tr. from the German by Richard and Clara Winston (New York: Alfred A. Knopf, 1971), 103.

degeneration of the soul that Mann so painstakingly calibrates, Aschenbach succumbs: to the sensual, the erotic, the forbidden. And everywhere, this is coupled with images of decay, of disease, of masks (Aschenbach in the barbershop—hauntingly portrayed in Visconti's film)—and of death.

At a critical turn in *Der Tod in Venedig,* inspired now by the physical presence of Tadzio on the beach and resolved to capture in prose—to possess, through an act of writing—the fusion of Beauty and Eros that his figure embodies, Aschenbach is consumed in this overwrought reflection:

> The writer's joy resides in the thought that can become feeling, feeling that can merge wholly into thought. Such a pulsating thought, such precise feeling possessed the solitary Aschenbach at that very moment: namely, that Nature trembles with rapture when the spirit bows in homage before Beauty.[12]

This epiphanous moment seems very close to just such a moment in Goethe's novella. Ottilie has been fixed in posture, statuelike, as the Mother of God in a tableau-vivant on Christmas eve. A thousand thoughts pass like lightning through her soul in these frozen moments:

> With a celerity with which nothing else can be compared, feeling and thought reacted one against the other within her. Her heart beat fast and her eyes filled with tears, while she strove to stay as still as a statue.[13]

Aschenbach, unlike Ottilie, translates his ecstatic moment into prose:

> Never had he known so well that Eros is in the word, as during those perilous and precious hours when he sat at his rude table, within the shade of his awning, his idol full in view and the music of his voice in his ears, and fashioned his little essay after the model Tadzio's beauty set, that page and a half of choicest prose,

---

12. "Glück des Schriftstellers ist der Gedanke, der ganz Gefühl, ist das Gefühl, das ganz Gedanke zu werden vermag. Solch ein pulsender Gedanke, solch genaues Gefühl gehörte und gehorchte dem Einsamen damals: nämlich, dass die Natur von Wonne erschaure, wenn der Geist sich huldigend vor der Schönheit neige." *Der Tod in Venedig,* in Thomas Mann, *Gesammelte Werke in dreizehn Bänden* [= GW], VIII: Erzählungen; Fiorenza; Dichtungen (Frankfurt am Main: S. Fischer, 1960/1974), 492. The translation, here and below, is my own, now and then borrowing from the translations of H. T. Lowe-Porter (New York: Alfred A. Knopf, 1930, and in many editions); David Luke (New York: Bantam Books, 1988); and Joachim Neugroschel (New York: Viking, 1998).

13. "Mit einer Schnelligkeit, die keinesgleichen hat, wirkten Gefühl und Betrachtung in ihr gegeneinander. Ihr Herz war befangen, ihre Augen füllten sich mit Tränen, indem sie sich zwang, immerfort als ein starres Bild zu erscheinen." HA 6, 405; *Elective Affinities,* 204.

so chaste, so lofty, so poignant with feeling, which would shortly inspire the admiration of his readers. Certainly it is a good thing that the world knows only the beautiful work, and nothing of its sources, of the circumstances of its origin; for a knowledge of the springs from which the artist's inspiration flowed would only confuse and intimidate it, and thus compromise the effects of its excellence.[14]

Then comes the poignant collapse:

Strange, curious hours! Strange, unnerving labor. How mysterious this act of intercourse and begetting between a mind and a body! When Aschenbach put away his work and left the beach, he felt exhausted, even broken, his conscience reproached him as though after a debauch.[15]

There is more than a whiff of irony in this transparent, furtive sighting of the shuddering moment at which art is born, even as Mann, through Aschenbach, protests the irrelevancy of such intimate knowledge to the appreciation of its beauty. And yet he wants us to know. He insists that we know. His work completed, the Aschenbach who comes up from the beach is spent ["erschöpft"]. The perfect work is the Death Mask of its intuition. In his little *scena* on the beach, Aschenbach act outs, dramatizes as though in parable, Benjamin's conceit.

III

This constellation of thought around the capturing, phenomenologically, of the *moment* of beauty comes alive for me in the image of a passage in the Andantino

---

14. "Nie hatte er die Lust des Wortes süsser empfunden, nie so gewusst das Eros im Worte sei, wie während der gefährlich köstlichen Stunden, in denen er, an seinem rohen Tische unter dem Schattentuch, im Angesicht des Idols und die Musik seiner Stimme im Ohr, nach Tadzios Schönheit seine kleine Abhandlung,—jene anderthalb Seiten erlesener Prosa formte, deren Lauterkeit, Adel und schwingende Gefühlsspannung binnen kurzem die Bewunderung vieler erregen sollte. Es ist sicher gut, dass die Welt nur das schöne Werk, nicht auch seine Ursprünge, nicht seine Entstehungsbedingungen kennt; denn die Kenntnis der Quellen, aus denen dem Künstler Eingebung floss, würde sie oftmals verwirren, abschrecken und so die Wirkungen des Vortrefflichen aufheben." GW VIII: 492–493.

15. "Sonderbare Stunden! Sonderbar entnervende Mühe! Seltsam zeugender Verkehr des Geister mit einem Körper! Als Aschenbach seine Arbeit verwahrte und vom Strande aufbrach, fühlte er sich erschöpft, ja zerrüttet, und ihm war, als ob sein Gewissen wie nach einer Ausschweifung Klage führe." GW VIII: 493.

of Schubert's Sonata in A major (D 959) of 1828. Hearing a performance of this music suggests how Benjamin's sense of the finished work, of a text, implicates performance as well: the performance, we might propose, in *its* realization, is itself a mask, emulating the process of mind that creates the text—acts out, that is, the life/death that Benjamin's definition of the work seeks to capture. This is not in any sense to suggest that the work itself "exists" only in such realizations. Rather, the phenomenon of performance excites us (as performers) because we reenact, each time uniquely, this intuitive process that the text suggests of its origins.

Schubert did not often leave behind the concrete evidence of such a process. But a draft for this movement has survived, and it has much to tell us.[16] (See ex. 15.1.) The placing of these two documents side by side will invariably inspire narratives toward a theory of "creative process": by one such script, the draft is shown to be but a naive, precritical glimpse at an idea not yet "perfected." In another, the draft is valued as a thing in itself, as rare evidence of primary, primal thought: fleet, spontaneous, unmediated by the meddling critical mind. To dismiss out of hand either or both of these views of the draft would be to miss something of value that each has to offer. And yet they are inadequate, and in this sense: to the written document is ascribed in each instance a fixity that traduces the complex privacy of creating—the silent internal colloquy, the torment, the euphoria, the play that is innate in it; a fixity that does not recognize the fluency of a dialectics that flow in the time and space between and around the documents. Construed as something definitive and finished, fixed in its notation, the document, whether of a draft or a sketch or of some perfected "final text," is made over into a mask that obscures the process of mind behind it.

This, however, does not get us very close to the funeral pyre that Benjamin conjures. Where is the truth content of this music? Where is its beauty? We follow Benjamin in the quest to separate out the luster, the appearance, the expression of beauty from something at once more abstract, more enigmatic, less open to cognitive grasp or visceral perception. We revisit the draft, its music telegraphically concise almost to a vanishing point. Is this really how the idea came to Schubert? Is the idea, in its irreducible essence, more closely captured in the draft, stripped of all semblance of the expression—of the poignancy of human

---

16. The portfolio of drafts for the last sonatas is published as Franz Schubert, *Drei große Sonaten für das Pianoforte. D. 958, D. 959, und D. 960 (Frühe Fassungen). Faksimile nach den Autographen in der Wiener Stadt- und Landesbibliothek,* text and commentary by Ernst Hilmar (Tutzing: Hans Schneider, 1987). For an essay on this publication, see my "Posthumous Schubert," in *19th Century Music* 14 (Fall 1990): 197–216.

EXAMPLE 15.1 Schubert, Sonata in A major, D 959, Andantino.

A Published version.

utterance—that moves us in the music that we all know? These are impossible questions, but in the asking, they expose the folly in trusting that we can nail down, cognitively, some identifiable moment in which the work coalesces. The problem seems to me at one with the Benjaminian riddle of an essential beauty that grows increasingly inaccessible as it is approached. If there is an essential

B Draft, Vienna: Stadtbibliothek, MH 171/c.

beauty—some essence that allows of apperception—it won't be found reified in the ultimate distillation that we theorists are forever burning out of the notes. Perhaps we must be content to imagine it, mysteriously inaccessible, embedded in the incessant play between faceless, formal abstraction and irrational, fallible expression.

Surely, it is a mistake to seek answers in the apparent opposition of draft to finished work. There is in effect no opposition here, but rather a fluid process of mind, hopelessly dialectical, obscure to the point of blankness. Benjamin provokes us to penetrate this impenetrable process, of which the draft captures but a single, fragmentary phase. It is not in the nature of the thing that we can ever succeed in the quest to locate that ineffable moment in the process at which Schubert will have found the "essentially beautiful" in this music. The moment itself—

Goethe's falling star—vanishes, as moments do, and we are left with the "voll-kommene Werk," and all that it masks.

IV

The porous boundary between the work, in what Benjamin calls its truth content, and what the author confides as to its meaning was of great concern to Benjamin. "To wish to gain an understanding of *Elective Affinities* from the author's own words on the subject is wasted effort," he writes. "For it is precisely their aim to forbid access to critique."[17] The second part of Benjamin's essay, now in close scrutiny of this boundary, opens with a set of maxims on the reading of the author in the text—and here I must again quote Benjamin: "The sole rational connection between creative artist and work of art consists in the testimony that the latter gives about the former." And, finally: "Works, like deeds, are non-derivable."[18]

Those "anderthalb Seiten erlesener Prosa" written by Aschenbach on the beach were years ago identified as the brief essay titled "Auseinandersetzung mit Richard Wagner" (Coming to Terms with Richard Wagner), a manuscript that bears the letterhead of the Grand Hotel des Bains, Lido-Venise (Aschenbach's hotel) and is dated May 1911.[19] In the essay, Mann is very hard on Wagner's theoretical writings, which he finds absurdly untenable. He doubts whether anyone actually reads this stuff. "Is it," he wonders, "because his writings are propaganda rather than honest revelation? Because their comments on his work—wherein he truly lives in all his suffering greatness—are singularly inadequate and misleading? There is not much to be learned about Wagner from Wagner's critical writings."[20]

---

17. "Das Verständnis der 'Wahlverwandtschaften' aus des Dichters eigenen Worten darüber erschliessen zu wollen, ist vergebene Mühe. Gerade sie sind ja dazu bestimmt, der Kritik den Zugang zu verlegen." GS I: 145; *Illuminationen,* 91. *Selected Writings,* I:313.
18. "Der einzige rationale Zusammenhang zwischen Schaffendem und Werk in dem Zeugnis besteht, das dieses von jenem ablegt. . . . Werke sind unableitbar wie Taten . . ." GS I, 155–56; *Illuminationen,* 101; *Selected Writings,* I: 321.
19. "Coming to Terms with Richard Wagner," in Thomas Mann, *Pro and Contra Wagner,* tr. Allan Blunden, ed. Patrick Carnegy (Chicago: The University of Chicago Press, 1985), 45, footnote: "There can be little doubt that this is the 'little tract . . .' whose composition . . . is assigned to Gustav von Aschenbach." Anthony Heilbut, in *Thomas Mann: Eros and Literature* (New York: Alfred A. Knopf, 1996), 249, writes: "This is the essay Aschenbach/Mann composes while on the beach . . . The result seems contradictory: a decadent occasion prompting a neo-classical manifesto."
20. "Coming to Terms with Richard Wagner," 47.

I call up the essay on Wagner for two reasons. For one, it worries this difficult question on the abuse of the author's privilege that Benjamin worries with Goethe. For another, the Wagner essay is itself implicated in just such a relationship, for the critic who is tempted to reveal the identity of Aschenbach's burnished prose will invoke the circumstantial evidence that implicates the Wagner essay. This is what I meant in referring to a porous boundary between work and author. There is much in the little Wagner essay that resonates sympathetically with the aesthetic problem in *Der Tod in Venedig*, and perhaps most notably, the opposition of Eros and classicism; even the "Auseinandersetzung" of its title is suggestive in this regard.[21] If we cannot know, if we are meant not to know, what it was that Aschenbach was writing on the beach, we can yet allow these two works, the essay on Wagner and the novella, to continue to resonate sympathetically, taking care, as we must, to respect the autonomy of their texts.

To mask is to disguise, to conceal, to obfuscate. But in an age before photography, the death mask sought to preserve the features of its subject in perfect fidelity: to reveal. Benjamin's metaphor is thus shrouded in further paradox, for if the finished work is a mirror held up to an intuition now vanished, it remains the only evidence of that intuition. It masks in these two contradictory senses, concealing, altering, disguising the throe of intuition even as it reveals, limits, sets the work in some formal language that allows of its apprehension. The death mask stands neither for the work nor our response to it, but for something less specific: a process, perhaps, internal to the creation of works, a mirror held up to the inner consciousness of the artist. How to figure this image in our efforts to write histories of art—to do criticism—is the difficult challenge that is Benjamin's legacy.

---

21. The title apparently was not Mann's. See the letter of 11 August 1911 to Ernst Bertram, given in *Pro and Contra Wagner*, 48–49.

LIST OF WORKS CITED

Music Editions and Facsimiles

Bach, Carl Philipp Emanuel. *Klaviersonaten. Auswahl.* Vol. 3. Edited by Darrell M. Berg. Munich: G. Henle, [1989].

———. *The Collected Works for Solo Keyboard by Carl Philipp Emanuel Bach.* Edited by Darrell Berg. 6 vols. New York and London: Garland, 1985.

———. *Carl Philipp Emanuel Bach Edition.* Series I, vol. 24, Keyboard Sonatas, ed. Claudia Widgery. Oxford: Oxford University Press, 1989.

———. *Kurze und leichte Clavierstücke mit veränderten Reprisen und beygefügter Fingersetzung für Anfänger von C. P. E. Bach.* Berlin: George Ludewig Winter, 1766; Zweyte Sammlung, 1768. Reprint edited by Oswald Jonas. [Vienna:] Universal Edition, [1961].

———. *Sechs Sonaten mit veränderten Reprisen (1760).* Edited by Etienne Darbellay. Winterhur: Amadeus Verlag, 1976.

———. *The Complete Works.* Los Altos, California: The Packard Humanities Institute, in cooperation with the Bach-Archiv Leipzig, the Sächsische Akademie der Wissenschaften zu Leipzig, and Harvard University, 2005–.

Bach, Johann Sebastian. *Neue Ausgabe sämtliche Werke.* Edited under the auspices of the Johann-Sebastian-Bach Institut Göttingen and the Bach-Archiv Leipzig. Kassel and Leipzig: Bärenreiter Verlag, 1954–.

Beethoven, Ludwig van. *Allegretto in h-Moll / Allegretto in B minor.* Preface by Martin Bircher and an Introduction by Stephen Roe. Munich: K. G. Saur, Fondation Martin Bodmer Cologny, 2001.

———. *Autograph Miscellany from circa 1786 to 1799, British Museum Additional Manuscript 29801, ff. 39–162* (The 'Kafka Sketchbook'). 2 vols. Edited by Joseph Kerman. London, 1970.

———. *Ein Skizzenbuch zu Streichquartetten aus Op. 18.* Edited by Wilhelm Virneisel. 2 vols. Bonn: Beethovenhaus, 1972–1974.

———. *Keßlersches Skizzenbuch.* Edited by Sieghard Brandenburg. 2 vols. Bonn: Beethovenhaus, 1976–1978.

———. *Klaviersonate e-Moll op. 90. Faksimile des Autographs.* Edited with commentary by Michael Ladenburger. Bonn: Beethoven-Haus, 1993.

———. *A Sketchbook from the Summer of 1800.* Edited by Richard Kramer. 2 vols. Bonn: Beethoven-Haus, 1996.

———. *Sämtliche Kadenzen. The Complete Cadenzas.* Edited by Willy Hess. Zurich: Eulenberg, 1979.

————. *Werke. Gesamtausgabe.* Edited by Sieghard Brandenburg and Ernst Herttrich, on behalf of the Beethoven-Archiv Bonn. Munich: G. Henle Verlag, 1955–.

Haydn, Joseph. *The Creation and the Seasons: The complete authentic sources for the Word-Books.* Foreword by H. C. Robbins Landon. Cardiff: University College Cardiff Press, 1985.

————.*Werke.* Series 15, vol. 2, *Konzerte für Klavier (Cembalo) und Orchester.* Edited by Horst Walter and Bettina Wackernagel. Munich: G. Henle Verlag, 1983.

[Mozart, W. A.] *Cadances* [sic] *Originales se rapportant a ses Concerto [sic] pour le Clavecin où Pianoforte* Vienna: Artaria & Co., 1801.

[Mozart, W. A.] *Cadence ou points d'orgue . . .* Offenbach: J. André, 1804.

Mozart, Wolfgang Amadeus. *Neue Ausgabe sämtlicher Werke.* Kassel: Bärenreiter Verlag, 1955–.

Neefe, Christian Gottlob. *Zwölf Klavier-Sonaten.* Leipzig: Schwickert, 1773. Facsimile reprint, Courlay: Collection Dominantes, 2004.

Schubert, Franz. *"Reliquie": Sonata in C für Klavier D 840. Faksimile-Ausgabe nach den Autographen in Cambridge, Paris und Wien.* Edited by Hans-Joachim Hinrichsen. Tutzing: Hans Schneider, 1992.

————. *Klaviersonaten.* Vol. 3, *Frühe und unvollendete Sonaten.* Edited by Paul Badura-Skoda. Munich: G. Henle Verlag, [1979].

————. *Drei große Sonaten für das Pianoforte. D. 958, D. 959, und D. 960 (Frühe Fassungen). Faksimile nach den Autographen in der Wiener Stadt- und Landesbibliothek.* Text and commentary by Ernst Hilmar. Tutzing: Hans Schneider, 1987.

————. *Sechzehn Goethe-Lieder.* Edited by Peter Hauschild. Leipzig: Peters, 1978.

————. *Werke. Kritisch durchgesehene Gesammtausgabe.* Series 21, Supplement. Revisionsbericht, ed. Eusebius Mandyczewski. Leipzig: Breitkopf & Härtel, 1897. Reprint, *Franz Schubert's Compete Works.* Vol. 19. New York: Dover Publications; Wiesbaden: Breitkopf & Härtel, 1969.

Documents and Bibliographies

Anderson, Emily, ed. and trans. *The Letters of Beethoven.* 3 vols. London: Macmillan; New York: St. Martin's Press, 1961.

————, ed. and trans. *The Letters of Mozart and his Family.* 2 vols. London: Macmillan; New York: St. Martin's Press, 3rd ed., 1985.

Bach, Carl Philipp Emanuel. *Autobiography* [with] *Verzeichniß des musikalischen Nachlasses* [see below]. Annotations in English and German by William S. Newman. Buren: Frits Knuf, 1991.

————. *Briefe und Dokumente: Kritische Gesamtausgabe.* Edited by Ernst Suchalla. Göttingen: Vandenhoek & Ruprecht, 1994.

————. *Essay on the True Art of Playing Keyboard Instruments.* Edited and translated by William J. Mitchell. New York: W. W. Norton, 1949.

————. *The Letters of C. P. E. Bach.* Edited and translated by Stephen L. Clark. Oxford: Clarendon Press; New York: Oxford University Press, 1997.

————. *Versuch über die wahre Art das Clavier zu spielen.* Part I, Berlin: Henning, 1753; and Part II, Berlin: George Ludewig Winter, 1762. Facsimile edition, ed. Lothar Hoffmann-Erbrecht, Leipzig: Beitkopf & Härtel, 1969.

————. *Verzeichniß des musikalischen Nachlasses des verstorbenen Capellmeisters Carl*

Philipp Emanuel Bach. Hamburg: Gottlieb Friedrich Schniebes, 1790. Reprinted as *The Catalog of Carl Philipp Emanuel Bach's Estate: A Facsimile of the Edition by Schniebes, Hamburg, 1790*. Annotated, with a Preface, by Rachel W. Wade. New York and London: Garland Publishing, 1981. Another facsimile, with annotations in English and German by William S. Newman, Buren: Frits Knuf, 1991.

Bartlitz, Eveline. *Die Beethoven-Sammlung in der Musikabteilung der Deutschen Staatsbibliothek: Verzeichnis*. Berlin: Deutsche Staatsbibliothek, [1970].

Beethoven, Ludwig van. *Briefwechsel Gesamtausgabe*. Edited by Sieghard Brandenburg. 8 vols. Munich: Henle Verlag, 1996–.

David, Hans T., and Arthur Mendel, eds. *The Bach Reader: A Life of Johann Sebastian Bach in Letters and Documents*. Revised, with a supplement. New York: W. W. Norton & Co., 1966. Revised and expanded by Christoph Wolff as *The New Bach Reader*. New York: W. W. Norton & Co., 1998.

Deutsch, Otto Erich. *Franz Schubert. Thematisches Verzeichnis seiner Werke in chronologischer Folge*. Kassel: Bärenreiter Verlag, 1978.

Helm, E. Eugene. *Thematic Catalogue of the Works of Carl Philipp Emanuel Bach*. New Haven and London: Yale University Press, 1989.

Hess, Willy. *Verzeichnis der nicht in der Gesamtausgabe veröffentlichten Werke Ludwig van Beethovens*. Wiesbaden: Breitkopf & Härtel, 1957. Edited, updated and translated from the original German by James F. Green as *The New Hess Catalog of Beethoven's Works*. West Newbury, Vermont: Vance Brook Publishing, 2003.

Hoboken, Anthony van. *Joseph Haydn; Thematisch-bibliographisches Werkverzeichnis*. 3 vols. Mainz: B. Schott's Söhne, 1957.

Johnson, Douglas, Alan Tyson, and Robert Winter. *The Beethoven Sketchbooks: History, Reconstruction, Inventory*. Edited by Douglas Johnson. Berkeley and Los Angleles: University of California Press, 1985.

Kinsky, Georg. *Das Werk Beethovens: Thematische-Bibliographisches Verzeichnis seiner sämtlichen vollendeten Kompositionen*. Completed by Hans Halm. Munich-Duisburg: G. Henle, 1955.

Klein, Hans-Günter. *Beethoven: Autographe und Abschriften*. Staatsbibliothek Preußisher Kulturbesitz, Kataloge der Musikabteilung, 1. Reihe, Band 2: Ludwig van Beethoven. Berlin: Merseburger, 1975.

Köchel, Ludwig Ritter von. *Chronologisch-thematisches Verzeichnis sämtlicher Tonwerke Wolfgang Amadé Mozarts*. Edited by Franz Giegling, Alexander Weinmann, and Gerd Sievers. 6th edn. Wiesbaden: Breitkopf & Härtel, 1964.

Mozart, Wolfgang Amadeus. *Briefe und Aufzeichnungen. Gesamtausgabe*. Edited by Wilhelm A. Bauer, Otto Erich Deutsch, and Joseph Heinz Eibel. 7 vols. Kassel: Bärenreiter Verlag, 1962–1975.

Schmidt, Hans. "Die Beethovenhandschriften des Beethovenhauses in Bonn." *Beethoven-Jahrbuch 7* (1971): ix–xxiv, 1–443. "Addenda und Corrigenda . . ." in *Beethoven-Jahrbuch* 8 (1975): 207–220.

———. "Verzeichnis der Skizzen Beethovens." *Beethoven-Jahrbuch* 6 (1969): 7–128.

Schmidt-Görg, Joseph. "Die Wasserzeichen in Beethovens Notenpapieren." In *Beiträge zur Beethoven-Bibliographie. Studien und Materialien zum Werkverzeichnis von Kinsky-Halm*, ed. Kurt Dorfmüller, 167–195. Munich: G. Henle Verlag, 1978.

————. *Katalog der Handschriften des Beethoven-Hauses und Beethoven-Archivs Bonn.* Bonn: Beethoven-Haus and Beethoven-Archiv, 1935.

Schubert, Franz. *Franz Schuberts Werke in Abschriften: Liederalben und Sammlungen.* (*Neue Ausgabe sämtlicher Werke.* Series 8, Supplement, Band 8, Quellen 2). Edited by Walther Dürr. Kassel: Bärenreiter Verlag, 1975.

Schulze, Hans-Joachim, ed. *Dokumente zum Nachwirken Johann Sebastian Bachs.* Kassel: Bärenreiter Verlag, 1972.

Solomon, Maynard. *Beethovens Tagebuch.* Edited by Sieghard Brandenburg. Mainz: v. Hase & Koehler, 1990.

Sotheby's. *The Pencarrow Collection of Autographs including the newly-discovered Beethoven quartet movement: London, Wednesday 8 December 1999.* London, n.d.

Tyson, Alan. *Wasserzeichen-Katalog.* In *Wolfgang Amadeus Mozart. Neue Ausgabe sämtlicher Werke,* Series 10, Werkgruppe 33, Abteilung 2. Kassel: Bärenreiter, 1992.

Unger, Max. *Eine Schweizer Beethovensammlung: Katalog.* Zurich: Verlag der Corona, 1939.

Primary Texts and Original Sources

Albrechtsberger, Johann Georg. *Gründliche Anweisung zur Composition.* Leipzig: Johann Gottlob Immanuel Breitkopf, 1790.

Aristotle. *Poetics.* Edited and translated by Stephen Halliwell. Loeb Classical Library. Cambridge, Mass., and London: Harvard University Press, 1995.

Benjamin, Walter. *Walter Benjamin: Briefe.* Edited by Gershom Scholem and Theodor W. Adorno. 2 vols. Frankfurt am Main: Suhrkamp Verlag, 1978.

————. *Gesammelte Schriften.* Edited by Rolf Tiedemann and Hermann Schweppenhäuser, in collaboration with Theodor W. Adorno and Gershom Scholem. Frankfurt am Main: Suhrkamp Verlag, 1972–1989.

————. *Illuminationen: Ausgewählte Schriften.* Edited by Siegfried Unseld. Frankfurt am Main: Suhrkamp Verlag, 1955.

————. *Selected Writing, I: 1913–1926.* Edited by Marcus Bullock and Michael W. Jennings. Cambridge, Mass., and London: Harvard University Press, 1996.

————. *The Correspondence of Walter Benjamin, 1910–1940.* Edited and annotated by Gershom Scholem and Theodor W. Adorno. Translated by Manfred R. Jacobsen and Evelyn M. Jacobsen. Chicago and London: The University of Chicago Press, 1994.

Burney, Charles. *A General History of Music.* Vol. 2. Critical and Historical Notes by Frank Mercer. New York: Dover Publications, 1957.

————. *An Account of the Musical Performances in Westminster Abbey in Commemoration of Handel.* London, 1785.

————. *An Eighteenth-Century Musical Tour in Central Europe and the Netherlands.* Edited by Percy A. Scholes. London: Oxford University Press, 1959.

————. *Tagebuch seiner musikalishen Reise.* Vol. 3. Translated by C. D. Ebeling and J. J. C. Bode. Hamburg: Bode, 1773. Reprinted in facsimile as *Tagebuch einer musikalischen Reise.* Vollständiger Ausgabe. Edited by Christoph Hust. Kassel: Bärenreiter Verlag, 2003.

————. *The Present State of Music in Germany, the Netherlands, and United Provinces.* London, 1773.

Claudius, Matthias. *Asmus omnia sua Secum portans, oder Sämmtliche Werke des Wands-*

becker Bothen. Vol. 3. Wandsbeck, 1777. In *Matthias Claudius. Werke*, ed. Urban Roedl. Stuttgart: J. G. Cotta'sche Buchhandlung Nachfolger, 1954.

Cramer, Carl Friedrich. *Magazin der Musik*. 2 vols. Hamburg: in der Musicalischen Niederlage, 1783–1786. Reprint Hildesheim: Georg Olms, 1971.

Czerny, Carl. "Über den richtigen Vortrag der sämmtlichen Beethoven'schen Werke für das Piano allein." *Die Kunst des Vortrags der älteren und neueren Klavierkompositionen*. Vienna: A. Diabelli u. Comp., 1842.

———. *Erninnerungen aus meinem Leben*. Edited by Walter Kolneder. Strasbourg & Baden-Baden: P. H. Heitz, 1968.

———. *Systematic Introduction to Improvisation on the Pianoforte*, op. 200. Edited and translated by Alice L. Mitchell. New York and London: Longman, 1983.

———. *Über den richtigen Vortrag der sämtlichen Beethoven'schen Klavierwerke*. Edited by Paul Badura-Skoda. Vienna: Universal Edition, 1963.

Diderot, Denis. *Diderot on Art*. 2 vols. I: The Salon of 1765 and Notes on Painting; II: The Salon of 1767. Edited and translated by John Goodman, with an Introduction by Thomas Crow. New Haven and London: Yale University Press, 1995.

———. *Entretien entre D'Alembert et Diderot; le Reve de d'Alembert; Suite de l'Entretien*. Edited by Jacques Roger. Paris: Garnier-Flammarion, 1965.

———. *Jacques the Fatalist and His Master*. Revised edition. Translated with an Introduction and Notes by J. Robert Loy. New York and London: W. W. Norton & Co., 1978.

———. *Leçons de clavecin et principes d'harmonie*, par Mr Bemetzrieder. Paris: Chez Bluet, 1771.

———. *Oeuvres complètes de Diderot*. Paris: Hermann, 1975–. Vol. 13 (1984): *Arts et lettres (1767–1770)*. Edited by Jochen Scholbach with Jeanne Carriat, et al.; Vol. 29 (1983): *Musique*, ed. Jean Mayer and Pierre Citron, with Jean Varloot. 47–387.

———. *The Paradox of Acting*. Trans. Walter Herries Pollack. 11–71. [With William Archer, *Masks and Faces?*] Introduction by Lee Strasberg. New York: Hill & Wang, 1957.

———. *Paradoxe sur le comédien précédé des Entretiens sur le fils naturel*. With a chronology and preface by Raymond Laubreaux. Paris: [Garnier]-Flammarion, 1981.

———. *Rameau's Nephew and D'Alembert's Dream*. Translated with an Introduction by Leonard Tancock. Harmondsworth and New York: Penguin Books, 1966.

———. *Rameau's Nephew and Other Works*. Translated by Jacques Barzun and Ralph H. Bowen. Indianapolis, New York and Kansas City: The Bobbs-Merrill Co., 1964.

———. *Salons*. Ed. Jean Seznec and Jean Adhémar. Vol. 2. 1765. 2nd ed., London: Oxford University Press, 1979.

———. *Selected Writings on Art and Literature*. Translated by Geoffrey Bremner. London: Penguin Books, 1994.

Forkel, Johann Nikolaus. "Ueber eine Sonate aus Carl Phil. Emanuel Bachs dritter Sonatensammlung für Kenner und Liebhaber in F moll, S 30. Ein Sendschreiben an Hrn. von * *." *Musikalischer Almanach für Deutschland auf das Jahr 1784*: 22–38. Leipzig: im Schwickertschen Verlag, [n.d.]. Reprint, Hildesheim and New York: Georg Olms, 1974.

———. *Allgemeine Geschichte der Musik*. Vol. 1. Leipzig: im Schwickertschen Verlage, 1788. Reprint, ed. Othmar Wessely. Graz: Akademische Druck- u. Verlagsanstalt, 1967.

————. *Allgemeine Litteratur der Musik*. Leipzig: Schwickert, 1792. Reprint, Hildesheim, Georg Olms, 1962.

————. *Johann Sebastian Bach: His Life, Art, and Work*. Translated with notes and appendices by Charles Sanford Terry. London: Constable & Co., 1920. Reprint, New York: Vienna House, 1974.

————. *Musikalisch-kritische Bibliothek*. 3 vols. Gotha: C. W. Ettinger, 1778–1779. Reprint, Hildesheim: Georg Olms, 1964.

————. *Ueber die Theorie der Musik in so fern sie Liebhabern und Kennern nothwendig und nützlich ist*. Göttingen, 1777; unauthorized reprint in Cramer, *Magazin der Musik* , I: 855–912 (Hamburg, 1783).

————. *Ueber Johann Sebastian Bachs Leben, Kunst und Kunstwerke*. Leipzig: Hoffmeister und Kühnel, 1802. Facsimile edition, with commentary by Axel Fischer. Kassel: Bärenreiter, 1999.

Freud, Sigmund. "The Moses of Michelangelo." Vol. 8, *The Standard Edition of the Complete Psychological Works of Sigmund Freud*. Translated and edited by James Strachey, in collaboration with Anna Freud, assisted by Alix Strachey and Alan Tyson. London: The Hogarth Press and the Institute of Psycho-Analysis, 1955.

————. *Moses and Monotheism*. Translated by Katherine Jones. New York: Vintage Books, n.d.

————. *On Creativity and the Unconscious: Papers on the Psychology of Art, Literature, Love, Religion*. Selected, with Introduction and Annotations by Benjamin Nelson. New York: Harper & Brothers, 1958.

————. *Studienausgabe*. 11 vols. Edited by Alexander Mitscherlich, Angela Richard, James Strachey, and Ilse Grubrich-Simitis. Frankfurt am Main: S. Fischer Verlag, 1969–79.

Goethe, Johann Wolfgang von. *Goethes Werke: Hamburger Ausgabe in 14 Bände*. Munich: C. H. Beck, 1981.

————. *Elective Affinities*. Translated by R. J. Hollingdale. Harmondsworth, Middlesex: Penguin Books, 1971.

Hamann, Johann Georg. "Metacritique on the Purism of Reason." In *What Is Enlightenment? Eighteenth-Century Answers and Twentieth-Century Questions*, ed. and tr. James Schmidt, 154–167. Berkeley, Los Angeles, London: University of California Press, 1996.

————. "Metakritik über den Purismum der Vernunft." In *Mancherley zur Geschichte der metakritischen Invasion*, ed. F. T. Rink, 120–134. Königsberg, 1800.

————. *Briefwechsel*. Edited by Walther Ziesemer and Arthur Henkel Wiesbaden: Insel-Verlag, 1957.

Herder, Johann Gottfried. *Abhandlung über den Ursprung der Sprache*. [Berlin: Christian Friedrich Voß, 1772.] Herder, *Sämtliche Werke*, vol. 5 (1891).

————. *Aelteste Urkunde des Menschengeschlechts*. Vol. 1. [Riga: Johann Friedrich Hartknoch, 1774.] Herder, *Sämtliche Werke*, vol. 6 (1883).

————. *Erläuterungen zum neuen Testament*. Riga: Johann Friedrich Hartknoch, 1775. Herder, *Sämtliche Werke*, vol. 7 (1884).

————. *On the Origin of Language (Jean-Jacques Rousseau, "Essay on the Origin of Languages"; Johann Gottfried Herder, "Essay on the Origin of Language")*. Translated, with afterword, by John H. Moran and Alexander Gode. Chicago and London: University of Chicago Press, 1966.

————. *Sämtliche Werke.* Edited by Bernhard Suphan. Berlin: Weidmann,, 1877–1913. Reprint, Hildesheim: Georg Olms, 1967.

Kant, Immanuel. "An Answer to the Question: What Is Enlightenment?" In *What Is Enlightenment? Eighteenth-Century Answers and Twentieth-Century Questions,* ed. and tr. James Schmidt, 58–64. Berkeley, Los Angeles, London: University of California Press, 1996.

————. "Beantwortung der Frage: Was ist Aufklärung?" *Berlinische Monatsschrift* 4 (1784): 494.

————. *Gesammelte Schriften: Akademie Ausgabe.* Vol. 8. Berlin, 1923.

Kirnberger, Johann Philipp. *Die wahren Grundsätze zum Gebrauch der Harmonie, . . . als ein Zusatz zu der Kunst des reinen Satzes in der Musik.* Berlin and Königsberg: G. J. Decker und G. L. Hartung, 1773. Reprint, Hildesheim and New York: Georg Olms, 1970.

Koch, Heinrich Christoph. *Musikalisches Lexikon.* Frankfurt am Main: August Hermann dem Jüngern, 1802. Reprint, Hildesheim: Georg Olms, 1885.

Kollmann, Augustus Frederic Christoph[er]. *An Essay on Practical Musical Composition.* London: "printed for the author," 1799. Reprint, with a new introduction by Imogene Horsley. New York: Da Capo, 1973.

Lessing, Gotthold Ephraim. *Hamburg Dramaturgy.* Translated by Helen Zimmern, with a new Introduction by Victor Lange. New York: Dover Publications, 1962.

————. *Hamburgische Dramaturgie.* 2 vols. Hamburg: In Commission bey J. H. Cramer, in Bremen, 1769. Reprint in *Sämtliche Schriften,* IX (1893): 1–177.

————. *Laocoön: An Essay on the Limits of Painting and Poetry.* Translated by Edward Allen McCormick. Baltimore: John Hopkins University Press, 1984.

————. *Laokoon oder über die Grenzen der Mahlerey und Poesie. Mit beyläufigen Erläuterungen verschiedener Punkte der alten Kunstgeschichte.* Berlin: Christian Friedrich Voß, 1766. Reprint in *Sämtliche Schriften,* IX (1893): 179–406; X (1894): 1–221.

————. *Sämtliche Schriften.* 3rd ed. Edited by Karl Lachmann. Stuttgart: G. J. Göschen'sche Verlagshandlung, 1886–1924. Reprint, Berlin: Walter de Gruyter & Co., 1968.

Mann, Thomas. *Death in Venice.* Translated by David Luke. New York: Bantam Books, 1988.

————. *Death in Venice.* Translated by H. T. Lowe-Porter. New York: Alfred A. Knopf, 1930.

————. *Death in Venice.* Translated by Joachim Neugroschel. New York: Viking, 1998.

————. *Der Tod in Venedig.* Vol. 8, *Gesammelte Werke in dreizehn Bänden: Erzählungen; Fiorenza; Dichtungen.* Frankfurt am Main: S. Fischer, 1960/1974.

————. *Letters of Thomas Mann 1889–1955.* Selected and translated by Richard and Clara Winston. New York: Alfred A. Knopf, 1971.

————. *Pro and Contra Wagner.* Edited by Patrick Carnegy. Translated by Allan Blunden. Chicago: The University of Chicago Press, 1985.

Marpurg, Friedrich Wilhelm. *Abhandlung von der Fuge nach den Grundsätzen und Exempeln der besten deutschen und ausländischen Meister entworfen.* 2 vols. Berlin: A. Haude and J. C. Spener, 1753–54. Reprint, Hildesheim and New York: Georg Olms, 1970.

————. *Historisch-Kritische Beyträge zur Aufnahme der Musik.* Vol. 2. Berlin: Gottlieb August Lange, 1756. Reprint, Hildesheim and New York: Georg Olms, 1970.

Mendelssohn, Moses. "Betrachtungen über das Erhabene und das Naive in den schönen

Wissenschaften." In *Bibliothek der schönen Wissenschaften und der freyen Künste*. Vol. 2, 2tes Stück. Leipzig: Johann Gottfried Dyck, 1758. Reprinted in M. Mendelssohn. *Gesammelte Schriften*. Vol. 1, *Schriften zur Philosophie und Ästhetik* I:203. Berlin: Akademie-Verlag, 1929.

———. *Phaedon[,] oder über die Unsterblichkeit der Seele[,] in drey Gesprächen*. Berlin und Stettin: Friedrich Nicolai, 1767. Reprinted in *Gesammelte Schriften*. Vol. 3, Teil 1, *Schriften zur Philosophie und Ästhetik*, 37–128. Berlin: Akademie-Verlag, 1932.

———. *Philosophical Writings*. Translated and edited by Daniel O. Dahlstrom. Cambridge: Cambridge University Press, 1997.

———. *Philosophische Schriften*. Vol. I (Berlin: Christian Friedrich Voß, 1761; verbesserte Auflage, 1771). Reprinted in *Gesammelte Schriften* 1: 468–469.

Mozart, Leopold. *A Treatise on the Fundamental Principles of Violin Playing*. Translated by Editha Knocker. London, New York, Toronto: Oxford University Press, 1951.

———. *Versuch einer gründlichen Violinschule*. Augsburg: Johann Jacob Lotter, 1756.

Neefe, Christian Gottlob. *Dilettanterien*. [n.p.], 1785.

Nicolai, Friedrich. *Allgemeine deutsche Bibliothek*. 1788.

Reichardt, Johann Friedrich. *Briefe eines aufmerksamen Reisenden die Musik betreffend*. Vol. 2. Frankfurt and Breslau, 1776.

———. *Briefe, die Musik betreffend: Bericht, Rezensionen, Essays*. Edited by Grita Herre and Walther Sigmund-Schultze. Leipzig: Verlag Philipp Reclam jun., 1976.

———. *Musikalisches Kunstmagazin*, I. Berlin: Im Verlage des Verfassers, 1782. Reprint, Hildesheim: Georg Olms, 1969.

———. *Ueber die deutsche komische Oper nebst einem Anhange eines freundschaftlichen Briefes über die musikalische Poesie*. Hamburg, 1774.

Rousseau, Jean-Jacques. *Essay on the Origin of Languages and Writings Related to Music*. Vol. 7, *The Collected Writings of Rousseau*. Edited and translated by John T. Scott. Hanover, N.H., and London: University Press of New England, 1998.

Schenker, Heinrich. *Das Meisterwerk in der Musik*: Ein Jahrbuch. 3 vols. Munich, Vienna, Berlin: Drei Masken Verlag, 1925–1930. Reprint. 3 vols. in 1. Hildesheim: Georg Olms, 1974. English as *The Masterwork in Music*. 3 vols. Edited by William Drabkin. Cambridge and New York: Cambridge University Press, 1994–1997.

———. *Beethoven, die letzten fünf Sonaten. Sonate E dur Op. 109. Kritische Ausgabe mit Einführung und Erläuterung*. Vienna: Universal-Edition, 1913. Reprinted as *Beethoven: Die letzten Sonaten. Sonate E Dur Op. 109. Kritische Einführung und Erläuterung*, ed. Oswald Jonas. Vienna: Universal Edition, 1971.

Schindler, Anton Felix. *Beethoven As I Knew Him*. Edited by Donald W. MacArdle. Translated by Constance S. Jolly. Chapel Hill and London: The University of North Carolina Press, 1966.

Schlegel, August Wilhelm. "Ueber Zeichnungen zu Gedichten und John Flaxmans Umrisse." In *Athenäum*, 2:193–246. Berlin 1798–1800.

Schlegel, Friedrich. "Athenäums-Fragmente." In *Kritische Friedrich-Schlegel-Ausgabe*, ed. Ernst Behler et al. Vol. 2, *Charakteristiken und Kritiken* 1 (1796–1801). Munich, Paderborn, Vienna: Ferdinand Schöningh, 1967.

———. *Dialogue on Poetry and Literary Aphorisms*. Edited and translated by Ernst Behler and Roman Struc. University Park: Pennsylvania State University Press, 1968.

————. *Friedrich Schlegel's* Lucinde *and the Fragments*. Translated by Peter Firchow. Minneapolis: University of Minnesota Press, 1971.

Shakespeare, William. *The Norton Shakespeare, Based on the Oxford Edition*. Edited by Stephen Greenblatt. New York and London: W. W. Norton, 1997.

Smollett, Tobias. *Travels through France and Italy*. 1766. Critical edition prepared by Frank Felsenstein. Oxford: Oxford University Press, 1979.

Sterne, Laurence. *A Sentimental Journey through France and Italy by Mr. Yorick*. 1768. Edited with an introduction by Ian Jack. Oxford and New York: Oxford University Press, 1968.

————. *A Sentimental Journey through France and Italy and Continuation of the Bramine's Journal: The Text and Notes*. Edited by Melvyn New and W. G. Day. Vol. 6 in *The Florida Edition of the Works of Laurence Sterne*. Gainesville: University Presses of Florida, 2002.

Sulzer, Johann Georg. *Allgemeine Theorie der Schönen Künste*. Neue vermehrte zweite Auflage. 4 vols. Leipzig: Weidmann, 1792–1794. Reprint, Hildesheim: Georg Olms, 1970.

Türk, Daniel Gottlob. *Klavierschule oder Anweisung zum Klavierspielen für Lehrer und Lernende*. Leipzig: Schwickert; and Halle: Schwetschke, 1789. Facsimile reprint, Kassel: Bärenreiter, 1997.

————. *School of Clavier Playing: or Instructions in Playing the Clavier for Teachers & Students*. Edited and translated by Raymond H. Haggh. Lincoln & London: University of Nebraska Press, 1982.

Vico, Giambattista. *The New Science of Giambattista Vico*. Abridged tr. of the 3rd edition (1774), edited and translated by Thomas Goddard Bergin and Max Harold Fisch. Ithaca, N.Y., and London: Cornell University Press, 1970.

Voss, Johann Heinrich. *Briefe von Johann Heinrich Voss nebst erläuternden Beilagen*. Vol. 1. Edited by Abraham Voss. Halberstadt, 1829. Reprint, with a foreword by Gerhard Hay. Hildesheim: Georg Olms, 1971.

Studies

Abbate, Carolyn. *Unsung Voices: Opera and Musical Narrative in the Nineteenth Century*. Princeton: Princeton University Press, 1991.

Adorno, Theodor. *Beethoven: Philosophie der Musik*. Edited by Rolf Tiedemann. Frankfurt am Main: Suhrkamp Verlag, 2nd ed., 1994.

————. *Beethoven: The Philosophy of Music*. Translated by Edmund Jephcott. Stanford: Stanford University Press, 1998.

————. *Essays on Music*. Selected, with introduction, commentary, and notes by Richard Leppert. Berkeley and Los Angeles: University of California Press, 2002.

————. *Gesammelte Schriften*. Vol. 7, *Aesthetische Theorie*. Frankfurt am Main: Suhrkamp Verlag, 5th ed, 1990.

————. *Mahler: A Musical Physiognomy*. Translated by Edmund Jephcott. Chicago and London: University of Chicago Press, 1992.

————. *Mahler: Eine musikalische Physiognomik*. Frankfurt am Main: Suhrkamp Verlag, 1960.

————. *Moments musicaux*. Frankfurt am Main: Suhrkamp Verlag, 1964.

————. *Notes to Literature*. 2 vols. Edited by Rolf Tiedemann. Translated by Sherry Weber Nicholsen. New York: Columbia University Press, 1991–92.

Albrecht, Theodore. "Beethoven and Shakespeare's *Tempest:* New Light on an Old Allusion." *Beethoven Forum* 1 (1992): 81–92.

Badura-Skoda, Eva. "Clementi's 'Musical Characteristics' Opus 19." In *Studies in Eighteenth-Century Music: A Tribute to Karl Geiringer on His Seventieth Birthday*, ed. H. C. Robbins Landon and Roger E. Chapman, 53–67. London: George Allen and Unwin, 1970.

———. "Eine private Briefsammlung." In *Festschrift Otto Erich Deutsch zum 80. Geburtstag am 5. September 1963*, ed. Walter Gestenberg, Jan LaRue and Wolfgang Rehm, 280–290. Kassel: Bärenreiter, 1963.

Badura-Skoda, Paul. "Possibilities and Limitations of Stylistic Criticism in the Dating of Schubert's 'Great' C major Symphony." In *Schubert Studies: Problems of Style and Chronology*, ed. Eva Badura-Skoda and Peter Branscombe, 187–208. Cambridge: Cambridge University Press, 1982.

Badura-Skoda, Eva and Paul. *Interpreting Mozart on the Keyboard.* Translated by Leo Black. London: Barrie and Rockliff, 1962.

Barford, Philip. *The Keyboard Music of C. P. E. Bach.* London: Barrie and Rockliff, 1965.

Barone, Anthony. "Richard Wagner's *Parsifal* and the Theory of Late Style." *Cambridge Opera Journal* 7 (1995): 37–54.

Berg, Darrell M. "C. P. E. Bach's 'Variations' and 'Embellishments' for his Keyboard Sonatas." *Journal of Musicology* 2 (1983): 151–173.

———. "Carl Philipp Emanuel Bachs Umarbeitungen seiner Claviersonaten." *Bach-Jahrbuch* 74 (1988): 123–161.

———. "C. Ph. E. Bach und die 'empfindsame Weise.'" In *Carl Philipp Emanuel Bach und die europäische Musikkultur des mittleren 18. Jahrhunderts*, ed. Hans Joachim Marx, 93–105. Göttingen: Vandenhoeck & Ruprecht, 1990.

Berlin, Isaiah. "Herder and the Enlightenment." In *The Proper Study of Mankind: An Anthology of Essays*, ed. Henry Hardy and Roger Hausheer, 359–435. New York: Farrar, Straus and Giroux, 1997.

———. *The Hedgehog and the Fox: An Essay on Tolstoy's View of History.* London: Weidenfeld & Nicolson; New York: Simon & Schuster, 1953; rev. 1978.

———. *The Magus of the North: J. G. Hamann and the Origins of Modern Irrationalism.* London: J. Murray, 1993.

Biba, Otto, ed. *Franz Schubert und seine Zeit.* Exhibition catalogue of the Gesellschaft der Musikfreunde. Vienna: Gesellschaft der Musikfreunde, 1978.

Bitter, C. H. *Carl Philipp Emanuel und Wilhelm Friedemann Bach und deren Brüder.* Berlin: Verlag von Wilh. Müller, 1868.

Bloom, Harold. *A Map of Misreading.* Oxford: Oxford University Press, 1975.

———. *The Anxiety of Influence: A Theory of Poetry.* New York and Oxford: Oxford University Press, 2nd ed., 1997.

Brandenburg, Sieghard. Reply to Douglas Johnson's "On Beethoven's Scholars and Beethoven's Sketches." *19th Century Music* 2 (1979): 270–274.

———. "Beethovens Streichquartette op. 18." In *Beethoven und Böhmen: Beiträge zu Biographie und Wirkungsgeschichte Beethovens*, ed. Sieghard Brandenburg and Martella Gutiérrez-Denhoff, 259–302. Bonn: Beethoven-Haus, 1988.

———. "Die Beethoven-Autographen Johann Nepomuk Kafkas: Ein Beitrag zur Geschichte des Sammelns von Musikhandschriften." In *Divertimento für Hermann J. Abs: Beethoven-*

Studien dargebracht zu seinem 80. Geburtstag, ed. Martin Staehelin, 89–113. Bonn: Beethoven-Haus, 1981.

———. "Die Beethovenhandschriften in der Musikaliensammlung des Erzherzogs Rudolph." In *Zu Beethoven: Aufsätze und Dokumente* 3, 141–176. Berlin: Verlag Neue Musik, 1988.

Brendel, Alfred. *Music Sounded Out: Essays, Lectures, Interviews, Afterthoughts.* London: Robson Books; New York: Farrar, Straus and Giroux, 1990.

Brown, A. Peter. "Haydn's Chaos: Genesis and Genre." *The Musical Quarterly* 73 (1989): 18–59.

Brown, Maurice J. E. "Schwind's 'Schubert-Abend bei Josef von Spaun.'" In Brown, *Essays on Schubert.* 155–168. London: Macmillan; New York: St Martin's Press, 1966.

Busch, Gudrun. *C. Ph. E. Bach und seine Lieder.* Regensburg: Gustav Bosse Verlag, 1957.

Christensen, Thomas, tr. and ed. "Johann Georg Sulzer. General Theory of the Fine Arts (1771–1774): Selected Articles." In *Aesthetics and the Art of Musical Composition in the German Enlightenment: Selected Writings of Johann Georg Sulzer and Heinrich Christoph Koch,* edited by Nancy Kovaleff Baker and Thomas Christensen. Cambridge and New York: Cambridge University Press, 1995.

Chrysander, Friedrich. "Eine Klavier-Phantasie von Karl Philipp Emanuel Bach mit nachträglich von Gerstenberg eingefügten Gesangsmelodien zu zwei verschiedenen Texten." *Vierteljahresschrift für Musikwissenschaft* 7 (1891): 1–25. Reprint, *Carl Philipp Emanuel Bach: Beiträge zu Leben und Werk,* ed. Heinrich Poos, 329–353. Mainz: Schott, 1993.

Churgin, Bathia. "Beethoven and Mozart's Requiem: A New Connection." *Journal of Musicology* 5 (1987): 457–477.

Clark, Stephen L. "C. P. E. Bach as a Publisher of His Own Works." In *Carl Philipp Emanuel Bach: Musik für Europa. Bericht über das Internationale Symposium . . . 1994,* ed. Hans-Günter Ottenberg, 199–211. Frankfurt (Oder): Konzerthalle "Carl Philipp Emanuel Bach," 1998.

Cone, Edward T. "Beethoven's Orpheus–or Jander's?" *19th Century Music* 8 (1985): 283–286.

Cooper, Barry, ed. *The Beethoven Compendium.* London: Thames and Hudson, 1991.

———. "The Newly Discovered Quartet Movement by Beethoven." *The Beethoven Journal* 15, no. 1 (Summer 2000): 19–24.

———. *Beethoven and the Creative Process.* Oxford and New York: Oxford University Press, 1990.

———. *Beethoven's Folksong Settings: Chronology, Sources, Style.* Oxford: Oxford University Press, 1994.

Dahlhaus, Carl. *Gesammelte Schriften in 10 Bänden, VI: 19. Jahrhundert III: Ludwig van Beethoven; Aufsätze zur Ideen- und Kompositionsgeschichte; Texte zur Instrumentalmusik.* Edited by Hermann Danuser. Laaber: Laaber-Verlag, 2003.

———. *Ludwig van Beethoven und seine Zeit.* Laaber: Laaber Verlag, 1987.

———. *Ludwig van Beethoven: Approaches to his Music.* Translated by Mary Whittall Oxford: Oxford University Press, 1991.

Danuser, Hermann. "Klaviersonate e-Moll op 90." In *Beethoven: Interpretationen seiner Werke,* 2 vols., ed. Albrecht Riethmüller, Carl Dahlhaus and Alexander L. Ringer; II: 25–34. Laaber: Laaber Verlag, 1994.

Darbellay, Etienne. "C. P. E. Bach's Aesthetic as Reflected in his Notation." In *C. P. E. Bach Studies*, ed. Stephen L. Clark, 43–63. Oxford: Oxford University Press, 1988.

Daub, Peggy. "The Publication Process and Audience for C. P. E. Bach's *Sonaten für Kenner und Liebhaber*." In *Bach Perspectives* 2: *J. S. Bach, the Breitkopfs, and Eighteenth-Century Music Trade*, ed. George Staufer, 65–83. Lincoln and London: University of Nebraska Press, 1996.

Feil, Arnold. *Franz Schubert: Die schöne Müllerin; Winterreise.* Translated by Ann C. Sherwin. Portland, Oregon: Amadeus Press, 1988.

Finscher, Ludwig. "Maximilian Stadler und Mozarts Nachlaß." *Mozart Jahrbuch* 1960/61 (1961): 168–172.

Fischer, Edwin. *Ludwig van Beethovens Klaviersonaten.* Wiesbaden: Insel Verlag, 1956.

Fox, Pamela. "The Stylistic Anomalies of C. P. E. Bach's Nonconstancy." In *C. P. E. Bach Studies*, ed. Stephen L. Clark, 106–109. Oxford: Oxford University Press, 1988.

———. "Toward a Comprehensive C. P. E. Bach Chronology: *Schrift-Chronologie* and the Issue of Bach's 'Late Hand.'" In *Carl Philipp Emanuel Bach: Musik für Europa. Bericht über das Internationale Symposium*, ed. Hans-Günter Ottenberg, 306–323. Frankfurt (Oder): Konzerthalle "Carl Philipp Emanuel Bach," 1998.

Fresenius, August. "Hamlet-Monologe in der Übersetzung von Mendelssohn und Lessing." *Jahrbuch der Deutschen Shakespeare-Gesellschaft* 39 (1902–03): 245–246.

Frimmel, Th[eodor] von. "Der Klavierspieler Beethoven." In Frimmel, *Beethoven-Studien, II: Bausteine zu einer Lebensgeschichte des Meisters*, 201–271. Munich and Leipzig: Georg Müller, 1906.

Frisch, Walter. "Schubert's *Nähe des Geliebten* (D. 162): Transformation of the *Volkston*." In *Schubert: Critical and Analytical Studies*, ed. Walter Frisch, 175–99. Lincoln and London: University of Nebraska Press, 1986.

Gay, Peter. *Freud: A Life for Our Time.* New York and London: W. W. Norton & Co., 1988.

Gay, Peter. *The Enlightenment: An Interpretation. The Rise of Modern Paganism.* New York: Alfred A. Knopf, 1966.

Georgiades, Thrasybulos. *Schubert: Musik und Lyrik.* Göttingen: Vandenhoeck & Ruprecht, 1967.

Gersthofer, Wolfgang. "Große Mannigfaltigkeit und Neuheit in den Formen und Ausweichungen." In *Carl Philipp Emanuel Bach und die europäische Musikkultur des mittleren 18. Jahrhunderts. Bericht über das Internationale Symposium der Joachim Jungius-Gesellschaft der Wissenschaften Hamburg 29. September–2. Oktober 1988*, 283–306. ed. Hans Joachim Marx. Göttingen: Vandenhoeck & Ruprecht, 1990.

Görner, Rüdiger. "Vom Wort zur Tat in Goethes 'Faust'—Paradigmenwechsel oder Metamorphose?" *Goethe Jahrbuch* 106 (1989): 119–132.

Grundmann, Herbert. "Per il Clavicembalo o Piano-Forte." In *Colloquium Amicorum: Joseph Schmidt-Görg zum 70. Geburtstag*, 100–117. Bonn: Beethovenhaus Bonn, 1967.

Gülke, Peter. Review of *Ludwig van Beethoven. Keßlersches Skizzenbuch*, ed. Sieghard Brandenburg. *Die Musikforschung* 36, Heft 2. (1983): 101–102.

Helibut, Anthony. *Thomas Mann: Eros and Literature.* New York: Alfred A. Knopf, 1996.

Helm, Eugene. "The 'Hamlet' Fantasy and the Literary Element in C. P. E. Bach's Music." *The Musical Quarterly* 58 (1972): 277–296.

Hinrichsen, Hans-Joachim. "Zur Bedeutung des Werks in Schuberts Sonatenschaffen." In

Schubert, *"Reliquie": Sonata in C für Klavier D 840. Faksimile-Ausgabe nach den Autographen in Cambridge, Paris und Wien,* ed. Hans-Joachim Hinrichsen, 7–18. Tutzing: Hans Schneider, 1992.

Huray, Peter, and James Day, eds. *Music and Aesthetics in the Eighteenth and Early-Nineteenth Centuries.* Cambridge: Cambridge University Press, 1981.

Jander, Owen. "Beethoven's 'Orpheus in Hades': The *Andante con moto* of the Fourth Piano Concerto." *19th Century Music* 8 (Spring 1985): 195–212.

———. "Genius in the Arena of Charlatanry: The First Movement of Beethoven's 'Tempest' Sonata in Cultural Context." In *Musica Franca: Essays in Honor of Frank D'Accone,* ed. Alyson McLamore, Irene Alm, and Colleen Reardon, 585–630. Stuyvesant, N.Y.: Pendragon Press, 1996.

Johnson, Douglas. "1794–95: Decisive Years in Beethoven's Early Development." In *Beethoven Studies* 3, ed. Alan Tyson, 1–28. Cambridge: Cambridge University Press, 1982.

Kavanagh, Thomas. *Enlightenment and the Shadows of Chance: The Novel and the Culture of Gambling in Eighteenth-Century France.* Baltimore and London: The Johns Hopkins University Press, 1993.

Kerman, Joseph. "Beethoven's Minority." In *Haydn, Mozart, & Beethoven: Studies in the Music of the Classical Period* (Essays in Honor of Alan Tyson), ed. Sieghard Brandenburg, 151–173. Oxford: Clarendon Press, 1998.

———. *The Beethoven Quartets.* New York: Alfred A. Knopf, 1967.

Kinderman, William. "Thematic contrast and parenthetical enclosure in the piano sonatas, op. 109 and 111." In *Zu Beethoven: Aufsätze und Dokumente* 3, ed. Harry Goldschmidt, 43–59. Berlin: Verlag Neue Musik, 1988.

Klein, Hans-Günter, and Douglas Johnson. "Autographe Beethovens aus der Bonner Zeit: Handschrift-Probleme und Echtheitsfragen." In *Beiträge zur Beethoven-Bibliographie: Studien und Materialien zum Werkverzeichnis von Kinsky-Halm,* ed. Kurt Dorfmüller, 115–24. Munich: G. Henle Verlag, 1978.

Klein, Hans-Günter. *"Er ist Original!": Carl Philipp Emanuel Bach. Sein musikalisches Werk in Autographen und Erstdrucken aus der Musikabteilung der Staatsbibliothek Preußischer Kulturbesitz Berlin.* Wiesbaden: Dr. Ludwig Reichert Verlag, 1988.

Knab, Armin. *Denken und Tun. Gesammelte Aufsätze über Musik.* Berlin: Merseburger, 1959.

Kramer, Lawrence. "Haydn's Chaos, Schenker's Order; or, Hermeneutics and Musical Analysis: Can They Mix?" *19th Century Music* 16 (1992): 3–17.

———. "Music and Representation: the Instance of Haydn's *Creation.*" In *Music and Text: Critical Inquiries,* ed. Steven Paul Scher, 139–62. Cambridge: Cambridge University Press, 1992. 139–62

———. "Primitive Encounters: Beethoven's 'Tempest' Sonata, Musical Meaning, and Enlightenment Anthropology." *Beethoven Forum* 6 (1998): 31–65.

Kramer, Richard. "'Sonate, que me veux-tu?': Opus 30, Opus 31, and the Anxieties of Genre." In *The Beethoven Violin Sonatas: History, Criticism, Performance,* ed. Lewis Lockwood and Mark Kroll, 47–60. Urbana and Chicago: University of Illinois Press, 2004.

———. "Between Cavatina and Ouverture: Opus 130 and the Voices of Narrative." *Beethoven Forum* 1 (1992):165–189.

———. "*Das Organische der Fuge:* On the Autograph of Beethoven's String Quartet in F Major, Opus 59, No. 1." In *The String Quartets of Haydn, Mozart, and Beethoven:*

Studies of the Autograph Manuscripts, Isham Library Papers 3, ed. Christoph Wolff, 223–265. Cambridge, Mass.: Harvard University Music Department, 1980.

———. "*Gradus ad Parnassum:* Beethoven, Schubert, and the Romance of Counterpoint." *19th Century Music* 11 (1987): 107–120.

———. "In Search of Palestrina: Beethoven in the Archives." In *Haydn, Mozart, and Beethoven: Studies in the Music of the Classical Period,* ed. Sieghard Brandenburg, 283–300. London and New York: Oxford University Press, 1997.

———. "On the Dating of Two Aspects of Beethoven's Notation for Piano." In *Beiträge '76–78: Beethoven-Kolloquium 1977,* ed. Rudolf Klein, 160–173. Kassel: Bärenreiter Verlag, 1978.

———. "Posthumous Schubert." *19th Century Music* 14 (1990): 197–216.

———. "The New Modulation of the 1770s: C. P. E. Bach in Theory, Criticism, and Practice." *Journal of the American Musicological Society* 38 (1985): 551–92.

———. "To Edit a Sketchbook." *Beethoven Forum* 12, no. 1 (Spring 2005): 82–96.

———. *Distant Cycles: Schubert and the Conceiving of Song.* Chicago and London: University of Chicago Press, 1994.

———. Review of Mozart, *Neue Ausgabe sämtlicher Werke.* Ser. 10, Supplement, Werkgruppe 30, Bd. 3, Skizzen. *Notes: Quarterly Journal of the Music Library Association* 57 (September 2000): 188–193.

Krause, Andreas. "Schuberts 'Reliquie,' Beethovens VII. Sinfonie und der 'Weg zur grossen Sinfonie.'" In Schubert, *"Reliquie": Sonata in C für Klavier D 840. Faksimile-Ausgabe nach den Autographen in Cambridge, Paris und Wien,* ed. Hans-Joachim Hinrichsen, 67–80. Tutzing: Hans Schneider, 1992.

Kundera, Milan. *Testaments Betrayed: An Essay in Nine Parts.* Translated by Linda Asher. New York: HarperCollins, 1993.

Kunze, Stefan, ed. *Ludwig van Beethoven: Die Werke im Spiegel seiner Zeit; Gesammelte Konzertberichte und Rezensionen bis 1830.* In collaboration with Theodor Schmid, Andreas Taub and Gerda Burkhard. Laaber: Laaber-Verlag, 1987; Sonderausgabe 1996.

Küthen, Hans-Werner. "*Quaerendo invenietis.* Die Exegese eines Beethoven-Briefes an Haslinger vom 5. September 1823." In *Musik, Edition, Interpretation: Gedenkschrift Günter Henle,* ed. Martin Bente, 282–313. Munich: G. Henle, 1980.

Landon, H. C. Robbins. *Haydn: The Years of 'The Creation' 1796–1800.* Vol. 4 of *Haydn: Chronicle and Works.* Bloomington and London: Indiana University Press, 1977.

Larsen, Jens Peter, Howard Serwer, and James Webster, eds. *Haydn Studies: Proceedings of the International Haydn Conference, Washington, D. C., 1975.* New York and London: W. W. Norton, 1981.

Leux, Irmgard. *Christian Gottlob Neefe (1748–1798).* Leipzig: Fr. Kistner & C. F. W. Siegel, 1925.

Levy, Janet. *Beethoven's Compositional Choices: The Two Versions of op. 18, no. 1, First Movement.* Philadelphia: University of Pennsylvania Press, 1982.

Lohmeier, Dieter. *Carl Philipp Emanuel Bach. Musik und Literatur in Norddeutschland.* Schriften der Schleswig-Holsteinischen Landesbibliothek, Bd. 4. Heide in Holstein: Boyens & Co., 1988.

Longyear, R. M. "The Minor Mode in Eighteenth-Century Sonata Form." *Journal of Music Theory* 15, nos. 1 and 2 (1971): 182–229.

MacIntyre, Bruce C. *Haydn: "The Creation."* New York: Schirmer Books, 1998.

Mann, Alfred. *The Great Composer as Teacher and Student: Theory and Practice of Composition.* New York: Dover Publications, 1994.

Marshall, Robert L. *Mozart Speaks: Views on Music, Musicians, and the World.* New York: Schirmer Books, 1991.

Marston, Nicholas. "Schenker and Forte Reconsidered: Beethoven's Sketches for the Piano Sonata in E, Op. 109." *19th Century Music* 10 (1986): 24–42.

———. *Beethoven's Piano Sonata in E, Op. 109.* Oxford: Oxford University Press, 1995.

McKay, Elizabeth Norman. "Schuberts Klaviersonaten von 1815 bis 1825—dem Jahr der 'Reliquie.'" In Schubert, *"Reliquie": Sonata in C für Klavier D 840. Faksimile-Ausgabe nach den Autographen in Cambridge, Paris und Wien,* ed. Hans-Joachim Hinrichsen, 43–66. Tutzing: Hans Schneider, 1992.

Mies, Paul. *Die Krise der Konzertkadenz bei Beethoven.* Bonn: Bouvier, 1970.

Miesner, Heinrich. *Philipp Emanuel Bach in Hamburg: Beiträge zu seiner Biographie und zur Musikgeschichte seiner Zeit.* Leipzig: Breitkopf & Härtel, 1929.

Misch, Ludwig. *Beethoven Studies.* Norman, Okla.: University of Oklahoma Press,, 1953.

Mörner, C.-G. Stellan. "Haydniana aus Schweden um 1800." *Haydn-Studien* 2, no. 1 (1969): 1–33.

Muxfeldt, Kristina. Review of *Nineteenth-Century Music and the German Romantic Ideology* by John Daverio. *Journal of Music Theory* 40 (1996): 149–160.

Neumann, Frederick. *Ornamentation and Improvisation in Mozart.* Princeton: Princeton University Press, 1986.

Newman, William S. "Emanuel Bach's Autobiography." *The Musical Quarterly* 51 (1965): 363–372.

Nottebohm, Gustav. *Beethoven's Studien.* Leipzig and Winterthur: J. Rieter-Biedermann, 1873. Reprint, Niederwalluf bei Wiesbaden: Sändig, 1971.

———. *Ein Skizzenbuch von Beethoven.* Leipzig: Breitkopf und Härtel, [1865].

———. *Zweite Beethoveniana. Nachgelassene Aufsätze.* Edited by Eusebius Mandyczewski. Leipzig: C. F. Peters, 1887.

Oster, Ernst. "Analysis Symposium I: Mozart, Menuetto K.V. 355." *Journal of Music Theory* 10 (1966): 32–52. Reprinted in *Readings in Schenker Analysis and Other Approaches,* ed. Maury Yeston, 121–140. New Haven and London: Yale University Press, 1977.

Ottenberg, Hans-Günter, ed. *Carl Philipp Emanuel Bach: Musik für Europa. Bericht über das Internationale Symposium . . . 1994.* Frankfurt (Oder): Konzerthalle "Carl Philipp Emanuel Bach," 1998.

———. *Carl Philipp Emanuel Bach.* Leipzig: Philipp Reclam jun., 1982. In English as *C. P. E. Bach.* Translated by Philip J. Whitmore. Oxford and New York: Oxford University Press, 1987; paperback ed., with new Foreword, 1991.

Panofsky, Erwin. *Idea: a Concept in Art Theory.* Translated by Joseph J. S. Peake. Columbia: University of South Carolina Press, 1968.

Plamenac, Dragan. "New Light on the Last Years of Carl Philipp Emanuel Bach." *The Musical Quarterly* 35 (1949): 565–587.

Plebuch, Tobias. "Dark Fantasies and the Dawn of the Self: Gerstenberg's Monologues for C. P. E. Bach's C minor Fantasia." In *C. P. E. Bach Studies,* ed. Annette Richards, 25–66. Cambridge: Cambridge University Press, 2006.

Price, Lawrence Marsden. *The Reception of English Literature in Germany.* Berkeley: University of California Press, 1932. Reprint, New York and London: Benjamin Blom, 1968.

Richards, Annette. *The Free Fantasia and the Musical Picturesque.* Cambridge: Cambridge University Press, 2001.

Riley, Matthew. "Johann Nikolaus Forkel on the Listening Practices of 'Kenner' and 'Liebhaber,'" *Music & Letters* 84 (August 2003): 414–433.

Rochlitz, Friedrich. *Für Freunde der Tonkunst.* 4 vols.. Leipzig: Carl Cnobloch, 3rd ed., 1868.

Rosen, Charles. *Sonata Forms.* New York: W. W. Norton, rev. 1988.

———. *The Classical Style: Haydn, Mozart, Beethoven.* New York: W. W. Norton, rev. ed. 1972.

———. *The Frontiers of Meaning: Three Informal Lectures on Music.* New York: Hill and Wang, 1994.

Schenker, Heinrich. *Ein Beitrag zur Ornamentik.* Vienna: Universal Edition, 1904, rev. 1908. English as *A Contribution to the Study of Ornamentation,* tr. Hedi Siegel (after Carl Parrish), in *The Music Forum,* IV, ed. Felix Salzer (New York: Columbia University Press, 1976), 1–139.

Schering, Arnold. "C. Ph. E. Bach und das redende Prinzip in der Musik." *Jahrbuch der Musikbibliothek Peters* 45 (1938): 13–29.

Schiedermair, Ludwig. *Der junge Beethoven.* Leipzig: Quelle & Meyer, 1925.

Schmid, Ernst Fritz. *Carl Philipp Emanuel Bach und seine Kammermusik.* Kassel: Bärenreiter, 1931.

Schmidt, James, ed. *What Is Enlightenment? Eighteenth-Century Answers and Twentieth-Century Questions.* Berkeley, Los Angeles, London: University of California Press, 1996.

Schmitz, Arnold. *Beethovens "Zwei Principe": Ihre Bedeutung für Themen- und Satzbau.* Berlin and Bonn: Ferd. Dümmler, 1923.

Schulenberg, David. *The Instrumental Music of Carl Philipp Emanuel Bach.* Ann Arbor: UMI Research Press, 1984.

Schulze, Hans-Joachim. "Carl Philipp Emanuel Bachs Hamburger Passionsmusiken und ihr gattungsgeschictlicher Kontext." In *Carl Philipp Emanuel Bach und die europäische Musikkultur des mittleren 18. Jahrhunderts. Bericht über das Internationale Symposium der Joachim Jungius-Gesellschaft der Wissenschaften Hamburg 29. September–2. Oktober 1988,* ed. Hans Joachim Marx, 333–343. Göttingen: Vandenhoeck & Ruprecht, 1990.

Schweizer, Hans Rudolf. *Goethe und das Problem der Sprache.* Basler Studien zur Deutschen Sprache und Literatur, Heft 23. Bern: Francke Verlag, 1959.

Serwer, Howard. "C. P. E. Bach, J. C. F. Rellstab, and the Sonatas with Varied Reprises." In *C. P. E. Bach Studies,* ed. Stephen L. Clark, 233–243. Oxford: Oxford University Press, 1988.

Simmel, Georg. *Goethe.* Leipzig: Klinkhardt & Biermann, 1913.

Sisman, Elaine. "Haydn, Shakespeare, and the Rules of Originality." In *Haydn and His World,* ed. Sisman, 3–56. Princeton: Princeton University Press, 1997.

———. *Haydn and the Classical Variation.* Cambridge, Mass., and London: Harvard University Press, 1993.

Skowroneck, Tilman. "The Keyboard Instruments of the Young Beethoven." In *Beethoven and His World,* ed. Scott Burnham and Michael P. Steinberg, 151–192. Princeton and Oxford: Princeton University Press, 2000.

Stanley, Glenn. "Voices and Their Rhythms in the First Movement of Beethoven's Piano Sonata Op. 109: Some Thoughts on the Performance and Analysis of a Late-Style Work" In *Beethoven and His World,* ed. Scott Burnham and Michael P. Steinberg, 88–123. Princeton and Oxford: Princeton University Press, 2000.

Smyth, David H. "Beethoven's Revision of the Scherzo of Opus 18, No. 1." *Beethoven Forum* 1 (1992):147–163.

Solomon, Maynard. "Beethoven's Tagebuch of 1812–1818." In *Beethoven Studies* 3, ed. Alan Tyson, 193–285. Cambridge: Cambridge University Press, 1982.

———. "The Rochlitz Anecdotes: Issues of Authenticity in Early Mozart Biography." In *Mozart Studies,* ed. Cliff Eisen, 1–59. Oxford: Clarendon Press, 1991.

Steblin, Rita. "Schwinds Porträtskizze 'Schubert am Klavier.'" *Schubert durch die Brille,* Mitteilungen 10 (January 1993):45–52.

Suchalla, Ernst, ed. *Carl Philipp Emanuel Bach im Spiegel seiner Zeit: Die Dokumentensammlung Johann Jacob Heinrich Westphals.* Hildesheim, Zurich, New York: Georg Olms, 1993.

———. "Die *Staats- und Gelehrte Zeitung des Hamburgischen unparteyischen Correspondenten* als unerlässliche Informationsquelle über C. P. E. Bach." In *Carl Philipp Emanuel Bach: Musik für Europa. Bericht über das Internationale Symposium . . . 1994,* ed. Hans-Günter Ottenberg, 212–220. Frankfurt (Oder): Konzerthalle "Carl Philipp Emanuel Bach," 1998.

Swain, Joseph P. "Form and Function of the Classical Cadenza." *Journal of Musicology* 6 (1988): 27–59.

Temperley, Nicholas. *Haydn: "The Creation."* Cambridge: Cambridge University Press, 1991.

Thayer, Alexander Wheelock. *Ludwig van Beethovens Leben.* 5 vols. Edited by Hermann Deiters. Revised and completed by Hugo Riemann. Leipzig: Breitkopf & Härtel, 1901–1911.

———. *Thayer's Life of Beethoven.* 2 vols. Revised and edited by Elliot Forbes. Princeton: Princeton University Press, 1964, rev. 1967.

———. *The Life of Ludwig van Beethoven.* 3 vols. Edited and translated by Henry Edward Krehbiel. New York: The Beethoven Association, 1921.

Thayer, Harvey Waterman. *Laurence Sterne in Germany.* New York: Columbia University Press, 1905. Reprint, New York: AMS Press, 1966.

Tovey, Donald Francis. *Essays in Musical Analysis.* Vol. 5, *Vocal Music.* London: Oxford University Press, 1937.

———. Preface to Johann Sebastian Bach, *Forty-Eight Preludes and Fugues.* New York: Oxford University Press, 1924.

Treitler, Leo. "Beethoven's 'Expressive' Markings." *Beethoven Forum* 7 (1999): 89–112.

Tyson, Alan. "The Mozart Fragments in the Mozarteum, Salzburg: A Preliminary Study of Their Chronology and Their Significance." *Journal of the American Musicological Society* 34 (1981): 471–510.

———. "The Problem of Beethoven's 'First' Leonore Overture." *Journal of the American Musicological Society* 28 (1975): 292–334.

———. *Mozart. Studies of the Autograph Scores.* Cambridge, Mass., and London: Harvard University Press, 1987.

Wade, Rachel W. "Carl Philipp Emanuel Bach, the Restless Composer." In *Carl Philipp*

Emanuel Bach und die europäische Musikkultur des mittleren 18. Jahrhunderts, ed. Hans Joachim Marx, 175–188. Göttingen: Vandenhoeck & Ruprecht, 1990.

———. *The Keyboard Concertos of Carl Philipp Emanuel Bach.* Ann Arbor: UMI Research Press, 1981.

Webster, James. "The *Creation,* Haydn's Late Vocal Music, and the Musical Sublime." In *Haydn and his World,* ed. Elaine Sisman, 57–102. Princeton: Princeton University Press, 1997.

———. "The D-Major Interlude in the First Movement of Haydn's 'Farewell' Symphony." In *Studies in Musical Sources and Styles: Essays in Honor of Jan LaRue,* ed. Eugene K. Wolf and Edward H. Roesner, 339–380. Madison: A-R Editions, Inc., 1990.

———. *Haydn's "Farewell" Symphony and the Idea of Classical Style.* Cambridge: Cambridge University Press, 1991.

Wedig, Hans Josef. *Beethovens Streichquartette op. 18 Nr. 1 und seine erste Fassung.* Veröffentlichungen des Beethovenhauses in Bonn, ed. Ludwig Schiedermair, 2. Bonn: Beethovenhaus, 1922.

Werner, Stephen. "Irony and the Essay: Diderot's 'Regrets sur ma vieille robe de chambre.'" In *Diderot: Digression and Dispersion,* ed. Jack Undank and Herbert Josephs, 269–277. Lexington, Ky.: French Forum, 1984.

White, Hayden. *Metahistory: The Historical Imagination in Nineteenth-Century Europe.* Baltimore and London: The Johns Hopkins University Press, 1973.

Wiemer, Wolfgang. "Carl Philipp Emanuel Bachs Fantasie in c-Moll—ein Lamento auf den Tod des Vaters?" *Bach-Jahrbuch* 74 (1988): 163–177.

Wilkinson, Elizabeth M. "Faust in der Logosszene–Willkürlicher Übersetzer oder geschulter Exeget?" In *Dichtung. Sprache. Gesellschaft: Akten des IV. Internationalen Germanistenkongresses 1970 in Princeton,* ed. Victor Lange and Hans-Gert Roloff, 116–124. Frankfurt am Main, Athenäum Verlag, 1971.

Winter, Robert S. "Of Realizations, Completions, Restorations and Reconstructions: From Bach's *The Art of Fugue* to Beethoven's Tenth Symphony." *Journal of the Royal Musical Association* 116, no. 1 (1991): 96–126.

———. Response to Richard Kramer's "*Das Organische der Fuge:* On the Autograph of Beethoven's String Quartet in F Major, Opus 59, No. 1." In *The String Quartets of Haydn, Mozart, and Beethoven: Studies of the Autograph Manuscripts.* Isham Library Papers 3, ed. Christoph Wolff, 266–272. Cambridge, Mass.: Harvard University Music Department, 1980.

Wolff, Christoph. "Bach's *Handexemplar* of the Goldberg Variations: A New Source." *Journal of the American Musicological Society* 29 (1976): 224–241. Reprinted in Wolff, *Bach: Essays on His Life and Music.* Cambridge, Mass. and London: Harvard University Press, 1991.

———. "Zur Chronologie der Klavierkonzert-Kadenzen Mozarts." *Mozart-Jahrbuch 1978/79* (1979): 235–246.

———. *Bach: Essays on His Life and Music.* Cambridge, Mass., and London: Harvard University Press, 1991.

———. *Mozart's Requiem: Historical and Analytical Studies, Documents, and Score.* Berkeley: University of California Press, 1994.

———. Review of two facsimile editions of Mozart's Requiem. *19th Century Music* 15 (Fall 1991): 162–165.

INDEX OF NAMES AND WORKS

Page numbers of music examples and illustrations are shown in bold.